FRANKIE HOWERD

FRANKIE HOWERD

STAND-UP COMIC

Graham McCann

FOURTH ESTATE · *London* and *New York*

First published in Great Britain in 2004 by
Fourth Estate
An Imprint of HarperCollins*Publishers*
77–85 Fulham Palace Road
London w6 8jb
www.4thestate.com

1 3 5 7 9 10 8 6 4 2

The right of Graham McCann to be identified as the author
of this work has been asserted by him in accordance with
the Copyright, Designs and Patents Act 1988

A catalogue record for this book is available from the British Library

ISBN 1-84115-310-9

Typeset in Monotype Bembo by
Rowland Phototypesetting Ltd,
Bury St Edmunds, Suffolk
Printed and bound in Great Britain by
Clays Ltd, St Ives plc

For

Mic,

who believed I could write it,

and

Vera and Silvana,

who believed I could complete it.

Contents

Contents

List of Photographs

ix

Acknowledgements

I would like to thank the following people not only for speaking to me, but also for trusting me to write accurately and responsibly about their late friend and colleague: Eric Sykes; Norma Farnes; Bill Lyon-Shaw; Ray Galton; Alan Simpson; Barry Took; Brad Ashton; Eddie Braben; Sir Bill Cotton; David Croft; Annie and Tony Clayton; Helen Walters; and John Ammonds.

I am indebted, too, to the following institutions and individuals for certain acts of kindness, advice and/or practical assistance: Tessa Le Bars; Fiona Cushley, Ruth Swindells, Ines Cavill and David Turnbull at the BBC; John Davis and Hazel Simpson at the BBC Written Archives Centre; Huw Martin at BBC Research Central; Elizabeth Dobson at ITN; Patrick Newley at the British Music Hall Society; Neil Hudson at the University of Cambridge Library; the staff at the British Library; the editorial staff at *The Stage* newspaper; Bill Pertwee; Sir Paul Fox; Bob Monkhouse; Ralph Montagu; Michael J. Simpson; Colin Bean; Dick Geary; Chris and Anne Lycett; Richard McCann; Irene Melling; Len Kelly; Mike Craig; Hugh Stuckey; and Jan Harvey. I am also pleased to have the chance to thank those people who helped me locate certain visual or audio examples of Frankie Howerd at work: Teddy Green; Susan Riley; Don Roberts; Geoff Thompson; and the staff at the British Library's Sound Archive.

My publishers, Fourth Estate, were both prudent and patient. I must acknowledge, in particular, Catherine Blyth, Nick Davies, Jessica Axe, Catherine Heaney, Caroline Hotblack and Christopher Potter.

My remarkable agent, Mic Cheetham, was as kind, as encouraging and as trusting an advisor and supporter as any author could hope to have, and without her faith I simply would not have seen this project through to its conclusion. Similarly, my dear mother, Vera McCann, and my dear friend, Silvana Dean, stopped me on countless occasions from giving up and giving in to the various irritations, frustrations and apparently irrational obstructions that seemed to arrive and multiply on a daily basis. Even if I did not thank them properly at the time, in my bewildered state, I happily do so now: whatever is worthwhile in what follows is due to the three of you – thank goodness that you cared.

I don't go for this business of the broken-hearted clown.
Because I think a broken-hearted clown would be a
damn sight more broken-hearted if he wasn't a clown.
FRANKIE HOWERD

THE PROLOGUE

Now listen, brethren. Before we begin the eisteddfod, I'd like to make an appeal . . .

Now, er, Ladies and Gentle-men. Harken. Now, ah, no: harken.
Listen, now. Harr-ken. Harr-ever-so-ken![1]

It was not so much the look of someone who did not belong. It was more the look of someone who did not belong up there.

He looked as if he belonged in the audience. He looked as if he had strayed on to the stage by mistake. He fiddled with the fraying fringe of his chestnut-brown hairpiece, fidgeted with the folds of his chocolate-brown suit ('Make meself comfy . . .'), and then he started: 'I just met this woman – no, oh no, don't, please, don't laugh. No. *Liss-en!*' He did not sound as if he was performing under a pro-scenium arch. He sounded as if he was gossiping over a garden wall.

That was Frankie Howerd. He did not seem like the other stand-up comedians. He seemed more like one of us.

The other stand-up comics of his and previous eras came across as either super-bright or super-dim.[2] Most of them, like Max Miller, were peacocks: slick and smart and salesman-sharp, they were happy to appear far more experienced, more assured and more articulate than any of those who were seated down in the stalls. The odd one or two, such as Tom Foy, were strange little sparrows: slow, fey and almost painfully gauche, they were the kind of grotesque, cartoon-like fools to whom even fools could feel superior.

No stand-up, until Howerd, came over as recognisably *real*: neither too arch a 'character' nor too obvious a 'turn', but almost as believably unrehearsed, untailored, unshowy, unsure and undeniably imperfect as the rest of us. Frankie Howerd, when he arrived, was genuinely different. He was the first British stand-up to resemble a real person, rather than just a performer.

3

He became, as a result, the most subversive clown in the country. What made him so subversive was not the fact that he dared to make a mockery of himself – any old clown can do that – but rather the fact that he dared to make a mockery of his own profession. He was the clown who made a joke out of the job of clowning.

Everything about the vocation, he suggested, was onerous, absurd, unrewarding and unbearably demeaning. He bemoaned, for example, the routine maltreatment meted out by the management: 'I've had a shocking week. Shocking. What's today? Tuesday. It was last Monday then. The phone rang, and it was, er, y'know, um, the bloke who runs the BBC. Whatsisname? You know: "Thing". Yeah. Anyway, he was on the phone, you see. So I accepted the charge . . .'

He also complained about his ill-fitting stage clothes: 'Ooh, my trousers are sticking to me tonight! Are yours, madam? Then wriggle. There's nothing worse than sitting in agony.' Similarly, he never hesitated to express the full extent of his resentment at being saddled with such an ancient and incompetent accompanist: 'No, don't laugh. Poor soul. No, don't – it might be one of your own. [*To accompanist*] It *is* chilly! *Yehss, 'tis!* [*To audience*] Chilly? I'm sweating like a pig!' He also always made a point of acknowledging the poverty of his material: 'What do you expect at this time of night? Wit?'

He never, in short, left his audience in the slightest doubt that he would have much preferred to have been doing something – anything – else. 'Oh,' he would cry, 'I wish I could win the pools!'

He did not even bother to turn up with, in any conventional sense of the term, an act. His act was all about his lack of an act, his artlessness the slyest sign of his art:

Now, Ladies and Gentle-*men* – no, look, don't mess about, I don't feel in the mood. No. I want to tell you – I've had a terrible time of it this week, and, er, I haven't been able to get much for you – so don't expect too much, will you? No, but I always try to do my best, as you know, but, oh, this week – it's been too much. Still, I've managed to knock up something – I'll do my best, I know you want to laugh – but, *oh*, the time I've had this week! Still, I won't bother you with it – I know you've got your own troubles and – mind you, it was my own fault . . .

4

These rambling perambulations revolutionised the medium of the stand-up comedian. They turned it into something much more intimate, intriguing and naturalistic, having less to do with the telling of gags and more to do with the sharing of stories.

So great has been his influence that nowadays, more than a decade after his death, the approach seems more like the norm than the exception. We have come to warm most readily to those who convey the core of their humour through character and context, while we have cooled on those who continue to rely on the creaky old conveyor belt of patently contrived one-liners.

Howerd, however, was the one who set the fresh trend. His decision to adopt such an extraordinarily 'ordinary' pose and persona back in the considerably less flexible show-business world of the mid-twentieth-century took real wit, imagination and guts. While his contemporaries remained content to step back and soak up the applause, he chose to step forward and make a connection.

That was his real achievement, his *great* achievement. Frankie Howerd really did make a difference. He was so much more than the casually patronised 'cult' figure, 'camp' icon and *Carry On* fellow-traveller who, according to far too many of the predictably trivial posthumous tributes and all of the tiresome tabloid nudges and winks, bequeathed us little more than a handful of over-familiar sketch shows and sitcoms, a few quaintly hoary catchphrases (all of which, thanks to their increasingly robotic repetition, have long since calcified into mirthless cliché) and a dubious fund of dusty double entendres.[3]

Frankie Howerd – the real Frankie Howerd – was truly special. A brilliantly original, highly skilful and wonderfully funny stand-up comedian – whose talent and impact were as prodigious and profound, in their own way, as those of Bob Hope, Jack Benny or any of the other internationally recognised greats – he deserves to be remembered, respected and celebrated as such.

Consider the extraordinary career: stretching all the way from the late 1940s to the early 1990s, and encompassing everything from the demise of music-hall and the rise of radio to the supremacy of television and the emergence of home video. Howerd stamped his signature upon each one of the media he mastered.

Consider, too, the incredible comebacks: written off by the producers, the press and more than a few of his fellow-performers on not one, not two, but on three profoundly harrowing and humiliating occasions, he returned each time not only to recover all of his old fame, fans and professional pride, but also to find himself a fresh generation of followers. Seldom has there been such a frail yet faithful fighter.

Consider, most of all, the exceptional craft. One critic called the on-stage Howerd 'a very clever man pretending not to be', and few descriptions could have been more apt. His comedy turned the traditional tapestry upside down: we were shown only the messiness – merely the 'ums' and the 'ers' and the 'ahs' – while the elaborate pattern – what Howerd liked (in private) to call 'a beauty of delivery, a beauty of rhythm and timing – like a piece of music'[4] – was kept well-hidden.

He acted more or less how most of us felt (and feared) that *we* would act, should we ever find ourselves forced into the spotlight up there instead of staying hidden in the dark down here. All of the key ingredients of Britain's peculiar post-colonial character – the defiant amateurism, the nagging self-doubt, the public primness and the private sauce – were caught squirming in the spotlight, stuffed inside a badly-fitting brown suit topped off by an exhausted-looking toupee.

The implicit admission was unmistakeable: 'I'm afraid I'm just not up to this job!' The phases of failure were similarly familiar: the nerve would falter, the words would fail and the half-hearted gags would invariably fall horribly, hopelessly flat. No one born British was ever moved to wonder why there was so much 'Oh *no*!' in the show, and so little 'Oh *yes*!' That was life. That was our life.

Most, if not all, of the humour sprang from this world-weary acceptance of our own insurmountable imperfection. Whereas 'proper' performers would always insist on being allowed to entertain you, Frankie Howerd was prepared to advise you to please yourselves.

The net effect was the creation of one of the most openly, endearingly, reassuringly *human* performances that modern comedy has ever produced. Every grumble, every groan, every grimace and every sudden solemn squeak of admonition would coax from us one more furtive snigger of recognition. We knew what he knew, and what he knew was us.

Howerd knew our sort all right. It is time now for us to get to know him.

ACT I: FRANCIS

Nervy — that was me. Nerves were the only thing that came easily.

CHAPTER 1

St Francis

Poor soul.

If we were to begin where Frankie Howerd would have wanted us to begin, we would be five years out of date. According to all of his own public accounts,[1] Frankie Howerd (whose proper surname, incidentally, was spelt 'Howard') was born on 6 March 1922. In truth, he was not: being painfully aware of the age-based prejudices of his own precarious profession, he arranged, in the first of many self-inflicted imprecisions, to have his real infancy erased.

The authentic beginning had actually arrived back on 6 March 1917, when Francis Alick Howard – the first child of the 30-year-old Francis Alfred William Howard and his 29-year-old wife, Edith Florence Morrison – was born in the City Hospital in York. An early photograph recorded the sight of a broad-browed, blown-cheeked and somewhat reproachful-looking baby, with a downy dome of fair hair, a pair of large protruding ears, and a mouth already puckered up into the now-familiar outraged pout ('I was,' the famous adult would always insist, 'quite beautiful'[2]).

The Howards' first family home was situated at 53 Hartford Street, a small but rather smart red-bricked terraced house not far from the city centre in the Fulford district of York. Both parents, right from the start, went out to earn a wage. Francis Snr was a private in the 1st Royal Dragoons; following in the footsteps of his father (a former sergeant at the Royal Military College at Sandhurst), he served as a staff clerk.[3] Edith, meanwhile, laboured long and hard as a 'cream chocolate maker' at the local Rowntree confectionery factory.

Before their child had the chance to acquire any real awareness of his loose northern roots – the solitary memory to survive to later life, apparently, would be of him tumbling down some stairs and bumping his head[4] – the family was obliged to move down south. In the summer of 1919, when the baby Francis had reached the age of two-and-a-half, his father was transferred to the Royal Artillery, promoted to sergeant and posted to the Woolwich Barracks at Greenwich in south-east London.

The need for the switch had been accepted with some enthusiasm by the newly-elevated Sergeant Howard, who recognised that he was not only taking a modest but none the less welcome step up the pro-fessional ladder, but was also, as someone Plumstead born and bred, on his way back to a place that struck him as so much more like 'home'. The acceptance of such a rude upheaval almost certainly came rather harder, however, to his wife, Edith, whose entire life, up until this point, had been lived in close proximity to her mother, father and seven siblings within the confines of the comforting walls of York.

The Howards' new family home was located at 19a Arbroath Road in Eltham (which in those days was a relatively quiet and rural area situated on the borders of London and Kent). Once the Howards had actually settled in, however, it soon began to feel like a home without a family. The problem was that Frank Snr had to spend his weekdays based six miles away at the Royal Artillery barracks, while Edith was left on her own in an unfamiliar environment to bring up their infant son. Although the ostensible head of the household would duly return, with his wage packet, each weekend to be with his wife, the stark contrast in their newly separate styles of life – his brightened by the clarity of its routine and the quality of its camaraderie, hers dulled by a creeping sense of loneliness and a palpable loss of purpose – would in time breed tensions deep enough to shake the base of the bond between them.

For a while, however, the couple worked hard to find ways to remain committed. Frank Snr not only behaved responsibly in his role as the family's sole breadwinner, but also invested a fair amount of effort into trying to make what little time he shared with his wife and son seem reasonably worthwhile. Edith, for her part, bit her tongue on all of the bad days, savoured each one of the few that were good, and buried herself in the business of being both a homemaker and a mother.

It was not just young Francis on whom she would dote. A second son, called Sidney, was born in April 1920, closely followed, in October 1921, by the birth of a baby daughter named Edith Bettina but known to everyone as Betty. Edith adored them all, and, making a virtue out of a necessity, she soon came to relish her role as the family's singular parental figure.

As a mother, she gave her children a generous measure of encouragement and affection. A short, slender woman with dark, vaguely 'gypsyish' good looks, discreet but deeply sincere religious beliefs and a quietly cheerful disposition, she made sure that her family had fun, sharing with them her great love of music, humour and the art of make-believe. When she could afford to she would take the children out, and when the money was tight she would stay with them inside, but, wherever they were, she always ensured that they would laugh, play and consider themselves to have been richly and warmly entertained.

Assuming those duties that had been neglected by their absent father, she also instilled a fairly strong sense of discipline in each of her children, and tried to teach them a simple but solid code of conduct. Echoing many of the lessons she had learned from her own father, David (a stern and very strict Scottish Presbyterian), she would always stress the importance of industry, frugality and self-reliance, and insisted on treating others with a proper sense of fairness and respect.

Of all her three children, it was Frank (as he preferred to be addressed) who appeared the one most eager to please her, as well as the one who was most closely attuned to her own personality and point of view. He loved to sit and listen to her singing snatches from all of her favourite musical comedies ('my first impression of show-business'), felt thrilled when she showed so much enthusiasm for any performance that emerged from out of his 'idiot world of fantasy', and was delighted to find that he shared her 'way-out sense of humour'.[5] In short, he adored her.

Even after he had started attending school – the local Gordon Elementary[6] – and begun to acquire a broader range of friends, potential role models and adult authority figures, this special allegiance stayed as firm and true as ever. He would remain, totally and openly, Edith's son.

He had never been, in any meaningfully emotional sense of the term, 'Frank's son'. Whereas young Sidney and (to a lesser extent) Betty would greet each fleeting visit from their strangely unfamiliar father with a fair degree of enthusiasm and excitement, their older brother never showed any pleasure at being in his presence, regarding him coldly instead as little more than a 'gatecrasher'.[7]

When Frankie Howerd came to look back on this formative stage in his life, he would confess that the only thing that he had shared willingly with his father (aside, perhaps, from their fair-coloured hair) was the recognition of 'a singular lack of rapport'. Frank Snr had seemed, at best, 'a stranger', and, at worst, a rival: 'I positively resented his "intrusion" in the relationship I had with my mother.'[8]

He also genuinely resented the emotional pain he could see that his father was causing her. It was hard enough on Edith when the sum total of the time she could hope to share with her husband amounted to no more than two days out of every seven. It was harder still when he was transferred to the Army Educational Corps, and began travelling all over the country, and spending far longer periods away, fulfilling his duties as an instructor and supervisor of young soldiers.[9] These many absences certainly hurt her, but then so too did her husband's apparent belief that the mere provision of his money would more than make up for the patent lack of his love.

Even if her eldest son failed to understand fully the intimate nature of the causes, he was mature enough to appreciate the true severity of the effects. His beloved mother was suffering, and his father was the man who was making her suffer.

This alone might have been sufficient to explain the adult Frankie Howerd's apparent aversion to any mention of his father, but, according to several of those to whom he was close,[10] there was another, far darker, reason for the denial: his father, he would claim, was a 'sadist' who not only used to 'discipline' his eldest son by locking him in a cupboard, but also (on more than one occasion during those brief and intermittent visits back to their home in Arbroath Road) subjected him to abuse of a sexual nature. While there is no conclusive proof that this is true, Howerd himself remained adamant, in private, that such abuse really did take place.[11]

The story, if one accepts it, certainly makes it hard not to reread the fragmentary autobiographical account of the first decade or so in his life as a coded insight into a profoundly traumatic time. So many tiny details about that 'incredibly shy and withdrawn child'[12] – including a fear of authority that grew so great as to make young Frank appear 'conscientious to the point of stupidity'; an early need to go off on long solitary walks 'just to be alone in my own private, dream world'; the unshakeable conviction that he was 'ugly and useless to man and beast'; and the longing for a place 'in which shyness and nerves did not appear to exist'

– seem to fit the familiar picture of someone struggling through the private hell that accompanied such abuse.[13]

It also appears telling, from this perspective, that towards the end of this period[14] Frank suddenly acquired a serious stammer. It first started to be noticeable, he would recall, whenever he was 'frightened or under stress, and in an unfamiliar environment': 'I'd gabble and garble. Always a very fast talker, I'd repeat words and run them together when this terror came upon me.'[15]

Failing health would gradually diminish any real physical threat posed by Frank Snr. Invalided out of the Army at the start of the 1930s following the discovery of a hole in one of his lungs,[16] he struggled on, increasingly frail and emphysemic, as a clerk at the Royal Arsenal munitions factories until his death, in 1935, at the age of forty-eight. Memories of past threats, on the other hand, would prove impossible for his son to expunge. The real damage had already been done.

When, in 1969, a young journalist had the temerity to quiz Howerd on his feelings about his late father, he merely responded with a slightly too edgy, and therapy-friendly, attempt at a casual putdown: Frank Snr, he muttered, 'was *all right*. He was away a lot. Look, I didn't let you in here to ask me Freudian questions.'[17] Seven years later, however, there was a far more obvious display of disdain in his autobiography, which all but edited out the father from the story of the son's life. In stark contrast to its lovingly lavish treatment of Edith, not one picture of him was included, and no description was provided: aside from the acknowledgement (apropos of nothing in particular) that Frank Snr was 'essentially a practical man',[18] the only recognition of his father's existence was to underline his absence: 'Most people have a mother and father,' Howerd observed, before adding, more with a sigh of relief than any hint of regret: 'I seemed to have only a mother.'[19]

His mother gave him a reason to focus on the future, and, more important still, a reason to believe that he still *had* a future. She represented precisely the kind of adult that he hoped he could become: someone kind, compassionate and honourable but also warm, amusing and refreshingly self-deprecating – 'a "good-doer" rather than a "do-gooder"'.[20]

Clinging tightly to this ideal, he heeded his mother's advice and, once enrolled for Sunday School at the Church of St Barnabas (known locally as the 'tin church' because of its run-down appearance and rusting corrugated roof[21]), threw himself into the culture of organised religion: 'It gave me a feeling of belonging; some comforting communal security.'[22] It was like, in his eyes, a Variety show with morals: lessons, songs, lantern slides and sermons. He loved it, and was spurred on to join 'the Band of Hope, the Cubs, the Society for the Propagation of the Gospel – I joined everything religious in sight'.[23]

His mother was impressed. Delighted – and more than a little relieved – to see the calming (and edifying) effect these spiritual activities were having on her shy and introspective young son, she began to harbour the hope that he might one day find his vocation as a clergyman. Frank himself, in fact, was already thinking along similar lines, although his sights were being aimed somewhat higher: his ultimate goal was to become a saint.

As improbable as it now sounds, the general drift of the ambition was sincere: 'I really thought in those pre-teen years that if I lived a good, pure life in the service of God I could end up as Saint Francis of Eltham, and go to Heaven.'[24] He knelt down each night to say his prayers, kept the Bible by his bed and never failed to read at least a page before setting off to sleep. The strong appeal that the idea of Heaven held for him centred on the belief that it promised to be 'this world without this world's miseries: its poverty and sickness and stammering shyness'.[25] The trainee St Francis might not have known much about where he wanted to go, but his understanding of what he wanted to leave behind could hardly have been any clearer.

Heeding his mother's advice that a good formal education, while no guarantee in itself of canonisation, was at least vital to becoming a vicar, Frank began studying hard to win one of the two London County Council scholarships that were then being offered by the local fee-paying Woolwich County School for Boys – soon to be renamed Shooters Hill Grammar[26] – to potential pupils from poorer backgrounds. Always an academically able young boy, with a particular aptitude for mathematics, he duly passed the entrance examination and, on 1 May 1928, Frank Howard, aged eleven, proudly took his place at the 'posh' school.

The first year proved difficult. He felt that he looked out of place – an unusually tall, very thin, slightly stooping scholarship boy – and feared that most of his middle-class, fee-paying classmates were mocking him behind his back for being nothing more than a mere 'charity' case.[27] His sense of discomfort was made even more intense by the fact that, having exchanged a 'safe' school environment that he had known so well for 'the terrifying question-mark of a strange unknown',[28] his stammer had started to worsen.

From the second year on, however, he began to feel more at home and increasingly happy, forming a fairly large circle of friends, producing consistently solid if unspectacular work in class and performing considerably better than he had expected at cricket. He even developed 'a great crush' on one of his fellow-pupils, a young girl named Sheila, although it led only to humiliation when the draft of a love letter was discovered by a mischievous classmate and subsequently displayed for all to see on the school notice board.[29]

His extra-curricular interest in religion, meanwhile, appeared stronger and deeper than ever. Indeed, he came to be regarded as so knowledgeable and enthusiastic about the subject that in 1930, when he had reached the age of thirteen, his vicar at St Barnabas, the Reverend Jonathan Chisholm, invited him to become a Sunday School teacher. It all seemed to be going smoothly and swiftly to plan: 'I was happy teaching, despite my diffidence, for being religious I was anxious to serve.'[30]

Religion, however, was far from being Frank's only serious interest. The world of popular entertainment had by now come to rival it as a source both of fascination and inspiration.

As with so much else that felt positive in Frank's young life, this appetite had been inherited from, and cultivated by, his mother. Although devoted to the solemn code of the black book, Edith was far from averse to sampling the odd bit of sauciness culled from the 'blue' book, and she was always happy to hear her eldest son repeat the latest jokes in circulation (though she did draw the line – and administer a crisp clip round the ear – when, without knowing quite what it meant, he included a certain four-letter word he had overheard being uttered by the local greengrocer).

She also introduced him to the potentially thrilling spectacle of live entertainment when, on 26 December 1925, she took him to the Woolwich Artillery Theatre to see his first pantomime, *Cinderella*, featuring the fragrant Nora Delaney as the principal boy: 'It was an exciting, glittering, over-the-rainbow world, and I instantly wanted to become a part of it: not specifically as an actor or comedian or singer or anything else, but just in order to escape to wonderland.'[31]

From that moment on, Frank seized every opportunity to see, hear,

out or re-enact the very best that the stage, screen and radio had
er. There were countless outings to the various local cinemas,
.h in those days ranged from the upmarket Palace (which boasted
a well-appointed' café lounge) to the downmarket Little Cinema (or
the 'Bug Hutch', as Eltham's youngsters preferred to call it,[32] which
during the silent years featured a piano accompanist called Lena Crisp
– a future Frankie Howerd stooge). There were also many sessions spent
in front of the wireless set, listening to all of the big dance bands (first
Jack Payne's, later Henry Hall's), plenty of revue and Variety shows
(such as *Radio Radiance* and *Music Hall*) and the first few broadcast
attempts at sketch and situation-comedy (starting off with *Myrtle and
Bertie*).[33] There were even, when Edith's meagre funds allowed,
occasional excursions to local clubs, theatres and fairs, as well as a visit
to the novelty 'Air Circus' that was held one summer on (and above)
Eltham's green and pleasant Nine Fields. In addition to all of this, of
course, there remained the keenly anticipated annual pilgrimage to the
pantomime.

The urge to imitate and emulate these glamorous forms and figures
grew stronger with each passing year. Inside the Howard home, Frank
started out by entertaining his mother and baby sister with peep-shows
created from old cardboard boxes, and original plays that came complete
with a miniature theatre (made out of rags, sticks and Edith's best tea
tray, and populated by a cast of cut-outs from well-thumbed copies of
Film Fun), as well as a selection of self-authored gags, funny stories and
painful puns grouped together under the banner of *Howard's Howlers*.

It was not long before he began hankering for a bigger and broader
audience, and he soon managed to persuade the girl next door, Ivy
Smith, to help him form a 'two-child concert party'. The duo managed
to perform several surprisingly lucrative Saturday matinées at the bottom
of his back garden, charging other children a farthing a time for the
privilege of admission, before a startled Edith stumbled upon the event
(or 'robbery' as she called it) and demanded that everyone present be
reimbursed without delay.[34] His response was to transform the operation
into a scrupulously charitable affair, performing a further series of concerts (first with Ivy and then later with his similarly-minded sister, Betty)
designed to benefit a variety of worthwhile local causes.

By the time, therefore, that Frank began his spell as a Sunday School
teacher, his strong sense of duty to the Church was already prone to

distraction from his even deeper desire to perform. Things soon grew worse, as far as spiritual matters were concerned, when he found himself obliged, as part of the preparation for his new duties, to join his fellow-tutors each Monday evening at Reverend Chisholm's home in Appleton Road for tea, cake and very, very, lengthy hermeneutical advice: 'I remember how I'd look at him, trying to be attentive, but with my mind wandering to films and music and the theatre.'[35]

The problem was not just that so little now seemed to be seeping in; it was also that so much that was already in seemed to be leaking out. With nothing more to rely on than a wafer-thin recollection of the basic theme of the kindly but rather dull Reverend Chisholm's latest briefing, Frank would find that he had no choice but to improvise his way through each one of his own Sunday School sessions, spending more time regaling his audience with tales of Robin Hood, Morgan the Pirate and Sexton Blake than he did engaging them with any pertinent biblical issues, axioms or events. His popularity soared as an unusually entertaining teacher, but so too did his sense of guilt as an increasingly heavy-lidded trainee saint: 'I thought I'd let God down in some way.'[36]

He soldiered on for a while in a state of stubborn denial, unable to face up to the fact that he was on the verge of disappointing a mother who seemed so proud that he had found what she had taken to terming his 'calling'.[37] Then, to his great surprise and immense relief, he stumbled upon a compromise: the deceptively perceptive Reverend Chisholm, sensing that his protégé was an extrovert trapped in an introvert's cassock, encouraged him to join the Church Dramatic Society. It struck Frank immediately as an inspired piece of advice: now, instead of having to abandon the Church for the theatre, he could accommodate the theatre within the Church.

The Society's upcoming project was a revival of Ian Hay's 1919 *Cinderella*-style drawing-room comedy *Tilly of Bloomsbury*, and the newest member of the company made no attempt to disguise the fact that he was 'pathetically eager' to take part.[38] Although the play had acquired a certain reputation for containing several roles that were suitable for the most 'wooden' of actors (even the BBC's notoriously teak-taut Director-General, John Reith, had managed to march his way through a recent amateur production without appearing too out-of-place[39]), it was immediately clear to the current producer, Winifred

Young, that Frank represented a serious casting challenge. Auditioning for the relatively undemanding part of Tilly's working-class father, he was excruciatingly bad, reading his lines 'in an incoherent gabble, flushing in a manner that would make a beetroot look positively anaemic, knocking over the props in my clumsiness – and embarrassing everyone in my anxiety to please'.[40]

When the ordeal was finally over, Mrs Young took him to one side, smiled a soft, sympathetic smile and then asked him: 'Will you let me help you?' Astonished that he was not being admonished, he stuttered an eager 'Yes' in grateful reply.[41]

From that moment on, this gifted and compassionate amateur director worked as Frank's private – and unpaid – tutor. Every Tuesday and Thursday evening, he would spend two taxing but hugely rewarding hours at her house, gradually learning how to overcome his stammer, start the process of mastering his role and, perhaps most importantly of all, begin believing in himself: 'She taught me how to "ee-nun-cee-ate", to be calm, to concentrate on the performance – and to forget myself as a self-pitying nonentity.'[42]

He would later claim that he owed 'as much to Winifred Young as to anyone else in my career', speculating that without her intervention 'there might not have been any career, merely bitter frustration'.[43] There was certainly no doubting her immediate effect: she transformed him, within a matter of a few short weeks, from a painfully awkward-looking nervous wreck into the show's most notable success.

Frank came through it all without offering the audience more than barely a hint of his former hesitation, anxiety and self-doubt, and, in spite of the modest size and nature of his role, his performance had drawn the warmest of all the applause. For the first time in his life, he felt triumphant.

Someone who happened to encounter him backstage after the show told him matter-of-factly: 'You should be an actor.'[44] Those five words, regardless of whether they were uttered out of honesty, politeness or perhaps even a playful sense of sarcasm, triggered a profoundly positive effect on the still-exhilarated novice performer, serving as 'a sudden and instant catalyst on all my vague hopes and half-dreams, fusing them into an absolute certitude of determination'.[45] That moment, the adult Frankie Howerd would always say, was the special one, the turning point, the moment when – all of a sudden – he really *knew*: '[F]rom that night on I never deviated from a sense of destiny almost manic in its obsessive intensity.'[46]

There would be no more talk of St Francis. The future was for Frank the Actor.

CHAPTER 2

A Stuttering Start

Well. No. Yes. Ah.

They coined a new nickname for Frank Howard at Shooters Hill school: 'The Actor'.[1] He loved it.

He loved the idea that an actor was what he was set to become. It might only have been 1932, three long and arduous maths- and Latin-filled years before he was due to leave school, but already, as far as he was concerned, acting was the only thing that really mattered.

Having acquired his initial theatrical experience under the auspices of his church, Frank now proceeded to advance his acting ambitions inside his school, joining its own informal dramatic society and establishing himself very quickly as one of its most lively and distinctive figures. Gone, in this particular context at least, was the insecure loner of old, and in his place was to be found a far more sociable, self-assured and increasingly popular young man: his whole manner and personality appeared to come alive, growing so much bigger and bolder and brighter, whenever the action switched from the classroom to the stage. Here, at least, he knew what he was doing, and he knew that what he was doing was good.

Right from the start, he made it abundantly clear that he was eager to try everything: acting, writing, direction, production, promotion – whatever it was, he was willing to do it, work at it and, given time, perhaps even master it. Everywhere that one looked – backstage, in the wings, centre stage, even at the table with the tickets right at the back of the school hall – Frank Howard seemed to be there, still slightly stooped, still slightly stammering, but now entirely immersed in the experience.

As a performer, he progressed at quite a rapid rate. Although he was hardly the type, even then, to lose himself in a role – his playful disposition, in addition to his distinctive voice and looks, conspired against the pursuit of such a style – his obvious enthusiasm, allied to his lively wit, ensured that each one of his stage contributions stood out and stayed in the mind. At his most inspired, such as the occasion when he played the spoiled and rascally Tony Lumpkin in Oliver Goldsmith's satire *She Stoops to Conquer*, he showed real comic promise, relishing the chance to release all of the dim-witted verve that he had found lurking in the original text.[2]

As a fledgling playwright, on the other hand, the great amount of faith he invested in his own ability struck most of those whose opinions mattered as gravely misplaced. An audacious attempt to squeeze a rambling one-hour play, entitled *Lord Halliday's Birthday Party*, into a tight ten-minute slot in a forthcoming concert was thwarted by the school's headmaster, the rather dour Rupert Affleck, who deemed the script (which featured a messy divorce, a brutal murder and several other striking themes lifted straight from some of the movies Frank had recently seen) 'far too outrageous and bold to be performed by young boys', adding (according to Howerd's own rueful recollection) that he was 'appalled that a fifteen-year-old could be so depraved as to write such filth'.[3]

Embarrassed but undeterred, Frank proceeded to write several more scripts that Mr Affleck, had he seen them, would no doubt have considered to have been of far too sensational a nature. When, however, a play that he did manage to get performed – his blatantly derivative murder-mystery, *Sweet Fanny Adams* – elicited nothing more audible (let alone encouraging) from the auditorium than the lonely sound of tumbleweed being blown through the desert, he resolved in future to keep the rest of his 'masterpieces' to himself.[4] Always a populist, Frank reasoned that if the current market demand was restricted to his acting, then his acting, for the time being, would have to be the sole commodity that he would seek to deliver.

In 1933, at the age of sixteen, he began attending an evening class in acting offered by what in those days was called the London County Council (or LCC). It was there that he first encountered his next great mentor: Mary Hope.

Hope – an experienced stage actor herself – became one of Howard's tutors, and, just like Winifred Young before her, she soon found herself intrigued by the young performer's quirky appeal. First, she encouraged him to join the LCC Dramatic Society – a vastly more serious and rigorous kind of company than either of Howard's previous two theatrical troupes – and then, after seeing how richly original was his potential (and also how open he was to instruction), she advised him to aim his sights on securing a scholarship at RADA (the Royal Academy of Dramatic Art). If he was interested, she added, she would be willing to work alongside him as his coach.

Howard, his eyebrows hovering high and his bottom lip hanging low, was, as he would later put it, '*a-mazed*'. Listening back to the phrase as it echoed around inside his head – '*Was I interested?*' – the only word that sounded out of place was the 'was'. He was almost too thrilled to speak: 'Choked with emotion, I managed to stammer that it was the most exciting prospect imaginable.'[5]

Before he could commit himself with a clear conscience, however, he knew that he would have to find a way to win his mother's blessing. This did not seem likely to be easy. Edith, after all, had set her heart on seeing her son acquire a good education and then pursue a suitably upright and worthy religious career; now he was set to dash both of these treasured hopes at a stroke. Frank's great sense of guilt grew even worse when he reflected upon the many sacrifices that had been (and still were being) made, not just by his mother but also by everyone else in his family, so that he could see through his education at Shooters Hill.

The loss of the ailing Frank Snr's Army salary, occurring as it did right at the time when the country was deep in the depths of the Great Depression, had forced Edith to find work as a cleaner in order to help pay the mounting pile of bills. A further, and far more painful, consequence of the family's shrunken income was the fact that it had made it impractical for either Sidney or Betty to match the length (or the quality) of their elder brother's education: both, it had become clear, would have to leave school as soon as they reached the then minimum age of fourteen (Sidney, as things turned out, for a career in the Post Office,[6] and Betty for a job in an office[7]). Everyone, it seemed, had suffered for the benefit of young Frank, and now young Frank was ready to risk it all on RADA.

'Children are inclined to take a tremendous amount for granted,' the adult Frankie Howerd would come to reflect, 'and for my part I never fully appreciated [. . .] the degree of the hardship involved in keeping me at Shooters Hill.'[8] The teenaged Frank Howard, however, in spite of his youthful self-absorption, knew enough to know how great a blow the news of his apparent recklessness would be, and how easily his sudden change of plan could be taken as a betrayal. He hated telling them, but he had to.

When he did, he could not have been more pleasantly surprised by his mother's outwardly calm and remarkably compassionate reaction. Instead of initiating a bitter debate or administering a furious rebuke, she just sighed, smiled resignedly, and said: 'That sounds like a nice idea.'[9] Frank's relief and gratitude were immense: if his redoubtable mother was still on his side, then she would ensure that the entire family remained on his side. 'I think she was disappointed that I wasn't going to enter the Church, after all,' he would recall, 'but since her primary concern was for my happiness, she gave me all the support she could.'[10]

He returned, suitably emboldened, to his coach Mary Hope, and started working hard – 'harder than I'd worked for anything in my life'[11] – in preparation for his forthcoming RADA exam. There were three set pieces to master: one a short speech from a contemporary play, and two soliloquies from Shakespeare. With the momentous event only a matter of months away, the schedule was unrelenting: day after day, week after week, the context of each discrete piece was studied, the character of each speaker explored and the rhythms of each line assessed. Hope also worked with Howard on keeping his nerve, controlling his stammer and coping in general with the unfamiliar experience of being up there on show all alone. Rehearsal followed rehearsal, critique followed critique, until both of them were happy that they had secured a strong start, a solid centre and a suitably big finish. When the time finally came, Frank Howard felt sure that he was ready.

The big day started cold and grey. Rising from his bed early, having barely slept throughout what had felt like an impossibly long night, Frank washed, fussed over his fine curly hair, and then put on his best, barely worn, brown suit – which hung limply off his tall, skinny frame like a large sack would have done from a stick. Studying the effect in the mirror, he thought that he looked rather good. There was just time to go downstairs for a quick cup of tea in the kitchen and some welcome words of encouragement from his mother, and then he was up, out and off to meet his fate.

Clutching the packet of cheese sandwiches that his mother had made for his lunch, he caught the train from Eltham to Holborn Viaduct, and then, with a growing sense of trepidation, walked slowly through Bloomsbury, with all of the lines from the three speeches rattling around inside his head, until he arrived outside the entrance to the grand-looking RADA building at 62 Gower Street. What happened next was an experience that Frank Howard would never, ever, forget.

Shuffling inside, he found himself at the back of a vast room that appeared to be almost full of his fellow-applicants. It only took one quick glance over at them – smart, smug, matinée idol types – and one furtive glance back at himself – suddenly revealed as a scruffy, shambling, 'sweating oaf'[12] – for all of the old demons to come crashing back. The others looked as if they belonged; he felt that he did not. As he stood there, rooted helplessly to the spot, he held on tightly to his packet of sandwiches ('I had to cling to *something*'), and felt sure that he could hear more than a few mocking laughs.[13] He knew what he had to do, but at that singularly vital moment, in spite of all of those months of lessons and learning and desperately hard work, he knew that he had lost all faith in his ability to do it.

Called in for his audition, he walked over to his spot, still clutching his packet of cheese sandwiches absent-mindedly to his chest, and then, sensing that he was having some trouble in keeping still, looked down and noticed that his left leg had started to tremble. The more he tried to stop it, the worse the quivering became. When he looked up in embarrassment at the examiners (one of whom – the imperious actor Helen Haye – he recognised immediately as the haughty wife of the master villain in Alfred Hitchcock's recent movie, *The 39 Steps*), he found that they were all staring back not at his face but straight down at his leg. Panicking, he took his right hand (which remained wrapped around his squashed packet of sandwiches) and slammed it down hard and fast against his left knee, praying that the violent gesture would at least bring the shaking to a stop.

It did not. The hand did not stop the knee; the knee started the hand. All that the attempt to end the action achieved was to provide the row of open-mouthed examiners with the even more peculiar spectacle of a crumpled young man and what was left of his crumpled sandwiches being shaken ever more wildly by a wildly shaking left leg. It looked a bit like a dance, and a bit like an exorcism, and a bit like a fit, but it was definitely a disaster. When, eventually, his leg, and the rest of him, finally came to a halt, his sandwiches had showered the examiners in a mixture of shredded cheese and breadcrumbs, and his suit was in almost as bad a shape as his frazzled nerves.

'Begin,' he was told, and so, red-faced and reluctantly, he did: 'Yes . . . Well . . . Um . . . To-to-to . . . er be . . . or not-not-not to . . . um . . . Yes, well . . . To be . . . Well, that's the question, isn't it? . . .' He was well aware that it was already over, right there and then, but, somehow, he struggled on to the bitter end: 'I should have thrown up my hands and run for my life,' he would recall, 'but beneath the panic lay that hard subsoil of determination, and so I stumbled and stammered and squeaked and shook my way through all of the three set pieces.'[14]

They thanked him. He thanked them. He went out. The next candidate came in. The grey day turned black.

Howard spent the train journey home slumped deep inside 'an anguish of desolation and shame': 'I'd let everyone down: my mother, my headmaster, my schoolmates, Mary Hope – and myself. I was a complete and utter failure.'[15] When he arrived back in Eltham, he found that he simply could not bear to face anyone, not even his mother, and so he went instead to a field at the back of his house, where he sat down in the long grass and started to sob. 'Never before or since,' he would say, 'have I wept as I did on that day.'[16]

He stayed there for two blank and miserable hours. Eventually, however, once the sobbing had stopped and the tears had started to dry, a bright thought burst through the gloom. Perhaps, he reflected, he had not reached the end at all, but had merely taken a wrong turn. Sitting bolt upright, he then said to himself:

You're a fool. A fool . . . You must have courage. Courage. The way you're behaving is absolutely gutless . . . Look, you believe in God, don't you? And you know that God seems to have given you talent. You *feel* that to be true . . . Now God is logical. He must be, otherwise life is stupid. Pointless. Without meaning . . . OK, perhaps RADA and straight acting aren't for you. What then is the alternative?[17]

It did not take long for this characteristically brusque internal inquisition to summon up an acceptable response: 'Comedy? Is that the alternative?

If you're not meant to be a great Shakespearean, are you meant to be a comedian? Is that it? . . . Why not try and see?'[18]

There seemed only one answer to such a question, and that was: why not, indeed? 'I didn't have anything to lose,' he concluded, 'except my pride – and that was wounded enough already after such a traumatic day.'[19]

He got up, dusted himself down and walked home, where his worried mother had been waiting most of the afternoon for her son to return. When he told her tearfully about his terrible day, she just held him for a while and gave him a consoling kiss on the cheek. When, a little later, he hinted at his belief that his 'calling' was now, yet again, about to change, and that this time it was set to be a career in comedy, she simply assured him that she still had 'an unswerving faith' in the inevitability of his eventual success.[20] Sensing how badly the fallen St Francis felt that he had already let her down, she did all that she could to discourage any further growth in guilt: 'As long as you're kind and decent,' she stressed, 'I don't care what you do.'[21]

According to the neat dramatic myth engendered by the memoirs, what the 16-year-old Howard did next was to leave school ('I'd betrayed the faith they'd had in me there: the Actor was now the Flop. No, I couldn't go back'[22]) and find a job while he waited impatiently for the arrival of some kind of bountiful show-business break. The unromantic truth, however, is that he returned to Shooters Hill, subdued and semi-detached, and, reluctantly but dutifully, saw out the last two years of his secondary education.[23] Although his academic studies never recovered (he would leave with only a solitary school certificate to count as a qualification), his actorly ebullience most certainly did: according to the fond recollections of one of his contemporaries,[24] Howard managed not only to strengthen his reputation as a much-talked-about 'character', but also somehow contrived to 'bring the house down' with his portrayal of The Wall in the school's 1935 production of 'Pyramus and Thisbe' (the play-within-a-play from Shakespeare's *A Midsummer Night's Dream*).

When, at long last, the day approached when he really was able to leave – at the start of the summer of 1935 – he intended to start scouring the local area for the kind of relatively well-paid but undemanding short-term job that would complement a young man's pursuit of a career in comedy. Before, however, he even had the chance to commence such a fanciful plan, his father died, on 12 May, and all of a sudden Frank Jnr, at the tender age of eighteen, found himself elevated to the position of the senior male in the Howard household.

Out of desperation, he took a menial job as a filing clerk with a firm by the name of Henry A. Lane, Provisions and Produce, at 37–45 Tooley Street in the East End borough of Southwark. The work was dull and the pay was poor (just £1 per week, which was meagre even for those days), and the only solace that Frank would find was within the walls of the nearby cathedral, where he spent most of his free time either sitting alone in prayer or sometimes listening to recitals.

He lived and longed for the evenings, when he could still feel, at least for an hour or two, that he was pushing on with his 'proper' ambitions: performing in local plays, pageants, concert parties, benefits, balls and revues – anything, in fact, that seemed to carry even the slightest scent of show business. He not only remained a keen contributor to the various productions put on by his colleagues at the local church, but he was also now an extremely active member of the Shooters Hill Old Boys' Dramatic Society (where he was free to test his acting talents on slightly more challenging forms of fare).

Not even the playful evenings, however, could make up for the laboured days. As he sat there in Tooley Street, shuffling papers and watching clocks, Frank Jnr could feel himself turning slowly but surely into Frank Snr – another career clerk, another man without any discernible drive or dreams or pride, just going through the motions, just getting on with getting through life. It was demoralising – and it was made even worse by the man who was Frank's boss.

As far as Frank Howard was concerned, the bluebird of happiness had never even come close to perching on one of Henry A. Lane's sloping shoulders. With wounds from the Great War that had left him with a tin plate secreted in his head, a patch wrapped over an eye and a limp in one leg, he was no stranger, Howerd would say, to moods of 'bitter malevolence'.[25] The one in-house factor guaranteed to trigger the eruption of such moods, it soon became clear, was the blatantly bored and permanently distracted Frank Howard: 'If a cup of tea stood ready to be spilled in his lap then I, in my clumsiness, spilled it. If a bottle of ink waited to be knocked over, I knocked it. He truly despised me and terrorised me, and the more sadistic his behaviour, the more of a gibbering idiot I became.'[26]

Lane was not the only one who found young Frank to be more than a fraction less than adequate. Most of his colleagues – noting his peculiar habit of suddenly making wild facial expressions in the direction of no one in particular, and his equally odd tendency to mutter, shriek and sometimes even squeak to himself behind the covers of a file – considered him slightly mad. The underlying reason for such eccentric behaviour was that Frank was actually spending the vast majority of each day's office hours furtively studying his scripts ('I simply had to,' he later explained; 'my nights and weekends were almost completely occupied with rehearsals and performances'[27]).

After ten weeks of trying to combine the day job with his multiple play jobs, Howard was tired, run-down and covered in a rash of unsightly boils. Something had to give, and it was no surprise what did. Thanks to the chronically distracted Frank, a large consignment intended for the United States of America ended up in the Republic of China, and a folder dispatched to Leningrad was found to contain, among other things, a programme for *Frank Howard's Gertchers Concert Party*. Henry Lane snapped, and Howard was sacked.

After he had endured the humiliation of a fortnight on the dole, his anxious mother intervened. Knowing that one of the wealthy people for whom she now cleaned was a part-owner of the United Friendly Insurance Company, she asked for – and duly received – a favour, and a suitable position as a clerk was found for her son at the firm's head office in Southwark Bridge Road. Frank had landed on his feet: not only was the pay (thirty shillings per week) a little better, but the hours were better, too: ten to six from Monday to Friday, with half-day shifts on alternate Saturdays. He was also greatly relieved to find that his new boss – a single woman aged about forty – was as kind as his old boss had been cruel ('I think she fancied me,' he would later claim[28]).

There was still not the slightest danger, however, of him ever wavering in his show-business ambitions and warming to his work as a clerk. He continued to pour all of his creative energies into his countless amateur performances, and even found the time, and the vanity, to form his very own tiny troupe – consisting of himself, his sister Betty, and one or two of their mutual friends – called *Frank Howard's Knockout Concert Party* ('the ego was in full flight again'[29]). This troupe went on to stage innumerable 21-sketch-long revues – all of them strictly for charity (Edith was still watching) – based on whatever Howard had time to write in the office and whatever he and the others found the wit and the will to improvise in front of the audience. They toured all of the scout huts, church halls and retirement homes in the Eltham area, carrying their homemade scenery, costumes and props along with them on the tram, and did far more good than harm.

Even when he was part of a group, however, Howard always remained, in spirit, an incorrigible solo artiste. His instructions to his fellow-performers tended to take the following self-serving form: 'Now you, Betty, will go on the stage and say something. Anything. Then I'll say something. Then Charlie here will say something. We'll make it up as we go along – always remembering that we're aiming for the tag-line . . . Which *I* will deliver!'[30]

Few talent contests in South London went ahead without the participation of Frank Howard. It was easy enough to execute: most of the old music-halls used to accommodate some sort of cheap and cheerful 'Talent Night' spot once a week on one of their bills, and all any amateur performer needed to do was to turn up, sign on and then try their luck. Such occasions were not for the faint-hearted – a bad act, or a good act that just happened to be having a bad day, would soon be loudly booed and crudely abused – but, for those with thicker skins or stronger dreams, these events were the places where hope would spring eternal, because, regardless of how awful it might have been on any one particular night, there would always be the promise of another week, another audience and another chance.

Howard, in spite of his notoriously pronounced susceptibility to stage fright, was one of those determined characters who kept going back for more. The first time, he walked on, delivered a comic monologue, and then walked back off again to the lonely sound of his own footsteps. The following week, he returned to try out a few impressions (the list included Noël Coward, Charles Laughton, Maurice Chevalier, James Cagney and Gary Cooper), but, once again, the act fell horribly flat. The week after that, he reappeared dressed like an overgrown schoolboy and proceeded to sing a novelty comedy song: that, too, sank like the proverbial stone.

One week, he even tried changing his name to 'Ronnie Ordex', but when that failed to change his fortunes, he promptly changed it back again, and then proceeded to try something else. He went on, and on, and on, into his early twenties, trying anything and everything that did not demand any great degree of physical dexterity. 'I kept trying,' he later explained, 'because the utter conviction that I did have talent was stronger than the flaws of personality that crucified me when it came to an actual performance.'[31]

Not even an exceptionally humiliating on-stage experience at the Lewisham Hippodrome would shake this underlying faith in his own potential. It was during a talent night here – on a bill that boasted some of the biggest names (including the band leader Jack Payne and the crooner and stand-up comic Derek Roy) on the current Variety circuit – that Frank Howard discovered just what it really meant, in the cut-throat world of show business, to 'die a death' in front of a large live audience.

The root of the problem was the fact that, as the slot for new talent came straight after the interval, Howard was obliged to follow the comedian who closed the first half – and the comedian who closed the first half was Jimmy James. Soon to be dubbed 'the comedians' comedian',[32] Jimmy James was already widely admired as an inimitable performer, an inspired ad-libber and an exquisite timer of a line. With his woozily lugubrious looks (suggestive of a bulldog whose water has recently been laced with Scotch) and downbeat demeanour, he was a masterful droll, and Howard, who watched him fascinated from the wings, was left, quite understandably, feeling utterly awestruck.

Then, after the short interval, it was his turn. The curtain rose back up, he strode on to the stage, and was immediately blinded by the most powerful spotlight he had ever encountered. He winced, blinked, shifted from side to side in search of a shadow, winced and blinked again, and then gave up and began his act. It was no good: whatever he tried to remember, whatever he tried to say, he could not get that blinding light from out of his eyes or out of his mind. His mouth dried up, the beads of cold sweat crept down his brow, the eyes froze open and one of his knees, inevitably, began to tremble. The stage seemed to be getting bigger, and he was getting smaller. He squinted out at the audience, and the audience stared back at him. For one puzzled moment, there was just silence and rapt attention, but then, as the unmistakeable scent of sheer naked fear drifted its way slowly out over and beyond the stalls, there came a reaction: 'The audience began to laugh, but it was the most dreaded of all laughter for a performer – derision. And the more they fell about, the worse I became. The orchestra leader hissed from the pit: "Do something, or get off!" I stumbled off – in tears.'[33]

He realised, as he sobbed backstage, that he could not take any more of this, but he also recognised, as he dried his eyes, that he would be unable *not* to take any more of this. He was trapped, and he knew it, and so, yet again, he resolved to go on.

He tried more talent nights, but won none. He staged more plays, concerts and revues, but most of them faded from memory soon after they were done. He auditioned on no fewer than four separate occasions for Carroll Levis, the powerful talent scout, but the result of each one of them was the same: rejection. The recurring problem was not that people failed to glimpse any potential; it was just that, far too often, the nerves kept getting in the way. No matter how many times someone said 'No,' however, Frank Howard never stopped believing that, one day, someone would say 'Yes': 'I was the most undiscovered discovery of my day!'[34]

This, for the foreseeable future, was what he would remain. A war was about to break out. His own personal breakthrough would have to wait.

CHAPTER 3

Army Camp

*So, anyway, he said, 'I was wondering if you could go to the
lads,' he said, 'and give them a turn.' Yes! That's what I
thought – cheeky devil!*

This time, he did not even need to audition: the British Army showed
no hesitation in signing him up for the duration. It had taken the
outbreak of a war, but, at last, Frank Howard was able to feel that he
was wanted.

The precise date of his admission is a matter of some dispute. Howerd
– that notorious biographical dissembler – would claim that it had
arrived one day in February 1940[1] – more or less a month short of his
twenty-third birthday, and a decidedly dilatory-sounding four months
after his name was first registered for conscription.[2] On this particular
occasion, however, he was probably telling the truth: his call-up papers
remain unavailable for public scrutiny, but, given the bureaucratic inef-
ficiency that is known to have dogged the entire process of mobilisation,
the date is not quite as implausible as, at first glance, it might seem.[3]

His initial hope, once war was declared, had been to join ENSA
(an acronym that stood formally for 'Entertainments National Service
Association', and informally for 'Every Night Something Awful').[4] The
motivation, he later took pains to explain, had not been 'to dodge
the column', but rather 'to try to be of service at something I thought
I was good at: entertaining'.[5] Even at that early stage, however, the
ENSA organisers were already managing to attract a sufficient number
of suitably-qualified applicants (ranging from ageing music-hall performers to a younger breed of actors, comedians and musicians) to make
them feel able to pass on such a raw and unconventional talent, and so
Howard was forced to try his luck elsewhere.

He ended up as just another regular soldier in the Royal Artillery – his father's old regiment – and was posted to Shoeburyness Barracks, near Southend-on-Sea, in Essex. It was there that, within a matter of days, 'The Actor' acquired a new nickname: 'The Unknown Quantity'.[6]

The name was first spluttered in exasperation by the latest authority figure to loom large in Frank Howard's life: a loud and irascible little man called Sergeant-Major Alfred Tonks. Howard – a gangling, slouching, stammering and startlingly uncoordinated creature in crumpled khaki – managed to make his Sergeant-Major angry, distressed, amused and confused in broadly equal measure.

He always struggled to look half-smart, made a shocking mess of stripping down his rifle, never seemed to know when he was supposed to march quick or slow, mixed up 'standing at ease' with 'standing easy', and was often a positive menace on the parade ground. 'Frank just couldn't get it together,' one of his former comrades recalled. 'When the sarge shouted "Right wheel!" once, Frank actually headed off to the left. And when the order came to "Mark time!" – guess who bumped into my back and sent me sprawling into the bloke in front? Right first time.'[7]

As if intent upon making matters even worse, Howard sometimes also failed to fight the urge to answer back. On one particular occasion, straight after Sergeant-Major Tonks had shrieked out his standard sequence of critical clichés – '*You 'orrible shower!*' – young Private Howard actually had the temerity to mutter in response: 'Speak up!' It was 'merely a nervous reflex', he later explained, but it was more than enough to spark another noisy rant from his ruddy-cheeked tormentor.[8]

The only thing that saved him from spending one long spell after another stuck in the glasshouse was the fact that Tonks, though clearly impatient to hammer this risibly unconventional soldier into some kind of vaguely acceptable shape, could never quite decide whether he was dealing with a 'truculent rebel' or merely a useless idiot.[9] He settled for thinking of Howard as his 'Unknown Quantity' – partly because the act of classifying the unclassifiable made him feel as if he was restoring at least the semblance of order to his environment, and partly because he was probably quite relieved to leave the true nature and extent of that 'quantity' undiscovered.

Once the trauma of basic training was finally over, Howard was transferred away from Tonks – no doubt much to their mutual relief –

and into B Battery in another section of the barracks. Accorded the rank of Gunner, Frank began busying himself with the business of providing a proper form of defence for an area of Essex surrounding Shoeburyness.

His thoughts, however, were seldom far removed from the much more pleasant world of show business. As soon as he started to settle, he found that all of the old 'passion' and 'fire' that had recently been 'damped down by the practicalities of circumstance' now suddenly 'burned hot again'.[10] Hearing that some of his fellow garrison personnel were putting on a concert each Sunday night in the local YMCA, he eagerly sought out the Entertainments Officer and offered his services as a stand-up comic. The out-of-his-depth officer, who had been anxiously patrolling the corridors asking anyone and everyone he encountered if they might just possibly be able to 'do anything', accepted the offer without hesitation. Frank Howard the performer was free to make his comeback.

When he stepped on to the stage the following Sunday, however, he was more than slightly surprised to hear himself introduced by the compère as 'Gunner Frankie Howard of B Battery'. He did a quick double-take: '*Frankie* Howard?' He had never allowed anyone to call him '*Frankie*' before – 'I didn't like Frankie a bit; it seemed positively babyish' – but, once the show was over, he soon came to find that it had caught on, and, in time, he would reluctantly become resigned to the fact that the name was destined to stick ('A pity, really').[11]

The performance itself had gone down rather well. Most of his four-minute spot was filled with the kind of tried and tested material that had been blatantly 'borrowed' from professional comedians – most notably Max Miller – but he did manage to make at least one elderly gag sound vaguely original:

> I was at a dance the other night in Southend. At the NAAFI. And this girl was there. Very nice, she was. Yes. So after the dance I said to her: 'May I see you home?' And she said: 'Oh, er, yes. Thank you very much!' So I said: 'Where do you live?' She said: 'I live on a farm. It's not very far from here. It's about a half-an-hour walk.' So I said: 'Oh, right, that's fine.' Then she said: 'The only thing is, you see, I've got a couple of packages to pick up, from my uncle, to take back home to the farm. Would you mind?' So

I said: 'No, no, we'll call in. What are they, by the way, these packages?' She said: 'Two ducks.' I said: '*Ducks?*' She said: 'Oh, it's all right. They're not dead. They're alive. But they won't flap. They're all sort of bound up a bit.' So we went down to this uncle, and he gave her these two ducks. So I – the perfect gentleman – said: 'Please, let me. I'll carry them.' So I put one under each arm. And then off we traipsed, down this lane and across this field. Pitch dark it was. And all of a sudden this girl fell back against a hedge and went: '*Ooo-aaa-eee!*' I said: 'What the *hell's* wrong with *you?*' She said: 'I'm frightened!' I said: 'What on earth are you frightened *of* ?' And she said: 'I'm frightened of you!' I said: 'Frightened of *me?*' She said: 'Yes. I'm frightened that you're going to try and make love to me!' I said: 'How the *hell* can I make love to you with a *duck* under each arm?' So she said: 'Well, I could hold 'em for you, couldn't I?'

He also sang the song, in his own inimitable style, for which he would later be infamous – 'Three Little Fishes':

> Down in the meadow in a little bitty pool
> Lived three little fishes and their mommy fishy too.
> 'Swim!' said the mommy fishy, 'Swim if you can!'
> So they swam and they swam right over the dam.

Each subsequent verse was disrupted with comic interjections, and each chorus became an excuse for a quite extraordinary array of high-decibel shrieks and yelps:

> There was Tom: 'Boop-boop-dittem-datten-wattem, choo!'
> And there was Dick: 'Boop-boop-dittem-datten-wattem, chooo!'
> And there was Cecil: 'Baa-oop-boop-dit-tem-dat-ten-wat-tem,
>   choooo!'
> (Oh, he was a snob! He was dying to get into an aquarium!)
> And they swam and they swam right over the dam . . .[12]

Snobbish Cecil, needless to say, met with a particularly grisly end.

It was the same routine that he had performed so many times before, but, on this particular occasion, it really seemed to work. There were relatively few noticeable stammers or stumbles, and plenty of well-rehearsed cues for laughs; compared to most of the others taking part, Howard looked as if he knew what he was doing – even when he was pretending not to know what he was supposed to do. His audience, though captive, was genuinely appreciative. He left them calling for more.

More was just what they were going to get. Buoyed by this initial success ('for me the smell of greasepaint had the same effect as a whiff of cocaine on a junkie'[13]), Howard threw himself back into his old routine, and, within a matter of a few short weeks, he had practically taken over the running of these Sunday night productions. He pestered his ostensible superiors until they agreed to let him improve the quality of the programmes; demanded – and received – a bigger say in the title, running order, writing and staging of each production; and he not only bossed about all of the officer-performers during rehearsals but also – much to the amusement of his many new friends among the audience – reduced them to mere stooges during the concerts themselves ('I treated them as bad performers and not as men with pips on their shoulders'[14]).

He also worked hard at improving his own act. Always a perceptive student of other performers, he was now able to stand back and think remarkably dispassionately about how best to shape and display his own peculiar talents. His stammer, for example – which had for so long been considered nothing other than a troublesome impediment – was now quite consciously transformed into a positive technique. Instead of struggling vainly against it, as he had done to such distressing effect in front of those grim-faced RADA examiners, he started using it, and sometimes even exaggerating it, along with all of the other obvious aspects of his general nervousness, to help accentuate his originality.

First, he thought of how much more distinctive and real and funny it would sound if, instead of just parroting the polished patter of a well-known professional, he actually appeared to relate the story to his audience as if it had really happened to him. Second, he realised how much easier it would be to fill up his allotted time on stage, and disguise the paucity of his original material, if he mastered the art of, as he put it, 'spinning it out'.[15] Max Miller, for example, would deliver the following joke, word perfect, at his normal rat-a-tat-tat pace:

'Ere's a funny thing happened to me this afternoon. A girl said to me: 'Hello, Max!' I said: 'I don't know you.' She said: 'It's my birthday. I'm twenty-one today.' She said: 'Will you come up to my flat for coffee and games?' I said: 'Don't bother with the coffee – but I will come up.' Well, it was raining outside, and there are only two things to do when it's raining. And I don't play cards. 'Ere![16]

Howard, however, would take this basic joke and, through hesitation, deviation and repetition, make it seem entirely his own:

Oh, no, don't, n-n-no, please, don't. No. *Liss-en!* Um. Ah! You'd have screamed! Oh, you would! Yes. I have to laugh meself when I think about it! Yes. I do. No, er, the thing was, th-th-there was this girl, you see. Yes. This girl. And, oh, she was pretty! What? Pretty? Oh! I should say so! *Pret-tee!* Yes. This girl. Oh! Ever so pretty. And, er – where was I?[17]

On and on he would go, moving forward, pulling back, stepping sideways, moving forward again, drawing his audience deeper and deeper into his distinctive comic world, until, when he sensed that they were ready, he finally hit them with the punchline.

He was no longer trying to hide his own inadequacies. He was no longer trying – and failing – to be like the other stand-up comics. He was now trying – and, increasingly, succeeding – to be more like himself. He started using everything – his arching eyebrows, his skewer-shaped mouth, his swooping vocal inflexions, his risible sartorial awkwardness, his occasional lapses of memory – to make a strength of his imperfection.

Most important of all, he began performing *with*, rather than *to*, his audience. They now became 'a vital part of the act':

I told these stories of misadventure in the form of a cosy 'just between you and me' gossip, as though leaning over an invisible garden fence or chatting to cronies in the local pub. And just as Mrs Jones can evoke laughter and sympathy by telling her neighbours about her troubles, so I found I could create laughter and sympathy by making the audience share the preposterousness of the improbable (but not impossible) situations in which I put myself as the innocent and misunderstood victim of *Them* (i.e. authority).[18]

It worked. It made 'Frankie Howard' work.

From now on, he would appear irrepressible. The Sunday concert parties grew to seem far more like 'The Frankie Howard Show' than any orthodox form of ensemble entertainment event. He appeared four or five times during each evening before, inevitably, returning yet again as top of the bill. Not content with his multiple solo spots, he also persuaded his sister, Betty, to take the train from Fenchurch Street to Shoeburyness every Sunday morning in order to join him on stage in an all-singing, dancing, joking double-act (she 'could have been a pro', he later reflected, 'but her energies were always to be channelled towards furthering my career'[19]). He was everywhere, he was always involved, and it was only a matter of time before he was completely, and officially, in charge.

It was the padre who did it. Howard was still a sincerely religious, churchgoing individual, and, from the moment he arrived at Shoeburyness, he had instinctively gravitated towards, and confided in, the garrison's resident chaplain, the Reverend Mackenzie. Mackenzie, in turn, followed Howard's progress with interest, and, after watching him blossom as an entertainer, helped facilitate a transfer to the Quartermaster's Office – a move that promised not only a promotion to the rank of Bombardier, but also, more importantly, the prospect of slightly more time for planning performances.

That was by no means the end, however, of the padre's well-meaning interventions. Keen (for the sake of camp morale in general as well as that of his protégé in particular) to encourage Howard's countless passionate plans to improve the standard of the garrison's in-house entertainment, Mackenzie arranged for him to write a letter to the Commander-in-Chief at Shoeburyness, setting out precisely what was wrong, what needed to be changed, and who should be charged with the power and responsibility to change it. It proved, recalled Howerd, to be 'an absolute stinker of a letter':[20]

In no uncertain terms I said that it was outrageous that officers should dictate to the men the way they should entertain and be entertained . . . That there was too much censorship . . . Too much patronising paternalism by the Entertainments Officer . . . That an entertainments committee should be set up on which the men should be represented – instead of this vital matter being left in the hands of an Entertainments Officer completely lacking in any semblance of qualifications for the job.[21]

The note went on, he would recall, 'florid with such adjectives as disgraceful, stupid, appalling [and] ridiculous'.[22] Naivety, rather than any conscious desire to cause offence, had prompted such a diatribe: 'Had I been more discreet in my wording, and wrapped the modified result in such phrases as "It seems to me, sir" and "May I respectfully suggest, sir" it might have been all right – but I was far too ignorant for such circumspect subtleties.'[23]

The result, unsurprisingly, was that Bombardier Howard was dispatched to the guardhouse and charged with gross insubordination. Luckily for him, the Reverend Mackenzie stepped in and saved the day: he sought out the furious Commander-in-Chief and sowed a few seeds of dubiety into his fevered mind, assuring him that the offending letter had, after all, been solicited by his good self, and, though its style and tone had obviously fallen far short of Sandhurst standards, its author had clearly only been trying to be honest. The General relented, and Howard was reprieved.

In fact, he was more than merely reprieved. He was actually given his head. As his letter had suggested, an entertainments committee was established, censorship was relaxed and a higher level of commitment was demanded. Bombardier Howard became the *de facto* controller of the Shoeburyness concert parties. His superior officers, having reasoned that it was better to have a character such as him operating on the inside instead of on the outside, then sat back and waited to see if he would sink or he would swim.

He swam. He swam length after length. He was practically amphibian.

Glorying in the greater stature, power and security that came (at least in his eyes) with his crowning as the unopposed 'Mr Sunday Night' of Shoeburyness, Frankie Howard pushed on with all of his brightly ambitious plans. The concerts grew bigger and bolder. The material became considerably more irreverent (a deliberate change of policy by such a playful anti-authoritarian) as well as a little 'bluer' (a trend whose start had far more to do with naivety than any conscious desire for greater vulgarity: 'Nobody realised that I was genuinely *innocent*,' he protested. 'Such is the way reputations are made!'[24]). There was also a change in sensibility: it gradually became more 'camp'.

'Camp' is one of those terms that has since been stretched to encompass everything from a marked preference for matching genitalia to a chronic weakness for placing words within quotation marks,[25] but, in the early 1940s, it meant little more than men mocking the supposed rigidity of their own masculinity – sometimes, but by no means always, in drag. It was a safe and playful form of release: a chance for homosexual men to behave less like heterosexual men, as well as a chance for heterosexual men, tired of going through the motions of military *machismo*, to behave less like heterosexual men.

It was a release for Frankie Howard, primarily, because it suited his overall comic style and sensibility. He had not been drawn to, and influenced by, other comedians because of their actual or supposed sexuality; he had been drawn to them because of their allegiances – always us against them, workers against bosses, women against bullying men, men against bullying women, the powerless against the powerful – and their devious methods of attack – such as George Robey's tactic of provoking anarchy by demanding order ('*Desist!*'), or Robb Wilton's use of characterisation as a means of critique ('The wife said, "You'll have to go back to work." *Oooh*, she's got a *cruel* tongue, that woman!'), or Jimmy James' subversive air of disingenuousness (STOOGE: 'Are you puttin' it around that I'm barmy?' JAMES: 'Why, are you tryin' to keep it a secret?').[26]

Howard was especially inspired, at this stage in his career, by the drag act of Norman Evans. As 'Fanny Fairbottom' – a mob-capped, bulbous-bosomed, voraciously nosey Lancastrian harridan – Evans would lean over a back-street wall and exchange gossip with an unseen neighbour:

What did you say? Who 'as? Her? That woman at number seven? '*As* she? *Is* she? Oooooh, *gerraway*! Oh, no, I won't say a word, no, I never talk. But, well: *fancy*! Mind you, I'm not surprised. Not really. I told her. She would go to those illuminations! It was the same with her next door to her. Oh yes, and that wasn't the first time. I knew what *she* was as soon as I saw 'er! Oh yes. That coalman was never away, you know! I mean, don't tell me it takes thirty-five minutes to deliver two bags of nuts! He's a bad lot! Oh yes. I knew what was goin' on when I saw him shout 'Whoa!' to his horse from her bedroom window . . .[27]

Off-stage, there was nothing remotely effeminate about Evans – and no one was in any doubt that he was a happily-married heterosexual[28] – but, on stage, he relished the role of this gossipy old woman. Howard was impressed by his acting skills: 'Even though [he] was talking to an imaginary person you could always hear the replies he was getting from his phrasing. He produced a personality on the other side of that garden wall without you ever seeing that person.'[29] Howard was also fascinated by the fact that Evans, when dressed as – and behaving like – a woman, could get away with the kind of material that, if it had been delivered by (or, in his case, as) a man, would have sounded far too 'blue'.

It was this sense of serving up an audience sauce through indirection, of sending out an encrypted signal of naughtiness, that drove Howard himself deeper and deeper into the camp sensibility, and often into drag. He wrote a new musical comedy routine, entitled 'Miss Twillow, Miss True and Miss Twit', and, alongside two of his male colleagues, performed it dressed up as ATS girls. The trio (with Howard centre-stage as Miss Twit) began the act as follows:

> Here we come, here we come,
> The girls of the ATS –
> Miss Twillow, Miss True and Miss Twit.
> (Repeat)
> The huge amount of work we do,
> You know, you'll *never* guess.
> But in Army life we fit . . .
> To bend we never ought,
> Because our skirts are short.
> But they really do reveal
> That we've got sex appeal.
> And if you want a date,
> Enquire at the gate
> For Miss Twillow, Miss True and Miss Twit . . .[30]

It went down well inside the boisterous barracks, and it also proved popular on those occasions when they were given permission to perform outside as part of a touring concert party called the Co-Odments.[31] It ran into trouble, however, when, right in the middle of one lunchtime performance in the Mess, the air-raid siren started up. As the audience stampeded for the exit, Howard had just enough time to remove his wig, the two balloons that passed for breasts and the painfully tight woman's shoes, and wriggle out of the borrowed ATS outfit and slip back into his own uniform – but, in the rush, the thick layer of make-up and the strip of ruby-red lipstick were forgotten. Out on parade, he stood stock still with his rifle, pack and painted face, looked straight ahead, and hoped for the best.

A young subaltern arrived to inspect the ranks. He approached Howard, gave him a cursory glance, moved on, stopped, shook his head, and then turned back for another, closer look. For a moment, neither man spoke: Howard stared blankly into the distance, trying his hardest not to twitch or tremble, and the officer, head cocked slightly to one side like a quizzical cocker spaniel, stared fixedly at his face. Finally, the officer managed a cough, which Howard took as the cue for him to offer some kind of explanation. 'C-concert party,' he stammered, the panic strangling his voice into a squeaky falsetto. 'The alert went,' he struggled on, 'in the m-middle of the c-concert party.' The officer seemed dazed: 'Concert party . . . Er, yes . . . Mmmm . . . Concert party . . . Jolly good.' He moved on along the line, stopping every now and again for a nervous glance back and a quick shake of the head, before departing hurriedly off into the distance. It had been a narrow escape, but it would not be the last time an officer would stare at Howard, in or out of drag, and shake his head and think: 'Er, yes . . . Mmmm . . .'[32]

The fact was that Frankie Howard was a homosexual. It seems that he had not always been entirely sure, in his own mind, about the true nature of his sexuality, but military life, with its all-male community, had started to draw out his deepest desires. He formed his first relatively intimate adult friendship with a fellow-soldier at Shoeburyness, a young man whom some of his contemporaries (reflecting the casual homophobia so common at that time) freely described as 'sissified'.[33]

There appears to have been little doubt, among the other soldiers in the garrison, as to what kind of relationship it was (or at least had the potential to become), but, fortunately, few seemed inclined either to report or condemn it. Although, in those days, homosexuality was illegal, it has since been estimated that at least 250,000 homosexuals served in the British armed forces during the Second World War, and, ironically, most of them were accorded a far greater measure of tolerance, compassion and respect, informally, than many of their successors would receive in peacetime. 'All the gays and straights worked together as a team,' recalled one who was there, explaining: 'We had to because our lives might have depended on it.'[34]

Howard and 'his right-hand man' (as some teases took to calling him) knew and understood the unwritten rule: so long as they were discreet, the relationship would probably remain safe. According to one of their old Army colleagues, Tom Dwyer, the couple never dared to attempt anything more demonstrative, in the presence of others, than the odd furtive touch of hands in the darkness between their beds. One night, Dwyer recalled, he noticed, as he drifted off to sleep, that each man was lying on his own bunk, but was still linked to the other by a shadowy outstretched arm: 'They were, like, holding each other's little finger.'[35] Such was often the sum of stolen intimacies to be treasured by those soldiers who sheltered 'secret' loves.

For Howard and his partner, however, there was always the unique freedom afforded them by the stage, with its licence for 'larger than life' personalities and playful poses, and, for a while, the relationship had room to thrive. 'They got on like a house on fire,' remembered Dwyer.[36]

Then came an enforced separation. Howard was posted to a new Ministry of Defence 'Experimental Station' over on Foulness – the largest of the six islands forming an archipelago in south-east Essex. He still returned each night to sleep in the barracks at Shoeburyness, but, with less time to spend with his partner and more time to spend on planning his concert parties, some of the original passion began to dissipate.

The camp attitude, however, did not. It was now part of him, as well as part of his act. It was the means by which he protected himself, preserved his sanity and made palatable his own occasionally prickly personality. A mixture of candour, sarcasm and self-parody, it could almost always be relied on to elicit a laugh, or at least an indulgent or confused 'Er, yes . . . Mmmm', when a blast of invective might otherwise have been expected.

It came in particularly handy when Howard, during one of his fleeting visits back to Southend to appear with the Co-Odments concert party, found himself on stage with a piano accompanist called Mrs Vera Roper (he had worked first, and often still did during this period, with another member of the party by the name of Mrs Blanche Moore, but on this particular night it was Mrs Roper who was seated at the piano). Although Roper had performed with Howard before without experiencing the slightest form of a mishap, on this particular occasion her mind seemed to be elsewhere – much to her young colleague's evident irritation. Cue after cue was missed, as she stared off into space and he stammered and struggled to cover up the mistakes. Howard's patience finally snapped after she twice failed to hear – or at least respond sufficiently promptly to – a carefully rehearsed question he had asked her. 'That's all I need,' he growled, 'a deaf accompanist!' and the audience, assuming it to be part of the act, laughed uproariously.[37]

That was all that was needed to spark another bright idea into life. What the conventional, sober sensibility responds to merely as an embarrassing error or unnecessary imperfection – something to be corrected or edited out and smartly erased from memory – the camp sensibility seizes on with relish, tweaks up a notch or two and then celebrates with a nudge and a wink. This was precisely what Howard did: he took the immensely frustrating experience of being ignored by a pianist who 'was pondering how many meat coupons she had left in her ration-book', and used it as the basis of a brand-new comedy routine: the 'daft situation' of him being saddled with an accompanist – 'Madame Vere-Roper, known to me as Ada', or 'Madame Blanchie Moore' – who appears incapable of providing any accompaniment.[38]

It would always progress (or, more accurately, fail to progress) along the following uneven lines: switching back and forth between a piercing shriek to make himself heard by his accompanist and the *sotto voce* tones required to confide two-facedly in his audience, Howard struggled in vain to get started:

I thought tonight, ladies and gentlemen, er, I'd give you a bit of music, yes, which, er, if my pianist has sobered up, we'll do now. It's called 'A Night in Old Vienna'. Yes. It's an operatic *aaaria*. Yes. It's lovely, this. Lovely. Here we go. [*Madame Vere-Roper, seated at the piano some distance back, prepares herself to play*] N-n-no, no, don't clap – she'll want money. I've told her this is an audition. Yes. No, the thing is, she can't hear very well. No, she can't hear much. And she's very bitter with it. Yes, she's a real misery guts. She really is. [*Turns, with a forced smile on his face, to acknowledge her*]

Evening. We'll do the song now. Yes, chilly. *'Tis,* yes. The song. We'll do the song. I SAID WE'LL DO THE SONG NOW! [*Turns back to audience*] No. Don't laugh. No. Don't, please. You'll make trouble. I beg of you. Don't laugh. No, she can't hear, and, oh, she's a *funny* woman, you know! Mind you, she's had a terrible life. Oooh, shocking life! Oh, yes, terrible! [*Shouts in her direction*] I'M TELLING THEM YOU'VE HAD A TERRIBLE LIFE. Yes, it *is* very chilly tonight! Yes! I know! *Chilly!* Yes! There's a wind blowing up the passage tonight! Yes! Very chilly tonight! *'Tis,* yes! Think winter's back! I SAID WINTER'S BACK! *Yehss!* [*Talking to the audience again*] Poor old soul! Well, she's past it, y'know – that is, if she ever had it! No, really, no, she should be in bed . . .[39]

It was what Howard did best: appearing to fail dismally at doing his best.

Over the course of the next half-century, he would use no fewer than eight of these 'deaf' pianists,[40] but the nature of the routine never changed. The attempt to produce 'a bit of culture' produced nothing better than a bit of chaos, and more or less everyone in every British audience, from the nervous young soldiers of the early 1940s to the not-so-nervous young university graduates of the early 1990s, could find something to identify with, and laugh at, in that.

Before Howard could expand and develop his promising act any further, however, he was uprooted once again. Early in 1942, he was posted to a new Army Experimental Station at Penclawdd – a small fishing village on the Gower peninsula near Swansea in South Wales – and assigned an uninspiring but time-consuming office job in Requisitions.

Penclawdd was hardly the most congenial of locations for an aspiring entertainer. The village itself consisted of a tiny, quiet and close-knit community of cockle-gatherers, while, on its outskirts, the Experimental Station amounted to nothing more than a cluster of Nissen huts. There was a small local amateur dramatic society of sorts (which a grateful Howard joined 'to keep my hand in, as it were'[41]), but precious little else to stir a performer's spirits.

Fearing that his ambitions would soon start to atrophy in such sleepily prosaic surroundings, he persuaded his Commanding Officer to allow him to apply to join the cast of *Stars in Battledress* – the big new Army

Welfare concert party (a sort of entertainment 'flying squad') that had been formed to tour all of the major fighting zones along the Allied Front.[42] He expected, bearing in mind all of the recent success he had enjoyed in front of audiences at Southend and Shoeburyness, that his act was now sound enough to assure him of a swift and easy admission. He was in, however, for a shock.

Auditions for *Stars in Battledress* were usually held in the nearest available cookhouse in front of an interviewing officer (and, invariably, it was only one) who had some kind of experience of show business. When, one dark and rainy morning, Frankie Howard arrived for his, he found himself at one end of a vast hall (still reeking of yesterday's soggy vegetables and watery gravy), and, far away at the other end, a stern-faced officer who had worked before the war as a part-time conjuror. Instantly, the old RADA feeling returned.

He suddenly realised just how helpless he was without a proper audience with which to interact. Alone in front of this single distant figure, in a room where every 'ooh', 'aah', and 'er' was left to die a lingering death of lonely echoes, Howard was beaten before he started. The left knee trembled, the stammer took over, the mouth dried up, the wide eyes glazed over: he conveyed nothing to the interviewing officer apart from the unbearable intensity of his frustration and fear.

He failed. Worse still, he went on to fail no fewer than four auditions in all. When the last of them was over, Howard went back reluctantly to the cockles and corrugated iron of Penclawdd, nursing an ego that had been badly bruised by the realisation that the very men who had been detailed to ferret out fresh talent 'didn't think I was worth ferreting'.[43]

He began to feel desperate. After having made so much progress as a performer, here he was, stranded in a rusty little Nissen hut in South Wales, shuffling papers and filling in forms. He had grown up coping stoically with just the lows, but now, after experiencing his first real high, the lows felt worse than ever. At the start of March 1944, following one too many dull and drizzly days, he cracked, and marched off to see his CO: '[C]an I please do *something* positive for the war effort,' he pleaded, 'even if it [is] my destiny only to get my name in the papers as one of yesterday's casualties?'[44]

The Commanding Officer smiled indulgently – he had grown used to this sort of thing by now – and assured Howard that the problem had already been solved. Earlier that very morning, he revealed, a new batch of orders had arrived on his desk – and one of them (relating to preparations for the imminent Allied invasion of France) entailed, among other things, a new posting for Bombardier F.A. Howard. He was off, without delay, to Plymouth: 'For the big show,' the CO added with the suspicion of a smirk, 'and I don't mean telling jokes, what?'[45]

A Commando course in Devon was not what Howard, in a cool hour, would have requested by way of a radical change, but, like everyone else in the services, he had to accept what he was assigned. It was just a relief to be doing something, *anything*, other than sitting around an office. Always fitter than he looked, he coped rather well with all of the shinnying up and down ropes and scrambling over assault courses. With neither the time nor the energy for the usual pursuit of stage-based activities, he got on with the job in hand, and the general opinion was that he did it 'jolly well'.[46] Indeed, such was his burst of enthusiasm (and temporary physical felicity) that he won a promotion to the rank of Sergeant, and was then sent off on a driving course.

That move precipitated a dramatic reversion to type: he proceeded to drive a large lorry full of soldiers through a hedge and into a tree. A certain loss of nerve was suffered as a consequence – not just on Howard's part, but also on that of his superiors – and he was shunted discreetly sideways to a role in which he could be trusted to do less damage.

There was little time, however, for further mishaps – at least on English soil. On 6 June 1944, Howard and his comrades boarded a merchant ship and set sail for Normandy as part of the D-Day dawn invasion force. Heavy seas prevented the vessel from disembarking its troops, and so it was left to wallow in its swell for no fewer than eleven days while the first wave of the invasion pressed on ahead. Howard – who was meant to be up on a conning tower manning a Bren gun – spent much of this frustrating and unnerving period coiled up on the floor, suffering from a combination of suspected influenza, undeniable seasickness and a mild form of malnutrition.

When, at last, he was back on dry ground, he was informed that he was being posted to Lille in northern France. 'Anyone speak French?' enquired an officer. Howard, somewhat impetuously, replied that, as he had been to a half-decent grammar school, he could manage the odd word. 'We're a bit short, Sergeant,' the officer said, 'so you're an interpreter.'[47] Before Howard had a chance to splutter any kind of protest, he was transferred to Brussels as part of the Military Establishment.

'Who are we governing?' he asked an officer when he arrived. 'The Germans soon,' came the confident reply, 'because we're winning the war.' 'Well,' said Howard, looking only a little less anxious than before, 'that's one blessing, anyway.'[48]

There were plenty of scrapes and narrow escapes. On one ostensibly straightforward assignment, for example, Howard accompanied a Major to a nearby village in order to ascertain how many women there were pregnant (and thus qualified as a priority for the soon-to-be-distributed food). The snag was that Howard the interpreter had absolutely no idea what word was French for 'pregnant', and so, in haste, he assumed a heavy Charles Boyer-style accent, improvised a phrase that he believed mistakenly to mean more or less the same sort of thing – '*Nous voulons savoir si une femme voulons avoir un enfant?*'[49] – and ended up asking a succession of women not if they were having a baby, but, rather, did they *want* to have a baby. Unsurprisingly, he and the Major were chased out of the village by a group of angry husbands brandishing cudgels, pitchforks and shotguns, and then, on their way back to camp, they almost got themselves lost hopelessly in a dense sea of fog.

The next thing that Howard did was to appear to liberate the Netherlands. As usual, it happened by accident.

The Germans were in the process of capitulation, and, on 5 May 1945, a convoy of Allied vehicles was due to set off from Brussels to enter the Dutch legislative centre. When the dawdling Howard was urged to hurry up and get into one of the cars, he chose, without the slightest hesitation, the one right at the front: 'It seemed logical.'[50] At some point *en route*, however, all of the vehicles lining up behind fell foul of navigational errors and disappeared from sight, leaving Sergeant Frankie Howard to enter The Hague alone in a chauffeur-driven staff car and be mobbed by a mass of grateful citizens ('the most appreciative audience I've ever had!'[51]).

As this surreal little period continued, Howard was sent with a young Army Captain to Stade, near Hamburg, to form a two-man Military Government. The Captain, facing one taxing challenge too many, promptly suffered a nervous breakdown, leaving a panicky Howard to tap out a signal for help. Reinforcements duly arrived, swelling the risibly under-manned Government of two to a risibly over-manned

Government of 200. Howard, relieved to find that his services were no longer urgently needed, redirected his efforts towards the far happier task of entertaining.

He organised yet another concert party. He tried, unsuccessfully, to inveigle a fleeting appearance in a movie – Basil Dearden's *The Captive Heart* – that he heard was being shot further 'up the road' in the British Occupation Zone. He performed the occasional one-man show. He did all of the things that he most enjoyed being able to do.

As far as Howard's Commanding Officer was concerned, he was pushing at an open door. During the summer of 1946, the War Office began a process whereby all of the old individual service entertainment bodies – including ENSA, *Stars in Battledress*, Ralph Reader's RAF Gang Shows and the many and various concert parties – were gradually merged to form a new, all-embracing, post-war organisation called the Combined Services Entertainment unit (or 'CSE' for short). With more than thirty separate shows to stage, the need for new talent was acute, and Howard's CO, hearing that the next audition was about to be held in nearby Nienburg, urged the obsessive performer to travel there and try his luck. 'With my record,' groaned Howard, 'I'll be back tomorrow.' His CO was more sanguine: 'Maybe you'll be lucky this time.'[52]

Howard drove there in a lorry. Although he had not applied for an audition, he managed to get his name added to the list, and just after lunch, before there had been any time for the customary build-up of nerves, he was instructed to take his turn in front of the judges.

There were two people in particular whom he had to impress. One was the officer in charge of CSE productions in Germany and Austria, Major Richard Stone: a former actor who would go on to become one of Britain's leading theatrical agents.[53] The other was Stone's assistant, Captain Ian Carmichael: a RADA graduate with a long and illustrious performing career ahead of him.[54]

Howard's routine revolved, somewhat idiosyncratically, around an old Ella Fitzgerald number called 'A-Tisket, A-Tasket'. Holding a slightly bent, smouldering Woodbine between the first two fingers of his shaky right hand, he interspersed the verses –

> A-tisket, a-tasket
> A brown-and-yellow basket
> I sent a letter to my mummy

On the way I dropped it.
I dropped it, I dropped it
Yes on the way I dropped it
A little girlie picked it up
And put it in her pocket.

– with his usual brand of rambling interjections, before bringing the song screeching to a close:

Tisket, tasket, I lost my yellow basket
Oh someone help me find my basket
Make me happy again, again.
(Was it red?) No, no, no, no!
(Was it brown?) No, no, no, no!
(Was it blue?) No, no, no, no!
No, just a little yellow basket
A little yellow basket![55]

'Thank you very much,' Major Stone said with the standard politely inscrutable smile, and then, once Howard had departed from the hall, he turned to solicit the views of his number two. 'Oh no, no,' sighed Captain Carmichael, 'he's too raw, with no timing, and I don't think he's particularly funny.'[56] Stone, sensing a negative, invited his colleague to clarify his position. 'I thought,' Carmichael replied with a grimace, 'that he was *death-defyingly* unfunny.'[57] Stone, however, disagreed: 'I think you've got it wrong. I'm going to book him for one of our shows.'[58]

Howard was duly installed as the compère of a concert party – *The Waggoners* – that was touring north-west Germany. For the next three months or so, from the end of 1945 to a short time after the start of 1946, he was in his element. Moving rapidly from place to place, he acquired a clearer sense of what it took to win over any audience, and he adapted his act accordingly. He improved the best of his old routines; dropped the rest; wrote, tried and tested several new jokes, sketches and monologues; and generally grew in confidence as a performer.

Those who watched him were impressed. One such admirer was a 21-year-old soldier and budding comedian named Benny Hill. Serving in Germany at the time with the Royal Electrical and Mechanical

Engineers, Hill was struck immediately by Howard's edgy originality, and made a point of seeking him out in the canteen shortly after the show had finished.

It was a brief but revealing meeting between two of British comedy's most significant stars of the future: Hill, the self-assured optimist, and Howard, the insecure pessimist. 'You've got a jolly good way with you,' gushed Hill, believing Howard (who was seven years his senior) to be a relatively seasoned professional. When it became clear that he was actually lavishing praise on a surprisingly shy and modest amateur, Hill urged him to consider pursuing comedy as a career: 'You ought to take it up,' he insisted. 'I think you would do very well.'[59]

Howard, blushing a little and fidgeting with his curly hair, mumbled a clumsily non-committal response – 'I don't know, really, you know' – but he was genuinely touched by the encouragement.[60] Indeed, having endured so many curt rejections up to this point in his life, he treasured every single one of the kind words that he now received.

Richard Stone, for one, would discover just how true this was some thirty-five years later, when the star Frankie Howerd, upon hearing a specious rumour that Stone had only grudgingly found a place for him in CSE, asked his former boss to meet him as soon as possible for lunch. 'It turned out,' recalled Stone (who had secretly been hoping that the reason for the meeting was to sound him out about acquiring Howerd as a client), 'that in all the years, through his many ups and downs, he had consoled himself with the thought that there was at least one man in show-business who believed in him. He then produced from his pocket a tired piece of Army notepaper which he had cherished. It informed those whom it might concern that Sergeant Howard was a very funny man, and was signed Richard Stone, Major!'[61] The insecurity would never go away.

Throughout that short tour during the winter of 1945/46, however, Howard was a relatively happy young man. The fears of wartime were finally over, and the anxieties of peacetime had not yet begun. All that he was required to do – and all that he needed to do – was perform, and he relished every minute. Then, with the arrival of April 1946, the brief but blessed interlude was brought abruptly to a close. Frankie Howard, after spending six years in uniform, was demobbed, and he returned to civilian life.

Finding himself back in Eltham, 'with less than £100, a chalk-striped suit, pork-pie hat',[62] and that precious one-page reference from Richard Stone tucked safely away inside his jacket pocket, he felt some of the old nerves start to stir. Now aged twenty-nine, he stood for a moment alone, took in all of the familiar sights, and then thought to himself: 'What now?'[63]

ACT II:
FRANKIE

They're mocking Francis!

CHAPTER 4

Meet Scruffy Dale

My agent. He's a very peculiar man, my agent.
He's got what they call a dual personality.
People hate both of them.

It was an extraordinary coincidence. Shortly after Frankie Howard departed from the Army, he met not only the man who would soon prove to be one of the best things to have happened to his early career, but also the man who would end up seeming like one of the worst. These two men were one and the same: Stanley 'Scruffy' Dale.

Of all the innumerable managers, promoters and sundry 'ten-percenters' who struggled to make a living out of post-war British theatre, none was quite as mysterious, unorthodox and downright odd as Stanley Dale. Invalided out of the RAF after sitting on an incendiary shell that had penetrated his aeroplane (an act of valour for which he was awarded the Distinguished Flying Cross[1]), he had since built a new career for himself in civilian life as a booker for the band leader-turned-impresario Jack Payne.

A whippet-thin man of average height with a sharp-featured face and short, curly hair that swept back over his head in shiny little ripples, Dale was notorious for his unpredictable office hours, his somewhat insalubrious personal habits and, most of all, for his chronically unkempt appearance. 'Scruffy *was* scruffy,' confirmed the scriptwriter Alan Simpson. 'I mean, nearly every time I saw Scruffy [he] was in bed! He used to conduct all of his office meetings in bed, with a fag hanging out of his mouth – he never seemed to puff it, it always seemed just to burn away until there was nothing there but a sort of grey stick – and he had all of this ash dripping down on to his pyjama jacket.'[2]

When, however, Dale managed to summon up the effort to rise from his bed and dress (which happened – if it happened at all – only very rarely earlier than noon), he was capable of giving off a certain 'loveable roguish' kind of charm, particularly when telling some of his extraordinary tales (many of them tall, a few of them positively colossal) about the remarkable things he had done, the astonishing sights he had seen and the impressive people he had known over the course of his improbably eventful life. Tony Hancock, for one, fell deeply under his spell for a while during the immediate post-war period, sitting around with him night after night, sharing cigarettes and drinks and listening wide-eyed and open-mouthed to his anecdotes about the countless narrow escapes he claimed to have experienced while serving in the RAF.[3]

A budding young stand-up comic by the name of Jim Smith was another performer who would find himself drawn into Dale's orbit. After seeing the teenaged Smith on stage at the start of the 1950s and quickly sensing his potential, Dale put him under contract, continued paying him a regular salary during his two years away on National Service, and, when he returned, gave Smith the 'gift' of his own surname – so Jim Smith became Jim Dale, and the comedy performer was promptly re-packaged as a pop star.

One of the qualities that friends and clients alike admired in Stanley Dale (at the beginning at least) was the extent of his apparent devotion to their cause. Behind the risibly indolent image lurked a lively and surprisingly imaginative champion of whomever he found worthwhile. If a performer needed someone to transport a cumbersome trunk, set up a prop or simply flick a particular switch, Scruffy, invariably, would agree to do it. If a friend fell into financial trouble, Scruffy would often be the first to volunteer to fix it. If a client required a change of style, Scruffy would go straight ahead and dream another one up. Nothing, it seemed, was too much trouble for Scruffy Dale – just as long, of course, as it did not need doing before noon.

What tended to dazzle people most of all about Dale was his claim to possess a special range of entrepreneurial powers. At a time when many of London's theatrical agents still seemed mired in the methods and manners of the pre-war Edwardian era, Stanley Dale appeared strikingly and excitingly progressive, buying and selling stocks and shares at both a speed and a level of complexity that rendered the average Variety artiste breathless and dizzy but also deeply impressed. He was regarded, recalled his former colleague Bill Lyon-Shaw, as 'a whizz-kid of his time'. Any up-and-coming performer would obviously have craved such lucrative expertise, but with Stanley Dale, Lyon-Shaw noted, there was a catch to the whizz-kid's promise of a boundless supply of cash: 'He whizzed quite a lot of it into his own pocket.'[4]

The full extent of Dale's many deceptions would only be discovered a decade or so later. Back in 1946, he struck most people as merely an eccentric but slyly effective wheeler-dealer, and there was one thing about this unconventional man of which no one was in any doubt: he had a genuinely sharp eye for new talent. It was this sharp eye that would soon spot Frankie Howard.

Howard first encountered Stanley Dale at the Stage Door Canteen in Piccadilly – a bustling little venue (based on the site occupied now-adays by Boots the Chemist) where Service men and women with a passion for performing could 'meet and see'. Howard, having recently been demobbed, should not, by rights, have been there, but he was already feeling desperate. During the brief time he had been out of uniform, Howard had failed yet another audition – this time at Butlin's holiday camp at Filey in Yorkshire – and then tramped his lonely way around most of Soho's well-known (and quite a few of the more obscure) agents' offices without eliciting more than the faintest hint of sincere encouragement. The problem was always the same: 'Where can I see you perform?' each cigar-chomping agent would ask. 'You can't,' came Howard's stock reply. 'I'm not working.'[5]

It was every young performer's Catch-22: in order to work, one needed an agent, but in order to get an agent, one needed to work. There was no hope to be found in logic; the only hope to be had was in luck.

Just before Howard met Dale, he sat up in his old bedroom in Eltham and hatched an audacious plan to actively make his own luck instead of continuing to wait passively for its possible arrival. Remembering that one of the most sympathetic (or least unsympathetic) agents he had so far encountered – Harry Lowe – was known to be a regular in the audience at the Stage Door Canteen, he resolved to try to sneak his way in.

Late one morning in the middle of the week, he put his old Army uniform back on, retrieved Richard Stone's short letter of recommenda-tion, passed politely on his mother's kind offer of another brown paper bag full of cheese sandwiches, and set off 'with nervous impatience' to catch the bus bound for Piccadilly.[6] Marching into the secretary's office in what he hoped resembled a suitably soldier-like manner, he introduced himself as Sergeant Frank Howard and handed over the positive reference from Major Stone. The ruse worked: he was told that he would be on stage next Friday night at seven o'clock sharp. Racing off to the nearest public telephone, he notified Lowe of the news, and Lowe assured him that he would make every effort to attend.

When Friday arrived, Howard – buoyed by the familiar sight of a boisterous military audience – gave what he felt at the time to be the performance of his life.[7] Immediately afterwards, however, he was crushed to discover that Harry Lowe had not been present to see it. Fearing that he would probably fail in the future to be as good as that again, he felt that his big chance had already come and gone.

Slumped in a chair back at his home in Eltham, Howard spent the next few days in a 'state of indescribable melancholy'.[8] Then, out of the blue, came a request from the Stage Door Canteen: as there was a shortage of performers for the following Friday night, the message said, would Sergeant Howard mind filling in? At first, he was disinclined to take up the offer, feeling that there would no longer be any real point to further exposure, but eventually, after being encouraged and cajoled by his mother, he relented: he would go, he mumbled miserably, but only in order to give 'a valedictory performance before abandoning all hopes of a show-business career'.[9]

Harry Lowe, once again, was not there, but this time Howard could hardly have cared any less. Expecting nothing of any consequence to come from the performance, he went on stage at his most relaxed, and he proceeded to have some fun. The act went even better than it had the last time: every gag, every routine and every semi-improvised comic exchange with certain individuals among the audience seemed to trigger another crescendo of laughter. Howard could do no wrong, and he knew it – and he loved it.

In an office elsewhere in the building, a visiting booker – there doing business on behalf of a major London agency – grew curious as to what, and more importantly who, was causing so much noise in the auditorium. Setting off along the corridor and down the stairs, he managed to slip inside the door at the back of the theatre and stood there to watch the remainder of Howard's act.

When it ended, the booker, who had been greatly impressed, raced backstage. 'Who represents you?' he panted. 'Nobody,' replied Howard, trying hard not to sound bitter. 'I'm with the Jack Payne office,' the man announced. 'Would you like us to represent you?'

Howard, who could still recall with a shudder that awful night at the Lewisham Hippodrome when he had shared the stage but none of the applause with the hugely popular Jack Payne and his band, was incredulous. Looking this stranger up and down for a few seconds – taking in the scuffs on the toes of the old shoes, the deep creases all over the trousers, the stains on the front of the open-necked shirt and the beads of sweat that were now sliding down the brow – he came perilously close to concluding out loud that the whole thing must be some sort of sick joke.

It soon became apparent, however, that the stranger was being serious. 'You'll have to see Frank Barnard,' he added matter-of-factly. 'He'll want to see your act.' Howard, now blushing beetroot-red and starting to lose control over his stutter, managed to reply: 'Of course . . . Yes . . . Um . . . Yes . . . Who's he?'

Informed that Frank Barnard was Jack Payne's general manager, Howard then asked where he could expect the great man to go to see him perform. 'In his office,' he was told. '*His office!*' a patently horrified Howard shrieked. 'I c-can't perform in an office! I need an audience.' After being told, somewhat tetchily ('Look, sonny . . .'), that Mr Barnard – a hugely experienced and no-nonsense old Geordie – already had more than enough people to see, he was handed his final chance: 'Are you interested, or aren't you?' This time there was no hesitation: 'You bet I am!' The stranger shook his hand and smiled: 'Then you will perform in his office.'

Howard was left in a daze. Even the daunting prospect of another audience-free audition failed to dampen down the tremendous feelings of elation: his talent had at last been spotted, and, on the very day that he had contemplated abandoning his long-cherished ambitions, he was finally getting his chance. Just before the unexpected meeting had ended, Howard suddenly realised that, throughout all of the heightened confusion, anxiety and excitement, he had not yet asked the visitor his name. 'It's Stanley,' the stranger revealed. 'Stanley Dale.'[10]

Howard would always claim, on the basis of this encounter, that Dale was the man who discovered him, but this was not strictly true. Dale may have been the first person from the agency to knock on the performer's dressing-room door, but it was one of his superiors within the Jack

Payne Organisation, the production manager Bill Lyon-Shaw, who had made the actual discovery.

Lyon-Shaw – responding to a tip from a talent scout – had gone down to the Stage Door Canteen on that particular day alongside Jack Payne to take a look at a promising young comedian and impressionist by the name of Max Bygraves. When they arrived, Lyon-Shaw noticed that Frankie Howard was also on the list of artists who were due to appear:

> I said to Jack, 'Oh, God, I know that chap, I've seen him before.' I'd actually seen him a few years before, during wartime, in a little concert party in Rochford. I used to live in Southend, you see, and a lady whom I knew there called Blanche Moore – who never gets the credit she deserves for finding Frank – had written to me and said, 'If you ever get a chance to come back again to Southend, you must come down and see my concert party. We have a very funny man called Frankie Howard.' So, one leave weekend, I went down, and saw this grotesque, in Army uniform, come on to the stage, do a whole lot of 'ooh-aahs' and the odd 'oh, no, missus', tell mostly Army-style jokes and then he ended up with the song 'Three Little Fishes' – which, of course, was unusual and very good. So at the Stage Door Canteen, after we'd seen and liked – and decided we'd book – Max Bygraves, I said to Jack Payne, 'Look, this Frankie Howard: he's quite funny. Let's just stay a bit and see what you think of him.' And so we stayed and saw Frank, and Jack liked him. He said, 'Yes, he's a funny man, he's different, not at all like the typical slick comic – let's have him, too.' And that's how we got Max Bygraves and Frankie Howard at the same time.[11]

Whether it was Payne, then and there, who dispatched Dale backstage to make the first official contact with the two new potential clients, or just Dale (in all of the noisy chaos of the moment) acting entirely on his own initiative, remains unclear, but it certainly seems that, during his time inside Howard's dressing-room, he made no attempt to undersell his own importance within the agency. The fact was that the comedian, who was struggling to believe his luck, was in no state to question anything his visitor said.

Howard was just delighted to have made the acquaintance of Stanley Dale. Admittedly, Dale did not fit the image of the conventional show-business intermediary, but then neither did Howard fit the image of the conventional stand-up comedian. What boded rather well, he reflected, was the fact that their relationship had been founded on such an encouraging convergence of opinion: namely, they both had faith in the star potential of Frankie Howard.

What brought Howard straight back down to earth with an abrupt and painful bump was the thought that this faith would still prove fruitless unless he now went on to win a similar vote of confidence from the notoriously gruff and bluff Frank Barnard. Having failed so many auditions in the past that had been held under similarly cold and unwelcoming conditions, he found it hard now to hold out much hope. Barnard was based in an elegantly capacious set of rooms two floors above Hanover Square in Mayfair. Howard had not even climbed the stairs before his big day started going ominously awry.

Vera Roper, his old friend and stooge, had agreed to accompany him there to provide some much-needed moral support, but, in an unwelcome imitation of her on-stage unreliability, she failed to turn up. The reality was that she had fallen ill, but, as neither she nor Howard owned a telephone, he was left to pace anxiously up and down on the pavement outside, waiting in vain until he very nearly made himself late.

Things went from bad to worse when, reluctantly, he entered the building alone and made his way up to Barnard's office. 'Got your band parts?' barked Barnard from behind a fat and angry Havana cigar. Howard (failing to grasp the full seriousness of the *faux pas*) confessed that he had not thought to bring any sheet music, but added that he would definitely have arrived with a pianist if only his accompanist had not reneged on her promise to accompany him. This provoked plenty of smoke from the scowling Barnard, whose face had just grown redder than the glowing end of his cigar.

Howard, still somehow oblivious to the obvious danger signs, then pointed a thumb over his shoulder in the general direction of the gleaming new office piano and enquired if there was 'anyone around who could play "Three Little Fishes"' for him. This provoked plenty of fire: Barnard, according to Howard's subsequent embarrassed account, leapt up from behind his desk and promptly 'went berserk'.[12]

Launching into a screaming tirade that rocked Howard back in his seat, Barnard told him that he was an unprofessional and impertinent timewaster, unworthy of begging the attention of a bored gallery queue in Wigan – let alone a top-notch metropolitan agent. 'He went on and on,' the traumatised performer would recall, 'whipping himself into a frenzy of near-apoplexy – while I sat literally shivering with terror.'[13] Eventually, having shouted himself into exhaustion, Barnard slumped back down into his chair, reached for another cigar, and, waving a hand dismissively in the direction of Howard, snarled: 'Wait outside.'[14] Howard did what he was told.

He ended up waiting outside for four solid hours. During that time spent sitting in silence on his own, he went all the way from quivering terror through meek contrition to angry resentment ('*Who the hell does he think he is?*'). When, at last, the call came that 'Mr Barnard will see you now', Howard was firmly in the mood for retaliation: 'The worm not only turned, but grew teeth.'[15]

'I wouldn't go near that man for all the tea in China,' he screamed at Barnard's startled secretary. 'I've never been so insulted in all my life, and I'm not so desperate that I'll go on my hands and knees to that ignorant pig. I'd rather not be in show-business at all – and that's that.'[16]

The secretary had obviously been screamed at before, because, once her ears had stopped ringing, she simply patted Howard on the shoulder and advised him to calm down: 'Swallow your pride. You may never get this sort of chance again.' Howard, however, was having none of it. With widened eyes and scarlet cheeks, he raged at all the rudeness, injustice and contempt he had suffered, not only that day but on so many, many days before, and then, folding his hands over the top of his head, moaned that he was in no mood now to put right what had gone so horribly, utterly wrong. 'Have a go,' said the secretary with a sympathetic smile, and guided him by the arm back to outside the door of the manager's office.[17]

So many thoughts, so many options, bounced around in Howard's head during the handful of seconds that he hovered outside that door: turning the other cheek; punching the other cheek; begging forgiveness; offering forgiveness; speaking his mind; biting his lip – countless ticks and an equal number of crosses. In the end, as he moved to open the door, he settled on speaking his mind.

Crashing into the office and racing straight up to the desk, Howard fixed his tormentor with his very best baleful glare and, stabbing the smoky air with his finger for emphasis, he screeched: '*I am now going to make you laugh, you clot. You're going to fall about with laughter, you idiot. Because I'm a very funny man, you oaf!*'[18] Then he noticed that Barnard was shaking.

He was shaking neither with fear nor rage, but rather with laughter. 'That's a great act. Great. It's a hoot,' he cried, shaking his head, wiping his eyes and smiling broadly. 'Can you do any more?'[19]

Howard, having purged himself of all fury, did a quick double-take and then proceeded to do his proper act. He was more disorientated than genuinely relaxed, but what he did went down so well that Barnard now thought nothing of summoning a pianist to support his rendition of 'Three Little Fishes'. When it was all over, Barnard shook Howard warmly by the hand and assured the exhausted performer that it had been the best 'cold' audition he had ever seen. He hired Howard on the spot, and then arranged for Jack Payne, the self-styled *capo di tutti capi* of the post-war Variety world, to see his newest client perform in front of an enthusiastic military audience at Arborfield in Berkshire. Payne (who had no recollection of his pre-war encounter with Howard) arrived in time to watch him steal the show.

Barnard's initial idea had been for Howard to make his debut as a professional in a relatively run-of-the-mill touring show in Germany. Payne, however, preferred to entrust the monitoring of his early career to Bill Lyon-Shaw, and so he was drafted instead into a far more prestigious new domestic revue by the name of *For the Fun of It*. Produced by Lyon-Shaw, it boasted such well-established names as the veteran stand-up Nosmo King, the comedy double-act of Jean Adrienne and Eddie Leslie and, topping the bill, the hugely popular singer Donald Peers. Howard joined two other fresh professionals – his fellow-comic Max Bygraves and a contortionist called Pam Denton – at the bottom of the bill in a special showcase for ex-Service performers entitled 'They're Out!'

Before the tour began, Howard sat down and invested an extraordinary amount of careful thought into how best to shape his on-stage persona. Desperate to get his professional career off to a strong and certain start, he analysed every aspect of his act – from what he should say (and how he should say it) to what he should wear (and how he should wear it) – and gradually built up an idea, and an image, of the kind of distinctive performer he wanted, in time, to become.

First of all, he reflected on what he most admired about his own comedy heroes – and what he could take from them and then adapt for himself. When he thought, for example, about two of his favourite American performers, Jack Benny and W.C. Fields, he drew inspiration from the prickliness of their respective images (Benny the hopelessly vain and miserly old ham, Fields the drunken and cynical old fraud) and the unusually sharp, self-aware and defiantly pathos-free nature of their material.

What he found especially refreshing was the fact that neither of these fine comedians (in stark contrast to the vast majority of their peers) was enslaved by any obvious need to be loved. It did not matter to Benny if anyone actually believed that he was waited on day and night by an African-American servant (whom he rarely, if ever, bothered to pay), or wore the cheapest toupee in Hollywood, or refused to acknowledge that he had long since passed the age of thirty-nine, or, when asked by a mugger to choose between his money and his life, resented being hurried – 'I'm thinking it over!'

Similarly, it did not matter to Fields if the odd person took offence when he knocked back one too many treble measures of bourbon, mumbled something insulting about his wife or aimed a large boot at little Baby LeRoy's backside. Like Benny, Fields was more than happy to use all of his various foibles, failures and flaws – whether they were real and exaggerated or imaginary and stylised – rather than try, like the more typical kind of comedian, to hide and deny them. The only thing that mattered to this exceptional pair of performers was the number of laughs they were able to generate. It was this attitude – a subtly smart, self-mocking and grown-up attitude – that Howard (the hypocritical 'friend' of elderly deaf pianists) was ready to emulate.

Turning his attention to the delivery of his material, Howard not only recognised the debt he already owed to George Robey, but also anticipated the impact to be had from studying the style of a more recent favourite, Sid Field. What both of these performers did was to dominate an audience through indirection, preferring to coax the laughs out rather than waiting for them to be handed over on a plate.

Robey had shown how much funnier a clown could be when he acted as if he was labouring under the illusion that he was not actually a clown. Once the first ripple of laughter had rolled towards him from over the stalls, he would stick his hands stiffly on his hips, hoist his nose high up in the air and then snort censoriously: 'Kindly temper your hilarity with a modicum of reserve.' When this act of pomposity summoned up an even louder and deeper splash of derision, he would, with an air of mounting desperation, urge the audience to '*Desist!*' – which in turn, of course, would succeed only in prompting an even bigger and more gloriously anarchic burst of playful mockery.

More recently, Howard had been deeply impressed by the classy comic artistry of Sid Field. Like Howard, Field was a peculiar mixture, on stage, of lumbering masculinity and camp effeminacy, of working-class toughness and middle-class gentility – the critic Kenneth Tynan summed it up rather nicely when he likened it to a strangely effective blend 'of nectar and beer'.[20]

Besides having the knack of being able to act with his entire body – with his nimble hands and knees as well as his brightly expressive face – Field also had a wonderfully playful way with words and sounds and idioms. Ranging freely from coarse, back-throated cockney, through the nasal, drooping rhythms of his native Brummie, to the tight-necked, tongue-tip precision of a metropolitan toff, he turned common words and simple phrases into a special repertory of colourful comedy characters.

Howard adored the way that Field (a master parodist of effete behaviour) needed only to cry a single 'Be-*ooo*-tiful!' or cluck a quick 'Don't be so *fool-haar-day*!' to trigger yet another gush of giggles. He warmed to the performer even more when Field paused to interact with the members of the pit orchestra ('And how are *yooo* today? *R-r-r-*reasonably well, I hoop?'), boast to an unseen acquaintance in the wings ('Did you *heah* me, Whittaker?') and bridle at an imagined insult aimed at him from the audience ('*Oh!* How very, very, *dare* you!'). Watching him, Howard felt that he had found a kindred spirit, and drew encouragement to follow suit.

When it came to deciding on how he would look, however, Howard had already arrived at some firm and subversive ideas all of his own. Aside from adopting the old Max Miller trick of applying plenty of blue to the lids 'to help the eyes sparkle',[21] he eschewed the custom of caking the face in layers of make-up. He also elected to do without any of the formal, garish or gimmicky styles of dress.

He chose instead to wear an ordinary, off-the-peg lounge suit and plain tie. The colour of both, he decided, would always be a medium shade of brown, because he thought that this could be relied on to be 'a colour that didn't intrude': 'It's warm and neutral and man-in-the-street anonymous,' he reasoned. 'If people *did* notice my suit or tie I thought it would mean that they were not concentrating on my face.'[22]

He also resolved to dispense with the way that other comedians 'framed' each performance by making a formal entrance and exit. There would be no opening announcements or closing bows from *him*: he would simply walk straight up to the footlights and start talking – 'No. Ah. Ooh, I've had such a funny day, today, have you?' – and then, when he had finished, walk off again in a similar fashion, without ever signalling the presence of quotation marks.

The key thing, he believed, was to create the impression 'that I wasn't one of the cast, but had just wandered in from the street – as though into a pub, or just home from work. And I'd emphasise the calculated amateurishness of my presence and dress with a reference to the rest of the acts on the bill: "I'm not with this lot . . . Ooh no, I'm on me own!" '[23]

With all of this, he was almost ready: an unusually informal, ordinary-looking, everyday kind of clown with a plausibly flawed personality, a deceptively artful style of delivery and a rare gift for engaging an audience. There was just one further thing, he felt, that still needed to be done: he needed to change his name. He knew that he was stuck with 'Frankie', but he decided, none the less, to alter the spelling of 'Howard'. There were, he was convinced, simply too many other, far more famous, Howards about.

It was, in fact, an erroneous belief: in the absence of both Leslie (the London-born Hollywood actor who had perished during the war) and Sydney (the portly Yorkshire comedian who had just died in June 1946), there was arguably only one notable Howard present in British show business at this time whose name had truly impinged on the public consciousness – and that was the actor Trevor Howard, who had only recently shot to stardom after playing the romantic lead in the 1945 movie, *Brief Encounter*.

Even one solitary Trevor, however, appeared to be one too many for Frankie, who proceeded to change the spelling of his surname from 'Howard' to 'Howerd'. Showing himself to be a surprisingly shrewd (if somewhat over-analytical) self-promoter, he reasoned that the minor alteration, aside from helping to distinguish him from the odd stern-faced matinée idol, would have 'the added advantage of making people look twice because they assumed it to be a misprint'.[24]

Along with the name change came the invention of what in those days was called 'bill matter' (the slogan that accompanied the name displayed on the poster). There were plenty of examples to study: Max Miller was 'The Cheeky Chappie'; Albert Modley 'Lancashire's Favourite Yorkshireman': Vera Lynn 'The Forces' Sweetheart'; Donald Peers 'Radio's Cavalier of Song'; Robb Wilton 'The Confidential Comedian'; and Sid Field 'The Destroyer of Gloom'. Frankie Howerd, after much careful thought, came up with an epithet all of his own: 'The Borderline Case'.[25]

Now, at last, everything really was well and truly in place. The professional career could commence.

It began in his native Yorkshire, at the massive and Moorish Empire Theatre in Sheffield, on the night of Wednesday, 31 July 1946. Even though he was placed right down at the base of the bill, the act that was 'Frankie Howerd: The Borderline Case' proved impossible to miss. It was not just that he was different. It was also that he broke every rule in the book – literally.

In *How to Become a Comedian* (a compact little manual that had been published in 1945), the veteran music-hall star Lupino Lane had spelled out the conventional code of conduct to be followed by any fledgling stand-up comic. Typical of his schoolmasterly instructions were the following sober decrees: 'Any inclination to fidget and lack "stage repose" should be immediately controlled. This can often cause great annoyance to the audience and result in a point being missed. Bad, too, is the continual use of phrases such as: "You see?", "You know!", "Of course", etc. These things are most annoying to the listener.'[26] Even if some people, at the time, might have resented the intolerant tone, no one really questioned the general advice. No one, that is, except Frankie Howerd.

For all of his myriad insecurities, powerful bouts of crippling self-doubt and near-paralysing second thoughts, when it came to the true heart of his art, Howerd always knew exactly what he was doing – and what he was doing, on that first and on subsequent nights, was walking out in front of as many as 3,000 people and redefining the very nature of what being a stand-up was all about. He made it seem real. He made it into an act that no longer appeared to be an act. He pumped some blood through its veins.

What made the newly professional Frankie Howerd so impressively *sui generis* as a performer was the very thing that made him seem, as a character, so very much like 'one of us'. He stood out as a stand-up by refusing to stand out from the crowd. For all of his many influences, the thing that really made him special was his willingness to be himself.

'In those days,' he would recall, 'comics were very precise: they were word-perfect, as though reading their jokes from a script, and to fluff a line was something of a major disaster.'[27] Howerd, in contrast, told these same jokes just like the average member of the audience would have told these jokes: badly. He shook up the old patter from within, via a carefully rehearsed sequence of increasingly well-timed stutters, sidetracks and slip-ups, until, eventually, the whole polished package was scratched and then shattered – leaving people to laugh not so much at the jokes as at the person who was trying to tell the jokes.

No audience, back in 1946, had anticipated such an approach, but, when it was witnessed, it worked. It worked, explained Howerd, because, unlike the conventional comedy style, the approach invited identification rather than mere admiration. By daring to appear imprecise, he brought his art to life:

> [The approach] worked, because the ordinary chap whom I was portraying *is* imprecise. You've only to listen to the answer when a TV interviewer asks what someone thinks of the Government: 'Well . . . You know . . . Yes . . . Well, the Government . . . Yes, well . . . What more can I say? . . .' People in real life don't talk precisely as though from scripts, and neither did I attempt to on stage. My act sounded almost like a stream of consciousness, which is why I often didn't finish sentences. 'Of course, mind you . . .' trailed away into silence – as again happens in real life.[28]

It was the perfect post-war comedy persona: a 'proper' person, with no airs or graces but plenty of fears and frailties – just like the vast majority of the people he was entertaining.

Right from the start of his nine-month run in *For the Fun of It*, he was rated a performer of rare potential. Semi-hidden in the small print at the bottom of the bill, he soon became many theatregoers' special discovery, the unknown performer who inspired them to ex- claim at work the next day: 'You should have seen this act!' He soon started winning even more admirers once Bill Lyon-Shaw had coached him in the craft of commanding, as a professional, an ever-changing audience:

> He was actually a very poor timer in the earliest days of the tour, and this was simply because he'd previously spent about two years playing in camp concerts to soldiers, who'd laughed the moment he went on. The reason they'd laughed was that they *knew* him, and they *knew* that he was going to take the mickey out of the Major, and the General, and send-up the Sergeant-Major. So they were a dead-cert audience to start with. Whereas once he went into Civvy Street, it was a different matter. When he got up North, for example, and into Yorkshire – where they're a bloody hard lot anyway – they'd be saying, *'What's this bugger doin' 'ere, ey? Does he not know what he's about yet?'* He had all of that carry on. And so he had to learn timing, and learn to adjust his pace to the audience he was playing – you've got to be much faster in the South and much slower in the North, and you've got to be impossible in Scotland – and learn to pay far more attention to that kind of detail.[29]

Grateful for the expert advice, Howerd proceeded to do just that, and, as a consequence, gathered an even greater quantity of praise as the tour progressed. The other two novice professionals on the bill, Max Bygraves and Pam Denton, were also attracting an increasingly positive audience reaction. Both of them, as the tour evolved, would grow increasingly close to Howerd.

The friendship with Bygraves was probably one of the firmest Howerd would ever have. Sharing both a dressing-room and digs throughout the duration of the tour, the two young comedians became each other's primary advisor, sounding-board, supporter and all-purpose 'cheerer- upper'.

The first time that Bygraves (a much more traditional type of com- edian) saw Howerd in action, he thought him 'the most nervous per- former I'd ever met'.[30] The act, however, impressed him – as, indeed, did the high degree of courage it took to do it – and he became very protective of his very talented but horribly anxious new friend. At the end of the tour's first week, for example, Bygraves discovered that an over-cautious Frank Barnard was attempting to pressure Howerd into cutting out the most audacious aspects of his act. 'Why don't you stop bullying him?' he shouted at the boss. 'You can see the boy's a nervous wreck, so why don't you leave him alone until he gets settled?'[31]

His intervention was only partially successful – Howerd did have to squeeze into his routine a few things that were more immediately recognisable as jokes – but the gesture, none the less, could hardly have touched the co-performer more deeply. 'I've always been grateful to Max for speaking up for me,' Howerd later said, 'and I've always admired his guts: after all, like me he'd been in the business just a week, yet there he was arguing the toss with the management and risked being tossed out of the show on his ear.'[32]

The pair went on to evolve together as performers. 'We were about the same age, same weight and height,' Bygraves reflected, 'and both had the same dreams of making our way in show business.'[33] Both certainly benefited from being taken under the wing of the senior pro on the tour, Nosmo King.[34]

An asthmatic, cigar-puffing stand-up comic in his sixtieth year (whose somewhat ironic stage name had been inspired by a 'NO SMOKING' sign he once spied in a railway carriage), King used to stand and watch his two young protégés every night from the wings, and then afterwards, over a cup or two of hot tea in his dressing-room, he would advise them on what they had done well and what he believed they could learn to do better.

One of his most useful tips of the trade concerned the art of voice projection. Sensing that both Howerd and Bygraves, as they began to work the large and noisy halls, were sometimes struggling to make themselves heard (and were therefore vulnerable to heckles of the 'Oi! We've paid out money – don't keep it a secret!' variety), King took each of them to the centre of the stage, made them look at the EXIT sign in the middle of the circle, and then said: 'Now pretend that sign is somebody's head. Don't talk like we are talking now. Don't shout, but throw your voice at that sign.' The increase in power, clarity and authority was evident, to both, immediately: 'It worked,' exclaimed Bygraves gratefully, 'it really worked!'[35]

While all of this comic bonding was going on, it appears that Howerd was also forming a far less predictable romantic attachment to the female third of the tour's troupe of youngsters: Pam Denton. How real (and how intimate) this relationship actually was remains unclear – he would make no mention of it in his memoirs, and she would subsequently disappear without a trace from public life – but, according to Max Bygraves, Denton was one woman with whom Howerd became 'totally enamoured'.[36]

He certainly liked her, and liked spending time with her, and she, in turn, appears to have enjoyed being with him. He had always been fascinated by speciality acts (he would be joined on a subsequent tour by strongwoman Joan 'The Mighty Mannequin' Rhodes), and had been drawn right from the start of the tour to Denton's carefully choreographed on-stage contortions. He also warmed to her calm, down-to-earth and friendly personality – and, like any other comedian, he loved the fact that she laughed so long and so loudly at so many of his jokes.

Tall and thin with an engagingly open face and a bright, gap-toothed grin, he had, in those days, a far from unpleasant physical presence, and, when his spirits were high, he was quite capable of exuding a considerable amount of charm. His problem, however, was that while it took something extraordinary to lift his spirits up, it only took something trivial to drag them down to the floor. As Bill Lyon-Shaw recalled:

Poor Frank was very shy, very introverted, and terrified of everybody – especially women. I think the main reason for this was that he'd been turned down by a lot of the girls of the ATS – let's face it, he was no oil painting! – and I gather that they'd been rather cruel to him. So that was the thing that had made him so frightened of women.[37]

Denton, however, was different. She admired his talent, and was touched by his vulnerability; whether she wanted ultimately to make love to him or merely to mother him, she certainly wanted to share many of her spare hours with him. He was gentle, attentive and very, very funny, and, in her eyes, he made even the toughest times of the tour seem tolerable.

He dubbed it 'Our Tour of the Empire – The Empire Sheffield, Wigan, Huddersfield, Glasgow . . .'[38] When things had gone well for both of them, he would relax, sit back, and entertain her with a selection of dialogue and one-liners he had memorised from the movies of W.C. Fields. When things had gone badly for her, he would put an arm around her shoulder, mock her critics and make her laugh. When things had gone badly for him, he would slump down, hold his head in his hands, and explain, in his inimitable gabbling manner, what he believed had actually happened – which often made her laugh even more.

Neither Denton nor Bygraves, for all of their deep affinity for their friend and fellow-performer, could ever quite fathom the full reason why a man so marked by self-contradictions soldiered on with such faith and fortitude. One day it was all about *carpe diem*: he would lecture all and sundry on the importance of making one's own luck, staying true to one's ambitions and never, ever, giving up. The next day it was all about embracing one's fate: fancying himself as a serious reader of palms, he would often grab Bygraves' hand, gaze at it for a moment and then assure him solemnly that he could look forward to one day becoming a millionaire ('Frank,' Bygraves would always say with a world-weary sigh, 'I think you've got your wires crossed').[39]

There seemed to be something equally contradictory about his attitude to his audience. He dreaded rejection, but, whenever he sensed that it might be about to happen, he appeared to actively invite it. If ever a routine or a gag threatened to fall flat, the heart would duly pound, the sweat would seep and the clothes would stick to his flesh, but there was never a wave of a white flag. 'What are you,' he would snarl into the darkness, '*deaf or something?*'[40] He was a vulnerable man who dared to live dangerously.

'Frank would go out and bait his audience,' Max Bygraves recalled with a mixture of admiration and incredulity. 'He was living on a knife-edge on that stage. Don't forget we were all unknown. He'd insult them, pretend to forget his lines – then miraculously remember them just before it got embarrassing. When it worked it was great. I've seen him tear the place up, and it was wonderful to watch. Other times . . .'[41]

There were quite a few of those 'other times'. One of them came at Sunderland.

It happened at the start of the week's run, right in the middle of Howerd's act. Just after his last 'um', and just before his next 'er', a loud cracking sound – like an axe cutting into a steel pipe – came up suddenly from the stage. It shook him and stalled the routine, and, even though Howerd soon recovered, he could barely wait to finish and leave. Once the curtain came down, someone found the cause of the noise: a ship's rivet, thrown down from the 'gods' by a distinctly unimpressed docker, had missed the top of the comedian's head by a whisker and left a large dent in the stage floor. 'Obviously they can't afford tomatoes up 'ere!' Howerd remarked once he was safely backstage, trying hard to laugh the incident off, but Max Bygraves could see that, beneath the show of defiance, the reaction had rendered him 'a nervous wreck': 'He was terrified of an audience like that.'[42]

Another one of those 'other times' occurred at the Glasgow Empire – the deservedly legendary 'graveyard of English comics' – where any performer not bedecked from top to toe in tartan could expect to be sent rushing back to the wings with the cry of '*Away hame and bile yer heid!*' ringing in their ears. Howerd knew all about the venue's terrifying reputation – indeed, as soon as he arrived at Sauchiehall Street, he felt an urgent need to find and make use of the nearest backstage lavatory – but he was determined to see all of the next six nights through.

He managed it, but only just. A combination of him stammering rather more speedily than usual, and the Glasgow crowd (bemused by the unconventionality of his act) summoning up its antiquated anti-English bile a little more slowly than usual, contrived to buy him some time, but, by the arrival of the dreaded second-house on the climactic Friday night, the customised 'screwtaps' (the sharpened metal tops from the bottles of beer) were being hurled at the stage with all of their customary velocity and venom. The conductor – hairless and blameless – was hit on the head, and was carried, bleeding profusely, from the orchestra pit, but Howerd survived, more or less, unscathed.

It was quite the opposite of the proverbial 'water off a duck's back': Howerd absorbed every single drop of negativity. It was just that he kept on going regardless of how much it hurt. Even when he seemed to lose faith in himself, he never lost faith in his act.

He also took comfort from the knowledge that, beyond the confines of the tour, there were people working hard on the advancement of his career. Apart from his sister, Betty, who (fresh out of the ATS) was now acting as his unofficial manager, script advisor and cheerleader, there was also Stanley Dale. Dale, in his own inscrutable, uniquely post-prandial way, was up to all kinds of schemes and tricks to enhance his client's profile. Contacts were nurtured, sympathetic critics were cultivated and – even though Howerd was only earning a paltry £13 10s per week – investments started being made in his (and Dale's) name. Whenever the comedian's spirits started to sag, Dale would invariably intervene, either in person or via the telephone, to reassure him that all was still going to plan.

To be fair to Dale, he did, through one means or another, get results. While Howerd was on tour, Dale called him with some extraordinarily exciting news: he had been sent an invitation, via the Jack Payne Organisation, from the producer Joy Russell-Smith (one of the most knowledgeable and perceptive judges of comic potential to be found in those days in British broadcasting) to audition for *Variety Bandbox*, the top entertainment radio show on the BBC.

There has been, in the past, some confusion as to the timing of this call. Howerd would remember it arriving a mere 'six weeks' into his professional career, which would have placed the date in mid-September.[43] It really happened, in fact, about three weeks after that.

Early on the morning of Wednesday 9 October 1946, Frankie Howerd travelled down to London and went straight to the BBC's Aeolian Hall in New Bond Street. It was grey and damp outside, and it was grey and damp inside as well. He found himself in a large empty room with a battered microphone in one corner, a pile of sandbags strewn around all four of the walls, and a dull plate of glass that passed for an audience. He struggled to suppress a squeal of horror: it was, after all, yet another audition without anyone with whom to play, and the atmosphere could not have felt more flat. This, however, was an audition for the BBC, and the show it was for was *Variety Bandbox*, and so he took a deep breath and went ahead: 'Now, Ladies and Gentle-*men*, I, ah, no . . .'

The act itself was something of a dog's dinner: some of the material had been taken straight from *For the Fun of It*, some had been invented expressly for the occasion and some had been 'borrowed' from other comics and tailored to suit his needs. It was rough around the edges, the timing was slightly off, but the impact was still there. At the end of the performance, the studio door opened, Joy Russell-Smith emerged, stretched out a hand and congratulated Howerd with a remark that showed him just how well she understood what he had been up to: 'A completely new art form'.[44]

The following day, Russell-Smith submitted her formal internal report:

FRANKIE HOWARD [sic] (Auditioned 9.10.46)
c/o Scruffy Dale.
Very funny, original patter and song.
Eric Spear and John Hooper present and agree. Seeded.[45]

It was brief but immensely encouraging: this time, without the chance to interact with a 'proper' audience, Howerd had managed to win the approval of not only the redoubtable Russell-Smith but also Eric Spear (an experienced producer and composer who would later be responsible for, among other things, the theme tune of *Coronation Street*) and John Hooper (another broadcaster with a sure sense of what it took to make any form of entertainment truly popular). As a consequence, he could now look forward to playing a part in the next, crucial, stage of the selection process – a recorded, 'seeded' audition in the form of a private 'show' before a special board of BBC producers.[46]

Howerd duly returned to Studio 1 at Aeolian Hall on the morning of Friday, 25 October, nursing a bad migraine but otherwise feeling – for him – fairly hopeful. Rehearsals took place at 9 a.m., followed at 3.00 p.m. by the recording itself. He only had five minutes to show what he could do, but he enjoyed being back on a proper stage, playing to what was admittedly a very special, but none the less reassuringly audible, studio audience, and he left believing that he had acquitted himself rather well.

He was soon proven right. Just over a fortnight later, a telegram arrived: '*YOU HAVE BEEN CHOSEN*'.[47] His career in radio was about to begin.

CHAPTER 5

Variety Bandbox

Liss-en!

The average listener, perusing a copy of *Radio Times* at the end of November 1946, would not have known quite what to expect. It was obvious enough that this new man, Frankie Howerd, was probably going to be something rather special, because the magazine described him as 'a comedian who is really different in that he doesn't tell a single gag!' It was not at all clear, however, what this difference would actually mean or amount to, because the magazine proceeded to reveal nothing more than the fact that Joy Russell-Smith 'wouldn't let us into the secret of Frankie Howerd's humour because it might take some of the surprise from the first show'.[1]

There was a real sense of anticipation, therefore, when, at 6 p.m. on Sunday 1 December, the latest edition of *Variety Bandbox* began on the BBC's Light Programme. Topping the bill that week at the grandly cavernous Camberwell Palace was the very popular singer, dancer and actor Jessie Matthews, supported by novelty comic monologist Harry Hemsley, singers Hella Toros and Edward Reach, jazz violinist Stephane Grappelli, comedy double-act Johnnie Riscoe and Violet Terry, Morton Fraser 'and his Harmonica Rascals', and, right down at the bottom of the bill, the mysterious young debutant, Frankie Howerd.

Bottom of the bill he might have been, but Howerd could not have found a more high-profile British programme in which to make his broadcasting debut. Established in 1944, *Variety Bandbox* had soon become the radio show on which every popular entertainer in the country craved to be heard. 'Presenting the people of Variety to a variety of people,' it was the most-listened-to programme of its type – overheard coming out from most of the houses in most of the streets in Britain each Sunday night, and discussed in countless workplaces each Monday morning. If ever there was an audition before the nation, then this, Howerd realised, was it.

As he readied himself in the wings before walking out to perform his first seven-minute spot, he thought of everyone who might be listening, somewhere, out there at home: certainly his devoted mother and his sister, and perhaps even his brother (although Sidney was never a great comedy fan) and innumerable other friends, acquaintances and relations; undoubtedly, from his agency and his touring company, Scruffy Dale, Jack Payne, Frank Barnard, Bill Lyon-Shaw, Nosmo King, Max Bygraves and Pam Denton would all be within hearing distance of the wireless; possibly, if the rumours that he had heard were right, such personal heroes as Jimmy James, Max Miller and Sid Field would also be tuning in; and, in addition to all of them, well, a frighteningly high proportion, it seemed, of the rest of the world and his wife. He felt nauseous – more so than usual – and his legs felt like lead, but, when the cue came, he puffed the air out from his mouth, clenched and unclenched his fists, took one last deep breath and then, with the help of a studio assistant, he pushed himself on to the stage to the sound of his new, aptly-titled signature tune: 'You Can't Have Everything'.

'Ladies and Gentle-*men*,' he began. They laughed. 'No ... Ah, no ... Now listen.' They laughed a little louder. 'No ... No, don't laugh ...' They kept on laughing. 'Oh, no, um, no, please, *liss-en* ...' He was off and running.

He did the usual routine, more or less, but this was the first time that it had been heard by the British public at large, and it went down extremely well. He seemed so new, so fresh, so ordinary, and, therefore, so odd. Instead of sounding like the 1,001st comic to come on and rattle off yet more of the same old gags – maybe a little faster, or slower, or louder, or quieter than the last one, but otherwise very much the same – Frankie Howerd lived up to his pre-publicity by coming over as a genuinely unusual comedian. He thought, at the end, that he had been 'far too twitchy to be good', but he had been good enough to impress most of those who had been listening both in the theatre and gathered around the radio at home.[2]

Some of them might have caught the odd comic novelty on the wireless before – such as the old Sheffield-born stand-up Stainless Stephen,[3] who had intrigued a small but loyal audience during the late 1920s and early 1930s with his downright peculiar brand of 'punctuated patter' (e.g. 'Somebody once said inverted commas comedians are born not made semi-colon') – but never, before now, had any of them encountered the sound of someone so original in the context of a prime-time mainstream show. What people had heard on this particular night had genuinely taken them by surprise.

Howerd could not have sounded less like the regular, rather more established, young stand-up associated with the show, Derek Roy. Later dismissed by an embittered Spike Milligan (who toiled for a spell as one of his many underpaid writers) as 'the world's unfunniest comedian',[4] Roy was a singer (nicknamed 'The Melody Boy') who had metamorphosed into a relatively slick but essentially old-fashioned teller of jokes. He was technically not much better than mediocre, but he was certainly full of cheek: if he doubted his ability to deliver a certain punchline, he would not hesitate to resort to donning a silly wig or a wacky hat in order to amuse the studio audience and thus ensure that the radio waves still registered the requisite laugh.[5]

His material revolved around a predictable cluster of comedy clichés: the shrewish wife; the dragon-like mother-in-law; the attractive but vacuous girlfriend; the bumptious boss; the slow-witted neighbour or acquaintance; and the latest celebrity sex symbol. 'Anyone here played Jane Russell pontoon?' went a far livelier than usual Derek Roy joke. 'It's the same as ordinary pontoon but you need thirty-eight to bust!' His style was somewhat Americanised – a kind of 'Bob Hope Lite' – and possessed all of the personality of a typed and unsigned letter.

With the memory of Roy's last stale routine still fresh in the mind, no listener would have failed to have been struck by Howerd's astonishing originality. It was like suddenly hearing modern jazz after a lifetime of tolerating trad: innovative, unpredictable and supremely individual.

The BBC had only booked Howerd for a three-week probationary period (paying him a paltry £18 per show), but a delighted Joy Russell-Smith wasted no time, after witnessing that truly remarkable debut appearance, in signing him up to the show as a regular. The residency would last for two-and-a-half extraordinarily memorable years.

Bill Lyon-Shaw, who was still responsible for Howerd on tour, was perfectly happy to share his energies with the BBC:

[*Variety Bandbox*] was good for him, good for the tour, and it wasn't like he was going to tire himself out. Frank was a young man, he'd been trained in the Army, and he was quite tough. It didn't take that much out of him to do our show [*For the Fun of It*], because he was only doing his own act – he wasn't doing any of the sketches or anything extra like that. So, twice nightly, it didn't take a lot out of him. And he'd just go off on either the Saturday night or the Sunday morning to London, to wherever the theatre was, and do his radio programme, and then he'd come back to us, wherever we were, on the Monday afternoon. So I don't think combining the two affected him much at all. But, I must say, he *did* start spending more and more time in the dressing-room preparing for the weekend. He used to sit there for hours on his own, making faces, and going, '*Ooooh! Aaaah! Yes! No! Missus! Ooooh!*' I mean, he worked very, very hard at it. It wasn't natural. That was acting. Off-stage, Frank was usually a very quiet and introverted person, and his stage presence was foreign, it really was an *act* in the true sense of the word.[6]

Joy Russell-Smith had decided that, from this moment on, Howerd would alternate on a fortnightly basis with Derek Roy as the show's top comic and co-compère. Inspired by the long-running mock 'feud' on American radio between Jack Benny and Fred Allen – a good-natured battle of wits that had been amusing both stars' audiences (and fuelling the imaginations of both sets of writers) since 1936 – the idea was for Howerd and Roy to cultivate a similar kind of sparring relationship.[7] It worked rather well, not only providing each performer with some welcome additional publicity (plenty of name-checks on the air during those weeks when one or the other of them was off it, as well as the odd mention in the letter pages and the gossip columns), but also furnishing them with an invaluable extra 'peg' for new comic material.

The need to keep coming up with fresh material, Howerd soon realised, would prove to be a chronic problem now that he was working in radio. The first few weeks were relatively easy – a combination of tried-and-tested routines, smart prevarications and a sharp rush of adrenalin each Sunday night saw to that – but then, all of a sudden, it felt as if he had run into a brick wall. He had used, and then subtly reused, more than a decade's worth – in fact, an entire life's worth – of comic material, and still people wanted, and expected, more.

'In Music Hall,' he reflected ruefully, 'you could use much the same script for the duration of the tour – it appeared new to each town played. But on radio the total audience heard it all at once, so I needed a fresh script for each broadcast.'[8] Since (unlike the considerably better-off Derek Roy) he could not yet afford to hire a scriptwriter (or pay, as Roy also did, for regular transcriptions of scripts that had already been used by the stars of top radio shows in the States), he got by, for a while, by studying a pile of joke books, cannibalising their contents and then inserting enough stutters, hesitations and digressions to ensure that every single joke could be relied on to go a long, long way.

Ironically, this craftiness eventually served only to make the problem even worse. So warmly received were his early performances that the BBC decided to reward him with two additional solo spots in each one of his shows – thus stretching his limited resources still further and thinner than ever. He responded by begging and borrowing on what seemed like an ever-increasing scale: Max Bygraves soon became used to his friend's anxious requests for 'spare' material, and never failed to respond with both promptness and generosity; Nosmo King was similarly obliging, even if much of what he offered dated back to shortly before the Great War; mother Edith and sister Betty jotted down dutifully every new joke, anecdote and one-liner they spotted in the papers or heard at the theatres; and Frankie himself spent long afternoons on his own at the movies, trying his best in the darkness to transcribe some of the best of the latest Hollywood *bons mots*.

The audience remained blissfully ignorant of his routine struggles behind the scenes. After all, they did not tune in each fortnight to listen to his jokes; they tuned in to listen to him.

The content might well have sounded commonplace, but it was the form that fascinated. Howerd's wonderfully characterful routines, delivered with such an unusual and lively manner, were drawing in as many as twelve million listeners each show, and the critics had started hailing him as 'the most unusual of all radio discoveries'.[9] It was clear that something special was happening. 'I was considered to be very much the alternative comedian at that time,' he would recall. 'I was different to everybody else: my attitude was different.'[10] In an era when radio was still Britain's pre-eminent mass medium, he was well on the way to establishing himself as one of its most popular, distinctive and talked-about young stars.

Those around him with a vested interest were quick to take notice.

Both Scruffy Dale and the Jack Payne Organisation, in particular, were keen to exploit their still rather 'green' client's increasingly propitious situation. Dale began urging Howerd to invest (or rather to allow him to invest on Howerd's behalf) in various stocks, shares and properties, and Jack Payne persuaded him to sign a dubious new 'rolling' contract (if things continued to go well, the star was fine, but if things started going downhill, the agency was free to drop him and walk away). Howerd did what he was told – he possessed at that time neither the head nor the disposition for serious business – and returned to his rehearsals.

He just wanted to be true to his ideals. He just wanted to keep sounding real. He had overcome so much to get where he was, and now he was desperate to ensure that he would stay there.

Preparation for the next show always began straight after the last. There were no boozy parties, no relaxing evenings out at restaurants, no lazy mornings in at home lapping up all of the positive reviews: there was just work. Plagued by doubts, the famously fastidious Howerd would spend hours walking up and down lonely country roads and wandering around local churchyards and cemeteries, mumbling to himself his lines and trying out all of his countless 'ums', 'oohs', 'ahs' and 'oh nos', in the manner of a text-book obsessive-compulsive. Each joke, monologue, sketch and supposedly throwaway remark was shaped and then repeatedly reshaped (often as many as seventy times) until every single element – the structure, the rhythm, the pace, the humour, the tone – sounded as good and as true as it could.

'The great paradox of show-business,' Howerd observed, 'is that you have one of the most insecure professions in the world attracting the most insecure people. In my case I was a nervous wreck with tremendous determination.'[11] The accuracy of this candid self-description was never more painfully evident than during these early days in radio. On tour, he said, when there was only one script for him to memorise, 'I could be relatively relaxed once I'd got over the terror of opening night.' On radio, however, where the script was always new, 'every broadcast was an opening night': 'I worked so hard on my material, and was so bedevilled by nervous insecurity, that after every *Variety Bandbox* I'd go home with a dreadful migraine.'[12]

Howerd was hard on himself, but then he was hard on his colleagues, too. Having worked so diligently on every detail of his act, he expected others to display the same high levels of professionalism, discipline and commitment – and he could be startlingly blunt and rude to anyone who (in his opinion) fell short of those exacting standards. Most of his angry outbursts soon blew over, and were followed more or less immediately by a completely sincere expression of remorse, but, none the less, not many of them were very easily forgotten. Working with Frankie Howerd was invariably a fairly tense affair.

What normally made all of the fussing and fretting undeniably worth-while – both for him and for them – was the finished product. At his best, the production team appreciated, Frankie Howerd really was worth it, and most of the rows, they realised, only came about because he always wanted so badly to *be* at his best.

By March 1947, however, a degree of fatigue was creeping in. Drained by the strain of having to continue to combine his touring commitments as a member of *For the Fun of It* with his current radio duties as an employee of the BBC, he began to sound a little stale. While millions of listeners remained happily captivated by the vibrant originality of his style, a slightly more knowledgeable minority had started to hear, just beneath all of those surface 'oohs' and 'ahs', the sound of someone scraping at the bottom of a barrel.

Howerd was running out of ideas. With no reliable supply of first-rate comedy material, he was gradually being forced into a number of bad habits: too many verbal tics, too few strong stories, too much waffle and far too many return visits to the well-trodden *boop-boop-dittem-datten-wattem-choo* territory of 'Three Little Fishes'. The whole thing was get-ting to sound a little bit robotic.

It was not that he had stopped trying so hard. He was trying harder than ever. It was just that he now had less than ever with which to work.

He did what he could. The rehearsals grew longer, the rows louder and the recordings more manic, but the act still seemed to lack some of its old joyful brio.

Things came to a head at Easter. Howerd was performing in *For the Fun of It* at a theatre in Peterborough, and also preparing for his next trip up to London to record another edition of *Variety Bandbox* (which by this time was moving its broadcasting base back and forth between the Camberwell Palace, the Kilburn Empire and the People's Palace in the Mile End Road). While he was resting in his dressing-room, an urgent message came from Jack Payne: the BBC, he was told, had recently conducted another one of its routine audience surveys, and the results contained bad news for Howerd. It seemed that, while Derek Roy's popularity (rated out of 100) was still, somewhat improbably, hovering just above the 70 mark, Howerd's had suddenly plummeted all the way down to the 30s.[13] According to Payne's unidentified contacts within the Corporation, the performer (and, more pertinently, his scripts) would have to improve, and soon, or else he risked being removed from the show for good.

'The news would have shaken even the most hearty extrovert,' recalled Howerd, who was patently anything but; 'I nearly collapsed on the spot.'[14] He had, deep down, been half-expecting the arrival of some sort of negative news like this, but nothing remotely as bad as this, and, now that it was here, he felt lost. Something had to change, he acknowledged, but the big question now was: what?

CHAPTER 6

The One-Man Situational Comedy

*In a way, desperation forced me into some small measure
of originality.*

If Frankie Howerd had merely been a fighter, he might well have fallen
and remained floored on that bleak day at Easter. The bad news that
he received could easily have felt like one blow too many. Fortunately, however, he was not merely a doughty fighter; he was also a
deep thinker, and he responded, once again, with intelligence as well
as grit.

After giving in, for a few hours, to an understandably powerful surge
of self-pity – during which he walked aimlessly through the streets of
Peterborough feeling dazed and 'miserable beyond words'[1] – he returned
to his dressing-room, tried his best to clear his head, and then did what
he always did when faced with such a problem: he thought. He thought
about every tiny aspect of his act, every element of his technique, every
decision he had either made or failed to make, and every gag, every
expression, every gesture, every routine, every show, every review,
every hope and every fear – everything. The search would not stop
until he had found the true causes of all the flaws.

The decline in the quality of his material, he acknowledged, had been
the obvious catalyst for the crisis, but he felt sure that there was more
to it than that – even though, much to his frustration, he could still not
quite make himself comprehend what, precisely, it was. Then, after
agonising over his analysis for countless hours, the answer suddenly
came to him: it was sound, not vision.

'It was ridiculous,' he later exclaimed, 'that neither the BBC nor the

Jack Payne Organisation had spotted it, and I was singularly stupid not to have been aware of it much earlier on':

> *I'd been giving stage, not radio, performances.* It was as simple as that. Listeners weren't able to see my expressions and gestures, and were baffled when the live audience laughed for no apparent reason – bafflement giving way to annoyance at the frustration of not knowing what was going on.[2]

Having at last diagnosed the cause, he wasted no time in devising a cure. Instead of continuing to stand back and project his voice at the studio audience (as he had learnt to do on tour), he now resolved to step forward and address the microphone. The aim, he explained, was not to ignore the live audience (without whose laughter he knew he would always be lost), but rather to develop a different technique: 'transferring from *visual* to *vocal* clowning'.[3]

As was so typical of him, Howerd laboured both tirelessly and obsessively to effect the necessary change. 'I used to do voice exercises, like a singer would do,' he recalled. 'I used to go up: "A–B–C–D–E, *A–B–C–D–E*, *A–B–C–D–E*". And then I used to go down: "A–B–C–D–E, *A–B–C–D–E*, *A–B–C–D–E*". So I learned to use my throat muscles as I would my face muscles.'[4] He ended up being able to switch in an instant from a dopey baritone to a goosed falsetto, and then slip straight into stage whisper.

There were also many hours spent studying the recognised masters of radio's more relaxed and intimate style of delivery – such as America's Jack Benny (who, through the use of his sublimely timed pauses, had taught listeners to pay attention to what he was thinking as well as saying) and Britain's Tommy Handley (who had the ability to race through reams of dialogue without ever sounding remotely rushed) – as well as many long and self-absorbed sessions in the studio, going over and over his act while practising standing relatively still and close up to the microphone.

Howerd did not stop there. He also took careful note of the seductive power of the well-spoken catchphrase. Having lived through the era of such hugely popular shows as *ITMA* – which, through weekly repetition, had coined several distinctive personal signatures out of common words and phrases, including, 'I don't mind if I do'; 'After you, Claude.' 'No, after *you*, Cecil'; 'Can I do you now, sir?'; and 'T.T.F.N – ta-ta for now!'[5]

– Howerd could see and hear for himself how beneficial the odd verbal 'gimmick' could be, and so he started to think up a few all of his own.

His playfully unconventional way of emphasising the opening phrase 'Ladies and Gentle-*men*' had already become something of a trademark, but he now took to mispronouncing on a grander scale, stretching some words close to their limits (e.g. '*luuud-i*-crous') while stretching the ends of others so far that they would snap off and shoot away like a stray piece of knicker elastic (e.g. 'I was a-*maaaazed*!'). He also cultivated quite a few catchphrases all of his own: 'Not on your Nellie!'; 'Make meself comfy'; 'Oooh, no, missus!'; 'Titter ye not!'; 'Nay, nay and thrice nay!'; 'I was flabbergasted – never has my flabber been so gasted!'; 'Shut your face!'; 'And the best of British luck!'

There were also some changes made (of a more subtle nature) to the ways that he shaped the 'saucier' sorts of material. The whole process now became far more devious and conspiratorial.

It had to be, because the code of self-censorship within the BBC was fast becoming even more neurotically draconian in peacetime than it had been during the war. Thanks to the efforts of the Corporation's Director of Variety at that time, Michael Standing, all of the BBC's producers, writers and performers who were working in the field of 'Light Entertainment' now found themselves saddled with a short but extraordinarily censorious 'policy guide' known informally as 'The Green Book'.[6]

According to this well-meaning but somewhat snooty little manual, 'Music-hall, stage, and, to a lesser degree, screen standards, are not suitable to broadcasting'. The BBC, as a servant of the whole nation, was obliged to avoid causing any members of the nation any unnecessary offence: 'Producers, artists and writers must recognise this fact and the strictest watch must be kept. There can be no compromise with doubtful material. It must be cut.'[7]

In order to ensure that all of its employees understood what this 'doubtful material' might be, the manual proceeded to spell it out in sobering detail. There must, it said, be no vulgarity, no 'crudities, coarseness and innuendo', which meant 'an absolute ban on the following': –

Jokes about –
    Lavatories
    Effeminacy in men

Immorality of any kind
Suggestive references to –
   Honeymoon couples
   Chambermaids
   Fig leaves
   Prostitution
   Ladies' underwear, e.g. winter draws on
   Animal habits, e.g. rabbits
   Lodgers
   Commercial travellers
Extreme care should be taken in dealing with references to or jokes
about –
   Pre-natal influences (e.g. 'His mother was frightened
   by a donkey')
   Marital infidelity[8]

As if that was not enough to completely obliterate the average red-nosed
comedian's act, there was more: no advertising; no American material
or 'Americanisms'; no derogatory remarks about any profession, class,
race, region or religion; no jokes about such 'embarrassing disabilities'
as bow-legs, cross-eyes or (a particular blow this for Howerd) stammering; and, last but by no means least, no expletives (which not only
meant no 'God', 'Hell', 'Bloody', 'Damn' or 'Ruddy', but also not even
the odd 'Gorblimey'). Writers and performers were also urged to keep
the jokes about alcohol and its effects to an absolute minimum.

Just in case these commandments had left any dubious comic spirits
still standing inside the Corporation, the manual went on to strike one
final blow for decency. All performers were warned that on no account
must there be any attempt to impersonate Winston Churchill, Vera
Lynn or Gracie Fields.[9]

The response of Frankie Howerd to these potentially suffocating
restrictions was ingenious. He simply took whatever the censors had
left and then proceeded to corrupt it.

Unlike most other comedians of the time, who remained prisoners
of their patter (and whose patter consisted of most if not all of those
topics that radio had now declared taboo), Howerd was not dependent
on gags, and therefore found it much easier, during the course of his
wireless ramblings, to slip in some of his own brand of sauciness just

under the radar. Max Miller's over-reliance on his so-called 'Blue Book' had already earned him a five-year ban from the BBC during an earlier, slightly more tolerant, era; now, in the age of 'The Green Book', the incorrigible directness of his material – (e.g. 'I was walking along this narrow mountain pass – so narrow that nobody else could pass you – when I saw a beautiful blonde walking towards me. A beautiful blonde with not a stitch on – yes, not a stitch on, lady! Cor blimey, I didn't know whether to toss meself off or block her passage!') – ensured that radio would render him speechless. Frankie Howerd, on the other hand, was able to survive by implying that it was the listeners, and not him, who were the ones with the dirty minds.

What he did was to make the audience – via the use of a remarkably wide range of verbal idiosyncrasies in his delivery – hear the sort of meanings in certain innocent words that no English dictionary would ever confirm. 'To say "I'm going to do you,"' he later explained by way of an example, 'was considered very naughty, yet I got away with the catchphrase: "There are those among us tonight whom I shall do-o-o-o".' Howerd would also respond more censoriously than the censors whenever one of his stooges, such as the show's band leader Billy Ternent, made a supposedly ambiguous remark: 'He'd say something like: "I've just been orchestrated," and I'd reply: "Dirty old devil!"'[10]

It all added up to a real mastery of the medium. Howerd's performances improved, and his popularity began, once again, to increase. The early crisis in his radio career was over.

As if to acknowledge this fact, the next *BBC Year Book*, in an article that hailed radio comedy's coming of age, included Howerd in an elite group of young British performers who had now earned the right to be considered 'true men of broadcasting'.[11] The turnaround was also recognised by the producers of *Variety Bandbox*, who responded to Howerd's soaring appreciation figures by promptly adding to the amount of airtime they apportioned to his act.

Howerd himself, however, was in no mood to rest on his laurels. He knew that he still needed – and now more urgently than ever – to find a way to start improving the quality of his scripts.

By this stage, he had started buying a few scraps of comic material from a man named Dink Eldridge. Each week, a sheet of about twenty or so one-liners would arrive from Eldridge, and Howerd would study them, pick the one that sounded least like it had been transcribed from short-wave radio, and then proceed to stretch it out into a full-length routine. It was not an arrangement that could be allowed to continue. With more time to fill, and his first summer season coming up in Clacton, it was obvious that he needed to hire a proper, full-time comedy writer.

By now, he could just about afford it. *For the Fun of It* may recently have finished, but he was now earning a sum (£20 per show) from radio that for the time was a reasonable wage (equivalent to about £500 in 2004), and he was ready to invest some of it in his act. Finding an available writer blessed with both the right type and degree of ability, however, was another matter, and Howerd spent much of the rest of 1947 trying in vain to track him down.

Finally, at the end of November, shortly before he travelled up to the Lyceum Theatre in Sheffield to star (as Simple Simon) in the panto-mime *Jack and the Beanstalk*, he came up with a suitable candidate. Casting his mind back to his days touring Germany with *The Waggoners* shortly after the end of the war, he recalled seeing – and admiring – a young fellow-comedian who was appearing in Schleswig-Holstein at the time in another CSE revue entitled *Strictly Off the Record*.

The comedian's name was Eric Sykes. Aged twenty-four, from Old-ham in Lancashire, he was now struggling to make a living as a straight actor in repertory at Warminster. He was still, however, hopeful of one day resuming his comedy career (as a performer rather than a writer), and took great delight in tuning in his wireless each fortnight to catch the latest broadcast by one of his great contemporary heroes, a stand-up comic who, coincidentally, happened to be none other than Frankie Howerd.

After making a number of casual enquiries, Howerd found that he and Sykes had a mutual friend: the comedian Vic Gordon. When Gordon called Sykes to tell him how keen Howerd was for the two of them to meet up, Sykes could not have felt more thrilled: 'It was as if,' he recalled, 'the King had contacted me for a game of skittles at Buckingham Palace.'[12] He did not actually know what Howerd looked like – he only knew the sound of his extraordinary voice and the 'sheer brilliance' of his special brand of 'happy nonsense' – but Gordon provided him with a suitably vivid description and then advised him to arrange to visit the star as soon as possible.

A few days later, an excited Sykes travelled by train to Sheffield, and
made his way to the Lyceum Theatre. There, in a dressing-room backstage, he set eyes on Frankie Howerd for the first time. He was more
than slightly taken aback when Howerd started to explain how much
he had admired the material Sykes had written during the war – because
Sykes knew that he had not written any material during the war. The act
that Howerd so warmly recalled had in fact been built from second-hand
material culled from American shows on short-wave radio – just like
Howerd's had. When Sykes pointed this out, he was rather surprised –
and very pleased and relieved – to find that his hero still seemed interested in finding a way to use him on the show: 'He said, "Do you
think that you *could* write for me?" Well, I'd never written anything
for anyone in my life! So I said, "Well, er, no doubt: when do you
want it?" And he said, "Eight days from now." So I said, "All right,
hang on a minute, have you got a bit of paper?" And then he went
out to do the matinée performance of the pantomime, and by the time
he came back at the end I'd written his first script.'[13] A new partnership
had begun.

It proved, almost immediately, a near-perfect union. Both men had
always gravitated towards the kind of comedy that came from character
rather than gags; both of them had lived through the absurdities of war
and then come to terms with the uncertainties of peace; both of them
had an affinity for the routine experiences of ordinary working people;
and both of them seized on any chance to cock a snook at pretension
and pomposity.

Each man understood the other, and while Sykes found in Howerd
someone who cared enough to champion his talent and support his new
career, Howerd found in Sykes someone who could provide him with
precisely the kinds of words, rhythms and images – right down to the
'ums' and the 'oohs' and the 'aahs' – that suited his distinctive style of
stand-up. 'He was brilliant,' Howerd would later say. 'I was able to
help him, I think [in the beginning]. He had great ideas for lines and
I knew something about construction.'[14] Sykes would make a similar
point about the dynamics of their collaboration:

> When I was first writing for him, Frank would say, 'The only
> thing is, Eric, you've got to have a beginning, a middle, and then
> the end's got to come *up* instead of just fizzling out.' He'd give

me very helpful little pieces of advice like that. But he was a gift
to me. I mean, just to *listen* to him, he was almost writing the next
script for me. Frank's *style* was his own, and I copied his style, but
I did have my own flights of fancy in my head.[15]

What Sykes did was to use these flights of fancy to craft scripts that
contained not jokes but *situations* in which Howerd's established comedy
character could at last come fully to life. He did not just 'use' words:
he made words work. He made them, via Howerd's captivating delivery,
act as a catalyst on the imagination. When one heard his words, one
saw.

The effect was electric: never before, and arguably never again, would
Frankie Howerd sound so sure, so bright, so right and so joyously alive.
One of the first and most memorable of these routines concerned a
surreal attempt to transport a couple of 'items' from London up to
Crewe:

> . . . And the boss came up and he said, 'Ah, good morning.' He
> said, 'I want you to collect some goods from the depot and deliver
> them to Crewe.' Ooooh, I thought! Ooooooh, good, y'see! No.
> 'Cos: *Crewe!* 'Cos, I've always wanted to go abroad. So. Yes. Any-
> way. Yes. Anyway. I went along to the depot, and I saw the
> foreman. I said, 'Look,' I said, 'I want to sign for these goods.'
> And he said, 'They're labelled and ready. Get 'em out of here,
> quick.' So I signed for them, y'see. I went along. They were
> labelled and ready all right. Two elephants! *Two elle-ee-phants!* I
> was a-*maaaazed*! I said, 'I shall never get these to Crewe!' He said,
> 'I don't care *where* you're getting' 'em to, but get 'em out of *here*!'
> He said, 'The place has been in uproar. *In uproar the place has been!*'
> So I got a bit of string. And I, um, tied it round their necks, y'see,
> and I led 'em out into the street. Oooh, I did feel a ninny! I tried
> to look as if I wasn't with 'em! Anyway. Well. *No!* But the way
> people stared! The way people *stared*! You'd think they'd never
> seen two elephants going down the underground before! And I
> had a shocking – *Liss-en!* 'Ere! *Liss-en!* Yes! Ye may titter! *Titter ye
> may!* – I had a *shocking* time with 'em down this underground. No.
> What I had to do, y'see, I had to tie one to a slot machine, and
> push the other one on to the tube train. 'Cos they'd only let me

take one on at a time. No. Well, it was rush hour. And, of course, the elephant was *furious*, because it had to stand! Yes! It played the devil! So, anyway, I got it to King's Cross station, and I parked it there, y'see, but then I came back for the other one that I'd left tied up. And when I got there, there it was: gone! So I said to a porter, I said, 'Look, I left an elephant here tied to a slot machine. It's gone!' He said, 'Yes – and so 'as our slot machine!' Anyway, I dashed into the street and looked for it, and I could soon see the way it had gone, because there were crowds of people lining the road – waiting for the rest of the procession. *What a silly thing to do!* I mean, you'd think they'd have more sense, wouldn't you? And, honestly, I've never seen such a silly crowd of people in all me life! None of you were in Tottenham Court Road, were you? No! I didn't think you were. No. Anyway. Um. Now where was I? . . .[16]

On and on the tall tale went, with its teller sounding like he was having the time of his life. '*Cease!*' he shrieked, as the audience's laughter grew louder and louder, '*Cease!*'

It was great stand-up, and great radio. Freed by the inspired Sykes from the onerous chore of scraping together a script, Howerd was finally able to relax (at least by his own nervy standards) and invest all of his intellect, invention and energy into eliciting from his audience the greatest possible quantity of laughs. Delighted that his bold comedic ideal had at last, more or less, been realised – the original anti-patter act had completed its evolution into what he now termed a 'one-man situational comedy'[17] – his powers as a performer rose up to reach their peak.

He made his Sundays on *Variety Bandbox* sound like everything that Derek Roy's, by this time, were not: funny, imaginative, unpredictable and quite often genuinely unforgettable. Each fortnight, he would take the audience by surprise with another one of Sykes' wild flights of fancy, and then, through the brilliance of his delivery, conjure up the kind of vivid verbal pictures that rendered many listeners both helpless and happy with laughter.

To hear him announce to his audience that he had just endured yet another 'shocking day' in yet another improbable place – such as a dense jungle, a rocky mountain range or a speeding train that had lost its driver – and then draw them into his fiction, orchestrate all of their reactions and maximise each one of their laughs, was to witness the art of a truly consummate comic performer. The justly celebrated 'lion tamer' monologue, for example, acquired an extra layer of irony from the sound of the studio audience being tamed so expertly while the tale of ineptitude was being told:

Now, ah, Ladies and Gentle-*men*. Harken. Now – harken. This is, no – harken! Now har-*ken*! *Har-ever-so-ken!* Now, that's the life: the circus! What? That's the life! If you live. I know! What? I'm telling you this. *Liss-*en! There's one phase in my life, there's one phase – and I never forget a phase! Ha ha ha ha! Every gag fresh from the quipperies! One day, y'see, there I was, I was cleaning me boots, and then the ringmaster came up, the ringmaster came up, and he said, 'Howerd, I've been watching you for some time. You are ambitious, hardworking and courageous.' Oooh, I didn't know what to say! I mean, I felt like such a fool, really, stood there in me nightie! He said, um, 'Put this uniform on.' I said, 'Look, it's a bit of a cheek, you know, after all I've done for you, asking me to sell ice-cream!' He said, 'Don't worry!' He said, 'Have you got your uniform on? Right, stand by – 'cos you're on in a minute.' I said, 'Well, what's the rush? There's plenty of time – the interval's not yet, is it?' I said, 'They've got this lion act to do first.' He said, '*Ah,*' he said, '*Aah*. Now, that's it.' He said, 'Now,' he said, 'follow me.' So we got to the ringside and there was this cage, with all the lions inside, snarling and roaring and growling and jostling. 'Oooh,' I said, 'a nice bunch of pussies, aren't they!' I said, 'They're waiting for something, aren't they?' He said, 'Yes: the lion tamer. So: when you're ready . . .' I said, 'I beg your pardon?' He said, 'Yes,' he said. 'You're it.' Yes. I walked up straight to the cage, and immediately all the lions ran toward me and I just stared at them. Yes! I-just-stared-at-them! And they all slunk away. They did! I said, 'How's that?' 'Oh, yes, it's very good,' he said, 'but you should be *inside* the cage.' I said, '*INSIDE?*' I said, 'They'll tear me to pieces!' He said, 'Look,' he said, 'I don't know what you're making all this fuss about. I can assure you,' he said, 'I can assure you we shall all be stood round the edge with guns. And if there's the slightest chance of you being

torn to pieces, we shall shoot you.' So, he said, 'Don't worry!'
And before I could argue – *Cease!* – And before I could argue –
Cease! – And before I could argue – *oooh*, you make me *mad*! Now
pull yourselves together! – Er . . .

Long before the end – thanks to all of his various little verbal tics, tricks
and tetchy interjections – he had the whole of the audience eating
sweetly from his hand:

. . . Before I could argue, he opened the door, y'see, and pushed
me in the cage! *Oooh!* That door clanged behind me, and something
ran up and down my spine – I was too frightened to scratch it!
Oooh, I was in a shocking state! And there's all these lions, all these
lions, crouching at the other end of the cage – *grrrrrrrraaaaaaghhh!* –
arguing whether they should play with me or get it over with.
The ringmaster said, 'Well, go on!' He said, 'Go on! Do something!
You've only got six lions!' I said, '*Six?*' I said, 'You want to look
again – I make it seven.' He said, *'Seven?* Oh, *no!* Not tonight!'
He said, 'Oh, no, tonight of all nights it's happened – Leo's got
in by accident! *Oooh*, I shall give those keepers such a scalding!'
He said, 'Leo only came from the jungle yesterday: he's still savage!'
Eh? I didn't know what to do. So he said, 'Look, take your tunic
off. Get your tunic off, quick!' I said, 'Why?' He said, 'Well, you
don't want to get blood all over it!' He said, 'I'll tell you what.
Let 'im taste you – that'll put 'im off.' *I was a-maaaaaazed!* Then,
without warning, there was a dead silence. There was a dead
silence. It was so quiet I could hear the light shining on me! And
the drums started to roll . . . Then, one of the lions came *slooooowly*
forward. And I went *slooooowly* backward. And I was right up
against the bars – I couldn't go any further. And it came forward,
this lion, it still came forward, then it stopped and opened its
mouth! The ringmaster said, 'Well, this is it: this is the big trick.
Yes, this is the "Head in the Mouth Trick".' He said, '*No!* You
put *your* head in the *lion*'s mouth!' He said, he said, 'Look, I'll
show you what to do,' he said, 'look, follow me, watch me,' he
said. 'I'll do it once.' So he came in the cage. He said, 'Look,
watch *me.*' And he put his head right in the lion's mouth! Yes! *In
the lion's mouth!* Top hat and all! *Yes!* The crowd applauded. The

band played. Everybody cheered. It was wonderful! And as I said to his widow at the funeral, I said – *yehss, oh yehss* – I said, 'If he'd only remembered to take his cigar out of his mouth,' I said, 'it would have been all right!'[18]

The impact of these routines grew deeper and richer as each fortnight gave way to the next, because, as Eric Sykes would observe, the characterisation of the on-air 'Frankie Howerd' was edging closer and closer to perfection: 'It was continuous, and that was important. When I started writing for Frankie Howerd, I was only ever writing Frankie Howerd's next script. I wasn't ever writing *my* script, and hoping that Frankie Howerd would do it. I was continuing, from one script to the next, Frankie Howerd's persona. So there was a clarity of purpose about everything I wrote for Frank.'[19]

Howerd's strikingly original solo spot, central to the show's appeal though it was, was by no means the only aspect of *Variety Bandbox* to benefit from his increasingly fruitful collaboration with Eric Sykes. There was also a marked improvement in the two other segments of the show that regularly featured the host: the opening routine, which usually took the form of a brief sketch or spot of crosstalk with the affable band leader Billy Ternent, and the later spot that he shared with whatever celebrity happened to be that week's special guest.

The opening section, pre-Sykes, had tended to suffer most from the old shortage of material. Whenever Howerd had struggled to stretch his 'borrowed' bits and pieces as far as an entire script, the initial badinage with Ternent had invariably suffered most. That changed now, however, thanks to the prodigious efforts of Eric Sykes. He somehow found the additional time and inspiration to spark that staged relationship into life, transforming those first few minutes from what was often a patently forced and perfunctory affair into a far more entertaining exchange between a comedian and his stooge:

HOWERD: Tonight's topic is 'How to Speak English'. And I shall be assisted – 'assisted' with the accent on the '*ass*' – by Mr William Ternent, a bachelor of, er, well, a bachelor. And when Mr Ternent heard what the subject was, he immediately left his college –
TERNENT: Thank you, Mr Howerd –

HOWERD: Wait a minute, let me finish! He immediately left his college pudding to come here and assist me in 'How to Speak English'. Now, Mr Ternent, tell me: how do you speak English?
TERNENT: I talk.
HOWERD: No, no, I mean: is your English good or bad?
TERNENT: I can safely say I stand out.
HOWERD: Yeah, you stand out all right! Now, er, very well, Mr Ternent, since English is your strong point, *you* ask the questions.
TERNENT: Right, right. First of all, vowels: *a, e, i, o, u* –
HOWERD: There's half of me last act gone now![20]

The improvement to the regular sketch with the celebrity guest was even more pronounced. There was nothing new about roping in a passing British actor, singer or movie star (with a project to plug) to show that he or she could be a good sport, but, up until now, it had all been terribly respectful and, as a consequence, not terribly funny. Howerd and Sykes changed all of that. Long before *The Morecambe & Wise Show* brought the same kind of playful irreverence to television,[21] Frankie Howerd's *Variety Bandbox* became the first peak-time show on British radio that dared to really tease its celebrity guests.

Every fortnight, the stars of stage and screen were brought rudely down to earth by the man who sounded like one of 'us' rather than one of 'them'. The ribbing was never remotely malicious, but, at a time when broadcasters were still expected to treat their guests with a 'proper' degree of deference, even this playful ruffling of feathers seemed refreshingly unconventional.

Describing himself as 'Professor' Howerd (the use of the term 'psychiatrist', thanks to 'The Green Book', had been refused on the grounds of its 'dubious' taste), he would invite each star to enter his consulting room and ask for some advice. One of the most memorable of these 'patients' would be Dirk Bogarde, who arrived in the guise of the violent criminal he had recently portrayed in *The Blue Lamp*:

HOWERD: Now come along, Mr Bogarde – don't be so kindergarten. You must take that mask off. Oh, *dear*! You have given me such a *shock*!

BOGARDE: Why? By pretending to hold you up?

HOWERD: No – by taking your mask off! Fancy you creeping in here like a bandit!

BOGARDE: Ha, yes, just fancy!

HOWERD: You even had a gun in your hand!

BOGARDE: Yes, ha ha!

HOWERD: Why, even if you *were* a bandit, I've only got a pound.

BOGARDE: Only a pound?

HOWERD: Yes.

BOGARDE: Put 'em up![22]

Howerd's mock 'analysis' duly started after it had transpired that Bogarde, having gunned down PC Dixon in the movie, now felt compelled to rob every stranger he encountered in the street.

The improved quality of all three of these comedy strands – the opening crosstalk, the guest slot and the closing solo spot – made *Variety Bandbox* seem more like a special event than merely a show, regularly drawing in an audience estimated to be at least 42 per cent of the total adult population of the nation (a percentage which in those days amounted to 15,120,000 people – but, if both children and those adults still in military service had also been included, the figure would probably have been nearer to 21,000,000).[23] It also helped to confirm Frankie Howerd's reputation as one of the biggest stars in British radio.

The timing, for both, could not have been any better. Radio was a medium that was about to reach its peak: the number of radio licences would rise from 11,081,977 in 1948 to a record 11,819,190 in 1950 before commencing its sudden and inexorable decline during the rest of a decade that (thanks to the advent of television) saw listeners transmutate into viewers.[24]

A sign of how vital the wireless had become in the life and leisure of so large a part of the nation was supplied at the start of 1949, when the death of Tommy Handley, the much-loved star of *ITMA*, was mourned by the British public: tens of thousands of people lined the streets of London to follow the six-mile procession of his funeral cortège, and then, a fortnight later, huge crowds gathered in and around the cathedral of his native Liverpool to listen to eulogies, while in London thousands more set off to St Paul's Cathedral for the national memorial service – the first time a humble comedian had been so honoured. In

July of the same year, Michael Standing, the BBC's current Head of Variety, sent a note to a number of his colleagues, informing (or reminding) them of the following pertinent fact: 'Unquestionably, as a result of his broadcasts on *Variety Bandbox*, Frankie Howerd has become a star of the first magnitude.'[25] Handley's heir could hardly have been more apparent.

No one felt more proud about this fact than Eric Sykes. Although he still hoped that the chance would eventually come when he could resume his fledgling career as a performer, a recent sobering experience had reconciled him, in the short term, to his current role as a writer:

> I had actually said to Frank one day, 'Listen, Frank, I don't want to spend *all* my life writing for you. I am a comedian in my own right.' So he said, 'Well, write a script for the two of us.' And so I wrote a double-act for us, and he paid for the recording studio in Bond Street, and we went and did it. And after it was over we listened to it back. And after about ten seconds I said, 'Turn it off! Turn it off, Frank!' He said, 'No. You are going to listen to this all the way through.' I was in agony, because Frank was, you know, Frankie Howerd, and I was, well, I was pathetic. As I sat there listening to it, I was sweating with embarrassment. And so, after it was over, he said something to me that was very sagacious – because he was a very perceptive, thinking man – he said, 'Eric, you have a gift for writing. Because writing comes easy to you, you *suspect* it. You probably think, "Well, if I can do it, anybody else can do it". Well, it's not true. Now, you've heard that recording. Concentrate on your writing.' So I said, 'Yes, yes, Frank, you're quite right.' And I did. It would be about two or three more years before I again had any aspirations to be on the stage.[26]

In 1949, therefore, the knowledge that he had played some vital part in his hero's achievement was a good enough reward, for the moment, for Sykes:

> I lived in Oldham, and I went home one weekend – it was a nice, warm, Sunday evening – and I walked along this street, and every door was open (because they used to be in those days when it was a warm evening), and out of every door – *every door* – I could hear

Variety Bandbox, and Frankie Howerd saying the lines that I'd written. And I had to hug myself – because I knew what the next line was![27]

In the space of little more than a year, Sykes had gone from being just another avid listener to a singularly artful writer, and now his words were being heard by almost half the nation.[28] Life was good, and he knew it.

Life was even better for Frankie Howerd, but, unlike Sykes, he never seemed able to sit back and savour the moment. He was grateful, of course, for the succession of renewed contracts, the rise in wages (from £26.25 in the middle of 1948 to £66 at the end of 1949[29]) and the recognition of his talent by listeners and critics alike (even Jack Payne was now boasting about – and doing his best to take much of the credit for – what he described as 'one of the great romances of show-business'[30]), but, none the less, Howerd remained far too insecure ever to pause and really enjoy it.

He had done barely anything during 1948 but work. Apart from *Variety Bandbox*, he had also been persuaded (by Scruffy Dale and Jack Payne) to tour the country in another gruelling but lucrative revue – a rather risqué affair called *Ta-Ra-Ra-Boom-De-Ay* – as well as appear in pantomime, once again as Simple Simon, in another production of *Jack and the Beanstalk*.

He did find the time to move out of the family home and into an apartment of his own (it was actually a rented top-floor flat in a large Victorian house – which belonged to the comedian Ben Warriss – at 6 Holland Villas Road, not far from Shepherd's Bush), but, when he did so, he did so alone: however serious his relationship with Pam Denton had really been, it had not outlasted the run of *For the Fun of It* (she left soon after to live and work in America, where she would end up marrying an 'acrobatic dancer'), and the only reason for Howerd's change of address was to provide him with a more convenient place to rest. He was closer to the theatres and studios, closer to Eric Sykes (who, as the occupant of the ground-floor flat in the same house, was now his new next-door neighbour) and closer to his newly-appointed personal manager, Scruffy Dale (who was based just a few doors along the road at number 12) – and what all of this meant, of course, was that he was now so much closer to the thing that consumed practically all of the hours in his waking life: his work.

Always, by his own admission, 'a compulsive worrier', the arrival of fame served merely to stop Howerd worrying about 'making it' and start him worrying about 'keeping it'.[31] There was no sudden craving to decorate himself with the conventional regalia of show business success: he was fairly content to remain in his cosy little flat, and was far more interested in supplying the rest of his family with some additional forms of support than he was in acquiring a more fashionable type of address; he no longer drove, so had no need for a large and glamorous car; he also retained relatively simple tastes in food, drank very little and, as he confessed to the great surprise of absolutely no one, he 'wasn't fussy about clothes'.[32] He wished for one thing and one thing only: the right to continue performing.

'Having got to the top of the bill,' he later explained, 'I sweated desperately to survive.'[33] No matter how big the box-office figures or how loud the audience applause, nothing would ever convince him that, when the next time arrived, things might not turn out to be different, and things might not turn out to be worse. 'What little fame I had acquired,' he reflected, 'had come astonishingly – improbably – quickly, and I was extremely aware that it could vanish with even greater rapidity.'[34]

There was a little more to his fierce persistence, however, than mere neurosis. It was not just the fear of failure that drove him on. It was also the deep and positive belief that he had in his act. During the tour of *Ta-Ra-Ra-Boom-De-Ay*, for example, Howerd dared to take on the mob at the Glasgow Empire. He had actually enjoyed, up until this point, a fairly successful week – indeed, he was one of the precious few English comedians who tended to fare well whenever a tour reached this notoriously intimidating place – but, on this particular Saturday, something went abruptly and horribly wrong. He told a joke that hinged on the fact that he was half-Scottish: it was meant to ingratiate himself with his semi-fellow-Celts, but, on this particular night, they chose to interpret it as an outrageous insult. The change in the atmosphere was immediate: '[S]uddenly the theatre exploded into a madness of boos, jeers, catcalls and a slow handclap. Absolute pandemonium: the audience dissolved into a shrieking, raving mob. At first I was baffled, then humiliated – then terrified.'[35]

He simply refused, however, to submit. He insisted on completing the act – even when the ear-splitting torrent of abuse drowned out every single line of his closing song – and then, once he had taken (far more slowly and deliberately than usual) his bow in front of the baying crowd, he stunned just about everyone in the house by daring to re-emerge from the wings and walk back out to perform an encore. When it was finally over, a wide-eyed Eric Sykes, who had been there to witness the event, raced backstage to tell his friend that it had been the bravest thing he had ever seen attempted in a theatre.[36] Howerd was probably too busy throwing up at the time to fully appreciate the tribute, but, once he was safely back on the train ('shaking, quite literally, during the entire journey south'[37]), he must have been inclined to believe that Sykes was right.

No matter how tired or vulnerable he might have felt, Howerd simply cared too much ever to let up. Now that, at last, he felt that he was in front, he was determined to maintain the pace.

Howerd's frenetic pace, of course, was also, necessarily, Eric Sykes' frenetic pace. The more pressure the comedian placed on himself, the more, as a consequence, he heaped on his heroically uncomplaining scriptwriter:

Whenever he was appearing somewhere, like, let's say, in Black-pool for a summer season, I'd write his act for that particular show, but then I would carry on with his radio material. I would write his usual opening spot with Billy Ternent [for the next edition of *Variety Bandbox*] and his own solo spot in my office in London, and then I used to get on the train and go up and see him in Blackpool or wherever he was, read out these two spots, and if he liked them, fine. Then we had to wait until Frank heard from the BBC who the next guest celebrity was going to be. When he knew, he would put me in a room in whatever villa he was hiring for the season, give me a bottle of Scotch and a typewriter, lock the door, and when I knocked on the door and asked to come out it meant that I'd finished writing the guest spot. And once I had read that out to him and he'd said that he liked it, I used to get the train back to London. It was done like that: straight up and straight back down. In fact, the train sometimes used to wait for me at Euston! I'd come rushing on to the platform and they'd say, 'Here he is,' and on the train they'd have a restaurant car with one particular table that always had three bottles of Double

Diamond beer on it, and one glass, and that was for me! No one would bother me. I was a regular. It was a lovely time.[38]

Howerd's provisional schedule for 1949 handed him and his writer a workload that was heavier than ever. Besides the prospect of another batch of *Variety Bandbox*, there was also another Payne- and Dale-initiated touring revue planned for the spring (*Ladies and Gentle-men*), a high-profile summer season booked at the Central Pier in Blackpool, a commitment to appear at the end of the year at the Liverpool Empire in another pantomime (*Puss in Boots*) and, in addition to all of that, an invitation would later arrive for Howerd to take part in a special private Christmas show at Buckingham Palace (it seems that, by this time, King George VI and Queen Elizabeth had become two of his most ardent fans[39]). The combination of Howerd's own reluctance to say 'No', and Payne's and Dale's readiness to exploit that reluctance, was threatening to burn the star rapidly out.

The warning signs had been there – at least for those who had been willing to look – since the middle of the previous year. Joy Russell-Smith, fearing that he was in danger of driving himself (and his colleagues) to the brink of both physical and mental exhaustion, arranged for him to take a complete two-month break from broadcasting over the summer,[40] but then Payne and Dale made sure that he stayed busy throughout that period, and when he returned to radio in September, he still looked as if he was in urgent need of a rest.

Howerd, however, had somehow managed to convince himself that all he really needed was a change. Dale, as Bill Lyon-Shaw recalled, was the most likely influence on Howerd's decision, because, by this stage, Dale was ensconced in his client's flat: 'Scruffy had moved in with Frank, because Frank badly needed friendship. That's what he wanted more than anything. It had nothing to do with sex at that moment. He'd just been terribly lonely. It was friendship he wanted.'[41]

Dale certainly supplied Howerd with friendship, of a sort, but he also supplied him with a further source of aggravation. The older, run-of-the-mill anxieties during each day, combined with the newer, routine machinations of Scruffy Dale during each night, contrived to make Howerd feel edgier than ever.

Afraid that he might end up going stale by remaining on *Variety Bandbox*, and curious to see what he and Sykes could achieve once freed from the rigidities of that particular format, he and Dale began pressing the BBC to allow him to leave the show in order to star in a brand-new programme all of his own.[42] Although, for a while, the Corporation held firm, and Howerd was persuaded to stay put and guide the show into 1949, the writing was now on the wall: the change, sooner or later, was bound to come.

The BBC, which was understandably disinclined to break something simply because one of its employees happened to have requested that it be fixed, did what it always did best in such situations: nothing. Howerd kept asking for his own show, the BBC kept agreeing to give the matter some serious thought, and he and *Variety Bandbox* kept on topping the ratings. Privately, the BBC would probably have preferred him to carry on doing what he was doing on the radio, while appearing considerably less on the stage for the Jack Payne Organisation. Jack Payne, on the other hand, would probably have preferred him to carry on doing what he was doing on the radio, but for double or more of the current money, while doing just as much as ever for him on the stage.

Howerd, fearing that neither party was ready to press forward, grew more preoccupied than ever with tortured thoughts about the vagaries of fame. Anxious not to outstay his welcome, and eager to keep edging in the right direction, he came to the conclusion that he would have to seize the initiative and leave the show. The BBC judged his decision perverse (why choose, at the age of just thirty-two, to go missing from broadcasting at the very moment when your broadcasts are being hailed as unmissable?) but, rather than lose its long-term hold on such a valuable commodity, it agreed, reluctantly, to release him – but only for a short 'sabbatical'[43] – after the completion of his last scheduled broadcast on 20 March 1949. Explaining his decision to *Radio Times* a few months on, he reflected: 'I came off the air because I didn't want people to get tired of me. Some comedians broadcast too much and go on too long. Even the greatest artists in the world have their own special tricks and surely the secret is trying to keep the act fresh.'[44]

By the autumn, however, having duly 'refreshed' himself via a long tour of the United Kingdom followed by an equally tiring season in the north of England, he came to the conclusion that his previous conclusion had been more than a little rash. On 16 October 1949, therefore, he returned to *Variety Bandbox*.

Now, much to the BBC's relief, Frankie Howerd took up his rightful place, albeit somewhat belatedly, as British radio's latest king of comedy. He still worried about all of his tomorrows, but even he could no longer deny the glory of his todays. What he and Eric Sykes were once again creating, every fortnight, was comedy of a quality that was – and will surely always remain – a privilege to hear.

The situations grew richer and weirder, the guest celebrities bigger and better, and the performances stronger, more audacious, and funnier than ever. Whatever listeners feared that they had lost irrevocably with the passing of Tommy Handley – a thoroughly British, endearingly vulnerable clown; a bright but kindly wit whose raillery was without malice; perhaps even (as the Bishop of London had put it during the memorial service for the star at St Paul's) a comedian 'whose genius transmuted the copper of our common experience into the gold of exquisite foolery'[45] – they had now regained with the return to radio of the nation's new comedy favourite.

Everywhere that Frankie Howerd went, on every street in every region of the country, people seemed to make a point of letting him know just how much he now meant to them. Like Handley had done before him, Howerd responded to these regular waves of warm praise and sincere affection with a degree of humility that served to strengthen still further the bond between him and his legion of fans. Delighted with his success, but puzzled and a little daunted by its size, he often sought out the sage advice of Eric Sykes: 'Don't *question* a gift,' his friend kept on telling him, 'just *use* it to its best advantage.'[46] It went against his notoriously hyper-analytical nature, but, throughout those final two remarkable months of 1949, he actually managed to do so, and the on-air effect was a delight.

Howerd ended the year, and the 1940s, by reprising his old deaf accompanist act with 'Madame Vere-Roper' for the benefit of the King ('Shut your face!') and the Queen ('No, *liss-en*, missus, *liss-en*!') and their family ('I was a-*maaaazed*!'). When it was over, he was presented first to Princess Margaret – 'who told me – thank God! – that she'd had to stuff a handkerchief into her mouth to stop herself laughing too loudly' – and then the Queen – 'as I began to bow she said how thrilled *she* was to meet *me*!' – and then the King – who congratulated him on this and all of his previous performances.[47]

It had been quite a decade. The nervous young working-class man with the stammer, who had started the period by undergoing the pain and humiliation of hearing himself being dismissed by every judge, talent scout and selection board before whom he had dared to audition, had ended it as the most distinctive, talked-about and popular stand-up comedian in the country. His triumph had been immense, but the only thing that he could think about was: 'What next?'

INTERMISSION: THE YEARS OF DARKNESS

It's bitter out.

CHAPTER 7

Ever-Decreasing Circles

Come along, come along: don't doze off!

Anyone who listened regularly to Frankie Howerd's act during the late 1940s would have been accustomed to the fact that every 'yes' was usually followed by a 'no'. During the 1950s, however, this little trade-mark tic in his delivery could have served as a commentary on the course of his career: a 'yes' that suddenly became a 'no'.

Having spent the last part of the 1940s mastering the medium of radio, he elected to spend the first part of the 1950s attempting to master practically all of the other popular media – including television, movies and 'legitimate' theatre – that would have him. Motivated by the familiar feelings of insecurity rather than the first stirrings of Chaplinesque mega-lomania, the aim was to seek out new ways to keep his career climbing steadily upwards. The actual result, however, would see his career do precisely the opposite: spiralling downwards, slowly but strangely inexorably, into a succession of ever-decreasing circles.

The irony was that the new decade started out so well. *Variety Bandbox* held on with ease to its place at the top of the ratings; a summer season at Great Yarmouth's Britannia Pier Theatre out-performed all of its rivals at the box-office; Howerd's wage for his radio work was raised to the sum of £100 per programme; and, in May, he was named as the 'Most Popular Comedian' on the BBC.[1] Then, in the middle of October 1950, Howerd made his West End debut at the London Palladium, topping the bill in a revue called *Out of this World*.

On the day that the production was due to open, he walked along to look at the huge promotional posters about him that had been plas-tered around Leicester Square. 'I was emotional almost to the point of tears,' he would recall, 'for my thoughts suddenly took me back through the weight of my days to my early struggles, and I realised that despite my success on radio and in the provinces, it was this that I'd really dreamed of.'[2]

As if all of this had not been sufficient to make 1950 an exceptionally memorable year for Frankie Howerd, he received another notable honour that November when the impresario Val Parnell arranged for him to make his debut in the Royal Variety Performance alongside two of his greatest comedy heroes: Max Miller and Jack Benny. All three of these comedians proceeded to conform to type on the night: Miller not only slipped in some material borrowed from his 'blue' book, but also overran by eight minutes and landed himself, yet again, in his boss's black book (when Parnell, anxious to move on to the big international acts, hissed at him from the wings, he hissed back: 'I'm *British!*'[3]); Benny – his eyes half hidden by their lids, his left hand cradling his left cheek and his lips pressed together to form that familiar look of graceful indignation – was a model of dry wit and sly precision; and Howerd (unnerved by the prospect of having to follow a crowd-pleasing routine by the Billy Cotton Band) fled the theatre straight after the completion of his act, 'devastated with shame' at the thought that he had failed to supply the show with more than a spot of 'drizzle' after Cotton's 'typhoon'.[4]

He was, as usual, far too critical of his own contribution, and Parnell, knowing how insecure the star was rumoured to be, made a point of tracking him down at the end of the night to reassure him that his performance had gone down far better than he had feared. 'Anyway,' Parnell added, 'the King said to me afterwards that you've got a very nice personality.'[5] This obviously cheered Howerd a little, but it failed to dispel all of his nagging self-doubts about the development of his career. After enjoying two extraordinary years of uninterrupted success, he believed that he had just experienced a narrow escape: dazzled by the sight of his name high up in the West End lights, he had found it hard to focus on his performance. Never again, he vowed, would he allow such a thing to happen.

When, years later, he came to look back on this night of the most modest conceivable degree of under-achievement, he would freely admit that he had 'over-reacted to the point of ridiculousness'.[6] At the start of 1951, however, he was adamant that there was an urgent need to shake up his career.

Howerd decided that, this time, he really had to take a gamble. He resolved to take control of, and then attempt to rejuvenate, his act.

Scruffy Dale had already persuaded Howerd that the best way to achieve autonomy would be to break away from the Jack Payne Organisation and pass all of its powers and responsibilities over to him. The advice had been half-right: there had certainly been a problem with Payne – during the run of *Out of this World*, Howerd had discovered that Payne was not only taking half of his £600 weekly salary, but was also (thanks to a separate contract he had struck in private with Val Parnell) receiving an additional £300 each week as 'compensation' for 'sub-letting' his client to the show – but the decision to hand over formal control to Dale would prove to be a case of leaping out of the frying pan and landing straight in the fire.

Howerd – egged on by Dale – initiated legal proceedings against Payne, claiming that there had been a breach of contract, and declared that Dale would now have sole responsibility for the management of his career. Payne, apoplectic with rage and indignation, responded by claiming that it was Howerd, and not himself, who was guilty of being in breach of contract – thus sparking a long-running sequence in the law courts of suits and counter-suits.

That particular battle would drag on for two bitterly difficult – and financially draining – years, but Howerd was in no mood to wait before pushing on with his other plans. He wanted change, and he wanted it now.

The act, he insisted, must on no account be allowed to atrophy. Convinced (in spite of his rock-solid, and strikingly high, listening figures) that he was in danger of becoming 'a bit of a yawn to the public', and curious to see how much further he (with the assistance of Eric Sykes) might 'extend' himself once handed a new challenge, he resolved to shake things up: he broke away from *Variety Bandbox*.[7]

'I would like to go forward, while retaining my present popularity,' he had already announced in a letter (dated 31 July 1950) to Michael Standing, the BBC's Head of Variety. 'By going forward,' he added, 'I mean to embark upon something a little more ambitious.'[8] Standing – his stiff upper lip turning frosty blue with *sangfroid* – had snapped back: 'I respect your views about your radio future, but I am afraid that I do not entirely share them.'[9] This time, however, Howerd proved implacable – 'I feel I must on principle dig my heels in over the matter'[10] – and, eventually, Standing agreed, with great reluctance, to release him from the show.[11]

Howerd's first broadcasting project, post-*Bandbox*, was a programme called *Fine Goings On*. It did not have an easy birth.

The basic problem was that, although Howerd was always very clear as to what he did *not* want the new show to be – namely, a *Variety Bandbox* Mark II – he remained frustratingly unclear as to what he *did* want it to be. Day after day, and week after week, he exasperated his colleagues by repeatedly asking for advice only to then dismiss it out of hand. Whenever it seemed that the team had finally taken a step forward, Howerd would suddenly change his mind and they would all take two steps back. The emphasis kept shifting from stand-up to sketches, then from sketches to situation-comedy, and then from situation-comedy back to stand-up (but with some sketches and a slice of situation-comedy). In the end, the format on which everyone settled – more for the reason of the approach of an imminent deadline rather than the arrival of a real consensus – turned out to be a very familiar kind of hybrid: part stand-up, part sitcom, part sketch show: a bit like *Variety Bandbox*.

The BBC certainly lavished a great deal of care, and money, on selling the new show to the public. Apart from having Frankie Howerd as its star, the programme boasted scripts written by Eric Sykes (with additional material by the up-and-coming Sid Colin), and a supporting cast that included the rising star Norman Wisdom, the comically gruff character actor Bill Fraser and an impressively adept young straight-woman by the name of Hattie Jacques. It also had, at its helm, not one but two of the safest pairs of hands currently available in British radio: first, Bryan Sears, who had worked with Howerd and Sykes before on *Variety Bandbox*; and second, Tom Ronald, whose other production credits included the high-profile sitcom *Life with the Lyons*.

When *Fine Goings On* finally went out on air, however, it fell rather flat. Running on alternate Thursdays for fourteen half-hour episodes, from 4 January to 5 July, it fared well enough in terms of ratings but did not really engage the imagination of the listeners. Howerd blamed himself, claiming that he had failed to cope with the show's relatively small (or, as he preferred to put it, 'claustrophobic and inhibiting') studio – the Paris Theatre in Regent Street – and should have tried harder to adapt his technique. That sort of admission struck Tom Ronald, who had spent the last few weeks of the run hearing the comedian complain about everything from the confused nature of the format to the supposedly unsatisfactory condition of the microphones, as more than a little rich: 'I would like to place on record,' he scribbled at the bottom of a memo bound for the BBC archives, 'that Frankie Howerd is the most difficult artist I've ever had to cope with.'[12] Howerd, to his credit, would almost certainly have concurred – he was inconsistent, but he also had a conscience – but no amount of contrition would prevent him from going on to make precisely the same kinds of mistakes, and infuriating precisely the same sorts of powerful people, over and over again.

His immediate response to what he took to be the 'failure' of *Fine Goings On* was the same as it had been to all of his earlier disappointments: he went for a long walk. Every new street that he reached seemed to prompt another theory as to why things had gone wrong. The further he walked, the more worried he became: was his career just experiencing a 'dip', or could it actually be starting to decline?

'I thought,' he later reflected, 'that if a tiredness is setting in, and if this means the danger of skidding on my backside down to the bottom of the heap, how can I apply the brakes?'[13] Although he was now beginning to acquire a certain amount of security – a company called Frankie Howerd Ltd, based at 130 Uxbridge Road, had been established in February (with himself, his mother and Scruffy Dale installed as its directors) to gauge and balance his earnings, followed soon after by a subsidiary company, Frankie Howerd Scripts Ltd (headed by Howerd, Dale and Eric Sykes), to deal with the commissioning of material – the state of his career was still a major worry.

Eric Sykes' career, on the other hand, was now going from strength to strength. Besides writing for Howerd, he was also (since June 1950) collaborating with Sid Colin on a new series called *Educating Archie*, starring the ventriloquist Peter Brough. An instant hit – it built up an audience of 12 million listeners, and won a national newspaper's 'Top Variety Show' award, in its first year on air[14] – *Educating Archie* had cemented Sykes' reputation as the most imaginative young comedy writer in British radio, and had also shown that, if he so wished, he could now pursue a career that would be independent of Howerd's.

Although he did not appear inclined to do so, Sykes certainly appreciated the fact that, at long last, his talent was being more widely – and publicly – acknowledged:

Frank had always been fine. It had been other people that had kept my contribution a kind of secret. I'd said to the BBC, 'I would like a credit, as Frank's writer, because, you know, he's reading out what I write word-for-word in every show.' But they said, 'Ah, well, if we gave you a credit a lot of people would be disillusioned, because they, the public, think that he makes it up as he goes along. If they thought for one minute that it was all written for him, he'd lose a lot of fans.' And then they said to me, 'Would you *like* Frank to lose a lot of fans?' Well, naturally, I said, 'No,' and that was it. It was emotional blackmail.[15]

Howerd had sympathised with Sykes, and so the comedian was the first to applaud his writer's new achievements:

He was happy for me, because he felt that he'd helped to 'create' me in a way. And I agreed with that, because without Frank I would never have considered myself to be a writer. He had opened the door for me to enter this profession. He made me understand that I was a writer and had a special gift for it. I always felt in his debt, and so, if Frank ever wanted anything, he knew that he only had to pick up the phone and ring me and, no matter how busy I was, I would always give him precedence. I was so grateful to Frank.[16]

Sykes had no intention of abandoning his close friend and first patron, but Howerd, though genuinely pleased to see his writer succeed, felt more insecure than ever when he compared the burgeoning appeal of *Educating Archie* to the underwhelming impact of *Fine Goings On.* Just when Peter Brough was hailing Sykes as the key to *Archie*'s success,[17] some critics were holding Howerd solely accountable for the failings of *Fine Goings On.* As he plodded along the back streets of Kensington, he kept asking himself the same couple of questions: 'Did this mean, as one critic wrote, that I was OK for scattered spots in a show like *Variety Bandbox*, but wasn't able to hold my own programme together? And having cut myself off from *Variety Bandbox,* what did the future now hold for me?'[18]

In the short term, he concluded, what the future held for him was the past: having kick-started his career by making himself the star of his

The infant Francis
Alick Howard: 'I
was quite beautiful'.

Gunner Howard:
The life and soul
of the concert party.

George Robey, whose mock
indignation at audience laughter –
'Desist!' – became a cornerstone
of Howerd's comic style.

Sid ('How very, very, dare you!') Field:
another rich source of inspiration for
Howerd.

Jack Benny and W.C.
Fields: neither man
feared making fun of
his flaws.

Frankie Howerd brought the art of the stand-up to life: real life – our life.

A rare sighting of a young Stanley 'Scruffy' Dale: the man who helped make and then almost ruined Frankie Howerd.

Jack Payne: the boss whom Howerd dared cross.

Bill Lyon-Shaw: one of Howerd's early mentors.

'Har-ever-so-ken!' Howerd recording a routine for the BBC's *Variety Bandbox*.

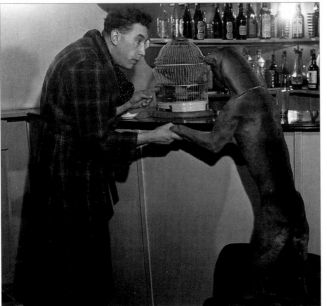

Top flat, 6 Holland Villas Road: Howerd's first home alone.

'I couldn't be an off-stage comic if I tried. I like heavy reading and symphony concerts'.

'Who's the master?' Howerd with his much-doted on dog, Red, in 1950.

Howerd and Sykes:
a peerless comedy
partnership.

Johnny Speight: 'I'll put in the "Oooh–aaahs,"
Howerd told him. 'Ah,' exclaimed Speight.
'This one can ad-lib!'

Galton & Simpson: plotting
Howerd's next half-hour.

'Every gag
fresh from the
quipperies':
Sykes, Galton,
Milligan and
Simpson, with
Beryl Vertue,
in action at
Associated
London Scripts.

The nation's latest favourite: 'I was a-maaaaaazed!'

own Army concert parties, he thought that he could now revive it in the same way. 'Frank never forgot all of the laughter that he got from his fellow-servicemen during the war,' recalled Bill Lyon-Shaw, 'and so, whenever he was in need of reassurance, he always knew, I think, that he could rely on that sort of audience. The concert party remained a "safe", friendly form of entertainment for him.'[19]

With the help of the BBC and the War Office, Howerd proceeded to work out an itinerary that took in flying visits to British troops stationed in Tripoli and Benghazi, Egypt, Jordan, Cyprus, Malta and Korea. He then enlisted his old friend from Southend, Blanchie Moore, as his stooge/accompanist, engaged the distinguished pianist/arranger Eric James and a young professional singer called Marcia Owen – the rest of each show's cast would be selected from volunteers at each military base – and inveigled the already over-worked Eric Sykes into writing him a set of scripts.

Contrary to the account given in Howerd's autobiography (and repeated in all subsequent second-hand accounts of his career[20]), he did not fly off immediately to record the concerts. Apart from a quick trip in the New Year to meet some of the troops that were stationed in Germany, he was unable to take his pet project any further until he had first honoured a more pressing commitment at home. He was due to make his television debut.

At that stage, however, Howerd – like so many of his contemporaries – harboured serious doubts about the potential appeal of the new medium. At the end of 1951, fewer than two million homes, grouped around London, Birmingham, Manchester, Glasgow and Cardiff, had access to a television set that was capable of receiving any actual television signal,[21] and most of those who worked in radio regarded the small screen with the kind of attitude that was very close to sneering contempt. When, for example, the writer and director Robert Barr, who had left radio for television back in 1946, returned to Broadcasting House for a brief visit at the start of the 1950s, a senior producer bumped into him in the foyer: 'Good Lord, I thought you were dead,' the former colleague exclaimed. 'No, I'm not,' Barr replied with a sigh. 'No?' the producer gasped in mock surprise, before adding smugly: 'Ah, yes: gone to television – same thing, old chap.'[22] Howerd had heard all of the jokes, and had been responsible for one or two of them himself. He expected his time on television, therefore, to be little more than a curious interlude – an interesting experiment – after which he would return to the more serious business of rejuvenating his radio career.

Called *The Howerd Crowd*, his first television series was set to consist of three hour-long monthly programmes, to be broadcast on what at the time was Britain's one and only channel, BBC TV. What had persuaded the performer to participate was the prospect of working again with the only producer-director that he knew he could trust: his old manager from *For the Fun of It*, Bill Lyon-Shaw.

The BBC had recently headhunted Lyon-Shaw from the Jack Payne Organisation to be one of the pioneers (alongside the likes of Michael Mills and Bill Ward) of what television's public service broadcasters chose to term, with a twitch and a grimace, 'Light Entertainment'. Already, however, he had overseen the small-screen debuts of Benny Hill (*Hi There!*[23]) and Beryl Reid (*Vic's Grill*[24]), as well as Norman Wisdom's first regular televised work (also in *Vic's Grill*[25]), and he could not have been better suited (technically and temperamentally) to the task of easing Frankie Howerd into the new medium.

Written by Eric Sykes and featuring the actor Bill Fraser, the tenor John Hanson, Victor Platt and Bunny Parish, the Beverley Sisters, the dancer and choreographer Ernest Maxin (who would later work on, and eventually produce, *The Morecambe & Wise Show*), Blanche Moore and the odd star guest, the show was designed to be a showcase for Howerd's special talent. True to form, however, Howerd fretted about every feature of the production.

His fears were, in this particular context, understandable. In the early 1950s, television was not only live, but also (thanks to the extraordinarily powerful lights) blazingly hot and blindingly bright, and, if one wilted, one wilted right in front of the viewing public. Howerd, as a consequence, bombarded Lyon-Shaw with anxious requests for everything from an extra, 'personal' camera (which would capture all of his reactions) to special hidden 'prompts' to help him with his lines. The director took it all in his stride:

> I was used to Frank, and he knew that, so we could be quite open with each other. And he *did* used to listen. He wanted you to help him. But, of course, what all stand-up comics find difficult, when making the transition from theatre to television, is getting used to the *intimacy* of the medium, and at the start Frank would struggle

to get it right, sometimes under-acting and sometimes – quite often, in fact – over-acting. But, by and large, I don't think the programmes turned out too bad, because, in those days, performers did what the director told them to do!

He did have to learn how to perform in front of the camera. Everything, obviously, is so much smaller on the television screen (and in those days, you have to remember, the screens were very, very small indeed). And time is different, too: ten minutes of television is like half an hour on the stage. That's something that people find it hard to understand even now: very often, performers over-play their hand. They want to go on and on. Television demands greater discipline.

You certainly had to be very disciplined back then. Everything was live in those days, of course, so you couldn't edit anything, and you had to come on and go off at the right time. There were no second chances. So it was hard for new performers, and quite nerve-racking for someone like Frank, but he picked it up pretty quickly – he did pay attention to what you told him, and he really thought about it, and he'd adapt.[26]

The first show (broadcast from 8.45 to 9.45 p.m. on Saturday 12 January) proved a success with both the public and the press. Featuring some good comic material by Eric Sykes (including what critics judged to be a particularly effective sketch – performed by Howerd and Victor Platt – that parodied the messy demonstrations given by the burly and bearded TV cook, Philip Harben), and assured contributions from the supporting cast, the programme, it seems, lived up to its billing as the highlight of the night.[27]

The second and third editions (broadcast, respectively, on 9 February and 8 March) were similarly well-received, and, at the end of his first mini-series, Howerd was not only congratulated by the critics (one of whom would later marvel at how quickly the comedian had mastered 'the hitherto untried trick of playing to the television audience while in front of a studio audience'[28]) but was also coveted by television's executives. Even BBC TV's Controller of Programmes, Cecil McGivern – a somewhat irascible man who believed (according to one of his colleagues[29]) that television 'was the greatest instrument for mind-bending since Caxton's printing press', and thus regarded much of what passed as 'popular entertainment' as a waste of valuable teaching time – had been struck by Howerd's potential. In a memo written on the Monday that followed the final show, McGivern told Ronald Waldman, his Head of Light Entertainment: 'This programme again emphatically demonstrated that Frankie Howerd is a television "natural" and you should do everything you can to get him and keep him.'[30]

Howerd, however, was in no mood to be wooed. Dismissing the very positive reaction as 'generous', and complaining that his nervousness had been 'shockingly emphasised by the TV cameras', he remained convinced that he still lacked the technique 'for projecting myself in this new medium'.[31] He would try it again, he averred, but only after he had revived his radio career.

The interlude was over. He was now free to fly off and commence his concert parties.

Accompanied by the producer Roy Speer, Eric Sykes and a small BBC sound unit, Howerd arrived at the first base in the middle of April, and the subsequent eight shows – which were recorded 'as live' – went out between 23 April and 11 June 1952 under the title of *Frankie Howerd Goes East*.[32] The powers-that-be at BBC TV thought that he was treading water, whereas their colleagues at BBC Radio (who judged the series to be both unprofessional and inadequate) thought that he was abusing their trust. Frankie Howerd ended up concurring with Both conclusions: the tour had seemed such a good idea when he first Thought of it back in London, but after he had recorded the opening show (outside in the open on a makeshift stage) alongside a hastily assembled group of sniggering young soldiers, it suddenly seemed more like an absurdly ill-advised vanity production. '[T]hese lads were complete and utter amateurs who'd never read a script before in their lives,' he complained (more to himself than anyone else), 'and while, as I've said, such a style had been great fun for the soldiery of Essex, it was another matter to offer it to the listening millions on BBC.'[33] When he then contracted dysentery, after eating an ice-cream in Port Said, he felt even more foolish for having dragged everyone out so far away from home in order to do shows of the sort of slipshod standard that he would not have tolerated back at any venue in the vicinity of Portland Place.

The listeners, however, seemed to love the programmes. Warming to their combination of an unpretentious 'Talent Night' format with a sentimental tribute to the young men who were still far away from home serving their King and Country, the audience ignored the negative reaction of the press and kept tuning into the series, and turned it into a ratings success. Howerd returned to England to find, much to his surprise, that one way or another his enterprise had paid off.

Radio still wanted him. Television now wanted him. There was even talk, according to Scruffy Dale, that one or two movie producers might be interested in using him. Howerd started to experience, he later acknowledged, an 'upsurge in good fortune'.[34]

It was just a pity that there was no complementary upsurge in self-confidence. He ended 1952 in the same mood that he had started it: very insecure, and very, very tense.

A journalist who knew Howerd during this period described him as a man who was often 'devastatingly serious' when away from the stage. A 'bachelor comedian who neither drinks nor smokes', who had come to prefer 'heavy reading and symphony concerts' to the company of his fellow-comics, Howerd struck him as curiously uneasy about the high esteem in which he was now held. 'It always worries me when people are shocked because I'm so serious,' the star said. 'I am not the aggressive type some people think: it takes me all my time to cover up an inferiority complex. I cannot help it if I am one of those who never have confidence in the present, but only lots in the future.'[35] He could not help it, but sometimes, like now, it could make him a difficult person to be around.

Starring as Idle Jack in an extraordinarily sumptuous production of *Dick Whittington* at the London Palladium, he was convinced that he was awful until someone showed him a review written by Kenneth Tynan, in which the critic praised him as 'the subtlest clod' he had seen in years, and placed him 'firmly in the great line of Jimmy James and Sid Field, whose bulk and strange vocabulary he shares'.[36] Not even Howerd could hide his pride at receiving a tribute like that.

He also agreed to give television another try, but then appeared determined to question every single detail of whatever proposals were sent him from the offices and studios at Lime Grove. *Frankie Howerd's Korean Party*, a far more polished reprise of his recent military routines (filmed – shortly after his return from yet another trip to see the troops – on 9 December in front of an audience composed of current and former servicemen and women at the Nuffield Centre in London) proved a relatively painless production, but the build-up to his next one-off project – *Television's Second Christmas Party* (an annual pro-gramme that was the precursor of the much-longer-running *Christmas Night with the Stars*[37]) was fraught with problems from start to finish.

Although the show's producer-director was his old friend and mentor Bill Lyon-Shaw, Howerd still found plenty about which to moan – and moan, and moan and moan. He was busy enough as it was, he grumbled, without having to endure an extra set of rehearsals, and then spend Christmas Day taking part in a sprawling, 105-minute, live television show in some hot and cavernous studio; he already felt tired out, he groaned, having to star in such a high-profile Palladium pantomime; and he also let it be known that he was not at all happy about the prospect of having to play to the cameras instead of the audience, his face turned a queasy shade of grey by the primitive make-up and his performance undermined by the absence of a 'proper' theatrical atmosphere.

What he was especially unhappy about, he claimed, was that the slot he had been allotted was about midway through the show, rather than close to its climax. It was his (and the increasingly tactless Scruffy Dale's) repeated protests about this that really niggled many of those who were working hardest on shaping the show.

The BBC's annual Christmas Party was meant to be the kind of event at which all egos (and there were usually at least a hundred of them) were left outside the studio door. It was meant to be a showcase for good sports: for one night in each year, viewers could expect to see, alongside some of the biggest current acts on the Variety circuit, such improbable sights as the classical actor A.E. Matthews downing in one a pint of ale with the triumphant cry of 'Bung-Ho!'; the popular singer Eve Boswell trying out a few traditional festive children's games; and strait-laced, sober-faced announcers like Sylvia Peters and MacDonald Hobley suddenly revealing a hitherto unsuspected talent for comic monologues, magic tricks or wild riffs on the washboard. By quibbling about billing, therefore, Howerd badly misjudged the studio mood.

News of (and complaints about) all of these countless moans, groans and tantrums eventually reached the cluttered desk of British television's very first *bona fide* Head of Light Entertainment, Ronald Waldman. Known to his colleagues as Ronnie, and to journalists as a 'tele-visionary',[38] Waldman could not have been less like the mean and aloof 'Thing' about whom Howerd would always complain in his act. A bright, decent and strong-minded man, he cared passionately about two things – high-quality popular entertainment and the principle of public service broadcasting – and it was his personal mission to convince the many sceptical people both inside and out of the Corporation that these two things, far from being mutually incompatible, would actually flourish if united within a happy (and prosperous) marriage.

Ever since he had been handed responsibility for this area of television, he had worked tirelessly to hire and train the most promising young producers, directors and technicians; overcome the hostility of a Variety theatre that was fearful of competition; and dream up a practicable (and affordable) way to fill the screen – every minute of every hour of every evening – with the kind of entertainment that pleased the public as much as it pleased the BBC.

Having already secured serious commitments to the medium from the likes of the established radio star Arthur Askey, the up-and-coming movie personality Terry-Thomas and the young Variety newcomer Norman Wisdom,[39] one of Waldman's top current priorities was to turn Frankie Howerd into his next television regular, but the performer was beginning to strain the patience of far too many people. Lyon-Shaw remained a sanguine champion of his talents, but Howerd's latest clashes (not only with authority but also, more pointedly, with expertise), added to the already sizeable fund of horror stories passed on from those with whom he had previously worked in radio, worried Waldman greatly.

He genuinely believed in Frankie Howerd – he genuinely *cared* about Frankie Howerd – but even he was growing weary of all the grumbles. Having already, within the space of slightly less than a single year, elevated him to the lofty position of the fifth-highest-paid entertainer on British television (with a fee of £84 per show – the equivalent of about £1,400 in 2004), Waldman expected, in return, a little more decorum.[40] He admired the comedian's fierce determination to get it *right* – it complemented his own ambition (as the man who had recently defined the role of BBC TV entertainment as 'to give viewers what they want – but better than they expect it'[41]) to push for greater quality and better programmes – but he was not prepared to countenance Howerd's scattershot outbursts of patently unjustified disrespect.

Desperate to save the self-critical star from his own neurotic excesses, Waldman watched and enjoyed the actual performance that Howerd gave as part of the Christmas Party, and then, in a cool hour, he sat down and wrote a far more measured, good-natured and constructive letter than the comedian's chronically impudent carping had really deserved:

29 December 1952

Dear Frank,

This letter is to say two things –

First, my very sincere and grateful thanks for the superb job you did at our Christmas Party. I was very sorry indeed that you had to leave so quickly afterwards because I wanted to express my thanks and congratulations in person. You gave us a tremendous and really outstanding performance and it seems to be the general consensus of opinion that you 'topped' the show in every way.

This, of course, leads me to my second point. The 'fuss and bother' we had about this show was most unfortunate. I do want you to realise that we are more than alive to your tremendous potential value on Television, but we want *you* to realise that we are not all complete clots (even though we may sometimes look it!) and that when we build a show like the Christmas Party, we build it with the greatest possible care both for the sake of the show and for the sake of the artists.

Even though you weren't prepared to see it, the spot we gave you in that show was the perfect spot for you and, what is more, nobody but you could have held it. I personally have been in show-business long enough (all my working life, in fact) not to make mistakes about elementary things like running-orders, and I would feel a whole lot happier if I could see signs of the fact that you were prepared to trust us a bit more to know our own job. If I make a mess of you, I deserve to be sacked, but I haven't yet – and Christmas Day was, to say the least, the very opposite!

I sincerely hope that 1953 will be a happier year for both of us. No more 'fusses', no more arguments, a little more belief from you that we *do* know what is right and what is wrong for Television, a little more understanding from us about your own particular nervous approach to your work and your desire for perfection (which we share) and a whole heap of TV successes starring Frankie Howerd.[42]

Howerd agreed with Waldman, and hoped, like him, that 1953 would indeed turn out to be much happier, as well as considerably calmer. Sadly, however, it would turn out to be neither. What 1953 turned out to be, for Howerd, was traumatic.

He had so much planned: more radio, more television, more stage work and even his first movie. He also, on the other hand, had an appointment booked at the High Court – and that unhappy event would end up eclipsing everything else that occurred during that exceptionally hectic year.

The headline in *The Daily Telegraph* spelt it out for all to see: 'FRANKIE HOWERD ACCUSES JACK PAYNE OF CHEATING'.[43] Actually, Howerd had done nothing of the sort – Scruffy Dale had been the one who had made the accusation – but, having gone along with Dale's dubious advice, Howerd now braced himself for a very public and potentially calamitous battle with one of the most powerful impresarios in Britain.

The case of 'Howard versus Payne' (the 'e' in Howerd's stage name reverted to the original, legal 'a') was heard in the High Court over a five-day period, from 16 to 20 March. Apart from the famous plaintiff and defendant, some formidable figures took part. Howerd's counsel was the 70-year-old Gilbert Beyfus, QC: a tall, florid, forceful man, with an owl-like face, an aggressively theatrical manner and a fund of crafty tricks, who would later win highly improbable victories (and improbably large sums in libel damages) for Liberace and Aneurin Bevan after certain journalists had accused the former of being homosexual and the latter of being drunk.[44] Payne's counsel was W.A. Fearnley-Whittingstall, QC: a far more restrained and conservative character who was widely admired in legal circles for the precision of his inquisitions. Presiding over the proceedings was Mr Justice Hilbery, a predictably stern but reasonably prudent individual with a reputation for showing unusual candour when summing up.

Neither of the men at the centre of the case had been looking forward to the occasion. Payne, thick-skinned though he was, had been genuinely hurt by what he took to be the ingratitude of such a notoriously 'needy' client. Howerd, in turn, believed that he had a right to be free from any further obligations to Payne, but harboured serious doubts about how his advisors had shaped his case.

The problem was that when it came to financial or legal matters,

Howerd was relatively easy for the so-called 'experts' to sway. He assumed that Dale and his various friends had known what they were doing, but he also recognised that, immersed in his work though he always was, he should have questioned them far more rigorously than he had. His anxiety grew deeper still when Beyfus, on the eve of the proceedings, remarked to him about Payne: 'The man's obviously a crook.' Howerd was appalled: 'I don't think that for a second,' he said in defence of his estranged manager. 'He may have faults, he may be guilty of misjudgement – but that's all. He's no crook.' Beyfus waved his protest away: 'He's a crook,' he insisted, 'and when I get him in the witness-box I'll tear him to shreds.'[45] Howerd's heart sank.

The basic claims that Beyfus put forward during the first day in the High Court were as follows:

- In March 1947, the Jack Payne Organisation had signed Howerd to a contract that guaranteed the performer a minimum weekly salary of £20 for the first six months, rising by £5 per week at the start of each new six-monthly period. The original contract also provided for Howerd to receive 50 per cent of any fees received (in excess of twice the amount of his basic salary) from any other management to which Payne consented to loan him out.

- In December 1950, during the run of *Out of this World*, Scruffy Dale received an anonymous letter that alleged: 'Jack Payne is being paid £900 per week for F. Howerd at the Palladium. The official contract is £600. The rest is paid privately to Jack Payne.' When Dale (who suspected the author was a bookkeeper whom the agency had recently dismissed) confronted Payne with the claim, the impresario denied it vehemently, saying that he was both shocked and deeply offended that anyone – let alone one of his own colleagues or clients – would believe such 'malicious rumours'.

- Convinced that Payne was lying, Dale urged Howerd to sever all ties with the agency immediately. When Howerd hesitated, Dale did some research into some of the other 'secret' deals it was rumoured Payne had struck, and uncovered a sufficient number of damning details to make his case, he believed, compelling. Presented with this 'evidence', Howerd, now feeling angry and betrayed, decided to act on Dale's advice. On 23 August 1951, therefore, Dale duly informed Payne that Howerd regarded their contract as terminated with immediate effect, and was taking him to court to demand a fair share of all the money Payne had made behind his back (with the addition of 4 per cent interest). Payne responded by counter-suing Howerd for breach of contract, claiming £9,000 in damages sustained between the break-up of their relationship in August 1951 and 10 March 1952 (the date when the contract would have expired) owing to the loss of the value of Howerd's services.[46]

Beyfus summed up with an analogy reminiscent of a routine from *Variety Bandbox*: 'Mr Howard's view is that even the owner of a performing elephant gives the elephant enough feed to perform properly, and Mr Payne should look after him so that he can maintain his good performances.'[47] By arranging a secret deal with another management, Beyfus insisted, Payne was not just guilty of greed: he was guilty of deception, too. 'Secrecy is the badge of fraud,' he observed, warming to his theme. 'The attempt was made to keep it a secret but it failed.'[48]

Howerd wriggled with embarrassment every time he heard his barrister refer to Payne as a cheat. He appreciated that Beyfus had a reputation for sometimes reaching logical conclusions via seemingly illogical means (he was well-known in the legal profession as 'The Old Fox'[49]), but the emphasis, in this context, seemed so wrong: the claim that Payne had acted improperly seemed rooted in fact, whereas the claim that he had done so deliberately seemed to rest on nothing more than speculation.

Howerd's sense of unease increased whenever he studied the judge's response to Beyfus' repeated use of the 'c'-word: his brow furrowed, his eyes narrowed, and his bottom lip jutted out as if to underline the alarmed expression above. It also worried Howerd that, whereas Mr Justice Hilbery addressed Payne throughout the proceedings as 'Mr Payne', he tended to refer to Howerd far more coolly (he thought) as 'Mr . . . er . . . the Plaintiff'.[50]

Then came Payne's defence, which saw Fearnley-Whittingstall list in careful detail all of the things that had been done to help turn Frankie Howerd from a complete unknown into one of the most famous (and best-paid) entertainers in the country. While Howerd found himself nodding in agreement at much of what was being said, he resented the insinuation by Fearnley-Whittingstall that he was just some kind of greedy and ungrateful puppet. Each mention of his 'phenomenal' rise to stardom seemed to lead straight back into yet another celebration of Payne's great talents as a manager. It felt as if all of his (and Eric Sykes') ability, industry and invention had suddenly been expunged from public memory.

Once again, as the sniping went on, Howerd sensed that there was precious little sympathy, but perhaps a certain degree of subtle condescension, emanating towards him and his legal team from the judge. 'Do they pay £900 a week for one artist at the Palladium?' enquired Hilbery of Beyfus. 'Yes,' said the barrister, who then added with an ill-considered chuckle: 'Why do we practise at the bar?' Hilbery eyed the old ham up and down and retorted, 'I suppose it is because you cannot give that other type of performance.' Turning his attention to Howerd himself, the judge then asked, 'Do people who write fan mail expect letters back?' 'Yes,' replied Howerd somewhat wearily. 'They expect photographs as well – for free.' Upon hearing this, Beyfus turned to the judge and added plaintively: 'It is not all beer and skittles being a Variety artist.' Hilbery, upon hearing this, hardly looked as if he was struggling to stifle a tear.[51]

When the judge began his summing-up, it was clear that he was unhappy about certain aspects of the case. Responding to Beyfus' claim that Payne was a liar and a cheat, Hilbery made a point of heaping praise on the impresario, declaring that he had seldom observed a witness who satisfied him more thoroughly that he had acted 'honestly and in good faith'. Whether or not Payne had been correct in thinking that he was entitled to make the collateral arrangements, Hilbery explained, his decision not to disclose these transactions had been entirely consistent with his belief that they had absolutely nothing to do with his client. It should therefore be acknowledged, ruled the judge, that nobody had the right to suggest that Payne's intentions had not been 'perfectly honest'.[52]

As for Beyfus' use of Howerd's 'under-fed elephant' analogy, Hilbery muttered, its incoherence seemed all too typical of a strangely confused campaign. 'An elephant does not live in a state of social security except in the zoo,' he snapped. 'The case is quite difficult enough without zoology.'[53]

Howerd listened to all of this and thought to himself: 'Hello, we've had it.'[54] What followed, therefore, came as a surprise.

The judge moved on to say that, in his opinion, the case really hinged on the answer to one particular question: namely, did Payne's unwitting breaches of contract amount to a repudiation of that contract? Admitting that he had vacillated in his mind throughout the trial as to his answer to this question, he announced that, 'after considerable hesitation', he had reached a definitive conclusion: 'On a cold point of law,' he said somewhat glumly, Frankie Howerd had indeed been right to regard the contract as repudiated, and so his subsequent action against Payne had been justified. Beyfus tapped Howerd's foot with his and smiled: they had won after all.

Mr Justice Hilbery awarded Howerd the costs of his claim and also Payne's counter-claim – which added up to a combined sum of £5,216 (equivalent to about £86,600 by today's values).[55] There was, however, a sting in the tail: Hilbery added that, as at least two of the five days spent in court had been taken up by the unfounded allegations concerning Jack Payne's supposed dishonesty, he was going to order Howerd to pay the costs of those two days (which were estimated to be about £800).[56] Howerd had still won – but now it felt as if no one had really won.

Outside, on the wide stone steps, Howerd reached out to shake his former manager's hand. 'I'm sorry it had to come to this,' he said quietly, feeling a genuine sense of regret. Payne just looked him coldly in the eyes, snarled 'I'll appeal,' and then headed off to address the many members of the press who had gathered together in the Strand.[57] 'My good name has been cleared,' he declared as the reporters scribbled and the cameras flashed, 'and that was what I fought hardest for. These charges of dishonesty were made and they have already done me a lot of harm. It has been a very worrying time.'[58] When asked what he planned to do next, Payne replied that he would fight. Howerd, meanwhile, just slouched off alone, wondering to himself whether it had really been worth all the worry and hurt.

There would be plenty of rumours whispered back and forth during the following few months about the case, including a claim that Hilbery and Payne 'were golfing chums'.[59] The truth, however, was that whereas Hilbery had been right, Howerd had been right but weak, and at least Howerd had the good grace, in private, to acknowledge it. His mind was made up: the next time that he was inclined to err on the side of caution, he was determined that he would (without, for once, so much as an 'um' or an 'ah') go straight ahead and err – regardless of what Scruffy Dale, or anyone else, might advise him.

While he waited for the dispute to be resolved once and for all, Howerd buried himself in his work. He did some more television: there was a special, Eric Sykes-scripted 'spring frolic', called *Nuts in May*, followed in September by another one-off programme (the result of a collaboration between Sykes and his friend Spike Milligan), entitled *The Frankie Howerd Show*. He also returned to the stage, in a grand and for the time somewhat daring, *Folies Bergère*-style production called *Pardon My French*, co-presented by Val Parnell and Bernard Delfont, and agreed to appear in another Royal Variety Show in the autumn. He began work on his first movie: a low-budget comedy-thriller (written, produced and directed by Val Guest) called *The Runaway Bus*. He even made plans to return to radio, working with his old friend Eric Sykes on a brand-new starring vehicle.

Life, however, did not seem to move on for Howerd until the middle of October, when Jack Payne's appeal was finally heard back in the Royal Courts of Justice. Starting on Friday the ninth, it dragged on without any sign of making progress until Thursday the fifteenth, when an exasperated Master of the Rolls expressed the opinion – not as the President of the Court, he said, but simply 'an ordinary human being' – that it was a great pity the two parties could not just sit down and settle their differences amicably.[60] Both teams of lawyers, and certainly Howerd and Payne, suddenly realised that they felt exactly the same, and so, after an adjournment, it was announced that a resolution had at last been reached. 'When Jack was finally convinced that I'd personally never questioned his honesty, only his judgement,' Howerd would explain, 'he reckoned his honour was saved and agreed to an out-of court settlement.'[61]

Howerd paid Payne £2,500, and publicly acknowledged his honesty, but their relationship was well and truly over. 'We never spoke again,' Howerd later said. 'Jack could not forgive me for that court action.'[62]

It had certainly been a spectacularly messy, and uncomfortably public, way for a client to free himself from his management, and now that it was finally over, many in the business were left with the feeling that Howerd and his advisors should have handled the whole affair not only better, but also differently. Big stars like Frankie Howerd were expected to rise above such unsightly squabbles – or at least keep them well-hidden behind closed doors – and there had been something depressingly amateurish about the manner whereby he and Scruffy Dale had bitten the hand that fed them and then plotted their means of escape.

Howerd was well aware that, in spite of his formal victory, a certain degree of damage to his professional reputation had probably been suffered. He also knew that Payne was now telling people (and would keep on telling people throughout the remainder of his life) that his former client was the kind of performer who should be regarded (and thus avoided) as 'trouble'.[63]

It did not bode well for a star who lived in fear of those ever-decreasing circles. Having made at least one influential enemy, he just hoped that he could hold on to all of his friends.

CHAPTER 8

Dennis

No, I think loneliness is a terrible thing, you know.
Oh, I do. Especially when you're on your own.

Frankie Howerd would lose many things during the 1950s, but he would gain at least one thing that he had always craved: a deep and lasting sense of companionship. It would arrive just in time for when it was most needed.

He had always had the unconditional love of his mother and sister. Edith, the proud and appreciative parent, remained his staunchest supporter, closely followed by the increasingly wise and witty Betty, and Howerd adored them both. There were times, however, when he needed someone else, and something else, to help him through his days.

Howerd knew that he could always rely on Eric Sykes for encouragement and advice, but he felt increasingly guilty about taking up too much of his loyal writer's time – not just because of his many and various other stage, radio and television projects, but also because he was starting to experience the serious hearing problems that were destined to dog him throughout the rest of his life and career. Sykes had also recently moved out and married – his wife was a bright and attractive young Canadian nurse named Edith Milbrandt whom he had met while recuperating from an operation on his right ear – and so Howerd was reluctant to burden the couple too often with his innumerable real, imaginary and anticipated problems.

There was still Scruffy Dale, of course, but, by 1954, even Dale was beginning to seem more like a distant manager than the intimate friend of old. He continued to be capable, on occasion, of some extraordinary gestures of selfless support – such as the time when he accompanied

Howerd to a tiny theatre in Clacton to perform a Sunday concert, and then spent over an hour perched high above the stalls on a dusty girder, with one of his hands hovering over a switch, simply to ensure that a certain lighting change coincided precisely with the delivery of a particular punchline[1] – but he was also starting to act, in a strangely deluded way, as if he was some kind of late-waking Jack Payne.

Spurred on by Howerd's friendship (and finances), Dale had begun to assemble his very own stable of Variety artistes. Aside from the single big name that was Frankie Howerd, one or two of them were reasonably good, several more of them were at best mediocre, and the rest were downright peculiar, but each one was pushed (after lunchtime) with more or less the same degree of dogged determination. By the middle of the decade, for example, Dale – under the auspices of Frankie Howerd Scripts Ltd – had started bombarding the BBC, amongst other potential employers, with invitations to hire such unlikely-sounding acts as: 'Rusty – with his Pigeon Friends'; 'Windy Blow – with his Balloons'; 'Mandy & Sandy – A Gal and Her Dog'; 'Bobby Collins – Personality Siffleur'; and the recently-renamed Jim Dale.[2]

As Howerd's personal manager, Scruffy Dale behaved in a manner that struck many of the comedian's oldest friends as unnecessarily paternalistic. Bill Lyon-Shaw, for example, was surprised to discover that Howerd, even after he had become one of the highest-paid entertainers in the country, continued to leave Dale in sole control of the purse strings: 'I remember asking Frank, "Are you all right for money?" And he'd say, "Oh, yes, Scruffy gives me an allowance every week, and he's investing some of the rest of the money." And, of course, he *did* invest the money – but he did so in his own name! Frank didn't know. Frank didn't ask. He never seemed to pay much attention to what Scruffy was getting up to.'[3]

It was a dangerous failing on Howerd's part, because, as another one of Dale's clients, his namesake Jim, acknowledged, Scruffy was the kind of character who thrived on careless inattention: '[H]e was always "doing deals". For instance, I wanted a car and he said, "Leave it to me," so we went to this second-hand car showroom and he haggled with the dealer and paid for the car [a pink Vauxhall Cresta] in cash. I repaid him over the next few months (with added interest), but I think it would have cost me less to buy a new car myself.' Scruffy Dale also persuaded his naive young namesake to let him look after his insurance:

'I have the feeling that he was an agent for the insurance company and got a rake-off.'[4]

When it came to offering financial advice to Frankie Howerd, Dale would tend to dismiss most of his friend's requests for an extra note or two to buy the occasional luxury item ('You don't need *that*, Frank,' he would say), but then would practically order him to buy something else at a slightly higher price – such as a complete set of the *Encyclopaedia Britannica*, bound in a particularly foul-smelling type of plastic – on the grounds that the unwanted purchase would one day come to represent 'an excellent investment'.[5] Howerd would just do what he was told, get on with his job, and try his best to settle for a busy, rather than a happy, life.

What little recreational time that he had tended to be spent either with Betty (they dined out together regularly) or on his own, wandering around the streets of West Kensington; watching the odd greyhound race at White City Stadium; attending classical concerts at the Wigmore Hall; swimming several lengths at the local baths; practising his tennis serve (he was an enthusiastic, and surprisingly aggressive, player); or sitting at home poring over learned tomes about philosophy, religion, psychology and history ('his only light reading,' recalled Eric Sykes, 'was novels by Agatha Christie'[6]). There was always plenty for Howerd to do; what made him seem somewhat melancholic was the fact that, far too often, he felt he had little choice but to do them alone.

He bought a dog – a large, slobbering and slyly flatulent boxer he named Red – and he doted on the creature. The actor Alfred Marks recalled a party at Holland Park Villas at which the veteran thespian Margaret Rutherford, turning away for a moment from her plate of roast chicken in order to deliver the punchline to one of her favourite theatrical anecdotes, was startled by Red leaping up on to her lap and gobbling up all of her supper. 'Margaret looked astounded,' Marks remembered, 'and complained loudly to the host. But Frankie only said: "Oh . . . Don't stop him dear, he's enjoying it!" That dog always did get priority to the guests.'[7] Not even the presence of Red, however, would make up entirely for the absence of regular human company.

The keen sense of guilt that he felt about the direction of his desires ('Don't think I like being the way I am,' he would confide to one close friend. 'If there was a pill I could take that would change my nature, I would take it'[8]) served only to exacerbate his isolation. Brief and impersonal flings were vaguely acceptable, even though they were usually so miserable, mainly because they were so forgettable. At a time when homosexuality was deemed illegal, anything that threatened to become meaningful, even though it was far more desirable, struck him as something that he had better try hard to resist. The absence of another, therefore, often seemed almost inevitable.

Sometimes, when he felt a little more battered and bruised than usual, he would try hard to convince himself, as well as others, that he simply did not care. 'Love is an emotion you can't *use*,' he once remarked coldly. 'If you love someone very much you're vulnerable. You aren't a winner: you lose control of the situation.'[9] None of those who knew him well, however, was ever really convinced, and neither, in truth, was Howerd himself. He felt alone, and it hurt.

The person who would change all of this was a young man named Dennis Heymer. When Howerd met Heymer, at a party in 1955, the former was starring in shows both on television and in the West End, whereas the latter was working as a waiter at Simpson's-in-the-Strand, but, within a year of finding each other, the two men had come together to share the same life.

Howerd had been in one relatively brief but tantalisingly hopeful intimate friendship before. Earlier on in the same decade, he had formed a fairly steady (but, given the prejudices of the time, a necessarily clandestine) relationship with a comic actor called Lee Young (when Howerd first met him, he was actually still using his 'proper' name of Jimmy Young, but after another performer of that name eclipsed him in terms of fame, he reverted to his middle name of 'Lee' – in spite of the fact that Howerd had complained that it made him 'sound like a Chinaman'[10]). Young, a competent but rather mannered comic 'feed' who had previously worked with the ageing music-hall ensemble act The Crazy Gang, supplied Howerd for a time with a great deal of affection, good humour and support, both at home and, more discreetly, at work (he appeared – usually in relatively minor roles – in a number of his partner's shows of this period, including *Frankie Howerd Goes East* and *Pardon My French*).

'He took everything personally,' Young would say of his old friend. 'He would yell and scream – but you knew where you were with him, unlike Benny Hill who always bottled things up. And he was a wonderful friend in a crisis.'[11] Young was good at lightening Howerd's moods and assuaging one or two of his fears, while Howerd provided Young with a fund of invaluable advice about comedy technique as well as expert guidance as to how best to cope with the hazardous world of show-business (a classic case of 'Do as I say, not as I do').

Theirs was the kind of friendship that would never really fade (they would still keep in touch, and sometimes work together, years after each, emotionally, had gone his separate way), but as time went on the differences that divided them, as a couple, grew harder for either to ignore. Young was far more open and relaxed about his sexuality than Howerd ever was of his (many were the times when the younger man's somewhat *chi-chi* choice of clothes caused the older man to growl that he was making himself – and, by association, his partner – look like a 'ponce'[12]), and, as a necessarily peripatetic jobbing actor, he had different needs, ambitions and interests. What Howerd, on the other hand, wanted most of all, according to Bill Lyon-Shaw, was the kind of relationship that made him feel like an integral part of a 'proper' family:

Frank was never what I'd call the 'effeminate' type of homosexual. I mean, you could say that he was 'camp' in his act, but off-stage he wasn't camp, and he didn't *want* to be camp. I suppose he rather wanted to be like everyone else. He *hated* the fact that he was considered by some people to be, as they would have put it in those days, 'not quite normal'.

He *always* wanted a home life. He often talked to me about that. He came from a good working-class background, and had been brought up to respect the idea of the family, and having a home, with a father and mother and children. And he realised that he was never going to get that. And I'm afraid that made him a very sad man.[13]

The closest that Howerd would ever approximate to that longed-for relationship was during his deep and unshakeable 36-year association with Dennis Heymer (surrounded by a small but stellar constellation of close female friends and their families). Writing in his autobiography, Howerd would describe Heymer as:

Basically . . . a Mr Fix-it, a super Jeeves who can drive a car and get me there on time, who deals with hotel bookings, supervises lighting and stage props, advises on my performance, timing and technique, and rehearses my lines with me. He's a keeper-out of unwanted visitors, and soother of troubled brows . . . a Godsend! Also, when you say that your performance was awful, he's there with a soothing: 'It wasn't all that bad' – then, when you've come to accept that 'it wasn't all that bad', he says: 'Actually, it *was* awful!'[14]

The description was accurate as far as it went, but it missed out one very important thing: Howerd loved him.

Heymer would go on to give real meaning to Howerd's private life. He would go on to make Howerd feel, for the first time since he had left his mother and sister in Eltham, as though he really had a home.

Just before Heymer came into his life, however, two other important people did. One of them was Ray Galton, and the other was Alan Simpson. Just as Heymer would go on to do in private, so Galton and Simpson now did in public: they encouraged him to enjoy being Frankie Howerd.

Galton and Simpson were two budding comedy writers from South London who, ever since 1948 (when they met at Milford Sanatorium while undergoing treatment for tuberculosis), had been hoping to establish themselves in radio. Their first commission, in 1951, had been for *Happy-Go-Lucky*, a new starring vehicle for Frankie Howerd's old sparring partner, Derek Roy. The title of the show proved to be a cruel misnomer, however, as not only did Roy's limitations as a performer cause some difficulties, but also its producer, Roy Speer, suffered a nervous breakdown in the middle of the run and the series ended up being cancelled.[15] The one good thing that came out of the whole unhappy experience, for Galton and Simpson, was their immediate rapport with one of the members of the supporting cast: Tony Hancock.

They had already started writing on an occasional basis for Hancock, among other comedians, when, while they were still in their early twenties, they began working for Frankie Howerd. It remains unclear who within the BBC had been responsible for putting their names forward – it could have been a combination of two of their earliest supporters, the script editor Gale Pedrick and the producer Dennis Main Wilson[16] – but, one way or another, they emerged as the favoured successors to Eric Sykes.

'I was asked to write a new radio series for Frank [*The Frankie Howerd Show*], and I just couldn't do it,' Sykes explained. 'As I've said, I'd always try and find time for Frank, but I was already committed to other things when they wanted me to do it.'[17] When Galton and Simpson were suggested as an alternative, Sykes was happy to hand the baton over to them, although he remained around to provide Howerd with a familiar presence in the background. He recalled: 'I said to the BBC, "I'll tell you what I'll do: if they write the script, I will edit it," and the BBC said, "Fine, if you edit it, that's okay." So they started to get some really valuable experience by writing for Frankie Howerd.'[18]

Howerd, reassured by Sykes' advisory role, soon warmed to Galton and Simpson, and found much to admire in what they wrote. Their first series together, which ran on the BBC for sixteen weeks from 23 November 1953 to 8 March 1954, represented a near-seamless transition from one source of comic material to another.

Galton and Simpson were drawn a little deeper into Howerd's world when they decided to join forces with Eric Sykes and Spike Milligan, with some assistance from Howerd and Scruffy Dale, to plan the formation of an ambitious and excitingly idealistic organisation they all agreed eventually to call Associated London Scripts.[19] Based, like Frankie Howerd Scripts Ltd had been before it, at 130 Uxbridge Road, in a cramped but cosy set of rooms five flights above a busy greengrocer's shop, Associated London Scripts was these four writers' inspired response to all of the agents who had been trying to get them to sign on to their books.

The basic idea was that their own organisation would be a non-profit-making writers' cooperative – or, as Alan Simpson described it, 'a mutual protection society':

> That was the original reason for setting it up. The four of us writers would look after our own affairs. Frank was a director, too, but he was sort of a sleeping director; he never got involved, never came to board meetings, but he was a director. We also tried to broaden it out a bit, and get Harry Secombe, Peter Sellers and Tony Hancock on board as part of it. Peter Sellers nearly did, but he didn't come in with us in the end because his financial advisor said it was unbalanced. The deal was that we all put in ten per cent of our income to run it, and Peter's agent pointed out that

ten per cent of *his* income would have been vastly more than, for instance, Ray's and my income. So Peter said he'd join if it was a set fee – if we all put in, say, £5,000. But he wouldn't come in at ten per cent. And Spike, to his credit, said, 'Well, if these two lads aren't earning as much money at the moment, it's totally unfair to make them pay the same as the rest of us – so it's ten per cent or nothing.' So Peter withdrew. Then Harry Secombe passed because he was tied up at the time with [his manager] Jimmy Grafton. And Hancock didn't come in because he said it was nothing to do with artists – it was a writers' organisation. So it stayed as it was.[20]

Each one of the four writers probably had his own take on what the organisation, in the long term, could and should achieve. Spike Milligan, for example, found himself drawn (on a good day) to the dream of being part of a community of individuals working in creative harmony;[21] both Galton and Simpson were keen on cultivating a context within which there would be greater artistic – and commercial – autonomy; while Eric Sykes was hopeful of fostering a 'comedy conglomerate':

I had great visions of what I was going to do with it. For instance, I wanted Associated London Scripts to have a big block of offices, and have the whole block full of writers. Because the thought process going through all of this building would be of comedy. Nothing but comedy. We would all do our own thing, but we would all subscribe to a fund that would be there when one of us hit a fallow period. We could go in to see each other and say, 'What do you think of this?' We could help each other. And we could find and help new writers, too. It would be a very special kind of conglomerate. And also, what I wanted was, where it would say 'Scripted by' or 'Written by', you'd have the person's name and then you'd have a circle with 'ALS' in the middle – so that everybody who saw it would say, 'Oh, what's "ALS"?' And then they'd get to know that this was the firm it was coming from.[22]

The Shepherd's Bush Green location might not have been grand or glamorous – not only was the street-level entrance to the rickety old staircase often blocked by several crates of pungent fruit and veg, but there was also a particularly gloomy-looking funeral parlour nearby (outside of which Milligan would sometimes lay down and shout: 'Shop!') – but the bold ambition was certainly admirable.

Frankie Howerd's far more prosaic vision for ALS (like Scruffy Dale's) would remain fixed firmly at the financial level. He was, however, more than happy to be able to lend some support to a venture that looked likely to find and assist more fresh talents like Galton and Simpson, because his new partnership with the pair of them was now going from strength to strength.

The Frankie Howerd Show was a finely crafted and wonderfully characterful comedy show that not only knew how to attract an exceptionally high calibre of celebrity guest, but also knew what to do with them once it had them. Emulating the example of Eric Sykes in *Variety Bandbox*, Galton and Simpson created the kind of playfully prickly routines that enabled Howerd to mock both the real and the supposed pretensions of such stars as Margaret Lockwood, Robert Newton, Cicely Courtneidge, Robert Beatty, Joan Collins, Dennis Price, Diana Dors, Robert Morley, Claire Bloom and, most memorable of all, Richard Burton (who found the experience so refreshingly down-to-earth, as well as funny, that he formed a firm friendship with Howerd that would last for the rest of his life).

'We'd have all of these big-name guest actors come on and say things to Frank like, "You're not very good are you?"' Alan Simpson recalled. 'And, of course, Frank would then explode, "How *dare* you!" He would be outraged at the suggestion that he wasn't a brilliant actor. And much of the comedy would go on from there.'[23] Just as Eric Morecambe would do a decade or so later ('Don't look now – a drunk's just come on'), Howerd would often fail either to recognise a star, or recognise what particular talent had made the person a star. When Richard Burton came on, for example, Howerd instructed the actor to get on with it and start playing his trumpet. 'He would treat them like dirt,' Ray Galton reflected. 'Burton would say, "Well, what did you think of my performance?" And Frank would say, "Well, er, ah, um, it was, er, um, ah, yes, it was, um, ah – I like your socks!"'[24] The teasing went down well on both sides of the microphone. 'We had great fun writing the scripts for all these great names,' Simpson said. 'It was a marvellous opportunity and, for us, a wonderful break.'[25]

A second, similarly warmly-received, Galton and Simpson-scripted series followed in the first half of the following year, and featured another set of celebrity guests (ranging from the brilliantined young movie personality Richard Attenborough to the crusty old classical actor Donald Wolfit), but by this time Howerd (his spirits having been buoyed by the success of his most recent venture) was ready to work with other talented young writers as well. 'Frank was always keen to encourage and open the door for others,' recalled Eric Sykes:

> He was probably the biggest boon for writers that British comedy's ever had, because most great comics, when they get somebody writing for them that they're really happy with, will stick with them for good, but Frank was always ready to try new writers. He knew, better than anybody, that writers are the lifeblood of comedy. Not the feller that's stood up there waiting to deliver it. Frank always put himself on the back-burner, because he knew that without good writers you'd be nothing. He used to say, 'It doesn't matter how great you are – you've got to be greater the next week.' And he meant it. So he really valued good writers.[26]

The next good writer with whom Howerd would work was a short, slightly stooping, slightly stammering, former-milkman-turned-insurance-salesman from Canning Town called Johnny Speight. A funny, quixotic and quick-witted autodidact with a passionate interest in culture, politics and, especially, comedy, Speight had first made contact with Howerd at the end of 1953, when a friend of his – a well-regarded professional masseur – was summoned to help cure the star's stiff neck during the West End run of *Pardon My French*. Howerd bought (for no great sum) the first joke that Speight ever sold – 'I'm livid – they're pulling down my house to build a slum!'[27] – and promised the budding writer that he would do what he could to help him kick-start his professional career.

Once Sykes, Milligan and Galton and Simpson had set up Associated London Scripts officially in the autumn of 1954, Speight was duly sent in their direction, but he almost fled before they had the chance to sign him up. On his first visit to the company's offices in Uxbridge Road, he climbed over a couple of crates of oranges, puffed and wheezed his way up all five of the narrow flights of stairs, and then took one look at the newly-dandified figures of Ray Galton (his short beard neatly clipped, his handmade Turnbull & Asser silk shirt open at the neck, his drooping pipe emanating the sweetest of smoky smells) and Alan Simpson (resplendent in a maroon bespoke corduroy jacket and a fashionably bright and narrow silk tie) flat out on the floor facing each other (which was the way, since they had launched *Hancock's Half Hour*, that they often preferred to work) and quickly decided that he had better think up some good excuses and then hurry off towards the exit. 'We later discovered,' recalled Simpson, 'that he was convinced that we were homosexuals and that we were going to have our wicked ways with him!'[28]

Once Speight realised that he would be 'safe' in the ALS offices alongside his two eminently heterosexual new friends, he joined the organisation and commenced his professional career as a committed writer of comedy. He started working for Howerd in the second half of 1955, shortly after the star had completed a second two-edition mini-series for television of the Eric Sykes-scripted *The Howerd Crowd*.[29] 'You don't have to write all of those "Ooooh-aaahs" in,' the comedian told him. 'I'll put those in myself.' The new writer just managed to stifle his instinctive sardonic response: 'Ah! This one can ad-lib.'[30]

It was not long, of course, before Howerd changed his mind and instructed Speight to ensure that all of the 'Ooooh-aaahs' *were* included in anything that he submitted (it was a little game that he liked to play with most of his new writers), but their partnership soon blossomed into an outstanding creative relationship. Just like Eric Sykes and Galton and Simpson had done before him, Speight benefited early on from Howerd's exceptionally sharp eye (and ear) for detail when it came to shaping a comedy script:

> He was a *big* help to me as a writer. It was like a young journalist joining a newspaper and having a marvellous editor . . . Working for a great stand-up like Frank was the same thing. I mean, Frank's attitude [towards a new piece of written material] was, 'Yeah, maybe a nice thought, but is it going to get a *laugh*?' You know, we all had such *trust* in him. We knew that if *he* said, 'Yes, it was okay,' then it *was* okay.[31]

Howerd, in turn, appreciated Speight's gift for bitingly sarcastic one-liners, as well as his ability to write the kind of comic monologues that contained so much of the performer's own refreshingly self-mocking spirit: 'It's not easy being a comedian,' went one of these routines. 'Some do it by wearing funny clothes. Some comedians have a funny face. Me? I have this curse of beauty!'[32]

Speight was the principal writer of the third series of *The Frankie Howerd Show* – which ran on BBC Radio from 2 October 1955 to 22 January 1956 – as well as (in collaboration with his friend Dick Barry) the two television shows that followed towards the end of 1956. Howerd, however, remained fascinated by the idea of ALS, populated as it was by such a rich variety of comedy writers, and came to think of it as a near-perfect answer to one of his most nagging professional anxieties: if ever he felt dissatisfied with a particular script, he now knew that he could always find plenty of potential script doctors tapping away on their typewriters five floors up in that incommodious little building on Uxbridge Road.

Apart from its core of directors and resident members – Sykes, Milligan, Galton and Simpson, Terry Nation and Johnny Speight (who between them would create such memorable shows as *The Goons, Sykes and A . . .*, *Hancock's Half Hour, Steptoe and Son, Till Death Us Do Part, Sykes, Q* and *Dr Who*) – ALS would also draw into its orbit many – if not most – of those young writers who were destined to dominate British radio and television comedy (and in some cases a number of other genres as well) during the course of the next two decades: the list of clients, informal associates and short-term visitors included Sid Colin (*The Army Game*); Eric Merriman (*Beyond Our Ken*); Barry Took and Marty Feldman (*Around The Horn*); and other talented contributors to a wide range of programmes such as John Antrobus; Dick Vosburgh; Charles Hart; Peter Bishop; Brad Ashton; Dick Barry; Maurice Wiltshire; John Junkin; Benny Green; and Lew Schwartz.

As Brad Ashton remembered, Howerd would not only drop in on Associated London Scripts to make use of a few of the perks of a major shareholder – 'Frank had a bad back, and next door to Eric Sykes' office was a nice big six-foot bath, and apparently the bath he had at his home wasn't big enough or comfortable enough, so sometimes he'd come in to have his bath in the office'[33] – he would also pay the odd visit to solicit a discreet 'improvement' to some of his scripts:

He knocked on my door late one morning, walked into my office and just said, 'Look at those!' And he threw four scripts down on my desk. I said, 'What are these?' He said, 'Read 'em.' So I said, 'Why?' And he said, 'Just read 'em.' So I said, 'But Frank, I'm –' and he said, 'Look: just *read* 'em! I'm going to lunch, I'll be back in a couple of hours, and I want you to have read them!' And before I could ask him why again, he'd left. So I read them, and then, eventually, he came back from his lunch, and he said, 'Well? Did you read them?' So I said that I had. He said, 'What's the name of the show?' I said, 'It's your show: it's *The Frankie Howerd Show.*' He said, 'Who gets all the laughs?' I said, 'Well, you get about 65 per cent of the laughs, and the other performers get the other 35 per cent.' He said, 'What's the name of the show again?' I said, '*The Frankie Howerd Show.*' 'Exactly,' he said. 'So I want more of the laughs!' So I said, 'Well, Frank, you know, it's nothing to do with me. It's not *my* show.' So he said, 'Do you know the writers?' I said, 'Yes, they're friends of mine.' He said, 'Do you want to save their jobs?' So I said, 'Well, er, yes.' So he said, 'Right then: I want you to rewrite those scripts. I'll pay you – you rewrite them!' I didn't get a credit – he just paid me and then swore me to secrecy – and then he told the other writers that he'd rewritten the scripts himself! He'd do that sort of thing, later on, quite a lot.[34]

Ashton could count himself fortunate to have been paid at all for his clandestine labours. As Ray Galton recalled, it was rare for such rewrites to lead to remuneration:

They tended to be looked on as favours. At least by Frank! Whenever Frank was in a hole, he'd call you and say: 'Ooh, would you mind? Could you possibly? Ah, er, ooh, if you could add, y'know, just a *touch* here and there, y'know, er, just a touch . . .' And, of course, the 'touch here and there' would nearly always end up as a complete rewrite, and I don't think he ever paid us for it. But you didn't mind. It was always a joy writing for him. We always got a lot of laughs out of it.[35]

'Frank was very generous in that respect,' Johnny Speight observed with real affection. 'He never left anyone out. He was willing to share our genius with the world. And I think he looked upon it as a comedy brook that flowed past his door, and he would put his bucket in and take out what he fancied for the day!'[36]

Howerd was not only experimenting with different writers during this period; he was also experimenting, rather less successfully, with different media. In the field of movies, for example, he was looking to build on his recent debut in *The Runaway Bus* (which had been released in February 1954 to a set of reasonably encouraging domestic reviews and a creditable response at the box-office), but, after making a couple of cameo appearances at the end of 1955 (a brief reprise of his radio persona in an instantly forgettable Rank Organisation comedy called *An Alligator Named Daisy*, and a similarly brief but infinitely more effective role as an angry barrow-boy in the classic Ealing black comedy *The Ladykillers*), followed by two more starring vehicles (a slight but fairly engaging greyhound-racing caper – also released in 1955 – called *Jumping For Joy*, and a woefully unfunny and badly acted hotel romp in 1956 entitled *A Touch of the Sun*), his faith in this particular ambition was already beginning to wane.[37]

On television, too, Howerd had tried to venture beyond the familiar stand-up and sketch-based formats. One of his attempts to move in this direction – a small-screen adaptation of the classic Aldwych farce *Tons of Money*, which went out on BBC TV at the end of 1954 – elicited a mixed response from the critics, but still struck him as a welcome breakthrough: he would later describe it as 'the first public demonstration of stirrings of restlessness: the feeling that had slowly grown over the months that I needed to diversify my talents'.[38] Another one of his attempts, however, resulted in a painfully traumatic experience.

The spectacularly unhappy incident came about, perversely, because of an invitation to appear on the most popular panel game of the time on British television: *What's My Line?* Emptying pubs up and down the country when it started in 1951, and then causing havoc with the nation's church attendance when the show was switched to Sundays, it was one of the country's first *bona fide* 'water-cooler' programmes.

Part of its appeal was the parlour game simplicity of its premise (an ordinary member of the public would come on, write his or her name on a blackboard, mime something in connection with his or her occupation and then challenge the panel to ask the right ten questions in order to determine the right job) and another part of it was the chemistry between the regular contributors: with the affable young Irishman

Eamonn Andrews in the chair, and a panel that consisted of the tough but urbane Canadian Barbara Kelly, the very elegant and restrained Englishwoman Lady Isobel Barnett, the calm and quietly genial Jerry Desmonde (later replaced by the similarly equable David Nixon) and the far from calm and far from quietly genial Gilbert Harding, the show always guaranteed enough incidents and outbursts to keep the country chattering from one week to the next.

Its key appeal, however, was the sheer outspokenness of the bespectacled, mustachioed, florid-faced Old Harrovian Gilbert Harding. Britain's first genuine television celebrity, Harding was bright enough, blunt enough and sometimes drunk enough to send millions of jaws crashing down to the floor in shock, admiration or self-righteous indignation.

A former schoolmaster-turned-broadcaster, who came to television via a spell as assistant to the BBC's general representative in Canada (where, when he was asked to supply an answer to the question in the application for an American visa that asked, 'Is it your intention to overthrow the lawful government of the United States by force and violence?' he had snapped: *'Sole object of journey!'*[39]), Harding had soon made a reputation for himself as a very bright man with a very short fuse and a very, very sharp tongue. Some people regarded him indulgently as a 'grumpy old teddy bear', while others considered him rather less charitably as 'the rudest man in Britain', but he was certainly the first in a long line of personalities whom most viewers seemed to find, for one reason or another, irresistible.[40]

Howerd had known Harding ever since they had worked together on an edition of *Variety Bandbox*.[41] After a decidedly inauspicious initial meeting at Holland Villas Road – which began with a clearly tired and emotional Harding reeling in and ranting at Eric Sykes for writing a script that was 'rubbish' and at Howerd for being 'neurotic', and then ended soon after with Harding suddenly hurrying up the stairs in urgent search of a lavatory (the 'trickle of liquid that appeared under the sitting-room door' alerted Sykes and Howerd to the fact that their guest had failed to locate one in time[42]) – the two men had gone on to form a fairly firm friendship.

The more that Howerd got to know Harding (or 'Gillie', as he preferred to call him), the more he realised how much they had in common. Harding, like Howerd, was far more complex than his public persona suggested, and was capable of great acts of kindness and generosity as well as the occasional outburst of anger and tactless invective; he was also the kind of tortured and closeted homosexual who was so sensitive, easily hurt and introspective that his feelings of guilt and unease would probably have been just as deep had he lived in a far more benign and permissive age. A woman once went up to Harding at a party and, in a whispered sneer, asked him, 'Tell me, Gilbert, are you or aren't you queer?' 'No, my dear,' he replied, 'I am merely maladjusted.'[43] He could not come to terms with the person that he was – nor the kind of people that certain other people seemed happy to stoop to be. 'I came to see him as a sad, basically very unhappy man,' Howerd would later say of his friend (whose premature death, at the age of fifty-three, came near the end of 1960), describing him as 'lonely, confused, and really very kind and soft under the abrasive public veneer'.[44] Had Harding ever recorded his impression of Howerd, his description would almost certainly have bordered on being identical.

It was, ironically, an agreement to act as Gilbert Harding's stand-in that led to Frankie Howerd's worst-ever moment on television. One Thursday evening in March 1954, Harding suddenly fell ill, leaving Dicky Leeman (his producer at the BBC) with just two days to find a replacement for the next live edition of the programme. Howerd – who had impressed as a guest on the show the previous year – was the first person Leeman thought to call. Howerd was happy to help out – after all, he thought, his previous appearance had been judged a great success, and it would be good to be seen doing something other than stand-up on what was probably the most popular show of the week – but, once again, it all went horribly wrong.

He arrived in good time at Lime Grove on the Sunday evening, chatted amiably to his fellow-panellists and then joined them beneath the sweltering studio lights. The time was counted down, the cue came, and the show went on the air – and Howerd froze. The first mystery guest came on, and Barbara Kelly, Isobel Barnett and David Nixon all asked pertinent questions and volunteered the usual sort of smart and witty remarks. Then it was Howerd's turn to interrogate the contestant, but all that he could offer was the odd 'um' and 'ah'. It was even worse when the second contestant appeared: this time, Howerd could not even manage a stammer. He looked, as he later said himself, 'like a rabbit caught in the headlights of a car, my mind an utter blank, incapable

of asking even the time of day'.[45] Barbara Kelly, recognising the seriousness of the situation, started slipping him scraps of paper on which she
had scribbled suggestions for questions, but it was all to no avail: 'I was
so paralysed I couldn't even read them!'[46]

It was not one of those performances that only the professionals
noticed was a little 'off'. It was one of those performances that everyone
– the other panellists, the contestants, the crew, the studio audience,
the viewers at home – noticed was painfully, horribly, shockingly 'off'.

As soon as the closing credits had scrolled down the screen, the angry
complaints started rolling in. For hours after the show was over, the
switchboard buzzed and flickered with angry messages for the BBC's
embattled Duty Officer. The following morning, the newspapers were
full of similarly scathing reviews of this small-screen débâcle, over-
reacting as the newspapers tended to do back in the days of Britain's
solitary television channel. It all amounted to a high-profile humiliation
for Frankie Howerd.

A full year on, a friend overheard a well-dressed gentleman holding
court in a bar in Bournemouth, berating Howerd for the 'exhibition
he made of himself on *What's My Line?*' and declaring – to many loud
shouts of 'Hear! Hear!' and countless clink-clinks of crisply-chilled gin
and tonics – how he would never forgive the hapless comedian's 'disgraceful conduct'. Howerd himself would receive – via one route or
another – countless similarly damning reports. 'It was generally agreed,'
he later recalled with a shudder, 'that I'd let down the entire nation:
compared with Frankie Howerd – Fuchs, Philby, Pontecorvo, Blake,
Burgess and Maclean were incidental trivialities.'[47]

He fared far better on the radio (where he continued to rely on some
of the best writers in the business), and by doing a more familiar (and
scripted) mixture of sketches and stand-up on the stage – a touring
version of *The Howerd Crowd* played to packed houses all over the
country throughout much of 1955 – but, none the less, the failures
elsewhere still really hurt. He was succeeding in those media (radio and
Variety theatre) that were now seen to be declining, whereas he was
either struggling or failing in those media (television and movies) that
were seen to be very much on the ascent. To a performer with such a
dread of being left behind, the portents could not have seemed more
bleakly depressing: ever-decreasing circles, he thought – nothing but
ever-decreasing circles.

It was at this point, mercifully, that Dennis Heymer came into Howerd's life. The son of Dolly Heymer, a former minor music-hall performer, Dennis was a tall, thin, good-looking man in his early thirties who, even though he had not forged a career in show business himself, understood the peculiar nature of the profession – with all of its soaring highs, swooping lows and cyclopean egos – very well.

Heymer was, in many ways, the polar opposite of Howerd. He was, for example, a smart and stylish dresser (unlike Howerd – a man who could put on a £1,000 bespoke suit from Savile Row and still somehow manage to look as if he had just been mugged in the doorway of a branch of Mr Byrite); he was also a person of considerable tact, blessed with a calm and stable temperament that bordered on the imperturbable (unlike the often tactless and notoriously mercurial Howerd); as well as something of a connoisseur of haut cuisine and fine wines (in stark contrast, once again, to Howerd – 'essentially a steak-and-kidney pie man' whose taste in tipples, in those days, did not stretch beyond the odd nip of gin or shallow tumbler of Scotch[48]). These opposites, however, held a surprisingly strong attraction for each other.

Heymer, by disposition, was drawn to the role of the unselfish and uncomplaining partner, whereas Howerd, by his own disposition, was eminently well-suited to the role of the needy, nervous, endlessly fascinating centre of attention. By the time, therefore, that Heymer had moved in with Howerd (late in 1956) to share his flat in Holland Villas Road, he had assumed much of the responsibility for organising his famous partner's life, work and leisure.

A quick course of driving lessons transformed him, publicly, into Frankie Howerd's ever-present chauffeur, and then, as time went on, the experience he acquired by Howerd's side would enable him to take over more and more of Scruffy Dale's old duties as personal manager. Howerd's longed-for 'Super Jeeves' had finally arrived, and so, crucially, had his even more deeply longed-for soul mate.

The need had always been there. In the next few years ahead, however, that need would become acute.

CHAPTER 9

The Breakdown

That's right – get your aahs out.

The bad times that Frankie Howerd had long been dreading but firmly expecting finally arrived towards the end of 1957 – and then showed no signs of leaving until the start of 1962. It was during this unremittingly dark and dismal period that Howerd would suffer a crushing loss of confidence in his looks, his image, his stature, his talent, his finances and, ultimately, his future as a professional. Every bad thing he had feared could happen now seemed to go ahead and happen, forming the sort of grimly remorseless sequence that felt as if it was destined never to end. 'It never rains but it pours,' Howerd would later reflect, 'and it poured for four years.'[1]

The loss of confidence in his looks came about because of a quirk of nature rather than the cruelty of any humans. Ever since the early days of his success on radio, Howerd had been suffering from a condition known formally as 'alopecia areata' – and informally as the gradual loss of hair from certain areas of the scalp. He had disguised it for a time by 'fluffing-up' his thinning locks to fashion a 'just-been-electrocuted' style of quiff, but, by the mid-fifties, he had no choice (seeing as he could not bear to be seen in public with a balding pate) but to start hiding the damage under a hairpiece.

He would actually have four toupees specially made, but, throughout the rest of his life, he would seldom wear any other than the first one. Right from the start, however, it seems that he was the only one convinced that it was practically impossible to see the join. Even Max Bygraves, one of his oldest and most trusted confidants, had to pretend not to notice every time a sudden gust of wind caused the hairpiece to hover slightly above Howerd's head, and plenty of other friends and colleagues found it similarly hard, at first, not to stare. In later years, when the wig came to resemble an elderly outstretched stoat, the effect would be even more risibly obvious. 'He used to scratch the back of his head when he was talking to you sometimes,' recalled the scriptwriter Barry Cryer, 'and [the hairpiece] would go up and down like a pedal bin.'[2]

Howerd's adoption of the toupee, though far from ideal, was an inevitable result of his *amour propre*. He would never feel particularly happy with it, but he knew that he would have felt unbearably unhappy without it.

It was not that he was entirely blind to his obvious facial imperfections (the overall effect of which, in the words of one critic, made him look like 'Simple Simon with mumps'[3]); it had more to do with his slightly exaggerated estimation of his overall physical charm, as well as his determination to preserve his reputation as an irrepressibly vivacious comic performer. Just when he felt that he most needed to prolong the sense that came from the supposedly careless ebullience of youth, he found that he had to fight against his prematurely aged physical appearance.

It represented, to him, yet another secret weakness, yet another reason to feel vulnerable and to worry, and he had already accumulated more than enough of those kinds of neuroses. The effect was to make him more edgy and depressed than ever, plagued by bouts of the sort of nervousness that made his mind feel like 'a disintegrating jigsaw'.[4]

This was merely, however, the first stage in the long and sorry sequence. There was worse – much worse – still to come.

The next thing to suffer was his image. Ever since he left *Variety Bandbox*, he had been looking to stretch himself and show the public that there was more to him than just stand-up. By 1957, however, he seemed to have stretched himself in so many separate directions that his original – and extraordinarily popular – image seemed to have lost some of the old sharpness that had helped to define its shape. The public still knew – still remembered – what they wanted from Frankie Howerd. The problem was that Frankie Howerd now appeared, as he reached the age of forty, to want something else – or at least something *more* – from Frankie Howerd.

'What you had there,' Eric Sykes said of Howerd during this period in his career, 'was a misfit: a man who did not want to be a comedian. After a time, someone like that can feel that people are laughing *at* you and not *with* you.'[5] Although Howerd's various adventures outside of the field of stand-up had failed either to win over enough of his old fans or attract enough that were new, he seemed disinclined to abandon the experiments, and, in his defence, there was a memorable precedent for his persistence. Had he not been told, time and time again, that he would never make it as a comedian, and had he not gone on to prove all of the countless doubters wrong? Why then, he reasoned, should any of the more recent rejections make him abandon his other, broader, ambitions? He would simply go on to prove them wrong again.

His reasoning, however, was specious. The unacknowledged difference was that, back in his amateur days, his stubbornness had no established reputation – or career – to tarnish, whereas, in the 1950s, it most definitely did. Probably the only person who still remembered, a week after it had happened, the first audition that Frankie Howerd failed for *Stars in Battledress* was Frankie Howerd. Probably a fairly large proportion of the British viewing public, in contrast, could still recall, two whole years on from the actual event, the night that Frankie Howerd froze as a panellist on *What's My Line?* There was no longer much room to run risks.

Howerd gambled on regardless. A spell in the West End (and then subsequently on tour) playing the leading role in the classic farce *Charley's Aunt* had paid off in 1956 – with the critics applauding the comedic consequences of 'an historic stroke of miscasting'[6] – as had a very short but enjoyable run in the autumn of the same year in another comedy romp called *Tons of Money,* but from then on things began to backfire.

His next project could have been a relatively undemanding but quite prestigious (and extremely well-remunerated) West End revue for Bernard Delfont entitled *Plaisirs de Paris*. Howerd, however, was by this time convinced that his 'destiny was now as a comic actor',[7] and he preferred to wait for the offer of a more taxing theatrical challenge. Delfont did manage to persuade him to try out some of the *Plaisirs de Paris* material (with the assistance of Blackpool's answer to Jayne Mansfield, the peroxide blonde and ample-bosomed Sabrina) on a short tour of provincial music-halls, but, even though the audience reaction was good, Howerd chose not to proceed. He decided against doing more of the same old stand-up material and sketches. He elected instead to pursue his dream of becoming a 'proper' comic actor.

'It proved,' he would later confess, 'to be the worst error of judgement I was to make in my entire professional life.'[8] Even at the time, straight after he had informed Delfont of his decision, he suspected, deep down, that he had probably made a mistake. 'My vacillating self-debate had been so intense,' he recalled, 'that I now found myself experiencing a reaction of terrible tiredness that manifested itself in self-pitying gloom.'[9]

Anxious, confused and depressed, he spent the first part of April 1957 in a private nursing-home in Harrow, Middlesex, where he was treated for a form of nervous exhaustion. After his release, he left London with Dennis Heymer to spend a few weeks of rest and recuperation in the country cottage he had recently bought at Reigate in Surrey. Some newspapers, after first noting his absence, speculated that he had suffered a full-blown nervous breakdown,[10] but his condition, though obviously a cause of some concern, was far from being anywhere near as clinically serious as that. Once he had calmed down his mind, and summoned up a little more courage, he returned to the capital feeling suitably emboldened and refreshed.

Following a brief trip to Cyprus in June, where he organised a number of concert parties for the British troops, he declared himself ready for his next major challenge. He had agreed to appear on stage in a touring production of Peter Glenville's adaptation of the Feydeau bedroom farce *Hotel Paradiso*. His role as Benedict Boniface – an upstanding citizen who finally decides, after more than forty years of prevarication, to do something about the lust he has always felt for his next-door neighbour's wife – had previously been performed by Alec Guinness to great acclaim in the West End.[11]

The tour was not a success, and neither was Howerd's performance. Many felt that he had fallen far short of the high standards set by his illustrious predecessor ('After Guinness,' he reflected ruefully, 'the public must have thought me pretty flat beer'[12]), and most considered the departure from his more familiar stage persona to have been a failure. His response, however, was yet again one of defiance: although he acknowledged that audiences had 'expected the "Ladies and Gentle-*men*" Frankie Howerd', and had not accepted him as 'a would-be comic actor', he refused to abandon the pursuit of his new image.[13]

It was Shakespeare who spurred him on. Ever since his days in the amateur dramatic society at Shooters Hill, he had claimed to revere the *oeuvre* of the Bard of Avon. He read the works, he attended the productions and he talked (and talked and talked) about all of the things that he found intriguing, moving and confusing in the classic Shakespearean canon. It never threatened to become an obsession, but it was certainly one of those abiding cultural passions that came as a surprise to those who met him armed with clichéd preconceptions. On one such occasion, for example, he spent a day with Kingsley Amis, co-judging (of all things) a cheese-tasting contest, and the novelist later complained that the comedian had 'talked to me about Shakespeare without stopping'.[14]

When, therefore, he received an invitation from the director Michael Benthall to appear at the Old Vic in *A Midsummer Night's Dream*, he could not have felt more flattered. There he was, twenty-two years on from the humiliation of that failed audition for RADA, contemplating an offer to join a cast composed of such distinguished 'proper' actors as Derek Godfrey, Joyce Redman, Paul Daneman, Edward Hardwicke, Coral Browne and a very promising young performer named Judi Dench in a *bona fide* classical theatrical production. It was certainly an enticing prospect.

It was also, he realised, a major gamble. If so many of his fans had found it hard to follow him from Sykes and Co. to Feydeau, it seemed highly improbable that more than a loyal few would favour moving on with him from Feydeau to Shakespeare. He would also, he recognised with a shudder, be earning far less in an entire week (a mere £30) than he could have earned in a matter of minutes on radio. Another issue that needed to be considered was how much prejudice his presence was likely to provoke – not only from the snobs but also from the inverted snobs. He was prepared to hear plenty of irritable tut-tutting from those purists for whom the term 'music-hall' was about as unwelcome in polite society as the description of a lavatory as a 'toilet'. He was also well aware, seeing as the role he had been asked to play was Bottom, that he would have to endure all of the lame old schoolboyish 'jokes' about playing a modest part in 'The Tit and Bum Show', as well as all of the predictable observations about the 'warm hand that the entrance of his Bottom received', and all of the variations on the theme of how 'the critics had never seen a warmer/colder/flatter/or funnier Bottom than Howerd's'. Finally, he knew that he would have to come to terms with the fact that, on this particular occasion, there could be no rewrites or ad-libs: he would have to heed the author's own directorial injunction – 'Let those that play your clowns speak no more than is set down for them'[15] – and refrain from 'Howerdising' the script.[16] None of this, however, seemed, on reflection, to matter: he simply could not resist.

The rehearsals were hard – he struggled both to learn and time his lines and then find their proper rhythms (and grew confused when someone suggested that he should attend to the latter before bothering too much about the former), and he also clashed more than a few times with his director – but, eventually, he found a way to acquire a degree of personal control over his role. He accepted the need for greater discipline when it came to the words and their manner of expression, but found a certain amount of freedom when it came to finding physical (and funny) things that it was appropriate for his character to be seen to be doing (verbally, Howerd may have been Shakespeared, but visually, Shakespeare was now Howerdised). He also started to relish the irony of playing someone who, like him, appeared to be suffering from such deep delusions about his aptitude for great acting.

When, on 23 December 1957, the opening night arrived, he was ready, and the production – and his performance – went reassuringly well. He never did quite master his lines, but what his short-term memory, as a budding classical actor, let him down on, his long-term memory, as an experienced comedian, more than made up for. As Judi Dench later said, he was often 'hysterically funny, though he just made it up a lot of the time'.[17]

The critics, in general, were similarly positive. According to *The Times*, for example, Howerd's contribution was 'poetic', while *Plays and Players* said that, even though there was probably 'more Widow Twankey than Bully Bottom about Mr Howerd's Old Vic creation', the unconventional casting still deserved to be considered an 'exhilarating' success, and *The Daily Telegraph* reassured its readers that 'Mr Shakespeare would have approved of Mr Howerd'.[18]

He felt sure that he was back on track. He knew that he had not quite reached the stage where he could say with any confidence to his critics, 'I told you so,' but he now believed that the arrival of such a moment was not too far away. 'It's what I call my transition period,' he informed reporters. 'I'm slowly changing from Frankie the Variety comic to Francis the comedy actor.'[19] The plan, he went on to explain, was to shed the 'one-man' part of the old 'one-man situational comedy' rather than to go entirely and irredeemably 'serious': 'I've no ambitions in the *Hamlet* line. It's just that I now prefer being funny in a situation.'[20] He then did his best to back up these words with deeds.

He appeared in another farce: a revival of *The Perfect Woman*, Wallace Geoffrey's and Basil Mitchell's crudely comical mixture of science-fiction and sexism, about an eccentric inventor, his frustrated young niece and a synthetic Galatea. He also worked (as a replacement for the unavailable Peter Sellers) on another movie – a hastily made sequel to the Naval comedy *Up the Creek* (1958) – called, with an entirely appropriate lack of imagination, *Further Up the Creek* (which was also released in 1958). The more adventurous his projects became, however, the cooler was the response.

Whereas, for example, another radio series of *Fine Goings On* (which ran for twenty shows during 1958, from the start of April to the middle of August, with scripts by John Junkin and Terry Nation) drew in a fairly solid audience, a second attempt at Shakespeare, this time on the radio, was generally judged a mistake. Playing the minor character of Launce, the clownish servant of Proteus, in *The Two Gentlemen of Verona* (broadcast on the BBC's high-brow Third Programme – the predecessor of Radio 3 – on 1 April 1958), his performance was criticised by Roy Walker in *The Listener* for its failure to 'communicate the many-sidedness of Shakespeare's gag-men', thus leaving the audience 'tickled' but not 'touched'.[21]

Howerd, however, pressed on. Venturing back on television again, but this time for the newly-formed commercial companies,[22] he accepted an invitation from Norman Marshall – Head of Drama at Associated-Rediffusion – to appear in an ambitious-sounding ninety-minute play called *The School for Wives*. Adapted by the old Ealing character actor Miles Malleson from Molière's seventeenth-century satirical comedy *L'École des Femmes*, it featured Howerd (sporting, somewhat ironically, a bald wig) in the central role of Arnolphe, an ageing roué who attempts to bring up a young girl as a perfect idiot, so that, by the time they marry, her only concern in life will be for his well-being.

It was not welcomed into the average ITV viewer's living room. Once again, it seemed, the audience had been attracted by the prospect of seeing a very familiar stand-up comedian, only to then be bemused by the sight of a fairly unfamiliar comedy actor. Everyone involved was guilty of a certain degree of naivety. Television had not yet learnt how to 'sell' a novel concept to its viewers and start shaping their expectations, and Frankie Howerd had not yet come to terms with that fact. It was another public, and very painful, failure. 'The sound of switched-off sets,' Howerd would recall, 'was like a thunderclap across the land.'[23]

The negative reaction shook him up without shaking his resolve. 'I knew I was beginning to flounder,' he later admitted, 'but fame has a certain momentum . . .'[24] The head told him to pull back, but the heart told him to push on.

He had little advice from Scruffy Dale, who now seemed more interested in managing the career (and the finances) of Tony Hancock than he did in attending to the man on whose fame he had fed for so long. Not only was Dale promoting Hancock's stage shows (and slipping in at the bottom of the bill one or two of his dodgy novelty acts while he was at it), he was also making full use of the association to draw more budding performers under his influence and on to his books. Howerd, meanwhile, was left largely to his own devices – and his own impetuosity.

He could, in fact, have turned his fortunes around in an instant. He could have gone to Eric Sykes, Galton and Simpson and Johnny Speight and returned straight to form with a beautifully written and brilliantly performed new stand-up act. What he did choose to do next instead, however, was to take one more shake of the dice, roll them out and then hope that this time the gamble would pay off.

The latest venture was the oddest one so far: a downright strange little mystical musical comedy called *Mr Venus*. Howerd's involvement was initiated by the internationally renowned impresario (and agent of Maria Callas) S.A. Gorlinsky. For some reason that he never made particularly clear, Gorlinsky had not only convinced himself that a folly of a script by Alan Melville (about a visitor from Venus who tries to preach love and peace, finds himself rebuffed by the average Earthling, and ends up spreading the message via a humble employee of a London publican) was worthy of a West End run, but had also reached the conclusion (once his first choice Norman Wisdom had turned him down) that Frankie Howerd was the best available actor to portray the Venusian's unlikely terrestrial mouthpiece.

Not even Howerd, to begin with, agreed. Once he had received and read the original script, he replied that it was 'not my cup of tea', and suggested Max Bygraves as a far more suitable alternative. 'We want you,' insisted Gorlinsky, and promised that the script would be rewritten according to his specifications. Howerd still had his doubts, and yet he found himself saying 'Yes'.[25]

He considered the pre-existing positives: Norman Newell had contributed some decent lyrics; Russ Conway had composed some pleasantly accessible music; and Paddy Stone's choreography seemed full of promise. Once, therefore, his own material had been tailored to suit his distinctive style and strengths, he hoped that he 'might indeed have found a passport back to the big time'.[26]

He was deluding himself. Everywhere he looked he should have seen warning signals. The plot called for a large, muscular, blond-haired Venusian (played by the German actor Anton Diffring) to be winched down from the gantry, wearing nothing but a sparkling cape, a shiny leather nappy and a pair of high-heeled, platform-soled shoes, and then start spouting platitudes about why there was nothing really funny about love, peace and inter-planetary understanding. That alone ought to have handed Howerd a clue. The other dubious outfits, the numerous tacky sets and the half-hearted sentiments expressed in the songs really should have been recognised as being fairly obvious clues, too.

Howerd, however, was too busy to notice, fussing as he was over the changes to his own particular sections of the script. He made the usual calls to his friends over at ALS: the multiple copies were sent out, the conflicting revisions came straight back in to be collated, Howerd offered his usual observations ('It's *craaaap!*'[27]), and then the process started all over again. Ray Galton, from this point on, oversaw most of the major alterations, working first as part of a stellar comedy trio with Alan Simpson and Johnny Speight, and then (after his regular writing partner had departed on a family vacation) as one half of an unfamiliar duo alongside the ever-dependable Speight.

'It had started in the usual way,' Galton recalled. 'Frank asked us to touch it up – "Y'know, just put a joke in here and there, yeah, y'know, just a few wheezes, nothing too fancy" – and then, of course, we got asked to do more and more and more.'[28] Eventually, the script became so blatantly 'Howerdised' (with the star now turning the show's many flaws into cues for additional comedy) that an outraged Alan Melville demanded that his name be taken off the credits.

When, on 1 October 1958, the production began a short provincial tour prior to commencing its prestigious West End run, it was painfully clear that so much was still seriously wrong. No one seemed to know what he or she was supposed to be doing. No one seemed to know what anyone else was supposed to be doing. Most worrying of all, for Howerd, was the fact that no one seemed to be laughing.

The root of all the problems, he concluded, was the absence of a single and all-powerful director. Apart from his own role as the unofficial editor of his 'talking' scenes, there were several more cooks in the crowded kitchen, including a (non-Howerd) dialogue supervisor, a dance supervisor and a song supervisor. The end result, he admitted, was that 'the dancing didn't fit in with the dialogue, and the dialogue scenes didn't really fit in with the musical numbers, and neither fitted in with the scenery or costumes. *Nothing* synchronised.'[29] No matter how hard they all tried to improve their respective sectors, the net result was merely an increase in incoherence. 'I was ready for a padded cell,' Howerd later reflected, 'as I ran around quacking like an eight-legged duck, telling everyone what was wrong and trying to put it right – and probably doing more harm than good in the process.'[30]

Frantic messages were sent down to London, and, eventually, a so-called 'overall director', Eleanor Fazan, was charged with the task of making something presentable from out of the mess. More revisions (this time by Eric Sykes, Johnny Speight and Galton and Simpson) were incorporated, one minor member of the cast was quietly dropped and a couple of the dance routines were tightened up. There was no time for anything more, however, because the tour had run its course.

Mr Venus opened in the West End at the Prince of Wales Theatre on 22 October. None of the cast had been looking forward to the occasion, and the assembled critics (who had heard all about the various crises during the tour) sat around the first few rows of the stalls looking like hungry vultures awaiting a kill. Howerd's nerves were so taut that he had to down large gulps of brandy before and after each scene, and there were one or two awkward on-stage moments before the effects of all the alcohol relaxed him for the later acts.

The verdict was never really in question. As soon as the audience caught sight of the hapless Anton Diffring (looking, as Howerd would put it, 'like a great big fairy queen lost on the way to the Christmas tree'[31]), the sound of countless snorts of derision became an integral part of the night. There was a little light applause at the end, but there were more than a few noisy boos.

The first-night reviews were damning: 'a dull, flat and vulgar entertainment,' declared *The Daily Telegraph*, 'with no beauty, no style [and] no comic resource'; 'disastrously unfunny', lamented Caryl Brahms in

Plays and Players, who excoriated the production for relying on 'the kind of plot that would sink a battleship' and 'the most tasteless, outmoded and ill-fitting sets that the West End can have seen for some time'.[32] There were more – many more – angry attacks, and although most of them tried remarkably hard to be kind about Howerd's contribution, the play as a whole was torn apart.

Mr Venus limped on for just sixteen more days before folding on 7 November. Howerd felt shattered. Before the run started, he had agreed to perform a couple of scenes from the show for television on the high-profile *Sunday Night at the London Palladium*; just before it ended, however, he persuaded the producer to let him do his old stand-up act instead. Ironically, he had to go on the programme the very night after the play had closed, and, just as the curtain went up, he suddenly found himself overcome by 'a wave of positively maudlin sentimentality for the disastrous show', and became so bogged down by his emotions that he overran by three whole minutes (a particularly big sin in those days on a live commercial broadcast).[33] Afterwards, the furious producer made a point of seeking Howerd out to inform him that he had given a performance that was 'just plain lousy'.[34]

The following morning, yet another pile of negative reviews landed flatly on his doorstep, but this time they were not about *Mr Venus*: they were exclusively about Frankie Howerd. There was no obvious sense of relish about the critical nature of the responses – on the contrary, there was a good deal of compassion and concern – but the overriding message, none the less, was that once again he had let down his firmest admirers, as well as his broadest audience, for no discernible reason. 'I'd blown it,' he later admitted, 'in a big, big way.'[35]

Fortunately, however, the BBC (in stark contrast to all of the ITV companies) was ready to step in and help him. On 10 November, Kenneth Adam, BBC Television's current Controller of Programmes, sent the following memo to Eric Maschwitz, the service's new Head of Light Entertainment: 'The disappearance of *Mr Venus* presumably leaves Frankie Howerd without work. I have considerable interest in this comedian. Do not let us be slow in seeing if we can make use of him.'[36]

No executive in British television at that time was better equipped than Eric Maschwitz to handle a performer of both the calibre and character of Frankie Howerd. Tall, suave and worldly, he was not only a near-legendary BBC man (during his first stint at the Corporation, which lasted from 1926 to 1937, he had turned the fledgling *Radio Times* magazine into a highly successful cultural enterprise, created and commissioned countless long-running radio formats, and been an exceptionally bright and canny pioneering Director of Variety), he was also greatly admired in wider show-business circles as the creator and producer of numerous musical plays and revues, as well as the writer of several successful novels and the lyrics of some exceptionally memorable popular songs (including 'These Foolish Things' and 'A Nightingale Sang in Berkeley Square'). Now that he was back for a second spell in broadcasting, he was determined to prove, in the new competitive era, that anything ITV could do, the BBC could – and would – do better.

As a long-time admirer of Frankie Howerd, therefore, Maschwitz needed no persuading to reach out and offer to help the fallen star plot a route back up to the top. He just hoped that Howerd was now in the right kind of mood to be helped.

Howerd was. He was surprised, and relieved, to hear that someone, somewhere, still wanted to give him a chance.

The next step was for the two men to meet, make use of Maschwitz's extraordinarily well-stocked office drinks cabinet, and discover what each of them was hoping to make of the collaboration. Maschwitz told Howerd that as far as he was concerned, the first priority was to find the right kind of vehicle to reunite the star with his old audience; once that had been achieved, he said, they could start looking at ways to progress and build on his broad appeal. Howerd told Maschwitz that he agreed. Then, as he began to relax, he started to confide in his new employer, and attempted to explain what he believed the underlying reason for his recent and very dramatic reversal in fortune had been.

The basic problem, he recounted, was that ever since the early fifties, he had felt unwilling to stand still but unable to go forward. As he would later put it: 'If, as I still believed, my sort of act was *passé* as far as the public was concerned, yet that same public weren't prepared to accept me as an actor, then I was in danger of moving in ever-decreasing circles until I disappeared up my own career.'[37] Maschwitz, understandably, was unconvinced that anyone other than Howerd had come to regard the original stand-up act as *passé*, but he nodded sympathetically none the less, and invited Howerd to go away and give some serious thought as to a possible, practicable solution.

He did just that, and he was soon back. The solution, he said, was a situation-comedy.

A situation-comedy, he reasoned, represented the perfect short-term compromise between what he, ideally, wanted to do (*viz* comedy acting) and what the public, ideally, wanted him to do (*viz* stand-up comedy). He even had a firm proposal for the pilot programme of a possible new series. He had solicited a sample script from Johnny Speight, who had dreamed up a format that would see Howerd carry – virtually single-handedly – a succession of self-contained situation-comedies.

Maschwitz was happy enough with the quality of the script – entitled *Pity Poor Francis* – and intrigued by its glimpse into a lonely bed-sit life of quiet, almost Hancock-like, desperation. He was keen, however, to have at least one other option available, so he commissioned a second script – but this time, oddly enough, from probably the only two British-based professional comedy writers of whom Howerd had never heard: a Canadian-born radio writer called Reuben Ship (who had recently been deported from the US following his defiance of the McCarthyite anti-communist witch hunts) and an American television writer named Phil Sharp (among whose credits were spells as one of the many contributors to *I Love Lucy* and *The Phil Silvers Show*).

Maschwitz's surprising choice of writers probably had something to do with his on-going attempt to compile an 'in-house' corps of relatively fresh writing talent expressly for BBC TV (an initiative that would lead, a year or so later, to the recruitment of Frank Muir and Denis Norden as full-time 'comedy consultants' to the Corporation), as well as, perhaps, a little to do with a slight anxiety as to Howerd's supposed influence over his various good friends and former protégés, like Johnny Speight, at ALS). A rejuvenated Frankie Howerd was undoubtedly an attractive prospect – but a rather more pliant and polite, as well as rejuvenated, Frankie Howerd must have represented an even more attractive prospect.

Ship and Sharp (the latter of whom would be unaccredited due to on-going contractual complications) were a competent and no-nonsense, if rather impersonal, pair of writers who could be relied on to come in, apprise themselves very quickly of what was required and then rattle off a workable script. They were as mechanical in their approach to crafting comedy as someone like Speight (or Sykes or Galton or Simpson) was organic, relying more on the clarity of structure and the quantity of funny lines than on the plausibility of the character and richness of the real life, but they knew how to deliver a reassuringly high number of audible laughs. The script that they now rattled off for Howerd was called *Shakespeare Without Tears*: a farce (with a nod to *A Midsummer Night's Dream*, a wink to *Charley's Aunt*, and a hefty nudge to those who knew something about the recent vicissitudes in Howerd's own career) about a humble shop assistant with Walter Mittyish aspirations to become a celebrated classical actor.

Howerd tried hard to hide his ambivalence about being asked to work with a brand-new brace of writers – although he was always happy to try out unfamiliar talent, he would have much preferred, at this uncertain period in his career, to have been given the right to have chosen such talent himself – but, understandably, he could not help but appear overtly resentful about being assigned (for both shows) someone – a young man named Eric Miller – whom he regarded as an unsuitably inexperienced director. 'I was sufficiently intelligent to realise,' he would complain, 'that at this stage of my career I needed an absolutely first-class director':

[A] man of good judgement who'd help restore my morale and self-confidence by virtue of *his* expertise and self-confidence when he put the show together. For such things *are* communicated: when someone has a doctor in whom he has faith he's often halfway to a cure. To extend the analogy: I wanted a top Harley Street specialist – and got a first-year student! In other words, a trainee director![38]

He had a point, but he had no power, and so the two productions went ahead as planned under the banner of *Frankie Howerd In . . .*

The first, *Pity Poor Francis*, went out on 16 December. The critics were not particularly impressed with Speight's script – which had Howerd barricade himself inside his room after receiving an anonymous death-threat – and doubted that it contained the seed of a successful series. Howerd felt sorry for Speight, whom he thought had been made into something of a scapegoat, and he also felt sorry for himself.

For the first time since he came to public prominence, his engagements diary was suddenly looking strikingly, horribly, bare. He did take up an offer to spend the end of December in Southampton appearing, yet again, in another revival of the less-than-perfect farce *The Perfect Woman* – 'I didn't do it because of residual yearnings to become a great comic actor,' he later confessed; he did it, he said, because 'there was nothing else on offer'[39] – but things were looking bleak beyond that booking. 'I was floundering,' he admitted. 'I had no sense any more of direction or purpose.'[40]

The second of his pair of sample sitcoms, *Shakespeare Without Tears*, was broadcast near the start of the New Year, on 28 January 1959, and it performed far better than Howerd had expected. The reviews hailed his performance as a return to form, and asked for more of the same.

Maschwitz responded promptly: he contacted Scruffy Dale to arrange for Howerd to meet up again with Ship and Sharp and himself, and start exploring the possibility of commissioning a full-length series. In a follow-up letter (sent to Dale on 3 February), Maschwitz tried his best to ensure that at least one supposed potential pitfall would be avoided:

> It was obvious from my talk with [Ship and Sharp] that both writers would insist upon a sort of partnership with Frankie in the preparation of the scripts; they are used to and would therefore not resent receiving suggestions and intelligent criticism from the stars they work with; the sort of relationship which Hancock and [Jimmy] Edwards both have with their writers. If I may be quite frank with you, Frankie has a reputation of being a little off-hand with writers and changing their scripts willy-nilly; if he were to insist upon doing this, then I think Ship and Sharp would not be interested in going ahead. Personally I hope and believe that Frankie will see the point of this.[41]

It was a rare error of judgement by Maschwitz, who appears to have been swayed, in this particular instance, by the opinions of one or two mediocrities instead of the testimonies of any of the greats, because there certainly had never been any complaints made about Howerd by the likes of Eric Sykes, Galton and Simpson or Johnny Speight.

'Those people who criticised Frank,' reflected Sykes, 'they were the nitpickers. They didn't understand the ability that he had. You don't achieve what he had already achieved without being something special. But for every tall man there's several little ones trying to tear him down.'[42] Ray Galton would make a similar observation: 'Frank just didn't suffer fools gladly. That's all. If you were good at your job, then Frank was fine, and if you were good at your job, then you knew that Frank would make you look even better. So you respected his contribution. It was like Eric Sykes always said: some comedians put 100 per cent into their delivery, but Frank put 110 per cent into his. He did splutter, and sometimes tread on the punchline of a gag, but he certainly made up for it when he didn't. No one could get laughs like him.'[43]

Howerd, understandably, was surprised and more than a little hurt to hear of such a slight: he accepted that he had often clashed with producers, directors, cameramen, lighting men, sound men, studio managers and just about anyone else he encountered on those days when things were going wrong, but, when it came to *writers*, he knew that no other comedian in the country had shown them, both as individuals and as members of a profession, so much trust, respect and support. He also knew, however, that he was in no position to dictate the terms of any deal, and so he decided to hide his wounded pride.

The meeting took place at 10.30 a.m. on Friday 6 February in Maschwitz's office at White City. Howerd went along with whatever was suggested: he really needed this new series. He was not happy with the writers, and he was not at all reassured by the choice of programme-maker – a journeyman producer-director called Harry Carlisle[44] – but he smiled, nodded a few times and made all of the right noises, and the contract was duly secured. He was going back to work, and back on television, and that, at the time, was what seemed to really matter.

As soon as he was back at work, of course, he was more concerned about the unsuitability of the scripts and the inexperience of the producer-director. It frustrated him to think that, although he was by far the most experienced figure associated with the show, it was his opinions that seemed to be most easily disregarded.

No matter how much he tried – coolly, calmly and tactfully – to teach Ship and Sharp something about what made him tick as a comedy character, they continued to care more about what suited his role than they did about what suited him. The most obvious example of this was their curious decision to provide Howerd with a regular on-screen girlfriend called Gladys (played by Helen Jessop), in spite of the fact that whenever he had been given a love interest in the past (such as in the movie *A*

Touch of the Sun) he had struggled to seem convincing. Like Tony Hancock (whose own sitcom girlfriend had been dropped early on from his show), Frankie Howerd was associated with a persona that thrived on rejection, not love and affection, but Ship and Sharp ploughed on regardless, and shaped each show more or less as they pleased.

Publicly, Howerd did his best to strike a positive note. In fact, he tried a little *too* hard to mask his true feelings, and ended up sounding on the verge of being smug. 'Television,' he told *Radio Times* on the eve of his return to the small screen, 'seems to be a medium in which familiarity no longer breeds contempt,' and then added, with a spectacular lack of tact, that the public, even if it does not know what it likes, 'certainly likes what it knows'.[45] If he expected that particular piece of PR to do the trick, then he was sadly mistaken.

Entitled *Frankly Howerd*, the six-episode series ran from 1 May to 5 June 1959, and, right from the start, it was widely regarded (both inside and outside the BBC) as a disaster. To Ship and Sharp, it felt like a setback. To Howerd, on the other hand, it felt like the end.

His spirit now crushed, he decided to get away with Dennis Heymer for a rest. They drove off to a remote corner of Wales in the foothills of the Brecon Beacons, not far from where Heymer had grown up, and booked into a quiet little hotel by the River Usk. Heymer, who was anxious to ensure that his demoralised partner did not just sit around and brood inside their suite, managed to persuade him to venture outdoors and try his hand at a spot of horse riding. Much to his surprise, Howerd found that he loved it – until he started falling off. The first time that it happened, the reins snapped, sending him crashing to the ground; then, the following day, he slipped off again when a stirrup broke; and then, on the third and final occasion, his horse bolted while he was high up in the mountains, shot down a steep slope, threw him off and then rolled on top – catching him, as it did so, on the side of his head with one of its hooves. He ended up in hospital, suffering from concussion, a broken wrist and severe multiple bruising, as well as a clutch of post-traumatic problems for which he would later claim to have required three years of treatment from a top London nerve specialist.

He returned home feeling, if anything, even worse than he had before. At the age of just forty-two, his career already felt as if it was in the process of fading away, and he had run out of rational ways to try to save it.

Scruffy Dale, by this stage, seemed in no kind of state to remedy the situation. When Bernard Delfont heard of Howerd's plight and offered to create a place for him in one of the least prestigious of his many summer shows, Dale gave every impression of being desperate and out of his depth. As his old ALS colleague Brad Ashton recalled, Howerd's eccentric manager and agent had taken to using the most peculiar form of preparation for his negotiations:

> I remember seeing him one night – the door was ajar and he didn't know I could see, and hear, what he was getting up to inside his office – and he was in there on his own, playing out a meeting he had planned the following day with Val Parnell. He was sitting on the 'wrong' side of his desk, and he was going, 'Look, Val, okay, Frank isn't as big a draw as he used to be, I know that, but he's going to really wow your audiences, believe me, you're going to want him back again, and so I think you should start off with a lot more than what you're offering.' And then he got up and went round to the opposite side of his desk, and he sat back, suddenly looked a bit bored, and he became Val Parnell: 'Yes, but as you yourself just said, he *isn't* such a big name now, and *I'm* giving him a big chance.' And Stanley just kept going back and forth around the table, haggling with himself! He'd go: 'Ah, you say that, but –' and then, 'Tch, come on, he's a –' and then, 'Look, Stanley,' and then, 'No, with respect, *you* look, Val . . .' And this was all a rehearsal![46]

The length of the meeting with Delfont was probably considerably shorter than it had been in rehearsal. Delfont said that, at a push, he could find a place for Howerd in a summer show at the Futurist Theatre in Scarborough, on a wage of £250 per week, co-starring alongside the less than stellar Cyril Stapleton and his Show Band. Dale thanked him for his generosity and then left.

Howerd knew that beggars could not be choosers, so he set off to Scarborough determined to make the summer season a success. Concluding that proud defiance had caused more problems than it was worth, he now hoped that meek submission would prove a more suitable short-term strategy. 'I was going to be nice to everybody,' he later said with more than a faint trace of bitterness. 'My behaviour would be impeccable. I'd be charming, polite, helpful, uncomplaining: in a nutshell I'd be my most lovable self – humble to the point of obsequiousness, and with no arguments about dressing-rooms or names at the top of the bill, and with forelock-touching deference to management.'[47]

For all the good that it did, he might as well have persisted with proud defiance. That summer – one of the warmest on record – was practically a heat wave from start to finish, and only the best shows did much business.

The show that Howerd was in, needless to say, was not one of the best. It lacked glamour, it lacked vigour and it lacked variety – and, as a consequence, it ended up lacking most of its aimed-for audience. What made the whole experience especially unpleasant for Howerd was the fact that his material was deemed to be 'inappropriate' for the delicate sensibilities of the kind of people who holiday regularly in a place like Scarborough.

'Your entrance,' complained a short, stout, cherry-cheeked Yorkshireman in a cheap powder-blue suit who was something to do with the management. 'It's far too vulgar for here.' Howerd (remembering his promise to himself to be scrupulously nice and polite) ignored the unintentional innuendo, took a deep breath and invited the uppity little man to put him right. 'What you should do,' the man said in all seriousness, 'is come on and say: "How are you? Are your cars parked nicely?"' Howerd, trying hard to stifle the realisation that he had gone from reading lines by Eric Sykes to taking advice from this humourless bureaucrat, composed a tactful response: 'That strikes me as odd.' He could see, however, that the conversation had run its course, and so he agreed to attend to the matter and then left.[48]

He altered his act, starting with something that he hoped was slightly less 'offensive' from seven years before, but it did little to ingratiate him with his bosses, who continued to blame him for any complaints they received about any aspect of the production. He then commissioned a brand-new sketch from another one of his young writer friends, Barry Took, but still his critics remained unimpressed. Nothing that he did throughout that sweltering summer seemed to meet with their approval. In spite of his best intentions, it had all gone horribly wrong, and he would later rate this Scarborough season as 'the unhappiest show I've worked in during my entire career'.[49]

When the run was finally over, he left immediately for London. He feared that the last door had now been shut on his career.

Acting on the advice of Dennis Heymer, who had urged him to invest in some property while he still could instead of frittering away what remained of his money on rent, Howerd moved out of his flat in Holland Villas Road and bought a smart little mews cottage situated nearby in Napier Place. It was here, in the hard weeks that followed, that he sat and wondered about what he could, and should, try to do with the rest of his life.

Desperate not only for a break but also a complete change of scene, he decided to fly off to America and spend some time in New York. Nobody over there knew who he was, and he rather enjoyed the experience of suddenly being anonymous – until, that is, it made him realise how much, if his career really was over, he would miss the recognition. He was relieved, therefore, when he encountered an old fan: the British-born musical comedy star (and former wife of Eric Maschwitz) Hermione Gingold. After learning of his recent problems, she arranged a meeting between Howerd and the producers of her forthcoming Broadway revue, *A to Z*, with a view to finding a place for him in the cast.

The negotiations seemed to go well, and he returned to London believing that some kind of deal had more or less been done. A fortnight later, however, he discovered that it had not: the producers informed him by letter that it had been decided, on reflection, that his brand of humour was 'unsuitable' for a Broadway audience.[50] Doors were now being slammed shut on both sides of the Atlantic.

Howerd rounded off a wretched year by playing the Dame in the pantomime *Mother Goose*, which was televised by the BBC, and the Mock Turtle, the Mad Hatter and two other roles in a new 'musical' adaptation of *Alice in Wonderland*, which proved to be the last show ever staged at the Winter Garden in Drury Lane. Neither production suggested that the bad times would soon be over.

The next decade started off, sure enough, with more of the same: a former big star scrabbling around for whatever bits and pieces of work that he could find at the bottom of the barrel. He managed to appear on one edition of the BBC's *Juke Box Jury*, but his obvious lack of interest in, or knowledge of, contemporary popular music ensured that he would not be invited back. He also passed an audition to appear in the pilot episode of a television version of the popular radio panel game *Twenty Questions*, but then failed to fit in with the basic aims of the show (he was looking for laughs while the others were looking for answers). Even a belated return engagement on *Sunday Night at the London Palladium* was only achieved by swallowing his pride and accepting a slot right down at the very bottom of the bill.

Apart from a handful of summer concerts planned for Folkestone, an apologetically back-to-basics radio series called *Frankie's Bandbox* (scripted by Barry Took and Marty Feldman) and a one-off television special (written by Took, Johnny Speight and Galton and Simpson) entitled *Ladies and Gentle-men*, Howerd's diary for the rest of 1960 contained precious little except blank pages. He descended into his deepest depression yet, convinced now that he would never be able to recover the lofty star status that had been lost. Then, just when he felt that he had at last reached rock bottom, the ground again gave way beneath him.

He suddenly discovered, to his horror, not only that a large portion of his savings had mysteriously disappeared, but also that he now owed thousands of pounds in back taxes. 'Someone,' Howerd would moan, 'had clearly fouled things up in a big way.'[51] There was no doubt, however, that the 'someone' in question was none other than Scruffy Dale.

Several friends and colleagues had been warning Howerd about Dale for some time. Spike Milligan, in particular, had never trusted this peculiar, and frequently pyjama-clad, figure, and increasingly resented his presence on the board of Associated London Scripts. Milligan had watched Dale branch out, during the second half of the fifties, into other fields of the entertainment business, such as music and, somewhat improbably, wrestling, and had grown more and more suspicious as to where he was finding the capital to invest in such ambitious and high-profile ventures as the national 'Stanley Dale skiffle contest'.

Howerd had also learned, via a number of people at the BBC, that his manager was getting increasingly remiss when it came to connecting the Corporation with his client. As long ago as the spring of 1957, for instance, Howerd had been alarmed to hear that an important letter sent to him by a producer had taken two whole weeks to reach him – all because Dale had forgotten that it was crumpled up in one of his pockets. He had been even more alarmed when he discovered sub-sequently that one executive, reacting angrily to Howerd's apparent disinclination to reply, had concluded that the comedian 'must either be a very bad businessman, mentally unstable or just not interested' to have allowed such a 'farcical' and 'insulting' situation to have arisen.[52]

There had been countless other hints, rumours, loose allusions and overt allegations made about Scruffy Dale over the course of the previous few years, but Howerd, blinded by a misplaced sense of loyalty along with a residual feeling of indebtedness, had managed somehow either to explain the claims away or just block them out of his mind. By 1960, however, not even he was able to remain any longer in denial, and the full extent of Dale's betrayal, once confirmed, hit him hard.

First, there was the matter of from where Dale's money had come. It transpired that most of the money had come from Frankie Howerd, Eric Sykes and, in varying amounts, several other members of ALS. 'He looked after Frank's money and he looked after my money, but it wasn't a very good idea,' recalled Sykes ruefully. 'He was always the one with the fist full of white fivers, and we were always the ones who had to ask him for one of them.'[53] It was found out, after some frantic research, that Dale had taken Howerd's and Sykes' money (and later some additional sums belonging to certain others at ALS) and struck a 'secret' arrangement with their bank manager to siphon off a percentage of their earnings and deposit the funds in a separate account (set up in Dale's name) in order to 'protect them from themselves': 'You know,' he had told the bank manager in confidence, 'how irresponsible these show-business people are. It'll be gone in a week.'[54]

Second, there was the matter of where this money had ended up. The answer to this was rather more complicated. Some of the money had gone into a haulage firm that Dale had set up discreetly and then run surreptitiously from his base at ALS. 'It turned out,' revealed Brad Ashton, 'that he'd got these two Italian brothers in to help him run it, and they'd sometimes be coming into the office to see him and use the office phones, chat up their girlfriends and all that sort of thing. Spike had hated their guts right from the start, but he could never quite find out why they were there.'[55]

Most of what money remained had been channelled into Dale's various projects as a budding promoter, and it was during his pursuit of this activity that he finally took one liberty too many. Dale had been managing a skiffle group fronted by his most promising young protégé, Jim Dale, and had secretly been benefiting from what he appears to have regarded as an ingeniously risk-free kind of arrangement: when the group made a profit, he pocketed it, but when it made a loss, his fellow-directors at ALS were asked to make up the shortfall (according to Jim Dale's former producer, George Martin, Scruffy had his client 'tied up in more knots than I could count, and poor Jim never had the vaguest idea what his financial state was'[56]). Eventually, Milligan and others, exasperated by so many apparent anomalies in their accounting, decided that enough was enough, and, following an internal investigation, Scruffy Dale's countless shady deceptions were at last brought to the light.

Shortly after this, Dale suddenly disappeared from the metropolitan show-business scene. 'He disappeared,' explained Eric Sykes, 'because we got rid of him. We voted him out because of several "misdemeanours". But then he got a very prominent lawyer to represent him, and Associated London Scripts had to pay for that lawyer! And we ended up having to pay him £5,000 redundancy money! So he was really . . . well, he was somebody who wasn't very nice.'[57]

Dale left Howerd to deal, among other things, with all of the massive tax problems that his own chronic negligence had caused. With no savings now to speak of and no work on the horizon, Howerd had no choice but to sell his treasured country cottage in Surrey and surrender an insurance policy in order to stay solvent.

Now, he feared, it really was all over. He felt that he had lost everything that he had earned.

Dennis Heymer remained steadfast by his side, as did his mother and sister, but Howerd seemed inconsolable. He struggled through to the end of the year, surviving on the paltry sum of £10 per week, and then somehow summoned up sufficient mental strength to complete a six-week spell in a poorly paid pantomime in Streatham. At the start of 1961, however, he crumbled.

Roger Hancock (Tony's younger brother) took over as his agent, but the telephone had long since stopped ringing, and the bookings diary remained depressingly bare. Whenever Hancock tried to find his client some work, the response from each potential employer was more or less the same: Frankie Howerd, they would say, *used* to be famous, but now, they declared, he was finished.

People had said this and similar things on various occasions before, but the difference now was that even Frankie Howerd appeared to agree with them. The combative spirit of old seemed to have been replaced by a sad sense of resignation. 'Comedians are a pretty neurotic bunch,' he admitted. 'When life's unkind the first thing that vanishes is your confidence – along with your salary. And that's fatal.'[58]

It was as if Howerd's life, in his mid-forties, had suddenly come to a standstill. He spent the empty days wandering around the streets of South Kensington, lost in thought, or else he stayed inside, reading, playing draughts or watching television, but saying little. He drank a little more than he used to do (especially brandy, gin and vodka), and came to rely on the odd pill or potion purchased from Harley Street to help deaden the pain that came with depression. He seldom slept well any more, and Dennis Heymer would sometimes have to sit for hours by his bed to comfort him through the night.

He looked lost, but was hard to help. Instead of seeking out the company of his many loyal friends at ALS, Howerd actually started avoiding them. The sights and sounds of old colleagues at work, with all of those telephones ringing and typewriters tapping, would only have made him feel even worse than he did before, and – although he knew that the likes of Sykes, Galton and Simpson and Speight would have willingly written for him without any prospect of financial reward – he feared that his presence there might seem (to him at least) 'like a begging bowl'.[59]

Desperate to bring to an end the period that he had taken to calling 'the years of darkness', Howerd preferred to withdraw completely from view. He felt that he had gone through quite enough humiliation for one lifetime. Although some small part of him still wanted to fight against the fact of rejection, he was now close to convincing himself that it was finally time for the fighting to stop. 'I had to give myself a talking-to,' he later explained, 'and say, "Look, maybe this is what you've got to face up to, and not go on hoping and hoping. And that's it. That's it." '[60]

The more that he thought about it, the more that it seemed to make sense. That, he agreed, probably was it. His career was over.

ACT III:
THE COMEBACK

The phone rang. Which made me jump.
'Cos I thought it had been cut off.

CHAPTER 10

Re. Establishment

Do you know: I could have taken my fist and banged on his desk in protest. But it's very difficult when you're kneeling.

During the spring of 1961, Frankie Howerd came close to abandoning his show-business career, selling his house and investing in a London supper club. When that particular deal fell through, he seriously considered the possibility of running a country pub. He was ready, at this stage in his life, to move on.

His new agent, Roger Hancock, had managed, through sheer stubborn persistence, to find the odd engagement here and there for his client over the course of the first half of the year – there had been a seven-minute spot in a Kenneth Horne-hosted radio special called *Variety Playhouse*, a couple of police benefit concerts and a brief tour of North Arabia in a service show for the troops – but that had been the sum of his recent involvement in the profession that used to treat him like a major star. There was still a summer season to come, and then there were plans for a pantomime at the end of the year, but after that, Howerd felt, the time would probably be right to bring the curtain down on his ailing career.

The summer season did nothing to change his mind. Booked by the provincial impresario Jack Jay to appear at the tiny Windmill Theatre in Great Yarmouth, he found himself relegated to the role of one of the 'supporting artists' to the young man at the top of the bill: the 24-year-old former pop star-turned-all-round family entertainer, Tommy Steele. Although Steele always treated Howerd backstage with rare thoughtfulness and respect, and insisted that the Number One dressing-room be given to the comedian instead of himself, the message sent out to the public by the playbills was that the once-great Frankie Howerd was now more or less washed-up.

So many of Howerd's old friends and former colleagues seemed to be working in one or another of Great Yarmouth's five theatres that summer – the list included Bruce Forsyth, Arthur Haynes, Ken Dodd, Bob Monkhouse and Roy Castle – but whereas their names were still very much in evidence at the top of the bill, Howerd's was now rooted right down at the base. Although they were all products of a fiercely competitive profession (in which it was not unknown for certain performers to take great pleasure from the misfortunes of their supposed rivals), there was no suggestion of *schadenfreude* in the reactions of any of Howerd's more prosperous peers: 'All in the business,' recalled Bruce Forsyth, 'were heartbroken for him.'[1]

Howerd spent much of the season keeping himself very much to himself. Some of his illustrious friends would catch the occasional glimpse of him, wandering alone around the seaside town in a pork-pie hat, a short-sleeved shirt and a pair of wrinkled brown slacks, looking like a cross between Banquo's ghost and an off-duty cab driver, but he rarely seemed to welcome any attempt to make contact.

One of the few performers in whom he confided during this period was Ernie Wise, who was appearing at the time in Torquay alongside his partner, Eric Morecambe. Wise (along with his wife, Doreen) had become friends with Howerd when they met for the first time earlier in the year, and, from that moment on, he would always make a point of getting in touch with his fellow-comedian every month or so in the hope of cheering him up. When, during the course of one of their conversations, Wise let slip the news that he and his partner were mulling over an offer from Lew Grade to make their television comeback (their previous, harrowing experience of this medium, back in 1954, had prompted one cruel critic to redefine the term 'TV set' as 'the box in which they buried Morecambe and Wise'[2]), Howerd understood his friend's apprehension. 'No matter how great your success,' he said with real feeling, 'you never get rid of the taste of failure. You wear your scars forever.'[3]

Howerd confessed that he could no longer bear to incur any more of these scars; he felt he already had more than enough to harm a lifetime. 'It's like a vicious circle,' he would say: 'you lose your nerve, and then you don't do so well and you're not wanted, so you lose your nerve even more, then you don't do so well . . . And so it goes on, and on, and you gradually spiral downwards.'[4]

He still had a number of shows to do, however, and he did them

because he needed the money, but, throughout the whole of that difficult and sometimes humiliating summer, he never felt truly at ease in
front of an audience: 'Mental turbulence,' he would say, 'precluded
such a possibility.'[5]

When it was over, he went home with Dennis Heymer to their
cottage in Napier Place, and settled back in the rooms where no telephone ever seemed to ring. The clocks continued to tick and tock, but
it felt as though time was standing still.

Old friends rallied round in a bid to boost his spirits. His latest 'deaf
accompanist', Sunny Rogers (whom he had known since the days when
she was dating Frank Barnard and touring the Variety circuit as a
'cowgirl' with a novelty rope-twirling act), offered him some of her
life's savings, and several other friends and former colleagues made similar
heartfelt gestures. Howerd was deeply touched, but he felt that he had
no choice but to turn them all down. '[N]ot only was borrowing no
solution to the problem,' he explained, 'but I had a horror of being in
debt – another imprint from my youth, for no matter how poor we
were my mother had always paid her way.'[6]

His writers, as always, were desperate to help him get back to work.
Eric Sykes not only offered free scripts, but also tried, manfully but
ultimately unsuccessfully, to persuade the major London promoters and
theatre owners to show a little faith in a truly great English stand-up. Ray
Galton and Alan Simpson were equally persistent, and they attempted to
find a place for Howerd in each new project that they proposed, but
their negotiations, just like Sykes', came to naught. Even a combined
offer from the cream of Britain's comedy writers – Sykes, Galton and
Simpson, Speight, Milligan, Barry Took and Marty Feldman – to supply
their services for nothing, on condition that Howerd could perform
their material, failed to entice any of the top executives or impresarios.
Every plea met with the same sneered response: 'Frankie Howerd? Why
on earth have him? He's finished. Dead as a doornail.'[7]

Apart from the writers, probably the only significant figure in broadcasting, during this barren period in Howerd's career, who continued
to offer him a reliable measure of support was Bill Cotton Jnr. Cotton
was working, in those days, as the producer of his father's very popular
prime-time television programme (later on in the decade he would
become Head of Variety for BBC TV, and then a quite brilliant Head
of Light Entertainment), and Howerd remained a firm favourite:

I tried my best to use him in every season of *The Billy Cotton Band Show*, because I genuinely believed that he was one of *the* great 'un-derivative' comedians in the country. He was always *hysterically* funny as far as I was concerned, and I felt exactly the same way about him when he was going through that time in his career when he really couldn't get himself arrested. Fashions changed, but he didn't. He was always a class act.[8]

Invaluable (and much appreciated) though such rare high-profile bookings were, it was just unfortunate for Howerd that Cotton had not yet made the transition from producer to executive, because it was at that lofty level that he now seemed to lack vital support.

Eric Maschwitz, although still formally in control of Light Entertainment on BBC TV, was now also working as a consultant to the Director of Television, and so had recently handed over responsibility for the day-to-day running of the department to his assistant, Tom Sloan.[9] The change did nothing to weaken the BBC, but it did do some harm to Frankie Howerd.

Sloan differed from his predecessors in the key sense that, unlike them, he had never really experienced what it was like to write or perform or produce (or succeed or fail), rather than simply manage, in the world of professional entertainment, and so, inevitably, he lacked that instinctive ability to understand, empathise with and sometimes indulge the talent inside his department. Whereas both Waldman and Maschwitz were, in effect, poachers-turned-gamekeepers, retaining an easy rapport with all kinds of creative individuals, Sloan was just a gamekeeper who had now been upgraded to head gamekeeper, and although there was never any doubt that he genuinely *admired* creative people, he found it hard sometimes to understand them.

He was actually a far more complex personality than his subsequent reputation would suggest. A rather military-looking figure, with a neatly-parted head of hair, a smart Ronald Colman-style moustache and a sober taste in suits, Sloan could certainly come over as fairly prickly on certain occasions, but he could also charm and disarm with his refreshingly self-deprecating sense of humour (particularly after he had downed a couple of snifters of Scotch in his office after lunch), and was even capable every now and again of the odd spasm of whimsical eccentricity (such as the time when he nibbled absent-mindedly on a tulip during a meeting at a television festival in Montreux[10]). 'He was a good, honest, decent man,' Bill Cotton recalled, 'with real integrity. A very effective and conscientious manager. People liked and respected him.'[11]

Sloan would prove himself to be an extremely successful Head of Light Entertainment, commissioning many of the BBC's most admirable, innovative and popular shows of the 1960s, but, especially in the early days of his reign, he had a tendency to err a little too readily on the side of caution. As part of his brief was to claw back as quickly as possible some of the audience that had been drawn away to ITV, he much preferred the apparent certainty of statistics to the vagueness of faith when it came to calculating which risks were worth running.

When, therefore, he invited two of his prized assets, Galton and Simpson, to nominate their next project after their collaboration with Tony Hancock had come to an end, he did not expect them to say that they wanted to team up next with Frankie Howerd. It was not that Sloan harboured any dislike for the comedian – on the contrary, he had liked and admired him for years – it was just that he could not understand the logic.

'He looked at us as though we'd just said something astonishing,' Ray Galton recalled, 'and then he said, "*Frankie Howerd?* Oh, no, no, he's finished. You don't want to do a series with *him*."':

So we said, 'Why not? We *like* him. We think he's great!' He said, 'No, he's finished on television – his last series for the BBC was an absolute disaster! Believe me, he's finished in the business!' So we said, 'Come on, Tom, don't be daft! Frank's a genius!' In the end, he buzzed his PA, Queenie [Lipyeat], and asked her to bring in this great tome with all of the charts and audience appreciation ratings and what have you for Frank's last series [*Frankly Howerd*], and then he said, 'Do you see? An absolute disaster! Terrible audience figures and even worse appreciation ratings. Look at the charts. Terrible! No, you don't want to do *that*.' What he suggested instead was that we fulfil a programme title he'd thought up: *Comedy Playhouse*. He said he'd got these ten half-hour slots, and that we could do anything we liked with them, so long as we used that title – which was a fantastic offer that was just far too good to turn down. And to be fair to him, he also told us, 'Look, if you want

Frank to do one of those, then that's fine, absolutely fine, it's entirely up to you – do what you want.' So we started out with *Comedy Playhouse,* and number four in the series turned out to be *Steptoe and Son.*[12]

They did write an episode for Howerd – a seed of a potential sitcom entitled *Have You Read This Notice?* – but by the time that this particular edition eventually went out on air, as part of a second run of *Comedy Playhouse* in 1963, the phenomenal success of *Steptoe and Son* precluded them from taking it any further.

Howerd understood. He knew how hard they – and others – had tried to help, and, remarkably, he refused to be bitter about those who were denying him a chance to stage a comeback. 'Managements,' he would say, 'they don't give a contract because I'm lovely and sweet and gorgeous. They do it because they think it's a good proposition.'[13] In 1961, he accepted that he no longer seemed like a good enough proposition. It was nothing personal, he reasoned, even though it certainly hurt. It was just a fact with which he would have to learn to live.

He just wanted the year to end. He just wanted it all to be over.

December saw him tread the boards again in a pantomime: *Puss in Boots* at the King's Theatre, Southsea. Although he had said nothing publicly, privately he had made up his mind that this was going to be his 'swan song': 'What was the point of working just three months of the year if I was lucky – and spending the other nine in self-pitying misery? The time had come to make a clean break.'[14]

While he was counting down the days, however, an invitation arrived for him backstage. Max Aitken, then Chairman of Beaverbrook newspapers, wanted him to give one of the speeches at the 1962 *Evening Standard* Drama Awards ceremony, which was due to be held in January at London's Savoy Hotel. Howerd had become something of a fixture at this famously convivial event over the course of the previous few years, having mastered the trick of making a custom-made script (crafted at the last minute by Sykes, Speight and Galton and Simpson) sound like a completely impromptu post-prandial routine, and he remained a great favourite of Aitken's. This time, however, Howerd was tempted initially to turn him down, but then, after giving the matter some further thought, he decided that such an engagement would represent a rather fitting final fling: 'I'd make my farewell appearance in evening dress, in posh surroundings, in front of a good-class audience!'[15]

It could hardly have gone any better. In the presence of such bright young things as the award-winning *Beyond the Fringe* satirical quartet – Peter Cook, Alan Bennett, Jonathan Miller and Dudley Moore – Howerd (fortified by the best part of half a bottle of Scotch) gave a *tour de force* performance. Apart from the odd newly-minted comical line care of his friends at ALS, most of the jokes were blatantly ancient (such as the one about the hard-of-hearing woman whose succession of pregnancies is explained by the fact that, whenever her husband turns to her in bed and says, 'Shall we go to sleep now, or . . . what?' she always replies, 'What?'), but the distinctive Howerd delivery proved, on the night, to be a rare and real delight.

Peter Cook was one of the first to come up afterwards and congratulate him, adding that he had always been a big fan ('As far as I was concerned,' Cook would later say, 'he was still an enormous star, and I'd felt very shy about approaching him'[16]). Howerd, his head still spinning with his success (and a fair amount of alcohol), felt, understandably, very flattered. When, therefore, Cook went on to invite his old hero to appear at the theatre club – the Establishment – he and one of his fellow-Cambridge graduates, Nicholas Luard, had opened recently in Greek Street in the heart of Soho, Howerd was happy to slur something vaguely positive in response. It had been so long since people had treated him like he meant something, like he was special, like he *mattered*, he could not bring himself to spoil the moment by announcing that he had just given the last performance of his career.

He remembered few of the details from the event when he woke up the following morning, and he could certainly recall nothing about any invitation to appear at a Soho club. Once the hangover had faded, however, he felt happy – happier than he had felt for a long, long time – as well as pleased and proud that his farewell performance seemed to have gone so well. He had gone out on a high.

That, then, as far as Howerd was concerned, was that. He paid a visit to his mother, who was now in poor health ('You'll get an award one day,' she told him, 'though I won't be there to see it'[17]). He assured her that those days were gone, told her that she – and she alone – was what mattered, and then he returned home. Prompted by Dennis Heymer, he auditioned for the role of Fagin in the Broadway production of Lionel Bart's *Oliver!* He was told to forget it, and so he did. Prompted by his old friend Alma Cogan, he appeared alongside her in a pilot of a possible new sitcom called *The Secret Keepers*, but the result of their efforts was shelved, and he was told to forget that, too, and so he did.

He went again to see his mother. She assured him that, sooner or later, he would make a triumphant comeback. He kissed her, squeezed her hand, and went back home again. He had a new life to plan.

His new agent, however, had other ideas. Beryl Vertue, an old school-friend of Alan Simpson's who was now working at Associated London Scripts as an over-worked secretary, fledgling agent and a sort of *de facto* general manager, had recently assumed responsibility for running what remained of Howerd's career after Roger Hancock had left to look after his brother Tony's various affairs. Although Howerd had made it clear that he was no longer interested in pursuing any new projects ('I mean, he'd been a worrier when things had been going *well*,' Vertue recalled, 'so now, when they weren't, he was really, completely, lost'[18]), his new agent, with the encouragement of all of her colleagues at ALS, was determined to prevent him from giving up show business.

She tried all of the usual suspects – the BBC, the ITV companies, the major metropolitan theatrical impresarios – but none of them had changed their mind: Howerd, they all repeated, was finished. Unde-terred, she used her intelligence and imagination, showed some initiat-ive, and started looking into what was left:

> I then got an idea. Thinking, 'Well, where *could* we work, then, if everybody else don't seem to want him?' So I thought of cabaret. That made him even more agitated, really, but I said, 'Well, look, let's *try* something new.' And he hadn't really done [cabaret] in London, and I didn't know much about it either, but I *had* heard of the Blue Angel – a nightclub. I'd never been there, but I'd heard of it. So I looked it up in the phone book, got the phone number and rang the man up and said could I come to talk to him about Frankie Howerd. So he was hugely intrigued by this, because they weren't used to having people of that calibre really.[19]

When the manager, Max Setty, confirmed that he would like to offer Howerd a month's residency at the club, Vertue called her client to inform him of the good news. 'No way,' he snapped. 'It's all over.

Finished. Done with. If you want to do me a favour you can come and buy overpriced champagne at the pub I'm about to open.' Vertue, however, surprised Howerd by snapping straight back: '*You-are-going-to-continue-in-show-business-and-you-are-going-to-do-well-again.*' He had no answer to that, which she took for a 'Yes', and so she booked him in at the Blue Angel for a month-long run from mid-May to mid-June.[20]

Howerd moaned that Vertue was 'a dreadful bully', but then added, under his breath, 'thank God!'[21] His plans for the pub were postponed.

Back at work, he paid a belated return visit to the offices at ALS (which had by this time relocated to far more elegant premises at 9 Orme Court, in Bayswater), and started collaborating with his old writers on the kind of act that he hoped would suit the unfamiliar venue. Although he continued to complain that the West End location was 'too high profile', and that the cabaret setting was 'too intimate', and that the engagement 'offered no long-term solution',[22] he heeded the advice of his 'incredibly tough' agent and prepared as thoroughly as he could for the month ahead.

The Blue Angel, in those days, was one of a cluster of London venues – Quaglino's, the Jack of Clubs and Esmeralda's Barn were among the others – where one could go to find late-night, and relatively mainstream, entertainment. David Frost had appeared there recently (and been spotted by a BBC producer), as had the cult crooner and pianist Leslie 'Hutch' Hutchinson, and it was not too unusual to spot the odd television personality, fashion model, top actor or pop star among the wealthy and well-dressed members of the audience. Howerd was right about the intimacy of the Blue Angel: based in Berkeley Square, it was a cosy little place, with a busy bar, packed tables and a small dance floor dimly lit with coloured lights. Cabaret started at 11 p.m. or slightly later, usually running on until about two o'clock in the morning, and the atmosphere was suitably relaxed.

Howerd found, somewhat to his surprise, that he rather liked it. As he grew more accustomed to the novel environment he came increasingly to command it, drawing confidence from the quality of his material and the apparent warmth of the audience reaction. He was getting laughs again. He was still only being paid a paltry £60 per week, but he *was* getting laughs again, and that made all the difference.

Before, however, he could start to consider the potential consequences of his return to form, he was rocked by the worst imaginable blow. On 7 June 1962, during the middle of his run, his beloved mother Edith died. Aged seventy-three, she had been in poor health for some time, suffering from a combination of heart problems and arthritis, but the news of her death still came as a terrible shock.

Howerd was devastated. 'Emotion and feeling dissolved into an utter and absolute sense of emptiness,' he later said. 'I felt that nothing material – but nothing – mattered any more. I'd lost someone I'd loved.'[23]

He did what all grieving children did: he went back to the family home, sat and stared at all the absences, and alternated between periods when the sadness seemed too deep for mere tears and times when it rose up to force them all out. Roaming aimlessly through the empty upstairs rooms, he came upon an old tin box his mother had kept by her bed: in it he found pictures of himself and his brother and sister; all of their old school reports; drawings and stories from childhood; and a thick bundle of yellowing cuttings from newspapers, each one of them chronicling some fresh triumph by her famous son. Feeling his emotions welling up once again, he went back downstairs, relieved to have resisted the temptation to surrender once again to the tears, but then caught sight in a cool corner of the pantry of a humble bowl of jelly, just like his mother used to make for him each weekend, and he broke down in a heap of grief.

He thought of all the countless sacrifices she had made for him, all of the times she had come to his aid and restored his faith, and all of the anxious first nights when the sight of her sitting alongside sister Betty in the front row, both of them smiling with pride, had helped assuage his jangling nerves. He would have done nothing, would have been nothing, without her, and he could not bear to think that now she was gone.

After the funeral was over, he attempted to withdraw completely from view. 'I didn't care about *anything* any more,' he said.[24] 'I suppose,' said Beryl Vertue, 'he had a kind of a breakdown, really, with one thing and another. It made him ill, all this worry. It was just really awful to watch.'[25]

He was racked by a misplaced sense of guilt. For all of the pleasure he had provided his mother he could not help thinking that he could, and should, have found more ways to have made her life better. 'When she died,' he later said of this time, 'I experienced death. I thought to myself, what does it matter, all this striving? It's people that matter, people that one loves or ought to love. If you are fond of someone who dies, part of you dies with them and your mind dulls and I didn't care.'[26]

The sense of loss, combined with the feelings of regret, exacerbated the spiritual crisis that had started shortly after the slow disintegration of his career. He began to question all of his beliefs, from the religious teachings gleaned during his childhood to the kind of hard professional platitudes passed down from one old pro to the next. None of them, any longer, seemed to make any sense:

> This led me to think that my obsessive determination to succeed in show-business – the very burdens and ego and all-consuming demands of it – had made me fail badly as a human being: had severely flawed my personality so that it had never truly developed outside of the strait-jacket confines of my professional career. My perspectives had become distorted: a combination of fanaticism and inferiority complex had given me nothing to aim for or cling to but fame . . .
>
> And I realised that even the measure of fame that I'd gathered *hadn't* brought me happiness, nor solved any of the problems I'd so naively supposed it would. I recalled how, even when I was a star of the day, my mother had privately told my sister that she wished I'd give it up: solely for the reason that, 'It seems to make him so unhappy . . . and has he got a clean vest on?'[27]

The question that he now found himself asking over and over again was: 'What had I lost on the way?' His answer, when it came, surprised even him: 'The answer was not so much a career: that was incidental to a greater loss – *myself*.'[28]

It was this realisation that plunged Howerd into a very private but very intense period of self-analysis – during which he would seek out assistance and advice from sources that ranged all the way from psychics to psychoanalysts. One of those in whom he sought solace was Doris Collins, a self-styled 'psychic healer' he took to visiting at her home in Richmond: 'He adored his mum,' she would say. 'He would sit with me, and she would come through and talk about his problems. It gave him a great deal of comfort.'[29]

Howerd continued to look to religion, but did so nowadays with a growing sense of doubt and disaffection. He kept going back to his old church in Eltham – St Barnabas in Addison Road – but not so much any more for the services as for the days when it was quiet and empty and he could sit on his own at the back and pray. Increasingly, as his soul-searching went on, he drifted away from things spiritual and placed his faith instead in science – or at least something that spoke to him with the authority of a science.

First came the psychiatrists and psychoanalysts, a succession of whom (at least twenty-four, according to some estimates[30]) he would consult from the early sixties all the way through until his death. 'He really came to fancy himself, after a while, as an amateur psychiatrist,' recalled Alan Simpson:

> He seemed to get deeper and deeper into it. He read about it, thought about it, and he used it. There was nothing he loved more, in a social set-up, than probing you about your private life as if he really *was* some kind of psychoanalyst. The few times that he came down to stay with my wife and me, he'd always be straight in there, after dinner, doing all of this 'on the couch' stuff.[31]

Shortly after his mother's death, as the grief began to grip, Howerd was moved to go even further: he decided to undergo a radically experimental course of psychotherapy that revolved around the use of LSD.

The hallucinogenic drug LSD-25 (lysergic acid diethylamide) had been used by certain psychiatrists in America (and particularly by those based in southern California) since 1949. Inspired by Freud's suggestion that 'The future may teach us how to exercise a direct influence, by means of particular chemical substances, upon the amounts of energy and their distribution in the apparatus of the mind,'[32] and pioneered by such figures as Humphry Osmond (who coined the term 'psychedelics'), Arthur Chandler and Oscar Janiger, the drug had been used in the treatment of a wide variety of conditions, ranging from alcoholism to writer's block. By the mid-1950s, a number of Hollywood actors, including Cary Grant and Jack Nicholson, and writers such as Aldous Huxley and Anaïs Nin, had undergone LSD sessions in the hope of curing their neuroses, enriching their creativity and pushing open the doors of perception.[33]

Similar experiments had begun in Britain at the start of the 1960s.

Psychiatrists such as R.D. Laing, R.A. Sandison and Joyce Martin were licensed to administer the drug to their patients in their private clinics; hospitals such as the Marlborough Day Hospital established an active section in which the drug was incorporated into certain forms of psycho-therapy; and a shady character by the name of Michael Hollingshead was in the process of setting up an unofficial centre for LSD apostles in his apartment in Belgravia (where members of both The Beatles and the Rolling Stones, among others, would later congregate).[34]

Once Frankie Howerd had heard of the supposed potential benefits of the drug, he was determined to try it under proper supervision. After making a few enquiries, he was put in touch with a psychiatrist named Thomas M. Ling, who was working in those days as a consultant at the Marlborough Day Hospital in association with his research colleague, John Buckman. Ling's central contention, that 'LSD helps the patient to see himself as he really is',[35] was precisely what Howerd wanted to hear, and so he arranged to meet Ling and organise a course of treatment.

Each fortnightly session began early on a Friday evening, when Dennis Heymer drove Howerd in their Mercedes to Ling's private clinic. At about 6 p.m., he was taken to a dark, medium-sized room and asked to swallow one grain of the sedative Sodium Amytal to allay any initial anxiety. Then he was laid down on a bed and given an injection of between 80–120 gamma of LSD. About fifteen minutes later, as the first effects of the drug (sudden flashes of light before the eyes, a slight fluctuation in temperature, an increased heartbeat, a tingling sensation all over the surface of the body and a general feeling of euphoria) started to be felt, a dose of Ritalin was administered intravenously to stimulate the central nervous system and thus achieve (it was hoped) a peaceful reverie.

He was then left alone in the locked room with a notebook and pen with instructions to explore his earliest memories and write down all of his thoughts ('Teddy bears, mirrors, family photographs, dummies and feeding bottles are available,' Ling had said, 'to help the patient act out his infantile feelings'[36]). About two hours into the session, a nurse entered the room to give Howerd a second, smaller dose of Ritalin in order to spark what Ling predicted would be a spell of 'penetrating self-understanding' during which 'the unconscious material that has been released earlier in the session is gone over with deep insight'.[37]

Finally, at around 11 p.m., the five-hour session was brought to an end when a nurse re-entered the room to supervise Howerd as he swallowed an anti-psychotic cocktail composed of 50 mg of the pheno-thiazine Largactil and three grains of Sodium Amytal to ease him back slowly to a relatively stable state of mind, and then he was left once again to drift off to sleep. The following afternoon, he would write up his scribbled impressions in the form of a report, which was then used during what remained of the weekend as the basis of his latest psycho-therapy session with Ling. By talking through the contents of each report, he was encouraged to attempt to distinguish between what among his LSD-induced visions, feelings and 'memories' had been actual, what had been symbolic and what had simply been fantasy. Dennis Heymer would then collect Howerd on Monday morning and drive him back home for a short period of rest and reflection (Ling had warned that patients were likely to be 'emotionally labile' and 'difficult' for two or three days after each session[38]).

This sequence of secret sessions ran over the course of a couple of months, with the odd follow-up session taking place during certain weekends later on in the decade, and it seems that, although one or two of his close friends judged most of the supposed results to be 'a load of balls', Howerd regarded them all as beneficial. He emerged from the sessions feeling very drained but slightly calmer than before, believing that he had acquired a much clearer understanding about (among other things) the impact of his father's behaviour on both the development of his personality and his attitude towards authority figures in general, as well as a better sense of his strengths as well as his weaknesses.[39]

He seemed no happier after, however, than he had been before, and he continued to grieve over the loss of his mother. Immersed in his memories, he cared less than ever about the future.

It was during this period that, with cruel irony, the telephones sud-denly started ringing once again. Word of Howerd's successful spell at the Blue Angel had reached television's consistently inconsistent execu-tives, who were now responding by trying to re-employ the man whom they had recently dismissed as unemployable. Offers came in from ITV (who wanted him as a guest in a forthcoming edition of Alma Cogan's *Startime*), BBC Radio (who wanted him to appear – this time at the top of the bill – in another *Variety Playhouse*) and BBC TV (who now had some series ideas that they hoped he would be willing to discuss). There was also yet another invitation from his loyal friends at *The Billy Cotton*

Band Show, as well as a polite reminder from Peter Cook about the forthcoming season at the Establishment club.

Howerd was not interested, initially, in doing anything, let alone a 'season', but, after much persuasion from Beryl Vertue and Dennis Heymer, he eventually came round to the idea that returning to work, rather than wallowing in sorrow, represented a more fitting tribute to the memory of his late mother. With a heavy heart, therefore, he duly did the guest spots, listened politely to the other offers and started talking to Vertue about what she thought he should now be looking to do with his renascent career.

Her first suggestion was more of an order: he was going to have to perform, she said, at the Establishment club. He tried his best to wriggle out of the commitment, protesting that he was surely the last person whom a young, predominantly university-educated and satire-obsessed audience would willingly pay to see. Vertue simply reminded him of two salient facts: first, he needed the money, and second, he could not break a professional promise (even if the promise had been made at the very end of a fairly boozy and woozy night). He had no choice but to accept that she had him trapped.

Before he was sent off to Soho, however, he was sent along to Shepperton to do a fortnight's work on a movie called *The Cool Mikado*. Directed by the would-be boy wonder Michael Winner, the movie offered audiences a nightmare vision of what Gilbert and Sullivan's original comic opera would look like after it had passed through the body of a large man with a small brain, a tin ear and an exceptionally irritable bowel. Howerd (who was cast as Ko-Ko) would say 'without equivocation' that 'not only was it the worst film ever made, but was [also] the one production in show-business that I'm positively ashamed to have appeared in'.[40] He was probably holding back.

After two weeks' work on *The Cool Mikado*, therefore, the prospect of spending the month of September at the Establishment suddenly acquired greater appeal. Howerd still felt a real sense of trepidation, however, about venturing into such blatantly alien territory – not least because he was due to start his spell there straight after a short season from stand-up comedy's latest *enfant terrible*, Lenny Bruce.

A 37-year-old Jewish New Yorker with a foul mouth, a sharp wit and a serious heroin addiction, Bruce had recently been accused of obscenity in the US, and had been allowed to enter Britain only after a prolonged period of edgy procrastination and prevarication by the Home Office. Armed with a reputation for being the 'hippest' and most iconoclastic young comedian in the world, he prowled around the stage at the Establishment clad in dark jeans and a black Nehru jacket, making starkly sardonic observations about politics, religion, race, sex, pornography, terminal disease and narcotics in a style of delivery that crackled with a mixture of crude Yiddishisms, tough Long Island street talk and drug-dealer slang.

There was no doubting his originality (even his solitary mother-in-law joke was distinctive: 'My mother-in-law broke up my marriage. One day my wife came home early from work and found us in bed together'), but some of those present took noisy exception, predictably, to his irreverence and vulgarity, and most nights ended up with flying fists and angry shouts. On one famous occasion, for example, the actor Siobhan McKenna rose to leave midway through Bruce's act in protest at his supposed attacks on the Roman Catholic Church. On her way out, Peter Cook tried to remonstrate with her, whereupon she grabbed and held on to his tie while one of her escorts punched him squarely on the nose. 'These are Irish hands,' shrieked McKenna melodramatically, 'and they're clean!' 'This is an English face,' replied Cook curtly, 'and it's bleeding.'[41]

Howerd followed the course of Bruce's progress at the Establishment with understandable interest, right from the rowdy opening night to the even rowdier closing date (straight after which Bruce was rushed back out of the country with a pack of tabloid hacks baying at his heels); the self-styled 'music-hall comedian' sat back and wondered how on earth he could hope to follow *that*. In a state of mounting panic, he did what he always did in an emergency: he called his writers.

As usual, they were more than happy to help, and so a meeting was duly arranged at Orme Court. Eric Sykes welcomed Howerd into the hall and took him up to reunite him with the others: 'Simpson and Galton, Johnny Speight and myself sat him down early one evening in my office, and I think that by about nine o'clock the same night we'd pretty much written, between us, a whole new act for him. And we did it for nothing. That's how much we respected Frank and his talent.'[42]

The act was inspired by Johnny Speight's initial suggestion that, rather than attempt to appear at home in his new environment, Howerd should make a point of behaving like a misfit. Once this conceit had been agreed, the script itself, in the hands of such a fine quartet of comedy writers, proved relatively straightforward to shape. 'A lot of it – most of the second half – was just his old stage act,' Alan Simpson recalled. 'It was mainly just the opening stuff that Ray and I were involved in, but I think Eric and Johnny wrote the majority of the new material.'[43] The result was a tailor-made text that inspired one of the very best performances that Frankie Howerd would ever deliver.

The opening night at the Establishment that September was a genuinely special occasion. Famous friends, powerful executives, curious critics and long-standing fans rubbed shoulders with college graduates, cabinet ministers, young metropolitan wits and fashion-conscious socialites as they all climbed the stairs, swarmed into the smoke-hazy former strip-club that now passed as the living room of English satire, settled into their seats and stared expectantly at the stage. The simple introduction was made by Peter Cook – 'And now, ladies and gentlemen, Frankie Howerd' – and then, right on cue, he wandered into view, blinked, twitched and grimaced as he fiddled with the microphone while the spotlight picked him out – and then proceeded, step by crafty step, like a wily old prize fighter, to take complete command of the event.

He began by surprising them with the comic equivalent of a swift left hook, confessing that he was only there because of a terrible mistake:

Er, brethren, before we start this little eisteddfod, I must make a little apology to you if I may – well, I say an apology, really it's an appeal, well, no, it's an explanation: well, no, it's an apology, I may as well be honest. I'll tell you why, because, er – you see, ah, I'd like to explain how I happened to get here in this place . . . before we start – because, as you know, well, if you do know at all, I'm a humble music-hall comedian, a sort of Variety artist, you know. I'm not usually associated with these sophisticated *venues* and I – no – well, a lot of people have said to me, 'I'm surprised at you going to a place like that.' And it *is* a bit different from a Granada tour with Billy Fury, ha-ha, and so I thought that if I could explain how I happened to be here it might take the blame off me a bit, you understand. It might disarm criticism . . .

He followed this by striking them with a solid right hook, recalling the set of circumstances that had led up to the moment when the unfortunate mistake had been made:

Y'see, every year, they have these drama awards, the *Evening Standard* drama awards, at the Savoy. The Hotel. Well, there are so many cafés of that name now. And they have a dinner there, a sort of dinner thing, you know, and they give these drama awards away, and it's a good *do*, a very good do, and it's free, so I'm there. And, um, at the end of this evening, I'm always asked to give a little speech. You know, I give just a few jokes and things. I always give this speech every year, you know, and I always look forward to it because it's the nearest thing I get to a West End appearance these days. It's like a sort of annual pilgrimage to Mecca, ha-ha! And this particular year, y'see, I'd done my stint, my little bit, and I was standing outside afterwards in the foyer looking sort of non*cha*lant, you know, and this young lad came over to me. Quite a presentable boy, you know, quite a nice lad, quite a nice *type*. And he said, 'I was wondering if I could introduce myself – I'm Cook.' I said, 'Oh! It was a *lovely* meal.' He said, 'No, no – I'm *Peter* Cook!' I said, 'I still enjoyed the meal.' Then, of course, the penny dropped. I suddenly realised that he's that chap who runs this place, or fronts for it, or whatever it is he does. I don't know – well, I don't *pry*, I don't pry. I take the money at the end of the week and I go. After all, whatever they do is their business – I wish to God it was mine, I tell you that! Anyway, so this lad, er, Peter Cook, he said to me, 'We were all watching you tonight, all four, and we thought it was rather amusing.' So I said, 'Oooh . . .' So I unbent as well. You see – I can be gracious too when I want to be. So he said, 'I was wondering if you'd care to do a season at the Establishment.' 'Well,' I said, '*weeell*, I, er . . .' I said, 'Ah, er, *weeell*, I, ah . . .' I thought if I stuttered long enough he might mention money.

Having established himself as the humble outsider, he powered in with a thumping uppercut, and started satirising the satirists:

He had the *audacity* to say to me, this boy, Peter Cook, he said, 'Of course, you must be original, you must have a different *slant*, because after all, the last solo entertainer we had here was Lenny Bruce.' So I said, 'Ah, now, you'd better be careful, I'm sorry, no, no.' I said, 'Look – I *live* here, *I've* got nowhere to flee *to*!' And ladies and gentlemen, I must tell you this – I hope you haven't got the wrong impression, ladies and gentlemen, if you've come along here tonight expecting Lenny Bruce, I'm sorry, I'm no Lenny Bruce. And if you've come here expecting a lot of crudeness, and a lot of vulgarity, I'm sorry, but you won't get it from me, so you might just as well piss off now! Admittedly, this is the home of satire, Peter Cook has made it very clear, he's said, 'You must be *satirical*, you must have a go, *knock*, you must be *bitter*, they must leave here *angry* – otherwise they aren't satisfied! Knock the establishment!' So I said, 'Look, I've done nothing else since I've been here!' He said, '*No!* Not *this* place – the people, the Establishment, the faceless ones!' It was a battle of wits from now on. So I said, '*Whom* had you in mind?' So he said, 'The Government. Macmillan. The Establishment. The civil service.' I said, 'Make them *angry*? But these are your *audience*. These are the people who come here. You don't want to make them angry. They think it's all rather sweet! They enjoy it! It's water off a duck's back!' After all, the whole place is only a snob's *Workers' Playtime*, let's face it. Instead of making jokes about the foreman we make jokes about Harold Macmillan – it's the same thing.

He had his knockout. The audience was his. He could now do entirely what he wished.

What he chose to do next, before he slipped all the way back into his old familiar act, was to show that he really could (with the help of his writers) incorporate contemporary politics into his act. Ned Sherrin, the BBC producer who would eventually, after a number of visits, make the less-than-Kierkegaardian leap of faith to find a place for the comedian back on television, got it spot-on when he said that the approach succeeded in reducing satire 'to the level of the kitchen sink'.[44] What Howerd did, mixing Norman Evans with Johnny Speight, was to satirise the whole political process instead of just the politicians of the day, or even just the Prime Minister, Harold Macmillan:

Why *should* I make jokes about Macmillan? Tell me. Why should I make jokes about Macmillan? I don't know the man. I don't know him. I mean, it's so unfair. And it's so easy. He's such an obvious target. Everyone has a go at Macmillan. After all, he's just one man against the Government. I mean, admittedly, well, I mean, I think he's silly to himself. I'm sorry, he's silly to himself. Well, I mean, his public image – I mean, let's face it, he's no Bruce Forsyth, is he? Pity, don't you think? Pity. I think it spoils him. He might be very nice, under that moustache. But it's a pity really, it spoils him. In any case, I mean, I've had no dealings with the man. I say 'no' dealings – there *was* this little, er, *fracas* we had about the Common Market. Wherever that may be. Well, no, we had a little argument . . . Well, no, ah, I thought, go to the top man, if you want to find something out, after all, we put him in. So I thought, right – he wasn't here, he was down in Chequers. Lovely place y'know. What? Oooh, a beautiful place! 'Cos, it goes with the job, that's why he's hanging on to it, naturally. You can't blame the man. No, I was, ah, no, *liss-en*, I was – no, honestly – I was out on a cycle rally, and we're passing – it can be fun, it can be fun – and we were passing by Chequers, and I thought I'll nip in. And, I'm sorry, I told him. 'Cos I'm very forthright. I'm too stupid to be anything else to be honest! I said, 'Harold, be careful, do! Don't rush, I beg of you. Don't rush!' But, you see, I don't think he got the message. No. I don't think he got the message. Of course, it's very difficult when you're shouting through a letterbox.[45]

Having proven a point, Howerd devoted the remainder of the night to a reprise of his old act (complete with Madame Blanchie Moore at the pianoforte: *'Tis chilly! 'Tis!*) and the laughs kept on coming. 'For many,' Howerd would recall with understandable delight, 'music-hall was so remote they took it to be even more "with it" than satire!'[46] It all added up to a glorious response to every single one of the jeers and sneers and snubs he had suffered over the course of the past five years. His perform- ance on that happy night had said it all: he was *not* finished, he was *not* out of date, he was *not* all washed up, he was still the same thing that he always had been – a truly great stand-up comic.

The *London Evening Standard* was quick to confirm this fact in the first of the following day's editions. Referring to the supposed chasm between Variety and satire that some had predicted would make How- erd's season in Soho an embarrassing débâcle, the paper reported on how easily, and speedily, he had actually closed the gap: 'He is able to step comfortably across any gulf which exists between these two poles of entertainment, and he had last night's Establishment crowd laughing just as unrestrainedly as any provincial coach-party.'[47]

The doubters were left shamefaced. Nicholas Luard, for example, had been appalled when his Establishment co-owner Peter Cook first expressed an interest in hiring Howerd, and had dismissed him as a mere 'pier-end comedian', but after that first night, and indeed throughout the rest of the triumphant run, he was more than happy to sing Howerd's praises (and celebrate the takings).[48] The critics were similarly quick to hold up two thumbs, and Howerd was sufficiently gracious not to respond with a thrust of two fingers.

The fans and friends, on the other hand, were left feeling vindicated. Kenneth Williams, for example, wrote of Howerd in his diary that night: 'He was v. good, but his performance was marred by an awful woman who kept shouting and interrupting him. I must say he bore it all with great good humour.'[49] The truth was that the real culprit, when it came to interruptions, had been none other than Williams him-self with his extraordinarily loud and unmistakeably nasal laugh – WILLIAMS: 'Nnnnnaaahha-ha-ha-ha-ha!' HOWERD: 'Ooh, Gawd help us!' WILLIAMS: '*Nnnnnnnaaaaahha-ha-ha-ha-ha-ha! Heeeeeen-neeeaahheeeeeeah!*' HOWERD: 'Ladies and Gentle-*men*, I want you to watch this, it's very rare – one comedian laughing at another one. And, of course, writing it all down at the same time!'[50]

Howerd was back, and so was his sense of purpose. After several increasingly unsuccessful years of experimentation and 'diversification', he had found his way back by finally accepting that stand-up was what he did best – and he seemed, at long last, to have realised that when it came to stand-up, his best was better than most of the rest.

'I think it is very dangerous to jettison one's personality,' he said as he reflected on the lessons that he had learnt from the years of darkness. 'If I go and see Jack Benny, who I admire very much, I want to see Jack Benny being Jack Benny with his meanness, his vanity and his struggle against the world. I don't want to see Jack Benny in Shakespeare or Restoration comedy.'[51] Many of Howerd's friends and colleagues had been saying precisely the same thing about *him* ever since his departure from *Variety Bandbox*, and now he appeared to understand the reasons why.

Eager to complete what he thought of as his professional rehabilitation, he first honoured an earlier commitment to appear in another pantomime (*Puss in Boots* at Coventry) with Sid James, and then started planning the months ahead with Beryl Vertue (whom he now acknowledged to be one of the 'great influences' on his professional life[52]). He was looking forward again. He had hope.

He began 1963 by accepting his customary invitation to attend the annual *Evening Standard* Drama Awards ceremony – and thus revisit the place where all of his bad luck had suddenly given way to good. He arrived at the Savoy armed with another memorised routine, but was then taken entirely by surprise when he found that the real reason why he was there was not to joke about the awards but rather to receive one himself instead.

Hearing his name called out, he rose to his feet, and, as he made his way to the front, he thought back to what his mother had said to him shortly before she died, assuring him that he would one day win an award even though she feared that she would not be around to see it.[53] Choking up, he collected the special award, read its heartfelt inscription – 'Frankie Howerd: Wit, Philosopher and Friend' – and then acknowledged the warm applause. He started talking about what his mother had said, and what he owed her, but, after struggling through the first few words, he broke down and fled the platform in tears. The applause grew even louder: those who were there knew what he had been through, and they were glad to have him back.

He would be as busy during 1963 as he had been idle in 1962. Offers, suddenly, were pouring in from television, radio, movies and the stage. He was suddenly right back in front of his old broad audience.

In March, the episode of *Comedy Playhouse*, written expressly for Howerd by Galton and Simpson, finally reached the small screen, and a year on from declaring Howerd to be box-office poison, an openly apologetic Tom Sloan opened negotiations with the duo for a full-length Frankie Howerd series. More good news followed at the start of April, when Ned Sherrin booked Howerd to appear one Saturday on what was probably the most talked-about show of the time: BBC TV's new late-night satirical weekly revue, *That Was The Week That Was*.

Hosted by the short-haired, shiny-cheeked, slippery-souled David Frost and featuring such wits and wags *du jour* as William Rushton, Lance Percival and Bernard Levin, *TW3* (to which the title was often abbreviated) was *the* show that the self-styled 'smart' people used to savour. Howerd (aided and abetted once again by Sykes, Galton and Simpson and especially, on this occasion, Johnny Speight) went on and teased the producer ('Nice man. Underneath'); mocked David Frost ('Yes. Hmm. He's the one who wears his hair backwards') and his fellow-satirists ('These days you can't be filthy unless you've got a degree'); ridiculed the more conventional pundits, such as the notori- ously austere Robin Day ('He's a strange man, isn't he? *Funny* man. Yes. Hasn't he got *cruel* glasses!'); moaned about the late slot ('I've been waiting a hell of a time here to get on. I thought I'd have to have another shave!') and then went on to do what he had already done at the Establishment, but this time for a national viewing audience, and proceeded to personalise national party politics.

Covering such topical themes as Harold Macmillan's controversial 'Night of the long knives' (when he responded to the Government's unpopularity by sacking no fewer than six members of his cabinet) and the latest budget of his Chancellor, Reginald Maudling, Howerd did not speak like a smug satirist. He did not sound like a slick opportunist. He sounded like one of the audience:

> Everyone blames Macmillan for sacking half the Government last year. You see. *Everyone* blames Macmillan. But, you see, I don't. No. *I* don't blame *him*. I blame *her*. No, I do! It's Dot. Yes, *Dot*. No. Dotty Macmillan. You can see what's happened: she's obviously got her knife into some of their wives and they've had to go, y'see. And, you see, that's where Beryl – Beryl Maudling – was so shrewd, because, I mean, she and Reg have this farm down in the country, this *smallholding*, down in the country, y'see, and so obviously what Beryl does is she brings up a few eggs, and a bit of pork, and a bit of, well, y'know, for Dot, you see, and keeps in with her.[54]

The audience loved it, and loved him. Although it was a live show, Howerd ran on, and on, and on: scheduled to do eight minutes, he kept going – ten minutes, twelve minutes, and still more minutes – clearly revelling in the spotlight, but this time no one complained. No one wanted him to stop.

'He was a revelation,' said the BBC producer (and son of Jimmy James) James Casey, because so few of the *TW3* team, and fewer still of their typical studio audience, had previously seen such a powerful, experienced and crafty old performer in action. 'Although it was very clever, a lot of the stuff [the young university-educated satirists] did was amateurish . . . But suddenly this old pro comes on, doing a *professional* performance, and they were all knocked out – and so were the viewers.'[55]

'It was a joy to see him relax and expand,' Ned Sherrin recalled. 'At the end, the battery of applause lasted so long that David Frost had to look down to check his notes to see what he was going to say next.'[56] What Frost was supposed to say next was a summary of the first editions of Sunday's papers, but he had been so engrossed watching Howerd's act that, for the first and only time, the papers had stayed unread. It had been that kind of night. It had been Howerd's night.

The following Monday – and, indeed, throughout the rest of that week – the papers were full of references to his tremendous televised success. Now there could no longer be any doubt about it: Frankie Howerd's triumphant comeback was complete.

CHAPTER 11

Musicals

Something familiar,
Something peculiar.

Just when it seemed as though Frankie Howerd had at last reconciled himself to the idea of devoting the rest of his career to stand-up comedy, someone went and asked him to star in a musical. In spite of all that he had been through, and all that he now had to lose, he found that he simply could not resist another gamble: he said yes.

The fact was that Howerd had always dreamed of being in a musical. It had never been his dearest dream – that had been about becoming a 'proper' actor – nor, of course, his most realistic dream – that had been about making a name for himself as a comedian – but, none the less, it had always been one of those dreams that had kept circling around inside his head.

He had grown up enchanted by the crisply choreographed and beautifully scored dance routines of Fred Astaire and Ginger Rogers and the sublime black-and-white glamour of the movies they made in the studios at RKO, and, like his mother, he had also adored all of the great West End show tunes from the same era. Although most of his childhood idols had been comedians, a few had been stylish song-and-dance men, like the British-born Hollywood star Jack Buchanan, and, as improbable as it seems, the stooping, stammering, hopelessly uncoordinated Howerd would never quite grow out of this early perception of himself as a potential new hoofer and crooner.

The delusion never failed to amuse his writer friends, who could see how strikingly ill-suited he was, in every sense, to that particular area of the profession. One problem was that Howerd, as Alan Simpson recalled, was as incapable of looking stylish as Fred Astaire was of seeming scruffy:

One thing that Frank had in common with Tony Hancock was the fact that they were two of the worst dressers I've ever come across in my life. Both of them were slobs. Frank could put a brand-new suit on, and within half an hour it looked like it had been worn non-stop for two weeks. Shocking. His stage suits were appalling, too, and he used to pick all of these weird colours, like tan and light blue, and they were all made out of material like *gabardine*. Oh, he was hopeless![1]

Another problem was that, as Ray Galton observed, Howerd was as ungainly as his idols were graceful: 'Frank was a terrible mover. He couldn't move more than a couple of inches at a time without bumping into something, tripping himself up or knocking something over. He was very, very clumsy.'[2] (It was true: once, when he was on holiday in the Canary Islands, the accident-prone comedian somehow managed to fall over the edge of his hotel balcony while leaning out to take in the view.)

A third problem was that Howerd possessed the kind of singing voice that could transform any song into an insult to the ear. A novelty such as 'Three Little Fishes' was one thing – Cole Porter was quite another.

The implausible dream, however, lived on. Eric Sykes was one of many well-meaning friends who tried to burst this particular bubble:

Frank once told me, in all seriousness, that he wanted to be another Jack Buchanan! *Another Jack Buchanan!* And I said, 'Frank: Jack Buchanan is probably eating his heart out because he can't be like Frankie Howerd!' He wouldn't have it. I remember him asking me to write something for a show he was doing in the theatre during the 1960s, but he said, 'I want this one to be more *sophisticated*.' Well, I realised what he was getting at, so I said no. But somebody else did it for him, and there was one routine where he had about eight boy dancers with him on the stage, and he was in the middle of them, and they were all in top hats, white ties and tails and holding fancy canes, and they did a 'sophisticated' dance! And Frank was trying – really trying quite seriously – to do it the same as they were! Well, of course, the audience were laughing. Laughing when he hadn't *expected* them to be laughing. It was *embarrassing*! It was like watching a fella with one leg enter the marathon.[3]

When it came to musicals, therefore, Howerd seemed fated to remain a misfit. Fortunately for him, however, there would prove to be one great exception to the rule – and it was this one that Howerd was offered.

A Funny Thing Happened On The Way To The Forum was an audacious and unconventional musical farce that had opened on Broadway in May 1962 and gone on to win rave reviews, innumerable awards and a fortune at the box-office. Based very loosely on aspects of the twenty-six surviving plays (and, in particular, the three texts *The Haunted House*, *Pseudolus* and *Casino*) of the third-century BC Roman playwright Titus Maccius Plautus, and featuring a libretto by Burt Shevelove and Larry Gelbart and a score by Stephen Sondheim, it had at its centre a character – Prologus, the vain actor-narrator, and his on-stage alter-ego, Pseudo-lus, the crafty slave – who was custom-made for a distinctive and experienced comedy actor.

Intended, originally, for the inspired comedic spirit behind Sergeant Bilko, Phil Silvers (who rejected it because of the complexity of the script), and then offered to the far more limited but very experienced old vaudevillian Milton Berle (who dropped out following a disagreement about the rewrites), the role had eventually been brought to life by Zero Mostel (a big, broad, bug-eyed comic actor who had recently clawed back his show-business career after spending the best part of the previous decade languishing on an anti-communist blacklist). Right from the start, when he first read through the script, Mostel had recognised the richness of the comic material.

Plautus – even when left ancient and untouched – was a relatively serviceable author of gags for the smart comic artist (e.g.: FIRST CITI-ZEN: 'How is your wife?' SECOND CITIZEN: [*sighs*] 'Immortal!'), but once both his words and situations had been updated and upgraded by Shevelove (a shrewd and relatively well-read writer and director) and Gelbart (an experienced comedy scriptwriter who would later find even greater fame as the creator, head writer and occasional director of the celebrated sitcom *M*A*S*H*), the lines seemed designed to suit the best kind of contemporary comic persona.

The basic two-act story developed as follows: when Pseudolus, a slave who will do almost anything to gain his freedom, is left in charge of his owner's young son, Hero (who has fallen madly in love with a beautiful courtesan called Philia), the action really begins. The young man promises Pseudolus his freedom if he can arrange a marriage before his father returns. Pseudolus, of course, agrees – but fails to foresee what a tangled web he is about to weave.

Punctuated by Sondheim's muscularly upbeat songs, adorned with clever sets and a fair amount of semi-bare female flesh, and driven on by Mostel's manic mugging, the play proved as crowd-pleasing as its opening number had predicted: 'Something that's gaudy, something that's bawdy, something for everybawdy: a comedy tonight!' It went on to accumulate, among other things, a cluster of prestigious Tony Awards (for Best Musical, Best Producer, Best Book, Best Director, Best Actor and Best Supporting Actor), and established itself as one of those shows that every keen theatregoer felt obliged to see.

Among the many people who did see it early on in its Broadway run during the summer of 1962 was the British comedian and writer Marty Feldman. Impressed by what he had witnessed, he called Howerd in London the following day, telling him excitedly that Mostel's role would be a perfect vehicle for him. 'Chance would be a fine thing,' Howerd had grumbled, and then thought no more about it.[4]

When, however, plans were announced to stage a second production in London, John Gielgud – who was working in New York at the time – sought out two of the men who were set to present it – Richard Pilbrow and Hal Prince – and recommended Frankie Howerd for the leading role. Howerd, who had just triumphed at the Establishment and on *TW3*, was currently appearing in *Puss in Boots* at the New Theatre, Coventry, so arrangements were made for Burt Shevelove and Larry Gelbart (both of whom had just flown over to England) to pay a visit to the pantomime and assess this potential Pseudolus.

Not only did the pair of them love their first experience of English pantomime, they also adored the performance by Frankie Howerd. When they met him afterwards backstage, they offered him the role of Pseudolus there and then. Howerd would later say that he had been so surprised and delighted that he 'nearly broke down in front of them'.[5] He really was going to star in a musical.

Following a busy beginning to 1963, he finally managed, in May, to fly off to New York and see for himself what was so special about the Broadway production. The cast knew that he was coming, and, according to the press, took exception to his unsmiling presence in the front row:

> [Howerd] cupped a hand over his mouth, as is his custom, and chuckled. But Mr Mostel, closely scrutinizing Mr Howerd, suspected that the visitor was not enjoying himself.
>
> 'He is not laughing,' Mr Mostel complained to colleagues in the wings between numbers. He had to be consoled with the explanation that the ostensible deadpan expression was probably due to Mr Howerd's preoccupation with details of the performance.[6]

Howerd (whom the New York media described as a 'British music-hall and pantomime artist') had to move quickly to defuse the embarrassing situation: 'I'm not a laugher,' he explained to reporters. 'I don't lean back and flash my teeth. Actually,' he added, 'if anyone was frightened that night it was me, seeing how good Mostel was.'[7] He then shook hands with the star of the show for the benefit of the cameras. Once this misunderstanding had been corrected, the rest of his trip, and his dealings with Mostel and Co., went without a hitch.

He learned his lines between performances for his summer season in Jersey. There were plenty of potential distractions (such as the night when Brian Epstein and The Beatles – all of whom, it transpired, were big fans – flew over to take in one of his shows and then join him for a party), but he managed to husband his time and his energy very well, working assiduously throughout the summer (with the assistance of Dennis Heymer and Sunny Rogers) at mastering the contrapuntal singing technique that he knew he would need for Sondheim's score.

Proper rehearsals were scheduled to start back in London at the end of August under the direction of the legendary George Abbott, and Howerd was determined to be ready. Abbott's intimidating reputation had preceded his arrival in England: a sprightly 76-year-old (he would live on to be 107), Abbott was the doyen of America's theatre directors, and was always addressed deferentially as 'Mr Abbott' (never 'George') even by the biggest stars and impresarios of the day. He was a tall, thin and austere New Yorker who issued instructions rather than offered advice, said little or nothing to those who lived up to his high expectations but reacted with ruthlessness to anyone who appeared to have fallen short.

Howerd was terrified of Abbott long before he had even met him, and was no less terrified after the first read-through in his presence. 'That's fine for the start,' the director announced unsmilingly, 'now we'll do it properly.'[8] As Abbott declined to elaborate on what else was required to do it 'properly', Howerd was left feeling terribly perplexed and inadequate about a part that would see him on stage for all but three minutes of the show's two-and-a-half hours. The next few days of rehearsal proved similarly tense and unfulfilling: Abbott would leave his assistant in charge of the morning sessions while he played a round or two of golf, then he would come in at 2 p.m., stare impassively for a couple of hours, and then make the odd gnomic remark before heading off to prepare for a leisurely dinner at The Ivy.

Howerd remained convinced that Abbott hated him until another member of the cast, Isla Blair (who was set to play the virgin Philia), revealed that the director had been singing his praises over supper. The news, though surprising, calmed him down and lifted his spirits, making the remainder of the rehearsal period far more enjoyable for all concerned.

Apart from Howerd himself, the cast included such artful comic actors as Jon Pertwee (in the role of Lycus, a dealer in courtesans) and Kenneth Connor (as the slave Hysterium), as well as two of British comedy's drollest personalities: Robertson 'Oh Calamity!' Hare (the diminutive Aldwych *farceur* with the voice of a tweaked oboe) and 'Monsewer' Eddie Gray (the anarchistic old vaudevillian who was notorious for his peculiar brand of pranks and practical jokes – which for some reason during this particular run included several attempts to butter the top of Robertson Hare's bald head). Abbott had not known a bunch quite like them, but, once he realised that there was no hope of denying their wild variety, he made the most of each little quirk.

The pre-London run got off to a hesitant start in Oxford, with Howerd 'drying up' in the middle of his opening song and then stumbling through a couple of his later routines. It did nothing to improve matters when George Abbott took him to one side the following morning, smacked him on his bad back and said: 'You know, if you could get rid of those music-hall mannerisms, you'd make quite a musical comedy star.'[9] By the time the tour reached Manchester, however,

Howerd was more or less word-perfect and in control, and the production as a whole was playing to warm applause. At the end of September, the company headed back to London feeling hopeful of West End success.

A charity performance, in the presence of Princess Margaret and Lord Snowdon, went ahead without any problems, but after it was over and the various VIP guests had left, Abbott called all of the actors on to the stage and declared: 'You've all worked very hard, but I think you'll get controversial notices. Half the press will like it, the other half will hate it.' Then he stunned the cast by adding matter-of-factly: 'I'm off to America now.'[10] That was indeed the last they would see of their distinguished director; he hopped straight on to the next available flight, leaving the cast to face their first-night nerves without him.

Howerd, in particular, was far from pleased about the abandonment, because he knew that his first-night nerves would be jangling long before the curtain went up. The intensive pre-publicity had made him anxious, and the painful memory of what had happened to *Mr Venus* was now making him panic. This time, he realised, it all simply *had* to go right. 'I had more than a first night at stake,' he would say. 'I had my personal life and my career in my hands.'[11]

When the opening night arrived, on Thursday 3 October 1963 at the Strand Theatre, Howerd, sure enough, was in a terrible state backstage. With less than an hour still to go, a huge pile of 'good luck' cards, letters and telegrams remained unopened in his dressing-room – because, he reasoned, the repetition of kind words would only have added 'to the burden of responsibility'[12] – and a couple of large brandies had been downed. As the doors were knocked and the cast began to assemble, his heart began to pound.

When the curtain went up, there was one toga but no slips: his mouth was a little dry, his voice a little forced and the perspiration was already beginning to trickle down his skin, but the words flowed, and the laughs followed – and the show was up and running. After the curtain closed again, however, he froze for a few seconds, paralysed by a combination of terror and cramp, before re-emerging (thanks to a shove from one of the three actors who were due to join him as a trio of eunuchs) for the next bit of business. From that moment on he was fine. This time, it all *did* go right.

At the end – 'Morals tomorrow. Comedy tonight!' – there was a thunderous ovation for the show, and then a separate one for Howerd's performance. He was overcome by the reaction, and left the stage in tears.

Back in his dressing-room, he locked the door for ten minutes, still feeling too emotional to welcome any visitors, and, as he draped a towel around his neck, he breathed a deep sigh of relief. Later on, after Betty and Dennis had arrived, the champagne was uncorked, and Howerd started opening some of his 'good luck' letters and telegrams. Among the first that he read was a real oddity: a TWA in-flight menu, which had been hand-delivered to the theatre by someone from the airline office, bearing a message that George Abbott had scribbled as he flew across the Atlantic − '*All the best. Thank you. George A*'.[13] It might not have seemed much, on the surface, but he had called himself 'George'. It meant a great deal to Howerd.

Abbott's prediction that the production would polarise critical opinion turned out to have been wrong, because the vast majority of the first-night reviews were fulsome in their praise of both the show and its star. Milton Shulman, writing in the *London Evening Standard*, declared that Howerd had been 'deliciously funny': 'Whether he is playing noughts and crosses on the midriff of a statuesque brunette or announcing his powers as a soothsayer ("Silence! I am about to say the sooth!"), there is a mad anarchy about his activities which are never less than hilarious.'[14]

Only Clive Barnes, among the most notable critics, expressed any real reservations about Howerd's contribution, saying that this 'wonderfully stylish comedian' had been hampered by a role that had seemed tailor-made for Zero Mostel but which fitted him 'like a second-hand suit of clothes'. Even Barnes, however, gushed about how much he had loved the show as a whole, calling it 'the funniest, the wittiest, the most resourceful, the bawdiest, the most boisterous and, yes, since we are ladling out the superlatives, the best musical to be seen in London for years'.[15]

Howerd was called at 11 a.m. the following morning to be told the good news that, even before any of the reviews had been widely read, reports of his success had spread sufficiently fast and far via word-of-mouth to cause the ticket agencies to strike a deal worth £40,000, thus guaranteeing the production a run of at least twenty weeks. Speaking to reporters later the same day, he admitted that he had been scared ('I had my fingers crossed all the two-and-a-half hours I was on stage that my nerves wouldn't let me down'), and acknowledged that the reaction he received at the end had been beyond his wildest dreams ('The tremendous personal ovation I got was too much – I just broke down'). He added, however, that his strongest feelings, the morning after, were of relief for his closest friends and family rather than elation for himself: 'People like my sister Betty deserve the medals. They were dying for me, but they were powerless.'[16]

Before leaving to walk his latest dog – a cairn terrier called Bunty – around some of the quieter streets near his London home, he vowed that he would not allow all of the praise to swell his head. Admitting that he had 'dashed' through a couple of his songs the previous evening – 'it was sheer nerves' – he said that he was ready now to try to make his music more effective in order to complement his comedy: 'I'm no Caruso,' he acknowledged, 'but I have got a good musical ear.' He would keep improving, he promised, and so would the show.[17]

Both of them did. *A Funny Thing . . .* went on to become almost as big a hit in the West End as it had been (and still was) on Broadway, running all the way through to the summer of 1965. Howerd would stay on as its star for no fewer than 21 months, winning along the way a Critics' Award for Best Musical Actor and an increased amount of international recognition, as well as a new generation of fans.

His extended spell on the stage did not prevent him, however, from also maintaining a high profile elsewhere. There was another six-part BBC radio series, *Now Listen*, in the autumn of 1964, followed on 18 October by an especially memorable return to television with what constituted the third and last part of his unofficial but brilliant trilogy of 'political' stand-up routines, *A Last Word on the Election*.

Using a script made up of ideas and lines that Howerd (the supreme comedy magpie) had gathered from a quite extraordinary roster of talented writers – the long list of official and unofficial contributors included Galton and Simpson (who were responsible for the core of it), Dennis Potter, Johnny Speight, Eric Sykes, Frank Muir and Denis Norden, David Nathan, Barry Took and Marty Feldman – he treated his late-night audience to another twenty-five-minute masterclass on the art of stand-up comedy.

First came the trademark preamble:

Ah, Ladies and Gentle-*men*, um, as you know, I've been asked to do this political commentary, and, ah, I must say, being political, I'm sure a lot of you are saying to yourselves: 'What the bleedin' hell does *he* know about it?' I'm sure a lot of you are saying that. I know I am for a start! No, I'll tell you how it happened. You see, I was sitting at home, and suddenly there was a knock on the wall, and it was the woman next door. So I put my head out the window and she put her head out of her window, and she said, 'You're wanted on the telephone.' Because, well, she's the only person in the street who has a telephone – and *that's* because she's in Civil Defence. She said, 'You're wanted.' So I went round there, y'see, and she said, 'It's the BBC who's on the phone.' So I thought to meself, '*BBC?*' So I said, 'Er, I wonder what *they* want?' She says, 'Well, actually, they want you to do a summing-up of the General Election.' So I said, 'I-*ah*-well-*er*-well, I know nothing about that!' She said, 'That's what *I* told 'em!' So I thought, 'Right, mate – that's the last time you'll get me on *your* stretcher!' So, anyway . . .[18]

He followed this by launching into the overtly political material, taking pot-shots at all three party leaders of the day: first, Jo Grimond of the Liberals – 'the sex kitten of politics'; then, the former Conservative Prime Minister, Sir Alec Douglas-Home – 'Of course, it's partly his own fault, I think, Alec. Oh, yes. I think he's silly to himself. I'll tell you why: it was going round, all this talking, and he *would* bring *politics* into it . . . But he's very upset. In fact, when he gets back to Scotland, God help the partridges!'; and then, of course, the victorious new Labour Prime Minister, Harold Wilson – 'All this business about adultery on the Labour front bench! That was all nonsense, of course – it's uncomfortable enough to sit there, let alone . . .'

He went on to cover everything from persistent canvassers ('I had one man here, he would not go! He was *determined* to sway me – he did my washing for three weeks for nothing!') to ubiquitous television pundits ('Robin Day was very good, I thought. You know, he kept his temper. Just. Well, you know, I suppose when the pills start to wear off, you get a bit . . .') with plenty of sideswipes at other political figures along the way. It was one of his most precise, assured and relaxed small-screen performances (even his voice, hardened by all of those daily on-stage exertions, sounded stronger and sharper than usual), and the combination of the high quality of the material (a good deal of which had been written in the two days that separated the day of the election and that of the transmission) and the novelty – for the time – of the irreverence made the programme such an unprecedented success that a recording was released subsequently in the form of a special 'extended play' single.[19]

After this – again in tandem with the West End run of *A Funny Thing . . .* – Howerd began a major new, eponymously titled, BBC peak-time television series – written by Galton and Simpson – at the end of the year. It was hard work for Howerd (who had to appear on stage every Monday through to Saturday, learning Galton and Simpson's new scripts between performances, and then rehearse and record in the studio every Sunday) but it was well worth it. Everything about *The Frankie Howerd Show*, from the classy direction from Duncan Wood to the composition of the supporting cast (which included such reliable character actors as Patrick Cargill, Frank Thornton, Hugh Paddick and Julian Orchard), underlined the exceptional quality at its heart: the best stand-up comedian in Britain at his most artful and self-confident, and the best pair of comedy writers in Britain at their most playful and slyly mischievous.

Running for six weeks, from 11 December 1964 to 15 January, the series not only managed to strike a reasonably happy medium between stand-up and sketches, but it also seized the opportunity to take revenge on all of those old doubters within the BBC ('*Frankie Howerd?* He's finished!') by returning, again and again and again, to that comically shady executive presence, 'Thing' (a measure of Tom Sloan mixed with a dash or two of irascible radio producer) – at the end of the opening episode, for example, Howerd asked the viewing audience to be sure to deliver a favourable verdict 'so that old "Thing" can have his extra six inches of carpet'.

Viewers, according to the BBC's own audience research reports, were 'delighted to welcome Frankie Howerd back to their screens', as 'far too little had been seen of this "engaging" comedian in recent years'. There was a particularly positive reaction to the way that his opening and closing monologues had dominated the show, and 'it was widely felt that his new scriptwriters – Galton and Simpson – had provided him with material that "suited him to a T"'.[20]

Another, arguably even more impressive series, would follow two years later, exhibiting the same fine style and strengths, attracting the same high ratings and winning the same warm reviews.[21] 'I think,' Ray Galton reflected, 'that those two series were the best thing we'd ever written for Frank. To be honest, I think they were among the best things that he would ever do on television.'[22]

Throughout this time, Howerd continued to earn the admiration and applause of those who saw him in the theatre in the West End, striding about the stage – and, subtly but increasingly significantly, ad-libbing as he did so – in the guise of either Prologus or Pseudolus. Contrary to Clive Barnes' initial cavils, Howerd proved, in the long run, far more flexible and sophisticated than Zero Mostel when it came to exploiting the potential both within and between the two roles for treating the characters and the context with a refreshing degree of self-mockery. Where Mostel tended to highlight the fragility and vanity of his on-stage persona with the theatrical equivalent of a brusque poke in the ribs and an abrupt bark in the ear, Howerd simply cleared his throat, raised an eyebrow and emitted a quick 'um', 'ah' or 'oooh' and everybody got the point.

When he finally left the show, at the start of July 1965, he did so as a *bona fide* musical-comedy star. He was still no Jack Buchanan, of course, and he knew it, but he had certainly further enhanced his reputation as Frankie Howerd, and, in his own crafty way, he had proven a point.

He had also greatly improved his financial situation. After the end of the run of *A Funny Thing . . .*, he and Dennis Heymer moved into an elegant four-storey Georgian house (found for them by Betty) at 27 Edwardes Square in Kensington, which they (or, rather, Dennis) went on to fill with expensive Persian carpets, fancy flock wallpaper, Roman columns, various Egyptian *objets d'art*, antique tables, deep settees and a set of tiny vases Howerd had inherited from his mother. Later on in the decade, an idyllic holiday home – based on a clifftop near Valetta in Malta – would be added, and named, in grateful memory of the show that helped buy it, 'The Forum'. It all seemed a long way from the dark days of Scruffy Dale.

There was no rush, however, to return to the West End. Howerd had struggled at times during the recent long run, requiring treatment at one stage for anaemia, sleeping difficulties and 'mental exhaustion' (his doctor had warned the BBC that without at least a brief break from his radio and television work, 'he will be forced to take a prolonged rest due to severe nervous exhaustion'[23]), so he preferred, in the short term, to treat himself to a little more harmless diversification.

There was a trip in August 1965 to entertain British servicemen stationed in Borneo with another one of his motley troupes (which on this occasion consisted of Sunny Rogers, zither player Shirley Abicair, singer Mary Murphy and a magician called Al Koran). A BBC film crew accompanied him on the month-long tour, recording material for a documentary, *East of Howerd*, to be screened on BBC 2 at the start of the following year.

There was also, in 1966, a minor role in a musical version of Oscar Wilde's *The Canterville Ghost*, which had been adapted for American television by Burt Shevelove and the duo responsible for the score of *Fiddler on the Roof*, Sheldon Harnick and Jerry Bock. It proved even less substantial than the spectral Sir Simon of Wilde's short story, but the episode left Howerd unscathed.

He decided, at last, to take a short vacation, and so, in the company of Dennis and Betty, he went on a leisurely trip across America, taking in New York, Las Vegas, Los Angeles, and then down to Acapulco and Mexico City. He felt tired but relatively contented: his career was in a better state than it had been for years, his self-confidence was higher than normal and, as he put it, he 'had a few pounds in the bank again'.[24]

On his return to Britain, his attention would turn to the one medium he had yet to conquer: the movies. It represented another challenge he found hard to resist.

CHAPTER 12

Movies

May I have the first slide, please?

Towards the end of 1965, Frank Launder, the very experienced British screenwriter, producer and director, asked Frankie Howerd to play the lead in a movie that he and his regular partner Sidney Gilliat were about to make: *The Great St Trinian's Train Robbery*. This time, Howerd felt, he did not have too much to lose: so, once again, he said yes.

Compared to his earlier, undeniably bold move into the realm of musical comedy, his return visit to the world of movies represented only a relatively modest kind of gamble. If it led to further success, all well and good: it would be a bonus. If, on the other hand, it resulted in him experiencing a certain measure of failure, there would surely be no real cause to feel any great shame: after all, plenty of significant stand-up comedians before Frankie Howerd – including Jack Benny, Henny Youngman and Fred Allen – had suffered setbacks when they tried to make the transition to the big screen. They survived – in fact, their failure served merely to add to their fund of comic material (the disappointment of *The Horn Blows at Midnight*, for example, helped keep some of Jack Benny's team of writers in work for years[1]) – so Howerd could expect to survive as well.

The only real puzzle was why he felt any strong need any longer to bother. He had been drifting in and out of the medium for more than a decade, but had never come close to matching his impact on the stage, radio or television.

He had been in, but then all but edited out of, one or two genuinely good movies. His part in *The Ladykillers*, for example, had promised much, and made the director Alexander Mackendrick laugh, but then certain other factors had intervened. 'Because the film was too long,'

Howerd explained, 'a lot of my part was cut down because it really had nothing to do with the film. They cut out the middle but left the beginning and end. It was almost sad to see what was left.'[2]

He had also been in, and, alas, been kept in, more than a few low-budget mediocrities. *A Touch of the Sun*, for example, saw Howerd act embarrassingly badly opposite a supposed 'love interest' – Dorothy Bromiley – who acted even worse, exuding all of the warmth and unforced sincerity of a woman languishing in an ancient commercial for powdered gravy.

He had also been in *The Cool Mikado* – and *that* had been a movie bad enough to make the most ardent moviegoer contemplate staying at home in future and sitting, head in hands, beside the radio. Apart from Howerd's involvement as Ko-Ko, the production also featured Stubby Kaye as the Judge Mikado ('Who *is* dis guy "Ko-Ko"? Dat sure is a strange-sounding name!'), Lionel Blair as Nanki, a brief cameo from Tommy Cooper (as Pooh-Bah, 'Private Detective') and a painfully over-long contribution from the joyless sibling double-act of Mike and Bernie Winters (cast in the challenging roles, respectively, of 'Mike' and 'Bernie'). Even Howerd's desperate last-minute enlistment of Lew Schwartz, one of his friends from ALS, to provide him with some gags failed to save his blushes (the best, or least-worse, that Schwartz could come up with, in the time available, was the following response to a waiter's admission that his restaurant did not have wild duck as a dish on its menu: 'Well, bring me a tame one and I'll aggravate it!').

The reason why Howerd not only started working in movies but also, in spite of so many disappointments, kept working in them was the example that had been set by another former resident of Eltham: Bob Hope. Howerd knew that Hope had struggled through several unsuitable movie vehicles (including chaotic revues – such as *The Big Broadcast of 1938* – and 'zany' musicals – such as *College Swing*) before coming up with a format that complemented his stand-up comedy style. Howerd was driven on by the belief that, one day, he might do the same.

It had been Hope's breakthrough movie – *The Cat and the Canary*, released in 1939 – that Howerd had tried to use as a template when planning his debut in the medium. This delightfully deft mixture of 1930s comedy, horror and thriller genres, cleverly lit in a shadowy style heavily influenced by German Expressionism, placed Hope in a context in which he could crack all of his countless one-liners ('Don't big empty houses scare you?' someone asks him. 'Not me,' he snaps straight back. 'I used to be in vaudeville') while driving the story on. After the success of this production, therefore, Hope had a format, and a persona (the likeable coward), that his huge team of writers (eight of them full-time, and five more of them part-time) could sustain from one movie to the next.

Howerd had seen *The Cat and the Canary* when he was in the Army, and had dreamed of appearing one day in something similar: a good comedy thriller, with a strong story and a funny character at its centre. When, therefore, he came to form a friendship with the screenwriter and director Val Guest in the early 1950s, there was a certain inevitability about their decision, once they had agreed to work together, to attempt something in this particular genre.

The result, *The Runaway Bus*, was a kind of cross between a cut-price version of *The Cat and the Canary* and a very half-hearted reworking of *The Ghost Train* (which Guest had already adapted for Arthur Askey back in 1941). Howerd played a relief driver called Percy Lamb, who, one dark and foggy night, finds himself obliged to transport half a dozen curious characters (who included Petula Clark as a no-nonsense stewardess, Margaret Rutherford as a bossy old woman and George Colouris as a shifty-looking gentleman with a foreign-sounding name) from London to Blackbush airport. Once he has set off, Lamb is informed via his radio that a stolen shipment of gold bullion has been stashed at the back of his bus, and the culprit (known to police only as 'The Banker') is probably one of the people with him on board. After running off the road, hitting a tree and falling into a stream, he and his passengers are forced to decamp to a deserted farmhouse, where the tension begins to mount.

Made on a very low budget (£45,000) and shot to a frantic schedule (under five weeks), it was all very slight and mechanical, but Howerd was actually quite competent in a role that required him to do little more than flit back and forth between expressions of surprise, fear, confusion and irritation. Probably his best and most relaxed moment came about, tellingly, by accident. On the last day of shooting, it was discovered that the movie's running time was only going to be seventy-two minutes − three minutes short of the minimum length, in those days, to qualify a movie as a 'feature' − so, rather than fill up the extra time with extended shots of fog, Howerd suggested improvising an additional scene. It was, in truth, just a sly variation on his stage routine with his deaf accompanist, except that on this occasion he was on his own in a cramped little telephone box shouting down to the other end of the line, but, when it was slipped into the final cut of the movie (about fourteen minutes in), it worked rather better than the scripted material:

Hello, Gran? Gran? *Grandma?* I can't hear a word you're saying, dear! – Ooh, I bet she's got her shawl in her mouth! – That's better. Yes. Gran – ah! – look, let *me* do the talking, dear, 'cause this is costing me money. I said *IT'S COSTING ME MONEY!* Now, look: I won't be home till late. 'Cause I'm going out on a job. Yeah. A *JOB*, dear! *Work!* You know – what Grandpa never did! Oooh! There's a cottage pie in the oven. *A COTTAGE PIE!* Oh, whatever's come over her! *CAN YOU HEAR ME NOW?* [*A man taps on the window with his coin, Percy turns to see him, mutters an acknowledgement and then turns back again*] Look, dear, don't wait up for me because I'm going to be late. No, ah, I'm not going out with a girl. I'm going out with a coach. Oh! *A COACH.* You know: a big thing on four wheels. No, not the girl! [*Another tap by the man*] Look, I must go now, dear, there's a woodpecker tapping at the window. Yes. All right. Yes, ta-ta, dear. Well, keep warm, yes – or get into the oven with the cottage pie! *Yes!* Ha-ha! [*Hangs up*] Ooh![3]

When it was released, in February 1954, the reviews were generally favourable, and Howerd received a fair amount of praise. *Picturegoer*, for example, judged that there was enough to admire in Howerd's debut performance to entitle the magazine to declare that 'Howerd the film comic has definitely arrived'.[4] Most critics, however, were far more circumspect in their estimation of his big-screen potential. *Monthly Film Bulletin*, in particular, felt that Howerd had failed 'to bring to the cinema those qualities which have made him so successful on the radio and in the music-hall, and relies on mannerisms and grimaces which, though often quite funny, are not sufficient to sustain a film'.[5]

Nothing that Howerd did during the next ten years would threaten to seriously advance his movie career. No matter what he achieved in

radio, on television or in the theatre, his chances of progressing beyond
The Runaway Bus remained slim.

He seemed, for a while, to have reconciled himself to his fate.
Although he continued to envy the size of the movie stars' international
audience, he preferred to stress the greater control that he had as a
stand-up comedian in the theatre.

When he did stand-up in the theatre, he explained, he might not be
his own writer, but he was certainly his own editor and director: once
he had his script, he was self-contained and self-assured; he was in
control. It was different, he acknowledged, when he worked in radio
and television; the broad audience was absent, the immediate impact
impossible to gauge, and the art was harder to protect. Television, of
the two, was especially frustrating, because the director 'can cut your
performance and light it in particular ways': 'You have to do what
you're told.'[6]

Movies, however, were by far the most frustrating medium, for the
stand-up comedian, of all:

> Films are even more technical. The camera moves there, the
> cameraman lights the scene, you rehearse, the area is lit again. You
> work from marks on the floor and you move from one mark to
> another. They may be chalk marks or bits of wood stuck in the
> floor and you're told exactly where to go, what to look at, and
> where to look in terms of camera technique. So you're much more
> like a puppet in film.[7]

The technical restrictions were not the only aspect of the medium that
Howerd found discouraging; he was also uneasy about the way that
each performance closed up as soon as it was shot. 'Once they're done,'
he lamented, 'you can't do it again. The films appear and that's it. But
if you do a stage show and it's not right one night, I've got a chance
to correct it on another night.'[8]

In the mid-sixties, however, after proving so many people wrong
about so many different things, he was ready to take on the medium
one more time. Offers were now coming in on a fairly regular basis,
and some of them struck him as worth pursuing.

Two of the first projects to intrigue him, however, ended up in disappointment. Both could so easily have worked, but, for one reason or another, neither did.

The first project, early in 1965, was a new movie directed by Richard Lester and featuring The Beatles. Called, provisionally, *Eight Arms To Hold You*, Howerd was cast in the role of Sam Ahab, an irascible and pretentious drama teacher who attempts to give John, Paul, George and Ringo some acting lessons.

Howerd felt that he was among friends – or at least well-intentioned acquaintances. He had worked with Lester before, briefly, when he wandered in and out of a scene in the gentle satire *The Mouse on the Moon* (1963), and they had made each other laugh. He enjoyed a similar rapport with all four members of The Beatles, having socialised with them on several occasions since that first meeting during his summer season in Jersey, and he was hopeful that the 'chemistry' they seemed to share would show up on the screen.[9]

Work on Howerd's ten-minute sequence began at Twickenham Studios on 22 April 1965. Set in 'The Sam Ahab School of Transcendental Elocution', the scene saw Ahab proceed to lecture the four men – and a young woman known only as 'Lady Macbeth' (played by Wendy Richard) – on the art of 'transcending' (as he prefers to call acting), urging them to prepare by having a quick 'limber and lope' before each one of them commences a brief recitation from Shakespeare. The session is interrupted, however, when several members of a mystical Asian cult emerge from a fireplace, put everyone in a trance and then attempt to steal one of Ringo's rings.[10]

Howerd said of the plot at the time, 'I couldn't make head or tail of it,' but he enjoyed his two days on the set, and looked forward to the international exposure the movie – which by this time had been retitled *Help!* – was certain to bring him. During the editing phase, however, he received a call from an embarrassed-sounding representative of Dick Lester: as the first cut looked as if it was going to be far too long, he explained, it had been decided that all ten minutes of Howerd's scene would have to be dropped. *Help!* thus went ahead without Frankie Howerd.

The second disappointment also involved Lester as the director: the Hollywood movie version of *A Funny Thing Happened On The Way To The Forum* (1966). There had been plenty of rumours on both sides of the Atlantic concerning which members of which cast had a chance of reprising their roles on the big screen, and Howerd's had been one of those in circulation. Agents, publicists, producers and reporters all contributed to the general sense of intrigue that ran throughout 1964 and then on into the first part of 1965, but, slowly and somewhat unsurely, certain names emerged from the gossip either as strong possibilities or even, in one or two special cases, near-certainties.

Although a fair proportion of the Hollywood cast ended up being drawn from British television and theatre (including, from the West End production itself, Jon Pertwee, but also, from elsewhere, Michael Crawford, Roy Kinnear and Alfie Bass), Frankie Howerd was not among them. He *had* been considered, he was assured, but not, it was admitted, for very long: 'the argument was that American audiences needed a known name,' and the name had to be American – so the leading role went to Zero Mostel.[11] Howerd's best chance of making a breakthrough into the world of high-profile, big-budget, international projects, in a role that he already knew inside out, had gone.

It was at this point that he accepted Frank Launder's offer to star in *The Great St Trinian's Train Robbery*. He recognised that, while it was hardly likely to turn him into a 'known name' in America, it at least represented a better-than-average prospect in terms of the British box-office, and, after all, it *was* a starring role.

The movie (the fourth in the *St Trinian's* series) featured Howerd as Alfred Askett, the proprietor of the Alphonse of Monte Carlo hairdressing salon and a would-be criminal mastermind. The actual plot (a train is robbed, the money is secreted in a deserted manor house, and the manor house is then taken over by St Trinian's – thus obliging Askett and his gang to come up with a way to retrieve their ill-gotten gains) did not amount to anything more than an undemanding romp, and the awkward mixture of 1950s whimsy with 1960s sauce rendered the overall tone and style an unfortunate mess, but the cast contained some watchable character actors (including Dora Bryan, George Cole, Reg Varney and Norman Mitchell) and the brisk directorial pace kept the narrative moving along. It found its intended audience – no more, no less – and finished the year as one of the top ten homegrown box-office attractions.

Just as importantly, as far as Howerd was concerned, the movie had been 'great fun to make', and had whetted his appetite for similar, but (he hoped) better, excursions in British cinema.[12] The problem was that there was so little else on offer in British cinema during the mid-1960s, and arguably next to nothing that was any better, so Howerd agreed to try a *Carry On*.

Co-produced by Gerald Thomas and Peter Rogers, the *Carry On* franchise had been running since 1958, and, after the first few character-driven class comedies, had come to represent (depending on one's perspective) either the cinematic equivalent of the old saucy seaside postcard or merely the boneyard of a once-vibrant British wit, but, none the less, they continued to find a large and very loyal domestic audience. Rogers — a staunch Howerd fan — had been hoping for some time to coax the comedian inside his closely-knit clique of regular actors (which included Sidney James, Kenneth Williams, Hattie Jacques, Charles Hawtrey, Joan Sims, Kenneth Connor and Barbara Windsor) and, in 1967, he succeeded with *Carry On Doctor*.

Cast in the leading role of Francis Bigger, a pompous fake faith healer with a damaged coccyx, Howerd's sudden intrusion into the settled little troupe served, in the beginning, to ruffle more than a few feathers as well as bruise the odd actorly ego. Neither Sid James nor Kenneth Williams, for example, was pleased to discover that the 'newcomer' was set to be paid considerably more (£7,500 for five weeks' work) than either of them could expect to receive, and Williams was even more rattled about the fact that Howerd had been handed the plum part ('It's really a v. good vehicle for Frankie Howerd,' he scribbled in his diary after reading through the script, 'but all the other parts are lousy'[13]).

There was no personal animosity aimed at Howerd himself, however, and he soon bonded with the established members of the team (especially Joan Sims, with whom he shared a 'mad chemistry'[14]). On the screen, however, he never seemed to blend in with the other characters, appearing instead to observe them like some strange kind of visitor from another world.

As a one-off 'star guest' performance, this distancing effect actually worked rather well, conforming as it did to Howerd's individualistic, and essentially reactive, style of comedy. He was able to keep stepping in and out of the *Carry On* world, glancing at the camera every now and again to register his connection with us rather than them. When, for example, he spots a nurse heading towards him holding a daffodil, he reacts with a reference to the scene in the earlier *Carry On Nurse* (in which the same type of flower ended up being planted inside the character played by Wilfrid Hyde-White): 'Oh, no, you don't!' he snarls. 'I saw that film!' A nervy ironist surrounded by contented stereotypes, his character supplied the familiar format with a welcome extra dimension.

As a bid to signal the arrival of Howerd as a long-term *Carry On* regular, however, the ploy backfired, because the rest of the ensemble were suddenly demoted to the role of a supporting cast. Repeating the conceit would not only have necessitated rewriting the lucrative formula but also replacing several disgruntled former co-stars.

Howerd did reappear in the series, three more instalments down the line, in *Carry On Up the Jungle* (1969), but he did so only as a belated replacement for Kenneth Williams (who was otherwise engaged as the host of a series on BBC 2) in a role that had been written expressly for the absent star. In spite of the odd last-minute nip and tuck, the character of the camply fastidious ornithologist Professor Inigo Tinkle never really fitted Howerd's familiar persona, and simply showed up the limited nature of his acting skills.

He enjoyed making it – in fact, he would claim that it was 'the happiest [movie] I have ever done'[15] – but it did nothing to suggest that his movie career had much of a future. Playing just another off-the-peg *Carry On* character, he was nowhere near as bad as Bernard Bresslaw's awful black-faced guide with the Welsh-Chinese-Cornish-Caribbean accent, but, apart from uttering the odd 'Howerdism' (e.g. 'My ghast has never been so flabbered!'), and parroting one or two of the gags that had been written for Williams (e.g. WOMAN: 'One would feel so much safer with a strong, fearless man beside one.' TINKLE: 'Oh, I agree – but where could we find one out here?'), he did relatively little, and looked rather lost.

His regular writers were not in the least surprised. 'Frank was not an actor,' said Eric Sykes. 'He was this wonderful, *big*, unique comic personality. He was *Frankie Howerd*. Like Tommy Cooper was always Tommy Cooper. Like Ken Dodd is always Ken Dodd. Frank was always Frankie Howerd. His talent was just too vast to hide behind another character.'[16] Ray Galton concurred: 'Let's face it: Frank was a rotten actor! He was terrible. There was no point in trying to get him to submerge himself in a role, because he couldn't do it – and there was no *need* for him to do it. It wasn't what he was good at. So when you wrote for Frankie Howerd, you wrote for a personality who was already there. You *used* it. It would have been perverse to have done otherwise.'[17]

There would be more movies, but the majority of them would be mere television spin-offs, and the big breakthrough seemed destined never to come. Even this brief flurry of cinematic activity in the mid-1960s was overshadowed by Howerd's far greater success on stage in the West End revue (written for him by Sykes and Galton and Simpson) entitled *Way Out in Piccadilly*.

Co-starring Howerd and Cilla Black, this lively mixture of stand-up, sketches and songs ran for 395 performances, from November 1966 all the way through to the end of 1967, making it one of the most popular shows of the decade. The respected writer and critic Hugh Leonard said in his review of the production that it had established Howerd ('the funniest thing since Mr Laurel and Mr Hardy') as 'a great performer; and, in the manner of old bores who drone on about the past magnificence of George Robey, Vesta Tilley and Co., anyone who goes to see Mr Howerd will find himself boasting about it fifty years hence'.[18]

The show not only won Howerd a prestigious Variety Club of Great Britain award – 'Show Business Personality of 1966' – but it also made him, ironically, one of those stage performers whom most of the major international movie stars passing through London made a point of seeking out. Richard Burton and Elizabeth Taylor, for example, descended on the Prince of Wales Theatre, along with their large entourage, to pay homage to Frankie Howerd, and then take him out for a late night on the town. 'Did anyone ever tell you,' asked Taylor, 'that you're the funniest man in the world? If they didn't, I'm telling you now!'[19] ('What a nice lady,' Howerd exclaimed. 'And so intelligent!'[20])

Such stellar encounters showed him, if he still needed to be shown, how little he really needed a movie career: what he had already achieved, what he already did, as a stand-up comedian on stage, radio and television, was recognised by his peers in other media as something genuinely rare and special. If he wanted a sideline, an occasional diversion, he could have it, but the core of his career would remain elsewhere.

ACT IV:
THE CULT

He said, 'Excuse me, are you Frankie Howerd?' I said, 'Yes.' He said, 'Dear God! I thought you were dead!' So I said, 'Ha-ha! No, I'm very much alive. And kicking – if you know what I mean!'

CHAPTER 13

Carry On, Plautus

A room full of heaving chests! Oooh!
It's very nice to look at!

Frankie Howerd's next trick was to perfect a technique that one critic would dub the 'Argyll Street alienation-effect'.[1] Like Brechtian *Verfrem-dungseffekt* but with laughs, it was a method that he had been developing, intermittently, for at least a decade, but now, in the latter part of the 1960s, he finally began to style it ('in my own quiet way'[2]) into a truly subversive comedic device.

It had first occurred to him more or less by accident, back in 1956, when he was appearing alongside Sheila Hancock in a production of *Tons of Money*. One night, quite by impulse, Howerd found himself doing the same thing to the play that he had already done to stand-up comedy: he broke the rules.

Suddenly, in the middle of a scene that he and Hancock had sailed through many times before, repeating the familiar script word-for-word and with all due and proper respect, Howerd stopped, stepped out of character, turned to the audience, jerked a thumb in the direction of Hancock and shouted: 'Oooh, she's a right cow!'[3] When this triggered a torrent of laughs (from his co-star – who could give as good as she got – as well as the paying customers), he spent much of what remained of the play pivoting back and forth between the characters on the stage and his confidants in the audience, providing a bitingly funny commentary on everything from the sub-standard scenery to the sup-posed inadequacies of the extras.

Although it had started out as a 'spontaneous fun thing', Howerd would later claim that the positive reaction to such 'unprofessional' behaviour encouraged him to become 'something of a pioneer'.[4] Instead of always trying to hide the distance that remained between himself and the character he was meant to be playing, he would now start looking for ways whereby, when circumstances allowed, he could *use* it to his comic advantage.

He flirted with it again the following year, after being informed of the imminent cancellation of *Mr Venus*, when he turned the anarchistic device into an invaluable form of on-stage therapy. 'Since there was nothing to lose,' he said of the ill-starred show, 'I started to fool about':

> *I came out of the show* and laughed at it. Sent it up. For instance, when a joke didn't earn a titter, instead of going on with the dialogue I'd turn to the audience and say: 'What did you expect – wit?' [. . .] All in all, I played *against* the show, as though its faults were part of a deliberate plot against me: *I* was being sabotaged by *them* – the cast, the scriptwriters, the management – and was striving to rise above it all.[5]

At this stage in his career, however, Howerd remained enough of a budding 'proper' actor to keep such an irreverent impulse in check (although, once a project had been perceived to have gone awry, he would not think twice before abandoning all such inhibitions). He knew, none the less, that, as a performer, he had stumbled on a conceit that had tremendous comic potential.

A Funny Thing Happened On The Way To The Forum, with its in-built distinction between Prologus the actor and Pseudolus the character, represented, in this sense, a scripted step in the right direction, but it was not until the mid-1960s, when he resumed his fruitful collaboration with Galton and Simpson, that the approach was seriously explored. In those two very successful peak-time television series, he and his writers (with the expert assistance of the director Duncan Wood) started to cultivate the seeds of his future technique.

He called it 'behind-the-back gossip to the camera'[6]: stepping in and out of a sketch in order to address the viewers directly. If, in the middle of a sketch, he and his writers wanted to draw the viewers' attention to, say, the significance of a particular prop ('*Psst* – look at this: *ooooh!*') or the supposed limitations of a certain guest performer ('What a *shocking* actor!'), they simply had Howerd glance into the camera and utter (sometimes *sotto voce*, sometimes anything but) his barbed remarks. It was quite a novelty for British television at the time – the likes of Groucho Marx, Bob Hope and Jack Benny had all done something similar before, fleetingly and sparingly, in the odd Hollywood movie, but on the small screen such routine audacity seemed curiously new – and it lent the medium the kind of intimacy that it usually seemed to lack.

The more that he did it, the closer it made him feel to his unseen audience. Ever since the early days of *The Howerd Crowd*, he had been looking for a way to make his television performance feel more like a cosy human encounter instead of just a cold electronic connection, and now, at long last, he was beginning to believe that he had found it.

Before Howerd could pursue it any further on the small screen, however, he had a couple of other matters to attend to elsewhere. One of these concerned business, and the other one concerned Broadway.

The business matter involved the future of Associated London Scripts, which Robert Stigwood, the hugely ambitious Australian-born music mogul, merged with his own company, The Robert Stigwood Organisation (RSO), in February 1968.[7] Although two of Howerd's fellow-directors and good friends, Eric Sykes and Spike Milligan, elected to stay independent and remain at their existing base in Orme Court (with Norma Farnes acting as their agent, manager and all-purpose life-support system[8]), Howerd chose to go with his agent Beryl Vertue (who was now established as the company's managing director), along with Galton and Simpson and the rest of the ALS entourage, to a smart new set of offices at the RSO headquarters in Brook Street.

The move suited Stigwood, who was keen to expand his production interests beyond the world of popular music and into the realms of theatre, television and, especially, movies. The move also appealed to Vertue, who was interested in developing some movie projects of her own (via the existing ancillary ALS company called Associated London Films) as well as selling the foreign rights to some of her clients' format ideas to television producers based in the US and Europe.[9]

The move had less obvious significance for Howerd, apart from making him feel slightly more financially secure, although it did lead to the odd 'synergetic' project with another RSO act (especially if that act happened to be the Bee Gees). In May 1968, for example, a carefully reasoned proposal by one of his oldest and most loyal supporters, Bill Cotton (who by this time was Head of Variety at the BBC) to bring him back to the Corporation for more comedy shows was snubbed by Howerd's new management in favour of a slight one-off special for the commercial Thames TV entitled *Frankie Howerd Meets the Bee Gees* (which was broadcast on 20 August 1968).[10] Another, far odder Howerd–Bee Gees one-off special – a woozily surreal medieval fantasy called *Cucumber Castle* – would follow in 1970 – and then, worst of all, Howerd would go on to agree to appear alongside the group (and, it seemed, most of the bearded inhabitants of southern California) in RSO's outrageously execrable 1977 movie 'adaptation' of The Beatles' album, *Sgt Pepper's Lonely Hearts Club Band*.

The second matter, concerning Broadway, had more of an immediate and meaningful impact on Howerd's career. It originated with an invitation from Galton and Simpson to star in a new play that they had written: *The Wind in the Sassafras Trees*.

Adapted from *Du vent dans les branches de Sassafras* – a predictably sarcastic re-examination of the American Dream by the distinguished French playwright René de Obaldia – the new production added another dimension to the play by having Howerd come out at the start to present it as the latest effort by his humble English repertory company – whose collective knowledge of the US has been gleaned exclusively from the old westerns the players have watched. The curtains then opened on a scene set in the American mid-west, circa 1879 'or thereabouts', where Howerd duly reappeared in the guise of John Emery Rockefeller, a crusty old Kansas dirt farmer who spent much of his time sitting inside his log cabin, puffing on a corncob pipe as he watched the various members of his family (comprised of a genteel pioneer wife, a rebellious son and an equally rebellious daughter) come and go.

Once the Red Indians (all 608 of them) invade the area, however, all of the other Hollywood western stereotypes start descending on the Rockefeller ranch: the mysterious stranger in white, the drunken doctor (a part that would be cleverly played, after the try-out run, by Peter Bayliss) and the saloon girl 'tart with the heart' (set to be essayed by Barbara Windsor). The whole play thus becomes the context within which every well-known cliché can be mocked.

Howerd liked the idea, and loved Galton and Simpson's script, but he was not entirely sure that the role of the somewhat laconic lead character ('a sort of cod Spencer Tracy type'[11]) was really right for him. It was agreed, therefore, that he could try it out first, at the Belgrade

Theatre in Coventry, before committing himself to a high-profile West End run.

The opening night (on Tuesday 27 February 1968) proved a great success, eliciting standing ovations and enthusiastic reviews, and Tony Clayton, who was the general manager of the theatre at the time, recalled that the rest of the run was a sell-out.[12] There was a certain amount of tension, initially, between Howerd and Windsor – 'It turned out he was pissed off,' she recalled, 'because I got more laughs than him'[13] – but once he had added a few 'Howerdisms' (which took the form of sly comic asides to the audience), and arranged to make *his* entrance, like hers, up centre instead of from the side, the *entente cordiale* was restored along with the equilibrium of laughs, and the short, three-week run seemed to progress to everyone's satisfaction.

When the play's two producers, Arthur Lewis and the powerful Broadway impresario David Merrick, came to discuss what step Howerd was prepared to take next, the feelings of optimism could hardly have been much stronger. London and the West End beckoned, but Merrick, immediately, wanted Howerd to aim his sights even higher, and go straight to New York and Broadway. Tony Clayton, in whose office the meeting took place, said that in his opinion the production would probably run for 'two or three years' in London, but Merrick's mind appeared to have already been made up.[14] 'Come to America,' Merrick said, 'and I'll make you as legendary as Bob Hope.'[15] It was an offer Howerd found impossible to refuse: 'I'll go to New York,' he replied. 'I've got nothing to prove in London.'[16]

He meant it. Five years before, while he was in New York to watch Zero Mostel in *A Funny Thing . . .*, he had told reporters: 'I've had three ambitions in my life. One, to buy a home for my mother, the other to appear before royalty and the last to play on Broadway. I've accomplished the first two. I hope before long to achieve the last.'[17] Now, finally, he had his chance.

Barbara Windsor, however, had other commitments (and, besides, Merrick had already decided that American audiences would not understand her accent), and so her role was taken over by Ann Hamilton (a very able young comic performer who had just become a regular on *The Morecambe & Wise Show*[18]), and so three of the original Coventry cast (Howerd, Simon Oates and John Golightly), along with Galton and Simpson themselves, set off in the autumn for the States – where

Howerd's old *Forum* associate, Burt Shevelove, was due to join them as the show's director. The plan was to fine-tune the production there during a short tour of Boston and Washington, and then open on Broadway – and then, it was hoped, run for many months ahead.

Galton and Simpson, in particular, were already well aware of how precarious such plans could turn out to be. Back at the start of 1965, when they were readying themselves to write the fourth series of *Steptoe and Son*, they had received a message from Wilfrid Brambell's agent informing them that the actor had just been cast in a Broadway show called *Kelly*, and would therefore almost certainly be unavailable for anything else for a period of two years or more. Faced with a strict deadline for the next series, the two writers had no choice but to kill off Brambell's character and replace him with Harold Steptoe's hitherto unknown illegitimate son (whom they hoped would be played by David Hemmings). What actually happened, however, was that *Kelly* opened on Broadway on one day, then closed a couple of hours later, and Brambell was back at Television Centre in time to record the next series of *Steptoe and Son*: 'Here I am – ready to go!'[19]

Merrick had assured everyone concerned that there would be no problems with *Sassafras* – after all, *he* knew what he was doing – but he had not counted on the tastes of certain theatregoers in Boston. As Ray Galton explained:

> The script had been sent off, ahead of time, to the Colonial Theater in Boston, and the people there, they loved it, they thought it was wonderful. And so, of course, they went ahead and recommended it to all of their members – it was all subscription-based at that theatre – and they all bought their tickets. And so, when we actually arrived, we had a 98 per cent full audience. But then they soon found out that they didn't like us. Worse still, they found out that they couldn't stand us. And so we had this big audience, every night, who *hated* us! It was terrible! Every night I'd watch the curtain go up and then go straight off across the road to the bar and get pissed![20]

Panic set in among the producers, and sections of the script were re-written, and then rewritten again, and then reordered, and then re-written again.

The name of the troupe was changed to the 'East Coventry Repertory Company' (sent to Boston from 'East Coventry, England, Europe' in cultural exchange for the American production of *Hair*) and Howerd was handed a slightly longer introductory monologue. There would soon be further revisions to the script (and the troupe would end up being renamed all over again – this time to the 'East Grinstead Repertory Company'), and there were even more directorial changes of mind.

Arthur Lewis decided (just after the curtain had gone up on the first performance) that the character of the saloon girl should no longer speak with a Cockney accent, and so he marched into the dressing-room and instructed Ann Hamilton to start playing her with the voice 'of a fairy-tale princess' (and so, without the chance to warn the rest of the cast, she had to make her first entrance delivering her lines in a cut-glass English accent). He also decided that Joyce Grant (who was playing the role of the wife and mother) would have to be replaced, and so Hermione Gingold was brought in, handed the latest version of the script and then sent straight off to the bar to rehearse with Howerd. Two days later, however, Gingold came to the conclusion that she was just going to be a supporting player in what was effectively 'The Frankie Howerd Show' in all but name, and so she walked away from the production – leaving Howerd in an even worse nervous state than he had been in before she arrived, and forcing Arthur Lewis to reinstate Joyce Grant.[21]

Nothing about the production, as a consequence, ever seemed to settle. Everyone had to keep relearning their roles, rethinking their performances and then go out to face the unsmiling hordes all over again. Howerd, Galton said, dug deep – inveterate worrier though he was – to keep the production going:

How Frank went on night after night, to a hostile audience in Boston, for two weeks, I don't know. I really don't know. He must have been on pills! He was having to learn new dialogue during the day, and then go back out again in the evening. He really had to push himself. Because they didn't understand him, and they didn't understand the play. They just didn't know what the show was all about. They didn't get it at all. They just thought, 'This man's a *terrible* actor!' But they'd all booked their tickets, so the place was pretty much full every night. Full of misery.[22]

It was miserable for the rest of the cast, too. Merrick, it seems, had made it a point of pride, as well as a show of power, that he could transport an entirely British cast over to America. The result was that from the moment the actors started rehearsing to the arrival of the opening night, members of American Equity marched up and down outside the theatre picketing the production, and the bad feeling continued throughout the rest of the run. 'They kept parading around with these placards,' recalled Ann Hamilton, 'telling us all to go home. It wasn't very nice, but we had our jobs to do, and so we just did our best to carry on.'[23]

Boston's critics were blunt. The *Globe*'s Kevin Kelly damned the play as 'witless, tasteless and thankless', and declared the evening to have been 'utterly worthless'. Samuel Hirsch, writing in the city's *Herald Traveler*, was just as brutal, dismissing the production as a 'long one-act sketch' stretched out to fill three whole acts – a move that had made it 'almost impossible to save the evening from interminable boredom'. There were a few kind words from the venerable Elliot Norton in the *Record American* – who described both Howerd and Joyce Grant as 'amusing and agreeable', and praised Ann Hamilton for her 'good comic performance' – but even he warned that 'the authors had better begin working night and day' if the play was to stand any chance of survival.[24]

It was a different story, Alan Simpson recalled, when the company (minus its director, Burt Shevelove, who had just been sacked) moved on to Washington: 'We closed on the Saturday at Boston and opened on the Monday in Washington, with a new title – *Rockefeller and the Red Indians* – but the same script, same cast, to a tremendous acclaim! Very strange.'[25] Once the first performance at the new venue had finished, everyone waited to hear news of the initial critical reaction, and, in particular, the verdict of the man whom the producers regarded as the most influential cultural opinion-former in the area: the chief drama critic of the *Washington Post*, Richard L. Coe. 'He was a right poseur,' Ray Galton recalled:

Merrick told us, 'If that guy likes the show, he'll appear in the restaurant that everyone goes to after the show. And if he *really* likes it, he will *read* his criticism out to the restaurant.' And so we had to be in this certain restaurant that night, and, sure enough, in came Richard Coe – I think he had a cloak on as well! – and said, 'Would you like me to read it?' So we said, 'Oooh, *yes*, if you don't mind!' And it was a rave.[26]

It was definitely a solid '8/10'. Although Coe preferred either to ignore or explain away the sharpest satirical barbs, he certainly found much in the play to commend: he praised the writers for coming up with the inspired idea of 'creating a new frame for their adaptation' (*viz* the amateurish English rep company); congratulated Howerd on his 'affability', his 'naughty guile' and his 'very neat performance within a performance'; and the critic also expressed his admiration in general for a production that he felt offered Americans an image of themselves as seen 'through the eyes of the world', communicated in a tone that was 'not one of bitterness nor criticism but a kind of affectionate awe, inspired by a throbbing, almost envious curiosity'.[27]

Coe's encomia (echoed by most of Washington's other major critics[28]) made the show seem practically unmissable to the city's keenest theatre-goers, and attracted such blue-chip VIPs as the then US President's wife, Lady Bird Johnson, who went to see it once and then returned to see it for a second time with her daughter Linda and what looked like half of the FBI.[29] 'It became the talk of Washington,' said Alan Simpson. 'You couldn't get in, tickets were sold out for a fortnight – a total reversal of the disaster we'd had, 400-odd miles away, in Boston. So it was now "one-all", and we were poised for the decider in New York.'[30]

The key critic who was lying in wait for them there was Clive Barnes of the *New York Times*. Although he was neither as brutal nor as crude in his criticism as his successor, the so-called 'Butcher of Broadway' Frank Rich, would prove to be, he was fierce enough to scare most actors and managements, and it was widely believed that if Barnes panned a production, it was certain to perish.

Howerd, for once, did not seem overly concerned. He knew and rather liked the British-born Barnes, and believed that the critic would be inclined to give the play a fair – and perhaps even a slightly generous – hearing, and so, while he was still performing in Washington, he remained relatively optimistic about how well the show might fare. It was only when they were about to move on, Ray Galton remembered, that the pessimism began to creep in:

What happened was that the day before we were due to go to New York, Friday, it was announced that Merrick had had this very public row with Clive Barnes. Merrick had said something like, 'I am only staying in the business so that I can kick the arse of this limey bastard out of this country!' So we thought, 'Oh, *God*! That's it, we're finished, we may as well go home!' Then we heard terrible rumours – 'Oh, they're at it again!' – then good rumours – 'It's okay, they've had lunch and made up' – then bad – 'No, they haven't!' – and good – 'Oh, yes, they have!' Oh, it went on and on like that.[31]

Ann Hamilton, in fact, had reason to suspect that Merrick had already resigned himself to closing the production prematurely:

He took us all out for a meal while we were still in Washington. I sat next to him, and at one point I happened to say to him that my son was so looking forward to coming out to America soon for a holiday. He looked at me and said, 'You must try to come with him.' So he seemed to know even then that we weren't going to last.[32]

The effect on Howerd of all these rumours and speculation was predictable: 'I was overwhelmed with inferiority complex, stammering incertitude, and sheer terror.'[33]

The play was due to open (after completing twelve preview performances) at the Ethel Barrymore Theater, on West 47th Street in New York, on Thursday 24 October. 'I was there for the first night,' Ray Galton recalled. 'Alan had buggered off back to England on the last ship to leave New York for the season.'[34] Clive Barnes duly arrived and took his usual seat, close to the front, on the left-hand side of the theatre.

When the curtain went up, Howerd came out and felt immediately as though he was giving a private audition before the all-powerful metropolitan critic. As a result, he spent his entire time on stage trying to avoid meeting his tormentor's gaze, and thus addressed his whole performance to the people seated to the right of the middle aisle. The audience, on the whole, was actually quite enthusiastic – and one possible reason for that was the fact that Merrick had scoured New York for stray visiting Britons and resident anglophiles to ensure that there would be plenty of people present on the night who actually knew who Frankie Howerd was – but the star was still somewhat ill-at-ease.

After the show had ended, Ray Galton was persuaded to accompany the actors and producers to Sardi's, the legendary post-theatre watering hole where most of Broadway's major movers and shakers gathered to take the temperature of every newborn venture. 'There was a room there, upstairs, with TV monitors,' said Galton, 'and all the local stuff was starting to come through on it – you know, the local paper reviews and the ones on the radio. Well, it soon became clear that the reviews in the lesser papers and the radio crits were pretty favourable about us, but, at Sardi's, they were only waiting for one review: the *New York Times* review from Clive Barnes.'[35]

When it finally arrived, it was obvious, right from the start, that it was not good news. '*Rockefeller and the Red Indians*,' began Barnes, 'struck me as very possibly the finest antidote to insomnia since the discovery of Pentothal. Sheer duty kept me pinching myself to remain awake, and it would not surprise me if I had bruised myself for weeks.'[36] Hearts sank at Sardi's.

A review of Barnes' review, in truth, would not have been any kinder, because its awkward structure – a classic first-night frantic journalistic scribble, 'topped and tailed' by observations that sounded suspiciously pre-prepared – and its large, uneven chunk of loose analysis – random, rambling and superficial – did neither the play nor the critic proper justice, but, none the less, the piece still had its intended effect. Every low blow brought a bruise ('The humor,' sneered Barnes with all of the stored-up contempt and the asinine over-generalisation of the chippy old ex-pat, was unlikely to appeal to New Yorkers as they were 'not so strongly conditioned as English audiences to find things such as hemorrhoids funny in themselves'); every apparent pat on the back ended up feeling like an angry slap (Howerd's front-of-curtain preamble 'sets you in a good mood', the critic conceded, and the introduction of the old clichés 'is quite funny', but then, he complained, 'the play continues, and continues and continues'); and every sharp line drew some blood ('having found themselves with a dead horse on stage,' Barnes said of the cast, they 'start flogging it for what it is worth. And, gratifyingly, once in a while it does twitch a little – but it sure ain't ever going to get up and gallop'). It hurt. All of it hurt.

Ray Galton watched and listened as each painful detail was reported via the screens, and thought to himself: 'Oh dear!' When the ordeal was finally over – 'Better luck next time for all concerned,' boomed Barnes[37] – Galton glanced down, took a deep breath and then tried to gauge the mood inside Sardi's: 'I said to this bloke who was by the monitor, "What do you think?" And he turned round to me and he said, "Go home, son".'[38]

That, as far as those who mattered on Broadway were concerned, was that: 'Go home, son'. The critics had defeated the company 2:1. It was not long before Alan Simpson, although absent on leave, was on hand to share the dismal news with his partner: 'I phoned New York from about 900 miles away, off the coast of Newfoundland. I'd booked a ship's telegraph thing, which seemed quite a technological marvel in those days, and spoke to Ray direct. And he told me the story: "Go home, son". So I said, "At least I'm already on my way!"'[39]

The show had opened on the Thursday, with a modest little bang, and then closed on the Saturday, with a miserable little whimper, after completing just four performances. It was not the only Broadway production to have closed during that period – no fewer than four shows folded inside that very same week, and several more had recently spent even less time open than any of them: earlier in the month, for example, *The Flip Side* (starring David McCallum at the height of his fame from the television series *The Man From UNCLE*), had its last night straight after its first night.[40] In those days, especially, it was almost more of a surprise if a show succeeded than it was if it failed.

Everyone associated with *The Wind in the Sassafras Trees*, or *Rockefeller and the Red Indians*, or whatever it was that they were now calling it, seemed quite stoical. Galton and Simpson had plenty of other projects to pursue, and countless other offers to consider. Similarly, most members of the supporting cast either had, or knew that they soon would have, a relatively full diary for the rest of the year. Even Howerd took the disappointment in his stride: claiming that he was 'now more philosophic about life's ups and downs', he comforted himself with the thought that he had achieved the last of his three dearest ambitions (even if his stay on Broadway had only been for a mere three days), and so he filed the least unpleasant of the notices away in the scrapbooks and then returned home to England, feeling as much of a star now as he had felt before, on the last leisurely voyage of the old RMS *Queen Elizabeth*.[41]

News of his premature departure had reached the ears of a real-life Queen Elizabeth, the Queen Mother, who shared her reaction with Bernard Delfont over tea, Dubonnet and canapés at Windsor Castle. 'Isn't it a shame about Frankie?' she sighed. 'I'm sorry, ma'am?' replied Delfont with a look of puzzled surprise. 'His show in America,' she explained. 'It's failed, you know. He was so wrong to try it. But I'm glad to see that at least the critics were kind to him.'[42]

While Howerd was making his way home, as luck would have it, Michael 'Dark Satanic' Mills, the BBC's idiosyncratic but brilliantly astute Head of Comedy, was on his way off to Italy for a few days' holiday in Sorrento in the company of his colleague Tom Sloan (Mills' alluring wife, Valerie Leon, was otherwise engaged filming *Carry On Camping*). One day, during a visit to the ruins of Pompeii, the two men wandered away from the main part of the tour and started exploring the places where all of the old shops and bordellos had been. 'It's amazing,' Mills suddenly exclaimed, recalling the West End success of *A Funny Thing* . . . 'I expect to see Frankie Howerd come loping round the corner.'[43] Sloan knew exactly what he was talking about: 'Why not?' he replied with a mischievous smile.

Once the cultured and worldly Mills was back in his cluttered office at Television Centre, he settled down and worked his way through a translation of the collected works of Plautus, jotted down his thoughts as to how certain themes and scenes could be used as the basis of a sitcom, and then sent a copy on to Talbot 'Tolly' Rothwell, the principal writer of the *Carry Ons*, with a note attached that said: 'What about this for Frankie Howerd?'[44] Rothwell thought it would be ideal for Howerd, and ideal for him, and so, with Mills' permission, he went ahead and wrote a script.

There was only ever really one basic Talbot Rothwell script: a one-dimensional, loosely plotted, fast-paced comedy romp which – with a nip here and a tuck there – could be made to fit practically any situation, provided there was enough room for some of his trademark silly names, painful puns, blatantly obvious double entendres and 'revived' jokes (his most often-quoted line from *Carry On Cleo* – 'Infamy! Infamy! They've all got it in for me!' – was actually used first by Frank Muir and Denis Norden in an episode of their 1950s radio show, *Take It From Here*). Mills had realised, however, that there was really only one basic Plautus script, too: someone is after sex, someone is after power, and, at the centre, a clever slave is busy manipulating his master. It seemed right up Rothwell's *vicolo*.

When Frankie Howerd read what Rothwell had produced, he laughed out loud. It struck him as 'cheeky, cheerful, seaside postcard bawdiness designed for a relaxed belly-laugh'.[45] He had seen and heard it all before, of course, in *A Funny Thing . . .* and in music-hall, Variety and the *Carry Ons*, but this was a script that had been written expressly for him, and, if he agreed to perform it, a major new series was almost certain to follow. He was slightly concerned about the apparent vulgarity of some of the material – he was happy enough to be thought of as a 'cheeky' comedian, but he had no wish to be considered crude (and thus be persecuted by Mary Whitehouse and her fellow 'Clean Up TV' zealots) – but the project, as a whole, was hard for him to resist. 'I'm prepared to take a gamble,' he told Michael Mills, 'but a cautious one for a change. Let's make just this pilot, and see how the audience reacts. If the viewers like it – OK, I'll do a series.'[46]

Before the preparations began, however, Howerd was handed the unhappy task of standing in at that year's *Royal Variety Show* for two of his friends, Morecambe and Wise, after Eric Morecambe had suffered a serious heart attack. Walking on stage as the 'surprise replacement', he acknowledged the thunderous applause and then launched straight into a fine routine about his dealings with the theatrical equivalent of 'Thing' – the Palladium's Bernard Delfont:

> The phone rang – which made me jump, because I thought it was cut off. No. There was someone in a call box, you know, so I said, 'Yes, hello?' And this voice said, 'Lord Delfont here.' So I said, 'Oh, yes?' I said, 'Er, hold on a second.' So I poured meself out a small schooner of tonic wine and I made meself comfy on the settee, then I said, 'Yes?' He said, 'Would you mind hurrying up, please? I've got a very important meeting at EMI!' So I said, 'Is this *really* Bernard Delfont?' He said, 'Yes!' I said, 'I'm *so* sorry! I thought it was an obscene phone call, and there was nothing on telly so I thought I may as well enjoy it!' He said, 'Do I *sound* like a man who'd make obscene phone calls?' So, um, I said, 'Well, look, let me hear you *pant* a couple of times, breathe in and out, and I'll let you know. Ha-ha!' No sense of humour. No. Not a titter.[47]

Deftly explaining the reason for his presence, he claimed that Delfont had informed him, 'We've got a couple of people unable to get here tonight – very *important* people – and we want you to take their place.' He reported his response: 'I said, "*Me?*" But I'd feel such a *fool* sitting in that box all on my own!' At the end, after wishing Morecambe well, he went back off to another great ovation.

'You must have been very moved by that reception,' his great fan the Queen Mother said to him afterwards. Howerd confirmed that he had indeed been very touched. 'And I hope America didn't upset you too much,' she added, and then wished him well for his next project. He thanked her, and told her how keen he was to make it a success – especially now that he knew who was likely to be watching.[48]

He felt very positive when he returned to work on *Pompeii*. He regarded the show as the kind of thing that, if it was handled in the appropriate manner, had the potential to draw back in the old broad audience – and, as he had always said: 'A majority gives you a living.'[49]

A crucial part of the appeal, for Howerd as a performer, was the chance to perfect the on-screen technique he had been developing prior to the interlude in America with *Sassafras*. The whole show, he sensed, could turn out to be far more innovative on the screen than it had seemed on paper, combining as it did elements from Variety theatre (his old front cloth monologue preserved in the form of 'The Prologue'), radio (the regular brief scenes he shared with the likes of the old sooth-sayer worked just like the crosstalk on *Variety Bandbox*) and television (the ostensible form was still that of a modern sitcom). In addition to this already rich and interesting mix, however, viewers would also witness the novelty of the daringly direct and intimate camera technique, with its playful disregard for television's so-called 'fourth wall', that would allow Howerd to transform the medium, for half an hour each week, from a box in the corner to a little theatre inside the living room.

Working closely with Michael Mills – who was overseeing the production of the pilot episode – Howerd kept reshaping the script until it gave him this freedom to step in and out of the sitcom to send up the show, the material, the other actors and even certain members of the crew, as well as engage directly with the audience both in the studio and also at home. When he and Mills were finally satisfied with the general effect, the programme was broadcast, at 9.10 p.m. on Wednesday 17 September, on BBC 1.

From the very first moment that Howerd sat down to address the camera as the slave named Lurcio, he looked to be in complete control:

> Greetings, noble citizens, simple plebeians, crafty artisans and arty courtesans. I think that's the lot. Good. Now, the bit I'm going to do now is called 'The Prologue'. And, er, you see, not only is it a quick way to get into the *fruity* part of the plot, but also it helps me to fill you in with who is who, who does what to who and to whom they doth what to. Y'see. And, um, in addition, *how* – which brings me back to the fruity part! Now, my name is Lurcio. How do you do? Yes, nicely, thanks![50]

Once the bond was established between himself and the viewers, he went on to set the scene ('Imagine Italy is the shape of a woman's leg. Well, Pompeii is situated not quite high enough to be interesting') and then introduce some of the show's other characters (all of whom remained oblivious to Lurcio's privileged link with the inhabitants of a world beyond their fiction).

First on the scene came his master, a Roman senator named Ludicrus Sextus: 'That's him now. Probably lost his laurel leaves, the old fool. Take no notice.' Then came the rest of the master's family: Ammonia ('She's my mistress. Well, I say "mistress", I don't mean . . . I mean, er, I serve her. Well, no, I don't mean I *serve* . . . I mean, if she fancies a bit, I mean, ah . . . I have to give her what she wants. Er . . .'), and their two children – Nausius, their son ('He is, if I may say so, a trifle "*odd*" – oh, yes, they had them in those days as well!') and Erotica, their daughter (LUDICRUS: 'Ah, sweet child! And so delightfully chaste!' LURCIO: 'Yes. And so easily caught up with!').

Without much of a plot to speak of, Howerd was able to devote most of what remained of the show to a demonstration of his special television technique. He made sarcastic asides to the studio audience, such as when one of his jokes received a delayed response ('Late – but welcome!'); he made similarly sarcastic asides to the audience at home ('But wait – you may as well, there's nothing on the other two channels!'); and, most memorably of all, he mocked the show's empty promise of ripe and fruity post-watershed sights by inviting the camera, and through it the viewers at home, to come in close behind him and try in vain to peer over his shoulder as he spied through the keyhole at a secret tryst:

Cor! 'Ere, quick! 'Ere, 'ere – look: *Ooooh!* [*Turns back to admonish the camera*] Don't push, don't push – form a queue! That's it. Ooh, *look!* Ah, control yourselves, please! Now, look: [*He takes a quick look and then turns back to face the camera*] *Ooooooh!* [*He takes another quick look through the keyhole, and then turns back again to the camera*] *Oooooooooh!* Come on, there's one more: *Oooooooooooh!* That's your lot! [*He shoos the camera away*]

The show ended in the same place that his stand-up act always ended: stranded somewhere near the start. By the time that the soothsayer returned to warn him that 'the end is near' – 'She's right you know – the end *is* here! Oooh, doesn't Tempus Fugit!' – the Prologue was still unfinished.

It was a sitcom that had been well and truly 'Howerdised'. One critic would sum up the secret of its appeal as 'pure one-foot-on-the-footlights music-hall technique adapted for television'.[51] Later on, in reference to this subversion of not only the rules of a genre but also the conventions of the medium as a whole, another writer would claim that Howerd was 'arguably the most Brechtian actor in Britain'.[52]

Watched by an estimated 11,261,500 people,[53] the reaction, on the whole, had been good. Mary Whitehouse, true to form, informed the nation that the programme it had just seen had been 'sordid and cheap',[54] but, much to her surprise, hardly anyone else seemed inclined to agree – let alone complain. The more popular view, in fact, was expressed by the critic who said that the show had proven the wisdom of 'the one belief held in common by all comedians: that in the right place and with the right timing there is no such thing as an old joke'.[55] Even the worryingly cautious and politically pliable Sir Charles Hill, then Chairman of the BBC's board of governors, responded relatively favourably to the programme, explaining that he had asked his wife about it and she had assured him that it was 'very funny'.[56]

The reaction of the public in general, judging by the results of the BBC's own audience research survey, was similar to that of Lady Hill. 'Corny it may well have been – bawdy, too (decidedly so!),' said one interviewee, but it was still one of the funniest things they had seen 'for a very long time'. Howerd, it was said, had shown himself to be a 'master of corn and innuendo', and had been 'at his hilarious best' in the role of Lurcio, playing it 'for all it was worth'. Some said that they would have preferred him in a stand-up show rather than a sitcom, but even they still judged it to have been quite enjoyable. A sizeable minority disliked Talbot Rothwell's script, which they felt – justifiably – had lacked plot and action: one complained that 'the writer had seemingly taken down his book of 500 corny jokes and succeeded in getting 490 into his 34-minute script'. It was certainly generally believed, however, that the show had the potential to go on to become a popular series.[57]

Howerd agreed, and so did Michael Mills. The pilot was deemed a success, and the team pressed ahead with the project.

The following year, not one but two full-length series of *Up Pompeii!* were produced and transmitted. The first (which went out from March to May) was again written by Talbot Rothwell and directed by the shrewdly effective David Croft (the man responsible, in partnership with Jimmy Perry, for *Dad's Army*); the second (running from September through to the end of October) was co-written by Rothwell and Sid Colin and directed by yet another fine programme-maker, Sidney Lotterby. In addition to these two small-screen series, work on a spin-off movie began at Elstree at the end of the autumn.

In most of the accompanying promotional interviews, Howerd affected the air of one who, though not displeased to find himself back in such demand, was far too battle-hardened to be influenced any longer by the transient highs and lows of show business. When told, quite matter-of-factly, that the imminent arrival on the screen of the first series of *Up Pompeii!* was set to be heralded with the appearance of his picture on the cover of the *Radio Times*, he sighed and said weakly, 'Oh, that's flattering,' and then sat back and launched straight into a bleak-sounding monologue about the cold and amoral nature of modern fame:

> People only do that sort of thing for their own convenience though, you know. They don't say I'm sure Frank would like that, they don't say he's a good lad. One gets used to taking it from whence it comes, do you know what I mean? I'm not saying I despise it, I'm not saying please don't put it on. But I'm a bit cynical.[58]

Howerd with Lee Young, one-time partner, occasional stooge and constant friend.

Dennis Heymer: the love of Howerd's life.

Making his small screen debut, alongside Victor Platt, in *The Howerd Crowd* on 12 January 1952.

Soldiering on: Entertaining the troops, yet again, this time in Cyprus in 1966.

'I have a device to make all well': Howerd as bully Bottom.

Howerd as Percy Lamb in his movie debut, *The Runaway Bus.*

One of the film roles that did not get away: Howerd's turn as guest misfit in *Carry On Doctor.*

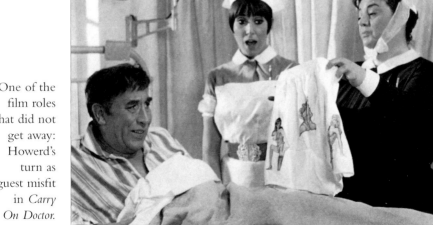

'Good evening': Peter Cook outside the strip club that would shortly become the Establishment.

Follow that: Lenny Bruce is escorted back out of Britain.

A Funny Thing Happened on the Way to the Forum: What the Romans did for Frankie Howerd.

Howerd with Cilla Black in *Way Out in Piccadilly*: their friendship never faltered.

'Did anyone ever tell you,' Elizabeth Taylor asked Howerd, 'that you're the funniest man in the world?'

'Yes, missus!' Frankie Howerd meets his biggest fan.

Ronnie Waldman: BBC TV's pioneering Head of Light Entertainment.

Top left to bottom:

Eric Maschwitz: a fine champion of foolish things.

Tom Sloan: you know – 'Thing'.

Bill Cotton: one of Howerd's firmest fans.

Talbot Rothwell: The King of Corn.

Michael Mills: The man who dreamed up *Up Pompeii!*

Eltham man
takes foreign
vacation, 1970.

Up Pompeii!:
'Howerding' up the
British sitcom.

'Why do it? Why not do what one is really able to do – what one is best at?'

He sat back, sipped from his glass of champagne, and recalled how he had been snubbed and rejected so many times in his early days, then reached the top on the stage and in radio and made his mark on television, then been written off, then rediscovered, and then rehired by the same people who had previously been so quick to write him off. Neither talent nor reputation, he reflected, offered much protection from the vicissitudes of taste and fashion. 'There's nothing spiteful or bitter about the way Frankie Howerd says this,' his interviewer reported. 'He says it with detachment, as though he were telling an anecdote about a bloke he once knew.'[59]

Inside, however, Frankie Howerd was feeling brimful with pride. He had started the 1960s at rock bottom, and, thanks to the success of *Up Pompeii!*, he had ended that decade right back at the very top, and now he had started the 1970s as one of the most popular, critically admired, best-paid and best-loved entertainers in the country. He could sigh and shrug his shoulders in public as much as he liked, but there was no doubt that, deep down, he was thrilled about being spoken of, once again, as one of the nation's favourites.

The full extent of his latest success, combined with a renewed awareness of how much he had gone through to achieve it, was brought home to him at the start of the new decade when, yet again, he took up his customary allotted place at the *Evening Standard* Drama Awards. First, he found that he had been promoted to the top table, where Laurence Olivier thanked him at length for teaching him so much about the art of comedy. Then, a little later in the evening, Howerd was surprised again when, without warning, he was presented with a silver key to celebrate his twenty-one years in show business (the award was actually a few years out of date, seeing as Howerd had made his radio debut back in December 1946, but the gesture still meant a great deal).

Once again, as the warm applause and loud cheers went on, he left the platform in tears. His stardom, at last, seemed assured.

CHAPTER 14

The Closeted Life

There's everything in my memoirs, you know: war, sex, politics, sex,
showbusiness, sex – my memoirs are so hot you could toast bread in
between the pages!

'I'm not a bag of nerves any more,' Howerd said at the start of the 1970s.
'Of course,' he added, 'you can't go on in a complacent haze and I'm
nervous about the reaction to a new show or a new film. But I accept ups
and downs. Nobody's consistently successful and the fact that I have failures occasionally doesn't worry me particularly. It must happen.'[1]

It had not happened, in truth, for some time, and it seemed unlikely
to happen again, in any serious sense, in the near future. Now in his
mid-fifties (although 'officially' he was still only nearing the end of his
forties), Frankie Howerd had become firmly established as one of those
well-known and well-liked personalities that the papers often described
as a 'national institution'.

There had been plenty of awards (apart from the recent *Evening
Standard* presentation, he had also been named as 'Show Business Personality of 1969' by The Grand Order of Water Rats, 'TV Personality of
1969' by the Radio Industries and 'Show Business Personality of 1971'
by the Variety Club of Great Britain); and there had also been plenty
of plaudits – not only from the critics (Bernard Levin and Kenneth
Tynan were two of Howerd's most avid admirers, and Hugh Leonard
had gone so far as to request that the comedian be nationalised[2]) but
also from some of his theatrical peers (Peter O'Toole said that the
sight and sound of Howerd in full comically self-righteous flow was
guaranteed to make him 'wet myself laughing'[3]). He had earned the
right, at this stage in his career, to relax a little, enjoy his life and be
more selective about his future projects.

He remained, however, as busy as ever, and seemed strongly disinclined to consider slowing down (one interviewer who met him during this period remarked: 'I never met a man who used the word "work" so often'[4]). When asked why he continued to push himself so hard, he simply replied that he felt compelled to keep doing what he did best: 'People need to do what they do. Doctors need to doct. Dentists need to dent. Actors need to act. And writers need to write.'[5] He was a performer, he explained, and so he needed to keep performing.

There was a little more to it than that. There was also the memory of those dreadful 'years of darkness', when the telephone stopped ringing and the bookings dried up. 'You wear the scars for ever,' he had told Ernie Wise back in 1961, and, one decade on, the sentiment remained the same. The momentum had to be kept going; the diary had to be kept full.

It was probably inevitable, because of this attitude, that Howerd would sometimes be tempted too readily into repetition. He did not, for example, agree to do just one movie spin-off of *Up Pompeii!* – he agreed to do three: the moderately funny eponymous first effort, released in March 1971, was thus followed later the same year by the Crusades caper *Up the Chastity Belt* (a far more forced and slapdash affair than its predecessor, and one of the cheapest-looking British movies of the second half of the twentieth century), and then, in 1972, by the Great War romp *Up the Front* (which, in spite of some good gags contributed by Eddie Braben, was anything but great). He also used the 'Up' tag for a send-up of Serge Gainsbourg and Jane Birkin's heavily panted hit single 'Je t'aime' – which he recorded with June Whitfield – called 'Up Je t'Aime'.

Similarly, after completing two series of the original sitcom itself – and scraping, in the process, the bottom of Talbot Rothwell's very deep barrel of puns, ancient jokes and increasingly silly names (which had ranged from the rather endearing 'Stovus Primus' to the clumsily obvious 'Pussus Galoria') – Howerd signed up to go over the same ground again in a new sitcom – broadcast in 1973 – called *Whoops Baghdad*. Based, supposedly, on 'an idea' of Dennis Heymer's (the idea being, presumably, to 'do *Up Pompeii!* all over again'), the show featured Howerd in the role of Ali Oopla, a chronically put-upon but quietly cunning bondservant to the Wazir of Baghdad. Instead of being written by Rothwell (who was committed to the latest *Carry On* project) it was scripted by his old colleague Sid Colin (along with a mélange of other contributors); instead of beginning with Howerd saying, 'The Prologue . . .', it now began with him saying, 'And it came to pass . . .'; and instead of wearing a toga he now wore a kaftan-style tunic and a pair of baggy pants – but this was the sum of the changes. Viewers saw the show for what it was – a fairly pointless, only intermittently amusing, ersatz version of *Up Pompeii!*, and, while plenty of them still watched it, few of them seemed to warm to it.

Howerd was by no means oblivious to any of this. He dismissed *Up the Chastity Belt* as a 'hotch-potch'.[6] He admitted to having shot some of the scenes for *Up the Front* while labouring in a state of 'alcoholic and physical exhaustion'.[7] He also acknowledged that, compared to *Up Pompeii!*, *Whoops Baghdad* was much weaker, with scripts of a standard that he deemed 'uneven' and lacking in 'proper continuity'.[8] He made no apology, however, for keeping himself in work. He had taken his gambles, he had run his risks, and, at times, had been made to pay heavily for his mistakes, and so he probably felt that he was now entitled, every once in a while, to play it safe. The crucial thing was to keep going.

He did allow himself a little leisure, but, unlike his labour, it often seemed unnecessarily chaotic and almost risibly *ad hoc*. Some of his evenings out with his sister Betty, for example, were arranged so near to the last-possible minute that they frequently threatened to descend rapidly into the realm of farce. On one occasion, for example, Barry Took and his wife Lyn were just putting their luggage down in the hall after arriving home from a holiday in France when the telephone rang: 'Oh, Barry,' said Howerd matter-of-factly, 'we were wondering, only you see it's Dennis's night off and Betty and I, well, I wondered if it's not too much trouble . . . if Betty and I could come round to supper.' Took cast a nervous glance over at his wife, mouthed the gist of the request, took note of her somewhat brusque but unmistakeable mouthed response, and informed Howerd that, as much as they would love to entertain him and his sister, the only edible things that they currently had in the house were a French loaf and a tiny piece of Camembert cheese. 'Oh, we'll bring the food,' said Howerd brightly. 'There's a little corner shop round here that's still open. We'll be right over.'[9] Fifteen minutes later, Frank and Betty turned up, as promised, bearing a flimsy plastic bag that contained one pre-sliced 'Tiger' loaf, a small tin of sardines, a tin of baked beans, a tin of corned beef, a tin of pea soup and, last but not least, a large tin of sultana pudding. After Took's wife had conjured up a relatively digestible three-course meal out of these disparate ingredients, and Took had passed around his bottles of duty-free wine and brandy, Howerd sat back in his chair, patted his stomach contentedly and said: 'Oh, by the way, there's a programme I'd like to see on the telly. Only, our set's broken.'[10] It was a long night for the tired Tooks.

Howerd tended to rely on June Whitfield and Cilla Black for most of his prearranged repasts. 'Frank had simple tastes and found my no-frills cooking palatable,' Whitfield recalled, 'but he had quite the strangest relationship with alcohol that I've ever come across. He would start the evening by downing a triple vodka almost before anyone else had time to get a glass in their hands, then he'd have one or two more in quick succession, and then he'd stop and not another drop would pass his lips for the rest of the evening.'[11] Cilla Black and her husband Bobby Willis started socialising with Howerd in the late 1960s, during the long and successful run of *Way Out in Piccadilly*. One weekend, he invited himself over to the Willis residence for Sunday lunch; after finding the roast lamb (as well as the relaxed family atmosphere) very much to his liking, he decided to invite himself over again, and again, and again – always expressly for roast lamb. One weekend, however, he called to say that, on this particular occasion, he would not be coming. 'Oh, why not?' asked Black. 'Because,' moaned Howerd, 'I'm sick of roast lamb week after week. Why can't you have liver and bacon?'[12]

If he dined out in London with Dennis Heymer and one or two of their mutual friends, the venue would often be his favourite local Italian trattoria, the Al Gallo d'Oro on Kensington High Street, although he was never very happy about the fact that his old tormentor from *The Cool Mikado*, Michael Winner, was also known to grace the place occasionally with his presence ('If that fellow Winner comes in here,' he used to whisper to the *maître d'*, Tony Malvasi, 'sit him as far away from me as possible!'[13]). When it came to indulging himself and his guests, however, he was (unusually for a comic) a generous host, although, as Ray Galton recalled, he relied on Heymer for guidance: 'Frank, who knew nothing about wine, would try and order Beaujolais, just because he knew that it was cheap, but Dennis, who did know his wines, would always say, "No, no, Frank," and then order the best wines in the place. Frank didn't mind. He just didn't know.'[14]

Tennis remained one of Howerd's favourite recreational activities. Most Sunday afternoons, he would team up with Heymer to play a game of doubles against a couple of their female neighbours on the bumpy little court hidden away behind the tree-lined railings of Edwardes Square. Dressed in a baggy top and over-long shorts, he would lumber his way around the court, puffing and panting, clearly desperate to win each point but often ending up as the loser. *'Sluts! Lesbians!'* he tended to scream and shout in mock-horror as the women kept on adding to their lead.[15] Heymer once bought him an expensive Dunlop graphite racquet, just like John McEnroe had used at Wimbledon, but then, in a fit of competitive pique, Howerd proceeded to smash it to pieces in the middle of a game, just like McEnroe had done at Wimbledon. 'I always beat him,' one of his regular female competitors remembered. 'He was a very good sport, though, and kept coming back for more.'[16]

Vacations abroad were few and far between, although, when he could, Howerd relished the chance to withdraw for a short rest at his elegant villa – 'The Forum' – in Malta, where, feeling protected from the rest of the world, he could sunbathe in the nude on top of the villa's large flat roof, swim or just idly float in his wide outdoor pool and go for a leisurely boat ride around the sheltered Blue Lagoon at the neighbouring island of Comino. He and Heymer would host the odd cocktail party at home in Valetta for such friends and fellow-entertainers as June Whitfield and her husband and Ernie and Doreen Wise (who had their own holiday home in the nearby village of Balzan), but most of the time they kept themselves to themselves, content to spend a few precious days of relaxation in the privacy of each other's company.

Howerd was never a great fan of formal show-business functions, but the ones that he did attend were invariably very special affairs. At the end of February in 1972, for example, he and Heymer were among the guests in Budapest for the weekend-long fortieth birthday party of Elizabeth Taylor. Socialising with the likes of Raquel Welch, Michael Caine, Ringo Starr and a surprisingly coquettish Princess Grace of Monaco, Howerd was happy to down his double vodkas, soak up the atmosphere and then return to London for more evenings in with tins of corned beef and sultana pudding.

It was not long after this trip, however, that he flew off to another glamorous-sounding setting – Los Angeles – but this time it was to mix pleasure with business. First, he had to call in on his former co-star from *Up the Front*, Zsa Zsa Gabor, at her gilded home in Bel Air (her redoubtable mother, it seems, had taken quite a shine to him), and then he moved on to a meeting with Bob Hope at the star's six-acre base in Toluca Lake (where, in addition to comparing notes with Hope about growing up in the terraced streets of Eltham, Howerd also got the chance to socialise with Jimmy Stewart and Alice Faye). The most pertinent reason for his brief stay in LA, however, was to commence informal talks with another British-born Hollywood actor, Ray Milland, about co-starring in a movie that Beryl Vertue was planning to produce called *The House in Nightmare Park*.

The project – yet another *Cat and the Canary*-style vehicle – appealed to Milland, in part because he liked the story but also because he happened to be a long-standing fan of Frankie Howerd (whom he always described as his 'favourite English comedian'[17]). His commitment was secured, as a consequence, without any need for strenuous persuasion.

Written by ALS stalwarts Clive Exton and Terry Nation and directed by the young Australian film-maker Peter Sykes, the movie (which was shot at Pinewood studios over the course of a mere six weeks, from 6 November to 16 December 1972) featured Howerd as an Edwardian ham actor named Foster Twelvetrees who is lured to a dark Gothic mansion by its owner, Stewart Henderson (Ray Milland), on the pretext of being needed to perform one of his awful 'orations' at a private family party. What he does not know at the time, however, is that he is actually the illegitimate son and heir of the family patriarch, whose recent death the others are concealing until they can discover where the Henderson fortune has been hidden and then do away with their unwelcome new relation.

Ably shaped and paced by Peter Sykes (who drew on his experience not only of the genre of Hammer horror but also that of mainstream British comedy[18]), the movie covered (and quietly mocked) most of the 'old dark house' clichés, while making the most of the somewhat laboured comic material, and pushed the plot on to its predictable conclusion. Compared to *The Cat and the Canary*, it was decidedly second-rate, but, compared to most of Howerd's previous efforts, it represented a well above average attempt (and, thanks both to Sykes and his cinematographer Ian Wilson, it *looked* far better than many other British comedy productions of the time).

Howerd, certainly, was unusually positive about the finished product, and described the making of it as the most rewarding experience of his movie career: it had been extremely physically gruelling, and Sykes had definitely been a hard taskmaster, but what ended up on the screen showed him that it had all been worthwhile, and the unusually appreciative reviews were the cause of considerable personal satisfaction.[19] It did not, however, change the course of his career. It did not spirit him off from Cricklewood to Hollywood. It amounted to nothing more, but also nothing less, than an intriguing and rather engaging interlude before he resumed his regular work in other, more familiar, media.

Back on television, he committed himself to his next (and, arguably, his last) genuinely and consistently high-quality television mini-series: three fifty-minute programmes for BBC 2's 'Show of the Week' slot entitled *An Evening With Francis Howerd*. Produced and directed by John Ammonds (the man primarily responsible for the overall quality of *The Morecambe & Wise Show* and one of the shrewdest and most attentive makers of comedy programmes in the business), this trilogy of beautifully made, broadly appealing, quintessentially *BBC* programmes – part stand-up, part sketches – demonstrated how good Frankie Howerd still could be when the scripts were right, the discipline was right, and the mood was right.

There were plenty of tantrums during rehearsals, and plenty of frayed nerves in and between the editorial meetings, but the result, when it came to the shows themselves, was an invaluable set of recordings of a brilliant and extremely experienced stand-up comedian – a stand-up comedian who was so sure of his material, and so sure of how his performance of this material was being presented, that he was able to relax and really enjoy the experience of entertaining a large group of people inside a studio. His monologues, in particular, were a delight to hear and watch, because, time after time, he would use the sound of the loud, unforced, joyful audience laughter to lift the humour up to a higher level:

Liss-en. The doorbell never stopped ringing from dawn till dusk. *Ring?* I thought I'd go mad! It's always the same, innit? First call was a gypsy. A gypsy, yes, with this bright coloured headscarf, y'see, and earrings, big earrings, and wellington boots. I thought to meself, 'Hello, it'll be a bunch of violets or a packet of shoelaces.' But before I could say anything, she said, 'Good morning: I'm your local Conservative candidate!' You could have knocked me down with a blue rosette! I said, 'I'm sorry.' I said, 'I don't take part. I'm not interested. I don't take part in any organised political bodies,' I said. 'I'm a Liberal.' [*Explodes with mock-indignation at the supposedly inadequate volume of audience laughter*] 'I'm a Liberal!' Y'see? That's supposed to be *witty*! That's *satire*! Now, come on: pull yourselves together! 'Liberal!' *Missus?* 'Liberal,' girl! You're Liberal, aren't yer? Yeah. *Very* Liberal, yes. We've heard all about you! No, um, the thing is, no, the second call – 'cause, I'd just sat down to lunch – *bang-bang* again! Gas man. Gas man, see. Out of breath. Puffing and panting, I thought he was ill: '*Hhhuuh-Hhhuuh-Hhhuuh.*' He said, 'Good morning,' he said, 'I'm from your local gas board. *Hhhuuh-Hhhuuh-Hhhuuh.*' I said, 'You're *winded*, aren't you? You're winded?' He said, 'So would you be after doing 400 meters!' [*Audience begins to laugh*] I could have smashed his face in! I'll tell you this, I'll tell you this, brethren: looking at – no, *liss-en!* – looking at him, it took me back – memories, memories! – to when I was a gas man. [*Loud audience laughter*] You will pardon you! When I was a gas man, I – [*A woman's loud laugh breaks in*] – Never mind '*Ha-ha-ha!*' She's as common as muck, that one there! Join her, over here! No, no, I used to – [*Again he is interrupted by a woman's laugh*] SHUT UP! LOOSEN SOMETHING, LOOSEN SOMETHING! Poor soul. There's nothing worse than your knickers out of focus![20]

There had been several memorable moments in other fairly popular but relatively patchily-made shows over the course of the previous couple of years – including two intermittently impressive specials for ITV (1971's *Frankie Howerd: The Laughing Stock of Television* – scripted by Took and Feldman, Galton and Simpson and Talbot Rothwell – and, later the same year, two quirky and sometimes extremely funny editions of *Frankie Howerd's Hour* written by Galton and Simpson) and a fine Bill Cotton-prompted, Terry Hughes-directed, 1973 special for BBC 1 (called *Frankie Howerd in Ulster*) – but these three BBC 2 shows, although still over-reliant at times on 'off-the-peg' sketches, really did provide viewers with overwhelming evidence of what a commanding performer Frankie Howerd still could be when a director pushed him to be great instead of just settling for very good.

He was similarly impressive at the end of the same year when he starred in Bernard Delfont's very expensive and high-profile production of *Jack and the Beanstalk* at the London Palladium – but the peak was prompted on this occasion by a sudden explosion of anger. He had been so petrified on the afternoon leading up to the opening night that he had gone for a long walk several times around the block and then returned to the Stygian gloom of the Palladium's windowless Number One dressing-room (or 'Hitler's bunker', as Eric Morecambe always called it[21]) to vomit violently and repeatedly into the sink. Fearing that his show was in danger of starting without its panicky star, Delfont asked his ebullient nephew, Michael Grade (who was about to make the transition from show-business agent to television executive), to go backstage and attempt to 'jolly' Howerd up:

> So I went into his dressing-room about half an hour before opening and said, 'It's great! It's all *kids*, Frank, you know – they'll *love* it! It's a *family* audience. You haven't got the *pros* in tonight. A few critics, but don't worry about it. It's going to be *great*! Bookings are *fantastic* . . .' You know, anything I could think of to put him at his ease. He'd heard all this before – this was all just kind of noise in the background – and his eyes were sunk into the back of his head. And suddenly, there was a knock at the door, and Vanessa Redgrave came in – and decided that this was the moment she was going to recruit Frankie Howerd for the Workers' Revolutionary Party! She started her pitch – about the overthrow of the class struggle and all this – and he suddenly got aggressive. Which was great, because he's got the adrenalin going. And he said [*sotto voce*], 'Who *is* this woman? Get her out of here! [*speaking up*] No, dear. Yes. Not you!' And he started performing! Anyway, eventually, I shushed her out, and, ooh, he was *so* indignant that a fellow-*thespian* would come into an actor's dressing-room, you know, minutes before opening night and start trying to flog them the Workers' Revolutionary Party! He went on the stage inspired – he forgot his nerves![22]

The performance that followed delighted the children, amused the adults and charmed the critics all at once. Michael Billington, writing in *The Guardian*, celebrated Howerd's 'luminous, unflagging presence' as an unusually lugubrious Simple Simon, stepping in and out of character, criticising the other actors, grumbling to the audience and even dressing up in drag and flashing his cocoa-coloured cami-knickers at the front row. 'This is Howerd in a king-sized pack,' the critic concluded, 'and I for one am grateful.'[23]

After this, however, there was a certain loss of momentum. Howerd kept working, doing a little of this and a little of that, but did nothing that stood out as essential.

He entertained British troops in Cyprus and Northern Ireland. He recorded several run-of-the-mill radio shows. He appeared in a couple of so-so television specials. He starred in an abortive pilot for ITV called *A Touch of the Casanovas*. He almost worked for the distinguished director Michael Powell on a movie version of *The Tempest*, but funding for the Anglo-Greek production fell through.[24] He reappeared in a toga for the one-off edition of *Further Up Pompeii!* He even tried his luck abroad, making a fourteen-part sitcom for Canadian television (originally called *Oooh Canada!*, but then retitled *The Frankie Howerd Show*[25]) and a four-part one in Australia (entitled *Up the Convicts*[26]). Once again, however, he seemed to have fallen out of fashion.

He had also started looking tired. Some of the old energy and hunger, as well as some of the old joy, had recently gone missing from his performances. By his own high standards, he was going through the motions. His career was beginning to drift.

One evening near the end of 1974, as he was sitting in his dressing-room preparing to do the same old club act all over again, he suddenly started to sweat – and not just slightly, but heavily and persistently – and the strength seemed to slip away swiftly from his body. When the stage manager arrived to tell him that it was time to go on, he found, to his horror, that he was barely able to move. His elbows bent, he pushed down on the arms of his chair, and nothing happened. Rejecting the offer of a doctor, he just asked for more time to gather his thoughts and summon his strength. Secretly, he was in a state of extreme panic, but he prayed that whatever it was that was wrong would soon go just as suddenly as it had come. Eventually, after half an hour or so, he forced himself up and, although his whole body still seemed to be shaking, he staggered out of his dressing-room and on to the stage, where he quickly called for a chair in which to collapse.

He somehow managed to struggle through his act – the audience, understandably, mistook his many grimaces and groans, along with his occasional memory lapses, for elements of his usual act – but it had been a long and draining ordeal. '[W]hen it came to taking my bow,' he would recall, 'the pains in my stomach were so excruciating I had to stand bent and with my legs astride to help combat the agony.'[27]

A check-up the next day revealed that there was nothing physically wrong; he was informed that (apart from some wear and tear in and around the knee joints) he was suffering from nothing more serious than a spastic colon that had been brought on by a sudden attack of nerves. In the weeks and months that followed, however, the sweating and forgetfulness kept recurring, and his anxiety increased. He started 1975, as a consequence, crippled by stage fright. 'I think I'm getting past it,' he confided to his doctor, and he meant it.[28] 'You're not senile,' he was assured. 'Your problem is psychological.'[29]

That was all that Howerd needed to know. He proceeded to talk his problems through with his regular analyst, as well as mulling them over at great length on his own, and began to dig deep in search of the possible causes of his current condition.

It was when he thought back to the first time he had been on stage that he sensed he was near to arriving at a plausible answer. Standing in front of an audience, he recalled, had filled him with terror, and yet so deep was his need to perform that he had gone on to overcome that feeling – his obsessiveness had held his fears in check. This was the realisation that sparked the answer: 'Now that the obsessiveness had gone,' he concluded, 'there was nothing to stop the basic fear from coming through. It was finally taking over . . .'[30]

Suitably enlightened, he did his best to shrug his shoulders and resign himself to his fate. He was fifty-eight years old: he had enjoyed the proverbial 'good innings', he reasoned, he had achieved all of his main ambitions, and he was now wealthy enough to call it a day.[31] Stand-up was a younger man's game; it strained the nerves and pained the heart. It was probably time for the suffering to stop.

He still had a few outstanding commitments, however, and one of these was to do a charity performance in aid of a local children's home. Full of trepidation, he set off with Dennis Heymer and Sunny Rogers, dreading what was waiting for him ahead. Shivering in the wings, he watched the lights go down and the spotlight fasten on the centre of the stage, and then, with his stomach feeling like 'a solid knot of fear', he took a deep breath and walked self-consciously out to face the crowd.

The initial applause, he was relieved to hear, was loud and sustained. He began his act – his act about his lack of an act – and he won some laughs. The heart started beating a little less hard; the mouth was no longer quite so dry; and the memory, all of a sudden, was razor-sharp. He caught sight of a tiny young girl in the front row, hugging herself with delight as she laughed at all of his 'ooohs' and 'aahs', and, as he pointed at her and smiled back, he realised that he was actually starting to relax.

Right there, right then, Frankie Howerd rediscovered enough of the old desire to overcome the old fear. As twee as it might sound to some, that moment really did summon back his self-belief. 'It was extraordinary,' he later said, 'but the sight of the innocence and happiness of that giggling child brought some strange chord of response from deep down inside me – almost an awareness that someone trusted me to bring them some needed measure of joy.'[32]

He almost had to be dragged from the stage at the end of that performance. He had learned to love being up there all over again.

There would be no more talk of retirement. Clowns had to clown. The plan, from now on, was 'to jog along for a few more years, but at a nice, quiet pace'.[33]

Before he moved on, however, he finally consented to do what he had been asked to do many times before. He agreed to write the story – so far – of his life.

In a way, it made sound commercial sense: prior to the phenomenon of the lucrative video/DVD/cassette/CD of the TV tie-in tour, the show-business memoir represented the main way (other than appearing in a successful new show) whereby a popular personality could bid to revive, preserve or enhance his or her career. In another way, however, it made no sense at all: to produce a memoir that was believable as well as readable, Howerd would have to be seen to reveal aspects of a private life that he had worked so assiduously over the past thirty years to keep hidden.

He squared the circle by writing about the closeted life, the supposedly heterosexual life, and redescribed whatever failed to fit in with that carefully cultivated public image. The countless peaks and troughs of the classic rollercoaster career, therefore, were admitted to the text more or less untouched, but the facts relating to his sexuality, on the other hand, were airbrushed out of existence.

It had been almost a decade since homosexuality had been made legal in Britain,[34] but it was understandable why Howerd remained so anxious about being 'outed'. He was a product of a deeply prejudiced era, which had damaged so many innocent lives and dashed so many decent dreams, and he was unconvinced by more recent claims of greater permissiveness – particularly after a proposed series in 1971 for London Weekend Television, which would have seen him perform a number of concert parties at various RAF bases overseas, was brusquely aborted after Rupert Murdoch, who had recently bought a large block of shares in LWT, declared that he could not countenance having such an 'effeminate' man 'roaming round the world with all those servicemen'.[35] The fear of being ostracised from both his profession and the broader society beyond it was thus probably almost as strong in the mid-1970s as it had been many years before.

He had, perversely, risked exposure on innumerable occasions throughout his long and eventful career, and been blackmailed by several representatives of the so-called 'rough trade' with whom he sometimes dared to consort, but somehow he had never been found out – at least, that is, by the public. Bill Lyon-Shaw, his old friend and tour manager, had managed to persuade one reporter not to publish a sensationalised story he intended to run about Howerd and an alleged boyfriend on the eve of the comedian's 1950 debut at the London Palladium in the revue *Out of this World*:

> I found out that this man liked to drink good claret, and so I invited him to lunch at the Savoy Grill. I can't remember how many bottles of Beaujolais-Villages he got through – but, well, it was certainly more than three – and, while he was putting it away, I tried to talk him round. I said, 'Look, Frankie Howerd is a great entertainer, a great *star*, a very *popular* star, and you want to *kill* him. You publish this, and there's no Frankie Howerd. You will have been responsible for wrecking a complete career, and *thousands* of people will turn away from your newspaper as a consequence of that – because you will have killed one of their idols.' Well, at the end of this long lunch, I could still walk unassisted to a taxi, but he certainly couldn't, and the story, thank goodness, was dropped.[36]

Such close escapes were extraordinarily common in those days, as the pressure of living a lonely and miserable lie led many closeted celebrities to crack at regular intervals and gamble not only with their public reputations but also with their personal safety. Howerd's good friend Gilbert Harding, for example, once found himself stranded stark naked – save for his horn-rimmed spectacles – in his room at Edinburgh's North British Hotel after the young man whom he had picked up in a nearby bar an hour or two before made off with his wallet and watch, his list of questions and answers for that evening's edition of the BBC's *Round Britain Quiz* and every single item of his clothing. A quick telephone call to his puzzled producer ('There're a few things I'll be needing . . .') led to a bundle of new clothes and a fresh pair of brogues being deposited outside his door, and his public humiliation (and probable arrest) was averted, but the gambling still went on.[37]

For some people, sometimes, the gamble went horribly wrong, and if they were especially famous the consequent embarrassment was immense. On 22 October 1953, for example, it was reported in *The Times* that 'John Gielgud, aged 49, described on the charge sheet as a clerk . . . was fined £10 at West London yesterday on a charge of persistently importuning male persons for an immoral purpose at Dudmaston Mews, Chelsea. He pleaded guilty.'[38] Gielgud survived the negative publicity – when he returned to the theatre, where he was appearing in a play called *A Day by the Sea*, his co-star Edith Evans merely remarked, 'Who's been a naughty boy?' – but the 'gentlemen' of the press would never allow the story to fade entirely away.

Similarly, on 22 November 1962 it was widely reported that Wilfrid Brambell, who had recently found fame as one of the stars of *Steptoe and Son*, had been arrested late one night a fortnight before – outside a public lavatory in Shepherd's Bush Green – on the same Sexual Offences charge. Although the fact of his homosexuality was well known within show business (as well as police) circles, he knew that only a complete and passionate denial would now have a chance of saving his career. Insisting in court that he was 'not a homosexual' and had 'never had the slightest desire to importune men for an immoral purpose', he claimed that he had simply ended up 'absolutely sloshed' at a cocktail party at the BBC's Television Centre, and had then walked a quarter of a mile in search of a taxi home to Acton when, feeling 'extremely fuddled', he decided to visit two lavatories in quick succession 'because it was necessary'.[39] In spite of the dubious nature of this defence, Brambell escaped in December with a conditional discharge and payment of twenty-five guineas in costs, but it was only after receiving a favourable response from the next studio audience he encountered that he was finally able to feel sure that his career had really been saved.

These, and other cases like them, had been sobering warnings for the likes of Howerd, but, in spite of the obvious dangers – as well as the great, steadfast and relatively 'safe' affection he was afforded by that paragon of discretion, Dennis Heymer – he could never quite curb his compulsion to flirt, or worse, with other men of either sexual persuasion ('a standing cock,' he would say crudely, 'has no conscience'[40]). This inexplicably brainless form of behaviour (though not quite as exhaustingly remorseless as certain of the more gossipy accounts would later suggest[41]) was made to seem all the more rashly irrational by the fact that Howerd, unlike those entertainers who had come to prominence in a later and slightly more tolerant age (such as the more openly effeminate John Inman and Larry Grayson), steadfastly refused to abandon the old carapace of camped-up heterosexuality.

On the stage and on the screen, he had always portrayed the vulnerable, fallible heterosexual: like a naughty schoolboy, his comedic alterego was a little scared of women, but attracted to them none the less, and quick to sneer at those whom he considered 'queer'. In one painfully ironic episode of *Whoops Baghdad*, for example, he shared a scene with a stereotypically sissified character – a genie of the lamp – who was being played by his dear friend and former lover, Lee Young, and, in accordance with the script, he mocked him remorselessly for his effeminacy: 'I hope this is not contagious,' Howerd's character growls, before remarking, 'One minute I was counting bubbles, and the next, *poof*: there you are!'

Contrary to many later perspectives on Howerd's public image, contemporary audiences were by no means uniform in their interpretation of his camply droll demeanour. His fellow-professionals had known, of course, since the earliest days of his career ('One thing about Frankie,' someone had said at a Variety Club lunch in his honour, 'he can certainly put bums on seats.' Tommy Cooper, one of Howerd's best friends in show business, replied, 'Safest place for them!'[42]), but the broader audience was by no means so sure. Some, of course, spotted all of the signs and saw straight through the disguise, but many more either did not or were not sure. 'I once wrote a very, very long analysis of Frankie Howerd based entirely on the idea that he was butch,' the critic Clive James confessed. 'Nobody told me. Usually with the camp comedians you could tell, but I couldn't tell with Frankie Howerd.'[43]

That was very much how Frankie Howerd wanted it to stay. When, therefore, he finally settled down to write about his life, he was prepared to tell some, but by no means all, of the truth. Time and again, when it came to the details of his love life, all of the notable trysts with men were rewritten as tender affairs with women, and poor Dennis Heymer was reduced to the role of a perennial and somewhat pathetic 'gooseberry', forever tagging along on Howerd's romantic trips with his imaginary girlfriends like some humble little valet. It was a cruel way to treat the most loyal and loving man in his life, and Howerd knew it, but Heymer was far too supportive to think of complaining about his shadowy fate in the text. If it would help protect his partner's career, he reasoned, then so be it.

Finally, when it came to supplying his readers with a reason for why (even though, as he blokeishly bragged, he 'never went short of it'[44]) he had never married, Howerd merely alleged that he had suffered three successive blows to the heart which had been of such severity as to leave it bruised and battered beyond all repair. The first time, he alleged, had been at the hands of an unnamed woman he claimed to have met when he was stationed in Wales during the war (she married someone else after he had been posted on to Plymouth);[45] the second time, he said, his heart had been damaged by 'a gorgeous girl' with whom he became 'so smitten' during his summer season in Blackpool in 1949 that he 'nearly married her' (she went off instead with a 'well-known writer');[46] and the third and final time 'in the late 1950s', he asserted, his heart had been well and truly shattered by 'a famous actress' (the identity of whom – along with the details of their past stage-managed affair – he knew the cuttings libraries would reveal to be Joan Greenwood) who, just like the others, had abandoned him in favour of marriage to another.[47]

Entitled *On The Way I Lost It*, Howerd's autobiography appeared in the autumn of 1976 to many warm and appreciative reviews, followed by a series of entertaining tie-in radio and television appearances. Whatever individual critics thought of the fairly obvious elisions and omissions relating to his personal life, the vast majority were happy enough to pay tribute to his extraordinary candour about other aspects of his life and career – including the questionable decisions in the second half of the 1950s and the heart-rending period in the wilderness at the start of the 1960s. No old scores were settled, no cooling coals were raked over, and the only person who was subjected to any real critical invective (apart from Michael Winner) was, engagingly, Howerd himself.

This part of the book, at least, was no act. The novelist Rebecca West – who had been a good friend of his for some years – discovered this when, one day after they had shared a leisurely lunch, she asked him if he had ever felt that the fates were set against him. She expected him to say that he always did, but instead he surprised her by insisting, with obvious sincerity, that most of the things that had gone wrong in his life had done so purely as a result of his own mistakes.[48]

It was typically, and admirably, perverse of Frankie Howerd: after hiding so much in the writing of his life, he still ended up being far harder on it, and on himself, than most other stars had dared to be in print on their own celebrated lives, images and careers. That was what made the book readable; that was what would make it last.

As for what Howerd did next: it was work. He just kept on working. The clown still needed to clown.

CHAPTER 15

Cult Status

I mean, it's too late to rehearse a new act now, innit?

'I want to live for ever,' Frankie Howerd once told his sister, Betty. 'Whatever for?' she asked. 'Why, when your health is poor and you're suffering excruciating pain in knees and legs, do you want to go on and on?' He replied, without the slightest suggestion of a smile, by saying: 'Because I want to find out who did it in the end.'[1]

He had always been a great fan of 'whodunits', but, as he slipped into his sixties, his search for answers to more spiritual kinds of issues became especially intense. The state of his career still mattered (and he was grateful to his new agent, Tessa Le Bars, for keeping his diary full), and public recognition still had the power to move him (he had choked back the tears when he was made the subject of *This Is Your Life* in 1976, and had given in to them completely when he collected his OBE the following year[2]), but, increasingly, it was the question of faith and its basis that seemed to feature most prominently in his thoughts.

'How can God be benign,' he took to asking, as he sat slouching over his second or third glass of brandy in Al Gallo d'Oro at the end of the evenings, 'when there's so much suffering in the world?'[3] He did not expect his guests to respond to such a clichéd yet heartfelt question; he was merely debating with himself – and the religion that he had inherited from his mother.

It was not just to do with any creeping intimations of mortality. It was also the inevitable consequence of the keen interest that he took in the broader world around him.

'It's people I'm interested in,' he said, 'not possessions. I am curious and nosey. If I do shows abroad I like to get out and about among

261

people because I like to know what is going on in any given situation, politically as well as economically.'⁴

He had always attempted to do just this on the countless occasions when he worked (without accepting any financial reward) for Combined Services Entertainment over the course of the previous three decades. He had performed, amongst other places, in Nicosia shortly after EOKA terrorists had shot dead several British servicemen in the streets;⁵ he had entertained troops in Borneo while a number of head–hunters looked on from positions high up in the surrounding trees; and he had braved an IRA-organised shower of bricks, rocks, stones and Molotov cocktails on his way to put on shows at border barracks in Northern Ireland. Some of the sights and sounds, as he travelled from one war-torn context to the next, had been heart-rending, while others had just been sickening, but, none the less, he kept making himself go back. 'Frankie was terrific,' recalled Derek Agutter (who, besides being the father of Jenny, was also, more pertinently, head of CSE from 1965 to 1985). 'He always wanted to go wherever the troops were serving in the most dangerous places, knowing they would be without their families, on their own and in real trouble spots. He had no regard for his own safety. I had to insist on going along to look after him.'⁶

Howerd had also been deeply moved, and more than a little distressed, by a recent visit he had paid to a home for emotionally disturbed children. 'The variety of tragedy,' he later said with a shudder, 'was seemingly endless.'⁷ He had been a fairly regular visitor, as well as a discreetly generous supporter, of such institutions for many years, but the sight of so much suffering was becoming increasingly hard for him to take. He would never stop going, but he did eventually stop expecting to find, upon returning home, any kind of comfort (let alone any acceptable form of explanation or justification) in his Christian faith.

'I'm religious,' he used to say. 'I like people and philosophy and dogs.'⁸ By the second half of the 1970s, however, he continued to care about people, still studied philosophy and kept on doting on his dogs, but he no longer seemed committed to his old religious beliefs.

'We used to have endless fierce arguments about religion,' recalled his friend Jeanne Mockford (a devout Catholic who had appeared with him, as the soothsayer Senna, in *Up Pompeii!*). 'Over the years something was gnawing at him. When I first met Frankie, he had a Bible by his bedside. But not at the end. The Bible had gone. He just turned away from it.'⁹

Rather than continue to rely primarily on the scriptures for insight, Howerd now immersed himself in those writings and research that related to metaphysics, ethics and anything else that promised to provide him with a measure of reliable guidance. He had his favourites (Plato, Aristotle and Aquinas were among them), but he was always open to each and every new approach that he encountered – no matter how improbable and unorthodox it might have seemed. On one occasion, for example, he delayed an important meeting with his radio producer in order to listen, goggle-eyed, to the ramblings of yet another over-excited psychic. 'Stupid old cow,' he growled as, at long last, she departed. 'Still,' he added, 'you can never be too careful.'[10]

As far as these existential interests were concerned, work was now more of an invaluable distraction than it was a therapeutic solution. Howerd had done it all before – many, many times before – and, while he (a firm believer in the reassuring old idea of 'Dr Theatre') still felt mildly reinvigorated whenever he walked back on to the stage to face another audience, he was far too self-aware and self-critical to think that he could ever again be anywhere near as good as he had been back in the days when his crafty art was so full of youthful energy and nervous wit. As his character in *Up Pompeii!* would doubtless have put it, 'How tempus fugits!' The old need remained, but a great deal of the old thrill had gone.

Part of him accepted this, but another part remained far too proud to accept it, and the result of this internal tension was an ageing, anxious, edgy performer who was hard to write for, hard to direct and, at times, almost impossible to please. In 1978, for example, the producer Richard Willcox, then BBC Radio's Deputy Head of Light Entertainment and a very decent and well-liked man inside the Corporation, was asked to preside over a rather grand and very expensive new eight-part series for Radio 2 entitled *The Frankie Howerd Variety Show*. As experienced and accomplished though he was as a programme-maker, however, Willcox did not make it past the halfway mark.

He had (by radio standards) a huge budget, a reasonably decent – if relatively inexperienced – team of writers (the up-and-coming partnership of Laurence Marks and Maurice Gran, supported by three young Cambridge graduates, Jimmy Mulville, Rory McGrath and Clive Anderson), a twenty-four-piece orchestra and a list of unexciting but fairly well-known future guests. In spite of all of this, however, and all of the

care and expertise that Willcox lavished upon the project, Frankie
Howerd never seemed remotely happy about any aspect of the production. The comedian had fallen back into the bad old habits: never
saying what he wanted, but making it abundantly and painfully clear,
over and over again, what he most definitely did *not* want ('*It's craaaap!*').

'He was extraordinary, the most amazing man,' Willcox would
remember. 'Yet he was so unsure of himself that he couldn't make a
rational judgement on a script.'[11] Each show evolved in the same excruciating way: Willcox would take the first draft of the material to
Howerd's home in Edwardes Square, where the star duly read it in his
brightly lit ground-floor morning-room, his bushy eyebrows bobbing
up and down in a mixture of puzzlement, boredom and horror as he
did so, and then the text would be handed back to Willcox with the
instruction: 'Take it away and rewrite it!' The producer would then
shuffle off, get the script rewritten and, three days after that, return to
Edwardes Square to hear the revised verdict directly from Howerd
himself: '*It's craaaap!*'

'In all,' Willcox recalled, 'I went back six times.' Exhausted and
exasperated, he decided to resort to an old producer's trick, and returned
once again – but this time armed with the very first script that the
performer had read and rejected. 'I think we've cracked it!' he said
hopefully as he passed the pages over. Howerd settled down with a
deep frown and an extra-large glass of gin and tonic, mumbled his way
through the text and then exclaimed: 'Now that's much better!'[12]

It was not the reaction, as Rory McGrath would somehow contrive
to suggest, of a man with 'no sense of humour'.[13] This was, after all,
the man who had revolutionised stand-up comedy; the man who had
spotted and sponsored the prodigious comic talents of Eric Sykes, Galton
and Simpson, Johnny Speight and countless others; the man whom
Peter Cook among others had regarded as one of his greatest comic
heroes; and the man who had inspired not one but several generations
of new comedy performers. The apparent irrationality of the reaction
of a man who had achieved all of that could hardly be attributed to an
inadequate sense of humour.

It was, on the contrary, the reaction of a man who knew, far better
than anyone else in and around Broadcasting House (let alone those
callow souls slumped around the bar at the Cambridge Footlights),
what Eric Sykes, Galton and Simpson and Johnny Speight – genuinely

imaginative, original and disciplined writerly wits – could do with a comedy script, and knew that what he was now being offered paled in comparison, but who now lacked both the energy and the patience (and perhaps also the basic enthusiasm) to sit down and attempt to help his young writers reach up to a higher level.

It was largely left to the already over-worked Richard Willcox, therefore, to try to improve the quality of the material, as well as enhance all other aspects of the show, and he duly did his best. Howerd, however, was seldom in the right frame of mind (nor, in truth, the right physical state) to contribute anything but negativity to the production.

He was, for one thing, drinking rather more than he should. The odd alcoholic drink had always been an option to help steady his first-night nerves, but over the course of the previous few years, the option had gradually come close to being a necessity, and too many of Howerd's performances were now overly reliant on the Dutch courage to be had from a double brandy.[14]

The drink did indeed help calm him down before he went on, but, once he *was* on, he needed something equally artificial to lift him back up. The over-reliance on drink, therefore, led eventually to an over-reliance on drugs in the form of amphetamines. Sometimes, as a consequence of this volatile cocktail, it would be several minutes into a performance before the various uppers and downers sloshed their way towards a relatively serviceable equilibrium.

He knew it. He was the most experienced person in the studio. The next time he was preparing to go on, however, the heart, once again, would start beating faster, the nerves would return, and the hand would reach back out for the bottle, and then, as his thoughts turned to his imminent performance, he would reach back out again for a pill. The sloshing would then start all over again.

Careful editing would help hide the more obvious stumbles and slip-ups, but there was a limit to what could ultimately be disguised. Howerd's delivery, for example, was less sure than it was before; he sounded as if he was reading from a script (which, of course, he was, but never before had he struggled so much to make his speech sound spontaneous), and the old verbal tics were now being used far too obviously – and far too frequently – as face-saving little tricks. He also sounded tired, sometimes even a little bored, and overly concerned with his diction, and the hour-long show's anachronistic Variety-style format (which not only made repeats of *Beyond Our Ken* sound dangerous in the late 1970s, but also proved far too indulgent towards a succession of bad impressionists, bland singers and rinky-dink pianists) did nothing to elicit any greater sense of urgency either from him or from anyone else.

Worst of all was the material, which was often either painfully uninspired or just patently unsuited to Howerd's peculiar style and strengths as a comic performer. The uninspired kind, delivered by a great but currently uninspired stand-up comedian, made the heart sink:

> Ladies and Gentle-*men*, I appeal to you – well, perhaps not all of you, or even any of you – I'm appealing tonight, ladies and gentle-men, for succour. *Succ-our!* Succour from all you succours! You won't believe this, but I have been charged with a crime of violence. Yes. I'm sorry. Ladies and gentlemen, your Francis, the gentle giant – oh, no, please, it's wicked to mock the afflicted . . .

The unsuitable kind, such as the gag that sounded as if it had been gathering dust dangling limply from the most distant peg in the office of *The Comedians* – 'I don't know, meself, very much about football, except I've heard that Brian Clough is going to become the next England coach. The coach, yes. They're going to take his teeth out and put some seats in! Ha-ha-ha!'[15] – or the one that appeared to have been rescued from the bin of *The Two Ronnies* – 'A Defence Ministry court of inquiry was told today that the Army is so under-strength that, should the Russians cross the Rhine tomorrow, they'll be faced by the Third Battalion: the Girl Guides. Which should take their minds off war. For a bit' – just made one wonder why Howerd was bothering to do a show of his own at all.

Richard Willcox certainly wondered just that, and after enduring all of the tantrums and traumas of the first desperately eventful month, dropped out, suffering from nervous exhaustion, and checked into a local hospital. His emergency replacement, a young Cambridge graduate by the name of Griff Rhys Jones, had no real time to effect any significant changes but, as he was already a great fan of the star of the show, he came to find the whole chaotic and often shambolic experience strangely enjoyable. Recalling the regular post-show inquests that Howerd used to hold at his home in Edwardes Square, Rhys Jones explained that each one tended to develop in more or less the same way:

He'd put an entire bottle of whatever it was that you'd asked for in front of you. So Rory [McGrath] was sat there with a great big bottle of whisky, and I sat there with a huge bottle of vodka and Clive [Anderson] sat there with a huge bottle of gin – and so the afternoon started! And, of course, we were only twenty, so we'd start hitting this stuff, because, you know, seeing a whole bottle of gin – even at university, we'd never seen one before. And he'd say, 'What did you think of the show last night?' So Rory would say, 'Well, I thought you were great, Frank. The monologue could do with a bit of work, but you were marvellous.' And he'd go round and say, 'What do *you* think?' And Clive would say, 'Ah, well, Frank, er, yes – right – okay, um, ah, yeah, it was all right.' Then Marks and Gran [would speak]. And then he'd say, 'Well, I'll tell you what *I* think: *It was craaaap!*'[16]

As for Howerd's own difficulties in front of the microphone, there was little that Rhys Jones (or 'the Welsh person', as Howerd sometimes preferred to call him[17]) felt able to do but just sit down and hope that his star had mixed the right quantities of drink and drugs:

I remember once we were watching him do this [monologue], and he said, 'Yes, and, um, I went to Debenhams, missus. Yes. Ooh, yes. No. Debenhams. Yehss. Debenhams . . . Deben . . . Debenaahherrum . . . Debennn . . . in the . . . aahhh . . . ooaahh . . . yehss . . . Debenham . . . – Anyway!' And then he went on with the act. We were all in the box going, '*What's happened?*' And then somebody said, 'It's all right, it's okay: it's only the brandy. Oh, look – it's okay, there's the pill knocking in now!' And off he went with the rest of the monologue.[18]

Miraculously, in spite of such problems, the series proved reasonably popular with a loyal core of listeners, and Howerd pushed on, unscathed, with his various other projects.

His various other projects, however, appeared to amount to little more than a rag-bag of relatively unenticing bits and pieces. In 1979, for example, there was a cabaret tour of New Zealand, a concert on the *QEII* and a tiny bit-part in the Eric Sykes TV movie *The Plank*; during the following year, there was a one-off special for Yorkshire

Television (*Frankie Howerd Reveals All*) and a guest spot on *Parkinson*; in 1981, Howerd appeared in a fairly patchy series of decent monologues and weak sketches (*Frankie Howerd Strikes Again*) for Yorkshire Television; filmed a couple of Gilbert and Sullivan operettas for the American television market (*Trial By Jury* and *HMS Pinafore*) and did a quick 'turn' as Frosch the drunken gaoler in the English National Opera's production of *Die Fledermaus* at the London Coliseum; and, in 1982, he made his choices for the BBC's *Desert Island Discs* (which were very similar, in tone and type, to the ones he made for his previous appearance back in 1959[19]), had a brief spell as one of the panellists on ITV's revival of *Does The Team Think?* and lent his name (but none of his effort) to a depressingly shoddy compilation of instantly forgettable one-upmanship anecdotes – published by J.M. Dent – called *Trumps!* (a new wartime sitcom he had recorded for the BBC, *Then Churchill Said To Me*, failed to appear – supposedly because of heightened political sensitivities following the outbreak in April of the Falklands/Malvinas conflict, but more probably because it was deemed to be embarrassingly poor[20]).

It was not that Howerd was being under-used during this period: he was popping up all over the place, in theatres, radio and terrestrial television channels, in chat shows, quizzes, panel games, pantomimes and extraordinarily repetitive ads (e.g. 'Naughty – *but nice!*'). It was just that, as an experienced and accomplished entertainer rather than merely a popular personality, he was often under-appreciated. In 1981, the Variety Club of Great Britain did present him with a Silver Heart to commemorate his thirty-five years in show-business, and he certainly appreciated the gesture, but would probably have preferred a decent offer of work.

There seemed to be no serious vehicles for him any more, no neat, simple and sensible showcases for his distinctive and enduring ability as a stand-out stand-up comedian. What made matters far worse, from Howerd's perspective, was the fact that certain aspects of his basic act were now being assimilated (without acknowledgement) by younger, and supposedly more fashionable performers.

His forty-year-old routine with his elderly accompanist, for example, was now being used by Barry Humphries, who, as Edna Everage, often mocked 'her' miserable old bridesmaid and hard-of-hearing accompanist, Madge Allsop. Howerd's equally venerable 'Ooh, I don't feel at all well!'-style monologues, along with his regular exchanges with various unseen managers, agents, impresarios and members of the audience, were also being reheated (along with the odd routine with yet another unspeaking pianist) by Larry Grayson. Howerd had been the man who originated these routines, and he was still the one who did them best, and yet the master was now being overshadowed by his imitators.

Grayson, in particular, had become Howerd's show-business *bête noire*. Although he was only six years younger than Howerd (and only one year short of Howerd's 'official' age), Grayson had only come to national prominence in the early 1970s, after Michael Grade had spotted him performing in a seedy London nightclub, signed him up as a client and then completely transformed his professional career.

Limper than a filleted salad leaf, Grayson brought a far more obvious kind of comical effeminacy – camp in single quotation marks – to ITV's peak-time schedules. He would lean for support on the top of a white wooden chair ('Well! I'm worn out before I start!') while he waffled on about his weakness for Wincarnis, his volatile relationship with his friends Everard, Slack Alice, Apricot Lil and Pop-It-In Pete the postman ('The things I've had through my letter-box over Easter!'), his strangely enervated pianist ('You look as though you're embalmed – I can smell the ferrets from here!') and his never-ending search for a special kind of ointment called Fiery Jack ('I've lost his address') – occasionally breaking off to complain about the draught ('Shut that door!') or the dirt ('Look at the muck in 'ere!'). 'What a gay day!' he would say, and his audience continued to laugh.

Howerd – who remembered the Nuneaton-born Grayson from the days when, under his previous stage name of Billy Breen, he used to slog his way around the old provincial club circuit, quite often appearing in drag – considered his rival to be overly crude, technically limited and shamelessly derivative. Of all the things that he disliked about the performer, however, the thing that he disliked most was the way that Grayson seemed to keep getting the jobs that *he* had expected to be offered.

Kenneth Williams was, if anything, even more resentful of such competitors. Writing in his diary at the start of 1977, he recorded the most salient point from a conversation he had just had with his agent:

> We talked about why there'd been no offers of work of any kind & he pointed out that the Grayson TV Show is a complete crib of my stuff, and that Inman is doing the same thing [. . .] It hadn't

hit me before! *Of course!* they've found other people to do it, and *cheaper* people in every sense.[21]

It was certainly a growing source of worry for both of these experienced performers – particularly when they reflected on the additional fact that Grayson, unlike either of them, had a reputation for being a relatively easy person with whom to work.

Williams, however, had never really succeeded in carving out a niche for himself on television as the kind of solo performer who could command his own starring vehicles. Howerd, of course, had done just that a very long time before, and so he, of the two of them, now had the more legitimate reason to feel aggrieved. Whenever he sat down and saw Grayson performing on the screen, he did not just think, 'I could have done that' – he also thought, 'I *did* do that!'

It was a game show, however, that ended up rattling him most. When Bruce Forsyth left *The Generation Game* – one of the most popular weekend shows on British television – in 1978, Frankie Howerd harboured serious hopes of replacing him, and so he was livid when Larry Grayson was chosen instead. Each Saturday after that, as he heard the emotional new host cry out at the end of the show, 'And I *love* you all!' Howerd tried his best not to sit back and think about what might have been – him appearing regularly in front of fifteen to twenty million viewers – but, none the less, the feeling that he had been overlooked in favour of a lesser, but more 'fashionable', figure cut deep. 'That man,' he grumbled, 'stole my bread and butter.'[22]

Unable to find a suitable challenge to galvanise both his creativity and his career, he struggled gamely on, doing what he could with what he was offered, and doing most of it quite well, but with little evident enthusiasm. When he was invited to appear as a guest on ITV's tortuous quiz show, *3–2-1*, he duly obliged. Similarly, when he was asked (along with the likes of Ian Dury and Jon Pertwee) to contribute vocally to what at the time was a novel kind of computer game called *Deus Ex Machina* (an elaborately odd Orwellian-style fantasy about authoritarianism, personal identity and genetic engineering, featuring a 'synchronised soundtrack' along with the on-screen graphics[23]), once again he agreed and then proceeded to do his best.

Physically, however, the years had started to take their toll. He had broken his coccyx (just like, ironically, his character had done in *Carry*

On Doctor) in 1978, and then his pelvis in 1980, and had put on some weight as a consequence of his restricted mobility; in 1983, he underwent a major operation after being warned that as his knee joints had begun to crumble and he would soon be wheelchair-bound unless he agreed to urgent surgery; and, even though he did indeed sometimes use it as an excuse to initiate a little physical contact, he really was suffering from an increasingly painful bad back.

All of these aches and pains, combined with his lingering fears about being struck down again by stage fright, made him more prone than ever to bad moods and petulant outbursts. He was angry and frustrated with himself, deep down, because he was now finding it so hard to move around, memorise his lines and time their delivery, but he still found himself taking it out, at times, on those innocent individuals who just happened to be around him. The drink and drugs made it worse instead of better, and probably prompted some of his increasingly sad, rash and impersonal passes at bemused young, and usually heterosexual, men ('You don't know what you're missing!' he would mutter as they fled the room[24] – to which a quick 'Likewise!' would surely have sufficed as a hurried response).

It upset his old friends and close colleagues to see him keep pushing himself on when he was clearly so unhappy and unwell. Barry Took, in particular, was depressed to find him in such a poor state when, in 1983, he agreed to adapt *Volpone*, Ben Jonson's classic Jacobean farce about an ageing con-man's bid to out-con his young pretenders, as a starring vehicle for Howerd at the Churchill Theatre in Bromley. Re-titled *The Fly and the Fox*, the actual process whereby Took and Howerd had collaborated on 'Howerding up' the text had proven to be quite enjoyable, but, when the production went ahead, the writer was taken aback by the apparent decline in the powers of the performer:

> He was, I'm afraid, dreadful. Maybe to say that he seemed without talent or timing is too harsh, but, by his own very high standards, he was really poor. Looking back, you see, it's not as surprising now as it was then, because, back then, I didn't know that Frank was several years older than he'd claimed, and I just couldn't understand why he was so sluggish compared to just a few years before, let alone compared to how electrifying he'd been when I'd first seen him perform. It wasn't easy to accept.[25]

The critics tended to concur, lamenting the absence of the play's traditional satirical bite and narrative drive, and complaining, reluctantly, that Howerd often appeared oblivious to the broader aspects of the story.

After this disappointment, Howerd licked his wounds while he drifted through shorter and less demanding engagements, such as a brief spell as a 'roving reporter' for ITV's new breakfast show, *Good Morning Britain*; an ill-considered role as the MC of Channel 4's ill-considered, and ill-timed, attempt to adapt for a British audience Chuck Barris' notorious US anti-talent contest, *The Gong Show* (which, in spite of a great deal of pre-transmission publicity, was 'gonged' itself straight after its pilot edition); a commission from Marks & Spencer to lend his name to a flimsy book of ghost-edited, and supposedly 'side-splitting', anecdotes called *Howerd's Howlers* (for which the discerning reader required a ghost laugher); and a job as the narrator of a Filmfair cartoon series for ITV called *The Blunders*. He even agreed to participate in a show called *Roland Rat's Yuletide Binge*, which really did make his heyday seem long ago and far away.

Sensing the need to reaffirm his reputation as a truly great comedy star – instead of merely the straight man to a woollen rat – Howerd decided to return to the scene of a past triumph and reprise his performance as Pseudolus in a revival of *A Funny Thing Happened On The Way To The Forum*. Presented initially as the centrepiece of the Chichester Festival Theatre's twenty-fifth anniversary season, the production ran there from 11 August to 27 September in 1986, before transferring to the Piccadilly Theatre in the West End of London (where it opened on 14 November).

Retrograde step though it was, the revival would have made sense, as a timely fillip for his flagging career, if he had still been able to cope with the show's considerable physical demands, but that was clearly no longer the case. The obligation to be on stage for all but a few minutes of the entire two-and-a-half-hour production had come close to hospitalising Howerd back in the 1960s, when he was still a fairly fit man in his early forties, but by the mid-1980s, when he was far from fit and on the verge of his seventies, the strain would prove too great.

He could still win plenty of laughs with his opening monologue, and could still deliver the best of the later comic lines with rare aplomb, but there was no hiding the frailty and pain that he was now feeling (he had to sit down for some of the musical numbers, and even wandered briefly off the stage when he sensed that his presence would not be missed), nor was there much hope of disguising the jaded nature of his overall performance. Although the critics had appeared keen to be kind when the show began its West End run ('I can think of no comic actor – with the exception of John Cleese – with whom I'd rather spend an evening,' opined one of them in *The Times*[26]), they wasted little time after the opening night in highlighting its obvious weaknesses, and the production closed prematurely, after a modest forty-nine performances, on 27 December.

Howerd was still struggling to get over this setback when, in 1987, he suffered another. Shortly after recording a version of his one-man show for Channel 4 (which broadcast it under the title of *Superfrank!*) and a short radio series for the BBC (called *Frankie's Forum*), he fell and damaged one of his fragile knees so badly that he had to have another operation that effectively put him out of action for the best part of half a year.

The enforced break at least allowed him to spend more time than usual in the most recent property he had purchased: a pretty, pink-walled cottage in the village of Cross, near Axbridge in Somerset, which he had spotted and snapped up on impulse while he was opening a new country club in the area during the mid-1970s. Filling the house and its grounds with some of his most cherished mementoes, including the two statues that had been salvaged from the bomb-damaged Palace of Westminster during the Blitz (which he now displayed proudly on his terrace), and, replanted in the garden, a fig tree that had been given him by Sir Winston Churchill, Howerd described the place as his special retreat: 'I can't believe how beautiful it is.'[27] Worries about work, how-ever, intruded even into this little idyll, and he spent much of the time mulling over what had recently gone wrong.

His agent Tessa Le Bars (described by one of her former colleagues, Helen Walters, as a person who was 'incredibly caring and extraordinarily patient, as well as extremely professional, with all of her clients'[28]) did her best to help Howerd through the gloom, but he remained restlessly self-critical and introspective. The act, he feared, had once again become a problem, and this time he could find no solution.

Life did not seem any easier when he resumed work in the middle of 1988. After warming up with a few low-key stand-up dates in

London, he went to Liverpool to perform at the city's Festival of Comedy. According to the journalist John McCready, who attended one of the shows, Howerd 'got heckled by some feminists. He was just doing his normal familiar act, all very gentle and playful, and suddenly this particular group of feminists started heckling him, shouting out "Sexist!" and "Sexist pig!" He looked really hurt and taken aback by it.'[29] Such a reaction, even though it was very much a 'one-off', would have mortified an entertainer who, by his own admission, always dreaded causing any offence ('I like to think of myself as a clown,' he once said, 'not a missionary'[30]). He managed, after an unplanned stuttering interlude, to complete that evening's act, but as he was already battling against stage fright, and he was no real ad-libber, the experience did him no good at all.

His luck at last began to change at the start of the following year, when a performance at the Hackney Empire's *Up the Festival* event met with an encouragingly positive reaction. The real turning-point, however, arrived in April, when he was invited to go to the Marriott Hotel in Mayfair to deliver a speech to the Gallery First Nighters' Club, a group of avid theatregoing faithfuls who were always happy to pay homage, each year, to their heroes. When it came his turn to talk, he felt his nerves (and his knees) go, and had to be helped to his feet by the club's president, Jack Rossiter. He flashed Rossiter a look of panic, but Rossiter, who had been around long enough to know how best to respond to an attack of stage fright, simply whispered to him, '*It's just another show – all right?*'[31] Howerd looked at him, mumbled, 'Just another show,' and then proceeded to deliver his speech.

When he finished, three hundred people stood up and applauded. 'What you said back there,' he told Rossiter as he shook hands and prepared to leave. 'It's what I wanted to hear.'[32]

He felt calmer after that, and started to reacquire much of his old appetite for performing in front of an audience. After easing his way back into circulation via a series of semi-private speaking engagements, the odd low-profile club date and even taking part in a mock-debate at the Cambridge Union (while everyone else addressed the rise and fall of the Roman Empire, he addressed the rise and fall of the Moss Empires), Howerd felt ready to take his stand-up act back out on a twenty-five-date nationwide tour (which he called *Frankie Howerd Bursts into Britain*).

He had barely begun when, in September 1989, his brother Sidney died, aged sixty-nine. Although they had never been particularly close, he still felt a keen sense of loss – which made him more attentive than ever to his last remaining sibling, Betty (who had been through both a marriage and a divorce and was now, once again, committed solely to her brother). Grateful for the distraction afforded by his tour, he pushed on, and soon came to find it far more rewarding than he had dared to expect.

What surprised him most of all, as he went from venue to venue, was the age range of his audiences. He was not just attracting the people who had been fans for twenty or thirty or more years. He was also drawing in some of the children, and even a few of the grandchildren, of such long-standing fans. He had won over the odd high-profile youth cultural figure before – the late Sid Vicious, for example, had hailed Howerd as the 'main man' back in the late 1970s, when the Sex Pistols were at their most self-consciously iconoclastic[33] – but not until now had he enjoyed the kind of extraordinarily broad multi-generational appeal that had so many ordinary young people flocking in to watch him perform. It suddenly gave him a heightened feeling of hope. It made him feel as if he still had a future.

Subsequent meetings with Tessa Le Bars – or 'Tess-*a!*' as he always called his agent – in her fourth-floor Queen Anne Street office became, as a consequence, rather brighter and busier affairs, with more offers to consider and more projects to plan and discuss. He agreed to do a spot at the Hackney Empire's *Holsten Funny Business Show*; he signed up for two series of a children's comedy-drama, called *All Change*, for Yorkshire Television (he played the cameo role of Uncle Bob, an eccentric million-aire biscuit baron and birdwatcher who only communicated with his avaricious relations via videotape); and he seemed more open than ever to quirkier, and supposedly more youth-oriented, kinds of proposals (even though his last venture in this area – a song called 'Sects Therapy' for Eric Woolfson's jaw-droppingly bizarre psychoanalytical concept album, entitled *Freudiana*, which also featured 10cc's Eric Stewart singing about the nature of the relationship between the ego and the id, The Flying Pickets on the interpretation of dreams and Leo Sayer on the analyst-analysand dynamic – had failed to excite even the loneliest young lover of 'deep' records in lyric-laden gatefold sleeves[34]).

Howerd took to calling his new student following his 'Frankie

Pankies', and they, in turn, started turning up to his shows wearing T-shirts on which they had printed such phrases as 'Get Your Titters Out' and 'Nay, Nay and Thrice Nay'. There was something strangely self-regarding and perhaps even depressingly smug about the way that many of them tended to laugh immediately and uproariously at the merest mention of one of his catchphrases, as if they were celebrating their own cleverness even more than they were his art, but Howerd seemed disinclined to mind. Although he was not having to really *earn* his laughs – which surely must have frustrated him, deep down, as a proud professional stand-up who was a true master of his craft – he insisted that he was just flattered that they kept coming back. 'Anyone who is a fan of mine cannot be anything but good,' he insisted with a sly smile. 'You understand what I mean? I appreciate them very much. I'd be stupid not to. Don't query it. Don't question it. Accept it. With gratitude.'[35]

He had known some dark days in his career. He knew what it was like to be written off and abandoned and ignored. Now he found himself back in demand once again, and, even though he might have wished that it had come from a more discerning kind of consumer, it was still a demand he was delighted to supply.

In 1990, therefore, he performed his stand-up show, *Quite Frankly, Frankie Howerd At His Tittermost!* (featuring support from 'Madame Sunny Rogers at the Piano'), first at the Lyric Hammersmith during April, then at the Garrick in May and then at various other venues as part of a national tour, and pitched his material primarily at his so-called 'cult following'. There was the odd new(ish) line (e.g. 'The worst thing about an orgy is you don't know who to thank afterwards'), but, as his younger fans had not heard his old act before, there was no need for anything more. Commenting on the wild reaction to his well-known phrases, he told an interviewer: 'They fell about. So I thought, "If they want it, I'll give it to them," So they got it.'[36]

They certainly did. At the start of each show, he would 'do' Frankie Howerd – or rather, *their* flattened-out, grossly simplified and, essentially, fairly patronising impression of 'Frankie Howerd' – expressly for them:

We'll get into the comedy act here now. We'll get into the comedy stuff now, all right, okay? [*Clears his throat and gets himself ready*] Go: *OH NO, OH NOOOO MISSUS, OOOH NO!* [*He is drowned out by a deafening ovation, accompanied by countless shrieks of laughter and shrill whistles and wild whoops of delight]* All right – I'll do an encore! I don't usually do encores till the end – if I get to the end! Um, all right: *NOT ON YOUR NELLIE! YOU SHUT YOUR FACE, YOU! OOOOH, TITTER YE NOT! TIT-TER-YE-NOT! OOH, NAY, NAY AND THRICE NAY!* – It's coming out now, y'see, it's all coming out in a torrent, now.[37]

After another long and loud ovation, he would then revert to his old, 'proper' act: 'No, actually, I don't – to be honest – I don't feel much like it tonight . . .'

His broader audience was just happy to see him back on form, and so much brighter, livelier and sharper than he had seemed during the course of the previous few years. Old fans came back to the fold, experienced critics returned to reaffirm their admiration and the new breed of devotee continued to fill up the first few rows (and yet another former Sex Pistol – this time it was John Lydon – was happy to be seen giving Howerd a standing ovation[38]). BBC 2's *Arena* arts documentary strand produced a splendid celebration of his remarkable career, the so-called 'alternative comedy' crowd hailed him as one of their own, and, yet again, people stopped taking him for granted and started rediscovering his very special talent.

'Can you believe,' he asked Barbara Windsor, half-jokingly and half-genuinely, when she visited his dressing-room to congratulate him after one of his shows, 'I'm still doing the same old rubbish I've been doing for years?'[39] 'I think he was stunned by the new adulation,' she reflected, 'but he wasn't complaining. Not one bit.'[40]

More 'Frankie Pankie' ventures followed, striking while the iron was hot, throughout the rest of the year, including the recording of a number of novelty 'dance' tracks (including 'Frankie's Grooving' and 'Get Your Titters Out') which would eventually see the light of day in such fashionable formats as extended and alternative mixes on coloured twelve-inch vinyl, and a line of 'Frankie Says' themed merchandise (produced by a company called Fishee Business). The climax of this youth-oriented campaign, however, came in November, when Howerd (at the age of seventy-three) made an appearance before a hall full of students inside the Debating Chamber of the Oxford Union.

Dressed uncharacteristically in a silver-coloured suit (but retaining the trademark brown for his open-neck shirt), he wandered on and, right from the start, assumed complete command over his audience. Treating the occasion – rather like he had done his season at the Establishment club – as a sort of upmarket *Workers' Playtime* (and drawing on material written by, amongst others, Barry Cryer, Dennis Berson, Steve Knight, Spike Mullins, Mike Whitehill, Peter Vincent and Galton and Simpson), he deferred to the undergraduates at the very same time that he showed them who was really the boss:

> Before we start the actual comedy act thing – what you've come to see, the sort of 'comedy' stuff – ah, I just wanted to say a word to you, er, which is, well, not serious, exactly, but, um, sincere. Yes. No, it's because, you see, I'm not – well, you know, no, you don't know, but I mean, no, but you'll believe me when I tell you – I'm not what you'd call an 'intellectual'. [*The audience starts to laugh*] No, no, I'm not, no, I'm not what you'd call 'brainy', er, you know, a sort of 'clever clogs'. I've not got levels – 'O' levels and 'A' levels – oh, no, nah, nothing like that. 'Cause, you're all students, so naturally, to you, I'm not what you'd call an academic. By no way at all could you call me an intellectual – [*A plummy-voiced plant at the back of the chamber cries out: 'Hear! Hear!'*] – which is why I feel so much at home here tonight![41]

He still indulged them with a quick burst of all the catchphrases, but, refreshingly, there was now slightly more of an edge to his attitude towards anyone who appeared to be trying to laugh *at* him rather than *with* him. The sharpness of his early put-downs showed just how expertly ruthless he could be, if he needed to be, and so there was a genuine sense of respect, as well as affection, for him long before the evening had reached its end.

The only flaw in what was in all other ways a superb performance came at the conclusion of a monologue in which he had played a vicar addressing a nudist colony. As he turned to head for the exit, he revealed that he was naked beneath his cassock – thus exposing his bare and elderly bottom. Even this sad and desperately unfunny lapse in taste, however, prompted yet another robotic sequence of ecstatic shrieks, squawks, whistles, hoots and cheers from an audience that, by this stage, would probably have applauded him had he relieved himself in the gallery.

It had still been, none the less, a triumphant night for Frankie Howerd, and fortunately, as a production team from London Weekend Television had been there to capture it on camera, the genuine brilliance of his performance would subsequently be seen and enjoyed by a much bigger, and almost certainly a more authentically appreciative, audience. The critical reaction could not have been much better − nor could it have been more well-deserved.

Howerd did not so much progress or regress in 1991 as just bask in the Indian summer that he had created for himself. He picked up another Silver Heart from the Variety Club − this one to commemorate his forty-five years in show business. He appeared on Channel 4's *Tonight with Jonathan Ross* to meet his younger fans, and on ITV's *Aspel & Co* and *Des O'Connor Tonight* to be reunited with the ones who were more mature. He played a flattering cameo role as the 'God of Comedy' in Channel 4's *The Craig Ferguson Show*. He also recorded a special performance of his quintessential stand-up act, in June at the Birmingham Hippodrome, for subsequent release on home video.[42]

The sole false move that he made during the year was to accept an invitation from London Weekend Television (after the BBC had passed on the project) to attempt yet another revival of *Up Pompeii!* Renamed *Further Up Pompeii* (ITV, in an unusually bold act of imagination, left off the old title's exclamation mark), this one-off special featured a plot (about Lurcio, having forged a clause in his late master's will making him a free man, trying to avoid prosecution for fraud) that was as wafer-thin as it had been twenty years before, and a corn-fed script (by Paul Minett and Brian Leveson) that was 'worthy' of Talbot Rothwell, but this very familiarity served only to underline the redundancy of the revival.

Howerd seemed to regret his decision as soon as work on the show began. Unlike on the stage, where he had recently regained a sense of purpose, energy and autonomy, he now found himself back in the kind of claustrophobic environment where there was so much that seemed beyond his control. All of the old testiness began to creep back: he was unhappy with the scripts, unhappy with his inability to remember the script, and unhappy with most other aspects of the production.

He started, once again, to behave irrationally − insisting, for example, on filming the show without a studio audience. Nerves were probably the cause of his reluctance to keep the very thing that he had fought so hard to retain ever since making his small-screen debut back in 1952: namely, a studio full of people to whom he could react. As soon as he won laughs from the technicians during the dress rehearsal, however, he realised the folly of his decision and announced that, on reflection, he wanted an audience after all – but it was too late: the size of the expensive set had left no room in the studio for the usual rows of seats (a laughter track was dubbed on instead at a later date). Howerd had effectively sabotaged his own performance.

The show that actually went out on air did him no favours at all. In the brightly-lit studio, Howerd – paunchy, puffy and liverish – suddenly looked every one of his seventy-four years, moving slowly and, thanks to absence of an audience, reacting slowly as well. There was the odd good moment, when he spoke conspiratorially to the camera about how awful a particular actor or line had been, but the overall impression was one of joyless fatigue.

Howerd had sensed it himself. After receiving a round of spontaneous applause from the crew on the last day of the production, he drew a line under the whole unhappy experience with a typical piece of melancholic mischief: 'Thank you,' he said. 'I've enjoyed working with all of you – except one,' and with that he walked off to collect his things from his dressing-room, leaving everybody else wondering, 'Did he mean *me?*'[43]

It had been an unexpectedly intense period of activity for Howerd since his 'elevation' to the status of a cult comedian (apart from the performances themselves, he had been averaging fourteen media inter-views each week[44]), and enjoyable though most of it had been, he now badly needed a rest. He therefore left for a short cruise of the Panama Canal – which he greatly enjoyed until he contracted a virus that caused him some respiratory problems during the latter stages of the trip.

He returned home to start work early in 1992 on his next project – a compromise between a television show and a concert party (produced by Trevor McCallum for Central Television) called *Frankie's On . . .* – but the effects of the virus were still being felt. He received hospital treatment at the start of February for problems with his heart and lungs, was given the 'all clear' to resume work, but then was back for more tests during the following month.

Max Bygraves, his oldest friend in show business, had heard conflict-ing rumours about the seriousness of Howerd's illness (they had ranged from influenza to heart disease), and was eager to check on how he was actually feeling. He called to arrange a leisurely meeting over lunch, and was pleased to elicit such an enthusiastic response:

> He said he would, and I chose one of the best restaurants in London, just the two of us. We talked mostly nostalgia and I asked if he still read hands. He said he did, and took my hand and gazed at my palm for a long time. 'Didn't I tell you that one day you'd be a millionaire?' I nodded. 'Didn't it come true?' I nodded again. He gave my hand back and said, 'Well, in that case, pay the bill!'[45]

Satisfied that there was nothing wrong with his friend's wit, and assured that the physical problems were being treated and would soon be resolved, Bygraves happily paid up and wished him well.

In truth, however, Howerd was hiding from himself, as well as others, just how severe these problems were. He tried to keep up with the demands of his taxing schedule – which saw him record shows in such diverse places as the *Ark Royal* aircraft carrier at Gibraltar, a colliery just outside Nottingham and a Fire Service College in Gloucestershire – but his health continued to remain poor, if not worsen, and after completing four of the six programmes, his strength was draining away. Something, clearly, was seriously wrong.

On 3 April, his condition suddenly worsened, and he was admitted to the intensive care unit of the Harley Street Clinic as an emergency. News of his frailty came as a shock to most members of the public, and it was not long before the pavement opposite the main entrance in Weymouth Street became the focus for photographers and fans alike. The mood among them darkened still more when it was reported that such old friends as Alfred Marks and Barbara Windsor had been denied the chance to visit.

Better news finally came four days later, when it was announced that Howerd had been moved out of intensive care and into a private room; his mood was said to be 'chirpy'.[46] Sister Betty, Dennis Heymer, Tessa Le Bars, June Whitfield and Cilla Black were all allowed brief visits to his bedside, and it was clear to each of them that, although he was trying hard to raise a smile, he was terribly weak. 'I want to go home, dear,' he whispered to Windsor. 'I've had enough of hospitals.'[47]

On Tuesday, 14 April, he was allowed to leave; the doctors had done all that they could. Outside on the street, the photographers huddled around him, their flashlights turning him even paler than he already was, and the reporters babbled away with questions. A young nurse by his side gave him a chocolate Easter bunny and a tender kiss on the cheek, and he smiled bravely for the cameras one more time before being driven away to recuperate at his home in Edwardes Square.

He longed to escape straightaway to his cottage in Cross, where he now felt most at home, but his specialist, Robert Donaldson, had ordered him to stay in London until he had regained a little more of his strength. Betty moved in for a few days to provide her brother and his partner with some support, a night nurse was hired, and Dennis monitored the telephone calls and ensured that Howerd was afforded some much-needed peace and quiet.

A few close friends, such as Bruce Forsyth, were allowed inside for a brief visit ('Thank God you brought chocolates,' Howerd cried when Forsyth arrived. 'I've had so many flowers. When I woke up I thought I was in a funeral parlour already'[48]), and several others, including June Whitfield and Alfred Marks, were put through to him by telephone. 'How are you feeling, Frank?' Marks asked. 'Not too bad, thanks,' Howerd replied, his voice sounding faint and frail. Marks suggested that the pair of them should meet up once the health problems were over, and Howerd agreed, proposing lunch the following week as a possibility. 'Fine,' said Marks, trying hard not to sound unconvinced, and then, after wishing his old friend well, he hung up. 'I just knew that he had been sent home to die,' he would later say, 'and he knew it too. I just felt most dreadfully sad.'[49]

On 17 April – Good Friday – Howerd felt fit enough to venture out round the corner and along the road to have one more dinner with his devoted sister. Seated beside her at his usual round table in the far corner of Al Gallo d'Oro, he drank a couple of double vodkas and ordered a starter of avocado with prawns, followed by a main course of calves' sweetbreads. Sharing a bottle of Frascati with Betty, he was quieter and more serious than the staff were used to seeing him, but he still managed to tease one of the waiters and crack the odd gentle joke with other members of staff before shaking hands with the *maître d'* and then setting off for the slow stroll home.

He did not talk about how much longer he expected to live, and the topic was not something about which any of those around him wanted to think. The only thing that anyone did, or wanted to do, was to continue to hope for the best.

Tessa Le Bars, therefore, continued to act as if there was still a possibility that her client would be well enough to film the cameo role (as the King of Spain) he had accepted in the forthcoming *Carry On Columbus*, as well as complete the outstanding two editions of *Frankie's On . . .*, and Howerd himself continued to talk positively about his latest project, *Holy J.O.* (a pilot for a possible comedy-drama series, scripted by Jeremy Burnham in the style of an updated episode of G.K. Chesterton's *Father Brown* stories, about Jocelyn Oscar Spottiswood – a country vicar who is also a part-time sleuth).

On the morning of Easter Sunday, 19 April, Robert Donaldson, Howerd's specialist, visited him at Edwardes Square and, much to his relief and delight, gave him the all-clear to journey down to his home in Somerset to continue his recuperation. Buoyed by the good news, he was still in good spirits at lunchtime, laughing and joking with Dennis and Betty over a few rounds of smoked salmon sandwiches and a small glass of wine. Early in the afternoon, however, he complained of feeling tired and slightly unwell, and so (after giving his current producer, Trevor McCallum, a quick call to invite him to visit once he had settled down in Somerset), he took a nap on the sofa in the lounge.

Heymer checked in on him every fifteen minutes or so, and, on the third or fourth of these occasions, found to his alarm that Howerd seemed to be experiencing difficulties breathing. Betty rushed to the telephone and dialled 999, while Dennis – in a state of understandable panic – tried desperately to help his partner to breathe. 'I tried everything,' he would later tell reporters. 'I gave him heart massage, kept thumping his chest, tried some breathing . . . everything. But there was no response.'[50] The ambulance arrived ten minutes after Betty had called, and Howerd was still alive when the paramedics hurried in and carried him out to the ambulance. Despite their efforts to resuscitate him, however, Frankie Howerd died of a heart attack on the way to the Charing Cross Hospital. He was seventy-five years old.

Reports of his death made the front pages of all the next morning's papers, as well as all of the regular bulletins of radio and television news. Tributes poured in from his writers, his fellow-comedians and his many friends, fans and critical admirers, and respectful obituaries appeared in the broadsheets as well as the tabloids. All of them agreed that the British people, and the wider world of comedy, had lost someone who was simply irreplaceable.

His funeral took place in Somerset, at St Gregory's Church in Weare (about a mile from his home), on Wednesday 29 April 1992. Although it was a modest and brief affair, in keeping with Howerd's wishes, there were still many of his closest and dearest friends in attendance, including Tessa Le Bars, Lee Young, Ray Galton and Alan Simpson, Cilla Black and June Whitfield, as well as, of course, the two people whose hearts were most obviously and irrevocably broken: Betty and Dennis. 'He taught us to laugh at ourselves,' said the vicar, the Reverend George Williams, of his celebrated subject, 'and he was loved by millions.'[51]

The burial took place in the same quiet little low-walled country churchyard where Howerd had so often wandered up and down, trying desperately to master his lines, emitting the odd audible 'oh', 'yes' and 'no' as he did so. Two months later, on 8 July, a memorial service was held for him in London at St Martin-in-the-Fields, and more than eight hundred people attended. There were many tender, funny and heartfelt tributes and recollections from the likes of Cilla Black, June Whitfield, Barry Cryer and Griff Rhys Jones, but perhaps the simplest, most moving and most apt observation came from Bruce Forsyth, who said that at a memorial service for a great entertainer, it was right for people to clap. Everyone who was there stood up and did just that: they all applauded Frankie Howerd.

THE EPILOGUE

Whimsicality upon whimsicality!
Will it never end?

And it came to pass . . .

At the end of Frankie Howerd's autobiography, he allowed himself two closing observations. The first was that his 'childhood ambition to become a saint resulted in spectacular failure'. The second was that 'it would be arrogant to believe that I acquired instead a monopoly of sin'.[1]

He was right on both counts. Frankie Howerd was no saint, and he was no sinner. He was wrong, however, when he concluded that 'the best that could be said of me is: "He means well"'.[2] We can do so much better than that. He did well, too. He was special.

'Every man in his lifetime,' wrote Emerson, 'needs to thank his faults,'[3] and Frankie Howerd certainly had good cause to do just that, because he found the source of his humour somewhere in those very faults and, as most of his faults were the same as most of our faults, by making us laugh at him he made us laugh at ourselves as well. That was what elevated him far above all of the slick little stand-up show-offs of his youth. He was profoundly different. He was not afraid to seem just as flawed, just as vulnerable and just as human as any of us. That was what made him one of the most distinctive, intelligent, influential and courageous stand-up comedians of all time.

That was what mattered. That is still what matters.

Most people seemed to know that at the time of his death. Les Dawson judged him 'a genius' and Ken Dodd described him as 'one of the greats'.[4] Every other stand-up supplied a similar superlative, and did so with rare sincerity, and the sentiments expressed by his writers were no less earnest or ardent. 'We'll all miss a great man,' said Eric Sykes, 'and it's a really sad loss – not just to me but I think to the whole country.'[5] Johnny Speight agreed, praising Howerd as 'one of the funniest men I've ever known',[6] and so, too, did Barry Took: 'The world has lost one of its dearest and rarest treasures,' he said – 'a true clown.'[7] Barry Cryer was another who concurred, describing him as the comedian who had best represented ordinary human beings: 'He was like an ombudsman. He was the rebel against all those people "Upstairs" who think they're very important. And he played that role for years – brilliantly.'[8]

Some people, however, seemed, as the time went by, to forget. Perhaps it had something to do with all of those awful, lifeless, asinine 'Oooh-Er-No-Missus!' so-called imitations by third-rate entertainers who were too dim to realise by how great a margin they had missed the point; or perhaps it had something to do with the strange reluctance of much of the media to recall Howerd in the prime of his life and at the peak of his powers (instead of near to the end of his life and during the decline of those powers). It almost certainly had something to do with the sewage stream of sensationalistic 'exposés' that collected every proven, presumed and patently fabricated piece of dirt and then magnified them all until they obscured every single act of selflessness and kindness, every scintilla of truly original talent and every precious hard-won laugh; and perhaps it also had at least a little to do with the pointlessly timid and patently elliptical 'official' or quasi-authorised hagiographies that seemed – deep down – to harbour doubts as to whether the reputation and achievements of their late friend and hero could withstand an open, honest and serious appraisal.

Whatever the causes, the salient point is that Frankie Howerd was far too good – and far too important – to be treated, in the public memory, either as casually or as cynically as this. He was far too good for craven coffee-table books and brain-dead retrospectives. He redefined an art and enriched millions of lives, and he deserves to be recalled with much greater clarity and in far richer detail – as well as with real affection and true respect.

The reductive clichés can safely be discounted. The reductive clichés only serve to obscure what they purport to reveal.

Frankie Howerd's sadness, for example, was not the key. Yes, he was indeed often sad, but then so, too, are many, if not most, of the rest of us. Sadness, alas, is a banality. As Howerd himself once wisely observed, 'Loneliness and the laugh-clown-laugh aspect of life is not a monopoly of comedians. You stray into a room full of people and see loneliness staring you right in the eye.'[9]

His sexuality was not the key, either. It might now intrigue, excite, titillate or perhaps even offend the immature, the prejudiced or just those without the slightest interest in stand-up comedians *per se*, but, none the less, it was not an *achievement*, and it does not provide an overwhelmingly powerful reason for us to keep thinking and talking about Frankie Howerd as a singularly notable human being.

The key, in reality, was his genius as a performer of comic material. That was what he had, and that was what he did, that made him genuinely exceptional. That, more than anything else that he may have said or done or thought, is what now makes Frankie Howerd worth remembering.

As Alan Simpson remarked, 'The way any man should be remembered, providing he's actually done something *worthwhile*, is through his work. "Was he any good?" That's the most relevant question.'[10]

In Frankie Howerd's case, the two main things that one needs to recall are the astonishing originality of his conception of stand-up comedy, and the sheer audacious brilliance of its execution, from the joyful days of *Variety Bandbox* in the late 1940s, all the way through to the courageous comeback at the Establishment and on *TW3* in the early 1960s, and then all the way on to the masterful reaffirmation of his talent at the end of the 1980s. That adds up to four decades of extraordinarily impressive and unusually treasurable work. It involved an enormous amount of effort, worry, clashes and crises, but then the best work always does.

It speaks volumes not only for his ability but also for his character that the people who assisted him so cleverly (and generously) throughout those four decades – his writers – remained his biggest fans. 'He was a joy to be around,' Ray Galton reflected. 'Any criticism would have to be done with great affection, because he really was a delightful man.'[11] 'I will always doff my hat when I think of Frank,' said Eric Sykes with the warmest of smiles. 'He really *was* unique.'[12]

Was Frankie Howerd any good? No. He was much better than good. He was wonderful.

List of Performances

Every effort has been made to assemble a list of performances that is as comprehensive as possible (although only the most significant guest appearances have been included); any unintentional omissions or inaccuracies will be corrected in a future edition.
(LP = BBC Light Programme; HS = BBC Home Service; TP = Third Programme; † = recording known to have been preserved in either the BBC or British Library Sound Archive; *V* = VHS copy exists; *DVD* = DVD copy exists; ★ = scheduled broadcast date delayed.)

STAGE

For the Fun of It
July 1946–April 1947
Tour

Summer Season at Clacton
1947
West Cliff Theatre

Jack and the Beanstalk
December 1947/January 1948
Lyceum, Sheffield

Ta-Ra-Ra-Boom-De-Ay
1948
National Tour

Jack and the Beanstalk
December 1948/January 1949

Ladies and Gentle-men
1949
National Tour

Summer Season at Blackpool
1949
Central Pier

Puss in Boots
December 1949/January 1950
Liverpool Empire

Christmas Show
December 1949
Buckingham Palace

Summer Season at Great Yarmouth
1950
Britannia Theatre

Out of this World
17 October–16 December 1950
London Palladium

Royal Variety Performance
13 November 1950
London Palladium

Babes in the Wood
December 1950/January 1951
Birmingham Royal

The Famous Frankie Howerd
4–10 June 1951
The Hippodrome, Coventry

Frankie Howerd
1952
Swindon Empire

Dick Whittington
December 1952/January 1953
London Palladium

List of Performances

Pardon My French
24 September 1953–11 December 1954
Prince of Wales, London

Royal Variety Performance
2 November 1953
London Coliseum

The Howerd Crowd
1955
National Tour

Charley's Aunt
22 December 1955–17 March 1956
Globe, Shaftesbury Avenue

Tons of Money
17–29 September 1956
New Theatre, Bromley

Hotel Paradiso
1957
National Tour

A Midsummer Night's Dream
23 December 1957–15 February 1958
Old Vic

Gala Night
18 March 1958
Old Vic

The Perfect Woman
24 March–4 April 1958
Northampton

Mr Venus
1–16 October 1958
Provincial Tour
23 October–8 November 1958
Prince of Wales, London

The Perfect Woman
December 1958
Grand Theatre, Southampton

Summer Season in Scarborough
1959
The Futurist

Alice in Wonderland
26 December 1959–23 January 1960
Winter Garden, Drury Lane

Royal Performance
16 May 1960
The Palace Theatre, London

Summer Season in Folkestone
1960
Leas Cliff Hall

Cinderella
December 1960/January 1961
Streatham Hill Theatre

Summer Season in Great Yarmouth
1961
Windmill Theatre

Royal Variety Performance
6 November 1961
Prince of Wales Theatre, London

Puss in Boots
December 1961/January 1962
King's Theatre, Southsea

Cabaret
May–June 1962
The Blue Angel, London

At the Establishment
September 1962
The Establishment Club

Alamein Reunion Concert
19 October 1962
Royal Festival Hall, London

Puss in Boots
December 1962/January 1963
Coventry

Glamorama of '63
1963
The Plaza, Jersey

A Funny Thing Happened On The Way To The Forum
3 October 1963–2 July 1965
Strand Theatre, London

Way Out in Piccadilly
3 November 1966–October 1967
Prince of Wales Theatre, London

Royal Variety Performance
3 November 1966
London Palladium

The Wind in the Sassafras Trees
27 February–16 March 1968
Belgrade Theatre, Coventry

List of Performances

The Wind in the Sassafras Trees/ Rockefeller
  and the Red Indians
14–28 September 1968
Colonial Theater, Boston
30 September–12 October 1968
National Theater, Washington
24–26 October 1968
Ethel Barrymore Theater, New York

Royal Variety Performance
18 November 1968
London Palladium

Royal Variety Performance
13 November 1969
London Palladium

Jack and the Beanstalk
December 1973/January 1974
London Palladium

Summer Season
1975

Jack and the Beanstalk
December 1976/January 1977
Theatre Royal, Bath

The Frankie Howerd Show
1977
National Tour

Royal Variety Show
November 1978
London Palladium

Cinderella
December 1978/January 1979
New Palace Theatre, Plymouth

Cabaret
1979
New Zealand

Robinson Crusoe
1979
Alexandra Theatre, Birmingham

Isle of Wight Holiday Spectacular
16 June–19 July 1980
Pavilion Theatre, Sandown

Cinderella
December 1980/January 1981
Wimbledon Theatre

Die Fledermaus
31 December 1981–January 1982
The Coliseum/English National Opera

Jack and the Beanstalk
December 1982/January 1983
Chichester Festival Theatre

Goldilocks and the Three Bears
December 1983/January 1984
Fulcrum Theatre, Slough

The Fly and the Fox
11 July–4 August 1984
Churchill Theatre, Bromley

Aladdin
December 1984/January 1985
Congress Theatre, Eastbourne

A Funny Thing Happened On The Way To
  The Forum
11 August–27 September 1986
Chichester Festival Theatre
14 November–27 December 1986
Piccadilly Theatre, London

Liverpool Festival of Comedy
July 1988
Liverpool Empire

Cinderella
December 1988/January 1989
Hanley

Up the Festival
5 March 1989
Hackney Empire

Frankie Howerd Bursts into Britain
1989
National Tour

Quite Frankly, Frankie Howerd At His
  Tittermost!
2–21 April 1990
Lyric Hammersmith
May 1990
Garrick Theatre

Frankie Howerd At His Tittermost!
23 June 1991
Birmingham Hippodrome

RADIO

1946

1 December *Variety Bandbox* (LP)
15 December *Variety Bandbox* (LP)
25 December *Variety Bandbox* (LP)

1947

12 January *Variety Bandbox* (LP)
26 January *Variety Bandbox* (LP)
9 February *Variety Bandbox* (LP)
9 March *Variety Bandbox* (LP)
23 March *Variety Bandbox* (LP)
4 April *Variety Bandbox* (LP)
20 April *Variety Bandbox* (LP)
4 May *Variety Bandbox* (LP)
18 May *Variety Bandbox* (LP)
1 June *Variety Bandbox* (LP)
15 June *Variety Bandbox* (LP)
29 June *Variety Bandbox* (LP)
13 July *Variety Bandbox* (LP)
27 July *Variety Bandbox* (LP)
10 August *Variety Bandbox* (LP)
24 August *Variety Bandbox* (LP)
7 September *Variety Bandbox* (LP)
21 September *Variety Bandbox* (LP)
19 October *Variety Bandbox* (LP)
2 November *Variety Bandbox* (LP)
16 November *Variety Bandbox* (LP)
14 December *Variety Bandbox* (LP)
24 December *Variety Bandbox* (LP)

1948

11 January *Variety Bandbox* (LP)
25 January *Variety Bandbox* (LP)
8 February *Variety Bandbox* (LP)
22 February *Variety Bandbox* (LP)
7 March *Variety Bandbox* (LP)
21 March *Variety Bandbox* (LP)
4 April *Variety Bandbox* (LP)
18 April *Variety Bandbox* (LP)
2 May *Variety Bandbox* (LP)
16 May *Variety Bandbox* (LP)
30 May *Variety Bandbox* (LP)
13 June *Variety Bandbox* (LP)
27 June *Variety Bandbox* (LP)
5 September *Variety Bandbox* (LP)
19 September *Variety Bandbox* (LP)
3 October *Variety Bandbox* (LP)†
17 October *Variety Bandbox* (LP)
31 October *Variety Bandbox* (LP)
14 November *Variety Bandbox* (LP)
28 November *Variety Bandbox* (LP)
26 December *Variety Bandbox* (LP)

1949

9 January *Variety Bandbox* (LP)
23 January *Variety Bandbox* (LP)
6 February *Variety Bandbox* (LP)
20 February *Variety Bandbox* (LP)
6 March *Variety Bandbox* (LP)
20 March *Variety Bandbox* (LP)
16 October *Variety Bandbox* (LP)†
30 October *Variety Bandbox* (LP)
13 November *Variety Bandbox* (LP)†
27 November *Variety Bandbox* (LP)†
11 December *Variety Bandbox* (LP)

1950

8 January *Variety Bandbox* (LP)
22 January *Variety Bandbox* (LP)†
5 February *Variety Bandbox* (LP)
19 February *Variety Bandbox* (LP)†
5 March *Variety Bandbox* (LP)
19 March *Variety Bandbox* (LP)
2 April *Variety Bandbox* (LP)

1951

4 January *Fine Goings On* (LP)
18 January *Fine Goings On* (LP)
1 February *Fine Goings On* (LP)
15 February *Fine Goings On* (LP)
1 March *Fine Goings On* (LP)
15 March *Fine Goings On* (LP)
29 March *Fine Goings On* (LP)
12 April *Fine Goings On* (LP)
26 April *Fine Goings On* (LP)
6 May *Festival of Variety* (LP)†
10 May *Fine Goings On* (LP)
24 May *Fine Goings On* (LP)
7 June *Fine Goings On* (LP)
21 June *Fine Goings On* (LP)
5 July *Fine Goings On* (LP)

1952

23 April *Frankie Howerd Goes East* (Nicosia – venue unspecified) (LP)
30 April *Frankie Howerd Goes East* (Canal Zone – venue unspecified) (LP)
7 May *Frankie Howerd Goes East* (Canal Zone – Moascar Garrison) (LP)
14 May *Frankie Howerd Goes East* (Fayid – RAF station) (LP)
21 May *Frankie Howerd Goes East* (Benghazi – The Berka Theatre) (LP)

28 May *Frankie Howerd Goes East* (Tripoli – The Miramare Theatre) (LP)
4 June *Frankie Howerd Goes East* (Malta – The Australia Hall) (LP)
11 June *Frankie Howerd Goes East* (Malta – Manoel Island) (LP)
28 September *Variety Bandbox* (final edition) (LP)†
1 December *All Star Bill* (LP)
15 December *All Star Bill* (LP)
22 December *All Star Bill* (LP)

1953

23 November *The Frankie Howerd Show* (LP)
30 November *The Frankie Howerd Show* (LP)
7 December *The Frankie Howerd Show* (LP)
14 December *The Frankie Howerd Show* (LP)
21 December *The Frankie Howerd Show* (LP)
28 December *The Frankie Howerd Show* (LP)

1954

4 January *The Frankie Howerd Show* (LP)
11 January *The Frankie Howerd Show* (LP)
18 January *The Frankie Howerd Show* (LP)
25 January *The Frankie Howerd Show* (LP)
1 February *The Frankie Howerd Show* (LP)
8 February *The Frankie Howerd Show* (LP)
15 February *The Frankie Howerd Show* (LP)
22 February *The Frankie Howerd Show* (LP)
1 March *The Frankie Howerd Show* (LP)
8 March *The Frankie Howerd Show* (LP)
30 August *The Frankie Howerd Show* (LP)

1955

22 February *The Frankie Howerd Show* (second series) (LP)†
1 March *The Frankie Howerd Show* (LP)
8 March *The Frankie Howerd Show* (LP)
15 March *The Frankie Howerd Show* (LP)
22 March *The Frankie Howerd Show* (LP)
29 March *The Frankie Howerd Show* (LP)
5 April *The Frankie Howerd Show* (LP)
12 April *The Frankie Howerd Show* (LP)
2 October *The Frankie Howerd Show* (third series) (LP)
9 October *The Frankie Howerd Show* (LP)
16 October *The Frankie Howerd Show* (LP)
23 October *The Frankie Howerd Show* (LP)
30 October *The Frankie Howerd Show* (LP)

6 November *The Frankie Howerd Show* (LP)
13 November *The Frankie Howerd Show* (LP)
20 November *The Frankie Howerd Show* (LP)
27 November *The Frankie Howerd Show* (LP)
4 December *The Frankie Howerd Show* (LP)
11 December *The Frankie Howerd Show* (LP)
18 December *The Frankie Howerd Show* (LP)
23 December *Christmas Crackers* (LP)
25 December *The Frankie Howerd Show* (LP)

1956

1 January *The Frankie Howerd Show* (LP)
8 January *The Frankie Howerd Show* (LP)
15 January *The Frankie Howerd Show* (LP)
22 January *The Frankie Howerd Show* (LP)
25 December *Puss in Gumboots* (LP)

1957

27 December *Son of Mother Goose* (LP)

1958

1 April *The Two Gentlemen of Verona* (TP)
2 April *Fine Goings On* (Series 2) (LP)
9 April *Fine Goings On* (LP)
16 April *Fine Goings On* (LP)
23 April *Fine Goings On* (LP)
30 April *Fine Goings On* (LP)
7 May *Fine Goings On* (LP)
14 May *Fine Goings On* (LP)
21 May *Fine Goings On* (LP)
28 May *Fine Goings On* (LP)
4 June *Fine Goings On* (LP)
11 June *Fine Goings On* (LP)
18 June *Fine Goings On* (LP)
25 June *Fine Goings On* (LP)
2 July *Fine Goings On* (LP)
9 July *Fine Goings On* (LP)
16 July *Fine Goings On* (LP)
23 July *Fine Goings On* (LP)
30 July *Fine Goings On* (LP)
6 August *Fine Goings On* (LP)
13 August *Fine Goings On* (LP)
25 December *Pantomania* (LP)

1959

28 September *Desert Island Discs* (HS)†

1960

5 April *Frankie's Bandbox* (LP)
12 April *Frankie's Bandbox* (LP)
19 April *Frankie's Bandbox* (LP)
26 April *Frankie's Bandbox* (LP)
3 May *Frankie's Bandbox* (LP)
10 May *Frankie's Bandbox* (LP)
17 May *Frankie's Bandbox* (LP)
24 May *Frankie's Bandbox* (LP)
31 May *Frankie's Bandbox* (LP)
7 June *Frankie's Bandbox* (LP)
14 June *Frankie's Bandbox* (LP)
21 June *Frankie's Bandbox* (LP)
28 June *Frankie's Bandbox* (LP)
25 July *Music Hall* (LP)
25 December *Leave It To The Boys* (LP)

1961

7 January *Variety Playhouse* (HS)
30 April *London Lights* (LP)

1962

25 August *Variety Playhouse* (HS)

1963

14 October *Variety Playhouse* (HS)

1964

27 August *Now Listen!* (LP)†
3 September *Now Listen!* (LP)†
10 September *Now Listen!* (LP)†
17 September *Now Listen!* (LP)†
24 September *Now Listen!* (LP)†
1 October *Now Listen!* (LP)†
8 October *Now Listen!* (LP)†

1966

24 July *Frankie Howerd!* (LP)†
31 July *Frankie Howerd!* (LP)†
7 August *Frankie Howerd!* (LP)†
14 August *Frankie Howerd!* (LP)†
21 August *Frankie Howerd!* (LP)†
28 August *Frankie Howerd!* (LP)†

1972

25 December *Frankie Howerd's Christmas Gala* (BBC Radio 2)†

1973

10 June *Frankie Howerd* (BBC Radio 2)†
17 June *Frankie Howerd* (BBC Radio 2)†
24 June *Frankie Howerd* (BBC Radio 2)†
1 July *Frankie Howerd* (BBC Radio 2)†
8 July *Frankie Howerd* (BBC Radio 2)†
15 July *Frankie Howerd* (BBC Radio 2)†
22 July *Frankie Howerd* (BBC Radio 2)†

1974

27 October *Frankie Howerd* (BBC Radio 2)†
3 November *Frankie Howerd* (BBC Radio 2)†
10 November *Frankie Howerd* (BBC Radio 2)†
17 November *Frankie Howerd* (BBC Radio 2)†
24 November *Frankie Howerd* (BBC Radio 2)†
1 December *Frankie Howerd* (BBC Radio 2)†
8 December *Frankie Howerd* (BBC Radio 2)†

1975

28 September *Frankie Howerd* (BBC Radio 2)†
5 October *Frankie Howerd* (BBC Radio 2)†
12 October *Frankie Howerd* (BBC Radio 2)†
19 October *Frankie Howerd* (BBC Radio 2)†
26 October *Frankie Howerd* (BBC Radio 2)†
2 November *Frankie Howerd* (BBC Radio 2)†

1978

16 August *The Image Makers* (BBC Radio 4)†
10 October *The Frankie Howerd Variety Show* (BBC Radio 2)†
24 October *The Frankie Howerd Variety Show* (BBC Radio 2)†
7 November *The Frankie Howerd Variety Show* (BBC Radio 2)†
21 November *The Frankie Howerd Variety Show* (BBC Radio 2)†
5 December *The Frankie Howerd Variety Show* (BBC Radio 2)†
19 December *The Frankie Howerd Variety Show* (BBC Radio 2)†

1979

14 August *The Frankie Howerd Variety Show* (BBC Radio 2)†
21 August *The Frankie Howerd Variety Show* (BBC Radio 2)†
28 August *The Frankie Howerd Variety Show* (BBC Radio 2)†
4 September *The Frankie Howerd Variety Show* (BBC Radio 2)†
11 September *The Frankie Howerd Variety Show* (BBC Radio 2)†
18 September *The Frankie Howerd Variety Show* (BBC Radio 2)†

1982

23 January *Desert Island Discs* (BBC Radio 4)†

1987

28 May *Frankie Howerd's Forum* (BBC Radio 2)†

4 June *Frankie Howerd's Forum* (BBC Radio 2)†
11 June *Frankie Howerd's Forum* (BBC Radio 2)†
18 June *Frankie Howerd's Forum* (BBC Radio 2)†
25 June *Frankie Howerd's Forum* (BBC Radio 2)†
2 July *Frankie Howerd's Forum* (BBC Radio 2)†

1990

22 December *Carry On Up Yer Cinders* (BBC Radio 4)†

TELEVISION

The Howerd Crowd (BBC TV)

12 January 1952   Frankie Howerd, The Beverley Sisters, Bill Fraser, Blanche Moore, John Hanson, Victor Platt and Bunny Parish, Marjorie Holmes, Peter Glover, The Peter Knight Singers, Ernest Maxin and Rae Johnson.
26 January 1952   Frankie Howerd, The Beverley Sisters, Blanche Moore, John Hanson, Victor Platt and Bunny Parish, Marjorie Holmes, Peter Glover, The Peter Knight Singers, Ernest Maxin and Rae Johnson.
8 March 1952   Frankie Howerd, The Tanner Sisters, Blanche Moore, John Hanson, Victor Platt and Bunny Parish, Marjorie Holmes, Peter Glover, Camilla Castelli, The Peter Knight Singers, Peter Daminoff and his Gypsy Music, Ernest Maxin and Rae Johnson.

[Writer: Eric Sykes]

Frankie Howerd's Korean Party (BBC TV)

9 December 1952   Frankie Howerd, Eve Boswell, Eddie Arnold, Clifford Kirkham, Vera Jessup, Steve Race, Geoff Lofts and Kenneth Carter.

[Writer: Eric Sykes]

Television's Second Christmas Party (BBC TV)

25 December 1952   Arthur Askey, Frankie Howerd, Tommy Cooper, Ethel Revnell, Norman Wisdom, Betty Driver, John Slater, Petula Clark, Eamonn Andrews, Joe Stuthard, MacDonald Hobley and countless surprise guests.

What's My Line? (BBC TV)

8 February 1953   Eamonn Andrews, Ghislaine Alexander, Barbara Kelly, Jerry Desmonde, Gilbert Harding and Frankie Howerd.

List of Performances

Nuts in May (BBC TV)

13 May 1953   Frankie Howerd, Gilbert Harding and Carole Carr.

[Writer: Eric Sykes]

The Frankie Howerd Show (BBC TV)

10 September 1953   Frankie Howerd and Joan Turner.

[Writers: Eric Sykes and Spike Milligan]

What's My Line? (BBC TV)

14 March 1954   Eamonn Andrews, Isobel Barnett, David Nixon, Barbara Kelly, Frankie Howerd.

Tons of Money (BBC TV)

27 December 1954   Frankie Howerd (Aubrey Maitland Allington), Eleanor Summerfield (Louise Allington), Jack Melford (Sprules the Butler), Rosemary Davies (Simpson), Joan Young (Benita Mullett), Lee Young (Giles), George Benson (James Chesterman), Barbara Shotter (Jean Everard), Bill Fraser (Henery) and Roland Green (George Maitland).

The Howerd Crowd *series two* (BBC TV)

11 June 1955   Frankie Howerd, Bruce Seton, Gladys Morgan, Lee Young, Saveen and The Tanner Sisters.
27 August 1955   Frankie Howerd, Bruce Seton, Gladys Morgan, Lee Young, Saveen and The Tanner Sisters.

[Writer: Eric Sykes]

Frankie Howerd (BBC TV)

11 October 1956   Frankie Howerd and Shani Wallis.
3 December 1956   Frankie Howerd and Joan Sims.

[Writers: Johnny Speight and Dick Barry]

Pantomania or Dick Whittington (BBC TV)

25 December 1956   Jean Kent, Sylvia Peters, Billy Cotton, Frankie Howerd, Hattie Jacques, Sam Kydd, David Attenborough, Roger Avon, Fred Emney, Edward Evans, Bill Greenslade, Peter Haigh, John Hall, Philip Harben, the Max Jaffa Trio, Jacqueline MacKenzie, Mary Malcolm, Spike Milligan, Freddie Mills, Robert Raglan, Nancy Roberts, Bruce Seton, Eric Sykes, Jimmy Wheeler and The Mitchell Singers.

[Writer: Eric Sykes]

The Howerd Crowd (ATV/ITV)

23 February 1957   Frankie Howerd.

[Writer: Eric Sykes]

The School for Wives (Associated-Rediffusion/ITV)

23 April 1958   Frankie Howerd (Arnolphe), Leslie French (Chrysalde), Kenneth Griffith (Alain), Joan Newall (Georgette), Zena Walker (Agnes), Charles Laurence (Horace), John Bailey (Enrique) and Frederick Farley (Oronte).

The Frankie Howerd Show (ATV/ITV)

17 August 1958   Frankie Howerd, Margaret Rutherford, Michael Denison, Sabrina and Joyce Shock.

[Writer: Eric Sykes]

Frankie Howerd In . . . (BBC TV)

Pity Poor Francis
16 December 1958   Frankie Howerd.

[Writer: Johnny Speight]

Shakespeare Without Tears
28 January 1959   Frankie Howerd.

[Writers: Reuben Ship and Phil Sharp]

Frankly Howerd (BBC TV)

1 May 1959   Frankie Howerd (Himself), Sidney Vivian (Fred Thompson), Helen Jessop (Gladys Thompson) and Sam Kydd (various roles).
8 May 1959   Frankie Howerd (Himself), Sidney Vivian (Fred Thompson), Helen Jessop (Gladys Thompson), Sam Kydd (various roles), Bruno Barnabe and Roger Avon.
15 May 1959   Frankie Howerd (Himself), Sidney Vivian (Fred Thompson), Helen Jessop (Gladys Thompson), Sam Kydd (various roles), Totti Truman Taylor, Denys Graham and Bernard Hunter.
22 May 1959   Frankie Howerd (Himself), Sidney Vivian (Fred Thompson), Helen Jessop (Gladys Thompson) and Sam Kydd (various roles).
29 May 1959   Frankie Howerd (Himself), Sidney Vivian (Fred Thompson), Helen Jessop (Gladys Thompson) and Sam Kydd (various roles).
5 June 1959   Frankie Howerd (Himself), Sidney Vivian (Fred Thompson), Helen Jessop (Gladys Thompson) and Sam Kydd (various roles).

[Writers: Reuben Ship and Phil Sharp]

Twenty Questions (Associated Rediffusion/ITV)

1960   Stuart McPherson, Stephen Potter, Isobel Barnett, Frankie Howerd and Muriel Young.

Ladies and Gentle-Men (BBC TV)

24 September 1960   Frankie Howerd, Richard Wattis and Dennis Price.

[Writers: Johnny Speight, Ray Galton and Alan Simpson and Barry Took]

Have You Read This Notice? (BBC TV)

29 March 1963   Frankie Howerd (Norman Fox), Bill Kerr (Customs Officer) and Edwin Apps (Passenger).

[Writers: Ray Galton and Alan Simpson]

That Was The Week That Was (BBC TV)

6 April 1963   David Frost, Roy Kinnear, David Kernan, Lance Percival, William Rushton, Bernard Levin, Millicent Martin and Frankie Howerd.

A Last Word on the Election (BBC 1)

18 October 1964   Frankie Howerd.

[Writers: Frankie Howerd, Ray Galton and Alan Simpson, Frank Muir and Denis Norden, David Nathan and Dennis Potter]

Frankie Howerd *series one* (BBC 1)

11 December 1964   Frankie Howerd, Patrick Cargill and Audrey Nicholson.
18 December 1964   Frankie Howerd, Norman Bird, Arthur Mullard, Anthony Sagar, Ken Roberts, Rita Webb, Margaret Flint, Lala Lloyd, Louis Mansi, Trevor Barrie and Walter Swash.
24 December 1964   Frankie Howerd, Colin Gordon, Anthony Sharp, Len Lowe, Alec Bregonzi, Don Smoothey and Stella Kemball.
1 January 1965   Frankie Howerd, Alfie Bass, Derek Francis, Frank Thornton, Delphi Lawrence, Bill Shine, Dennis Chinnery, Bill Maxam, Barney Gilbraith and Frank Littlewood.
8 January 1965   Frankie Howerd, William Kendall and Terence Edmond.
15 January 1965   Frankie Howerd, Hugh Paddick, Arthur Mullard, Yootha Joyce, Julian Orchard, Felix Bowness, Barbara Archer, David Grahame and Marian Collins.

[Writers: Ray Galton and Alan Simpson]

East of Howerd (BBC 1)

1 January 1966   Frankie Howerd, Shirley Abicair and Al Koran.

Frankie Howerd *series two* (BBC 1)

22 February 1966   Frankie Howerd, Arthur Mullard, Anthony Sagar, Julian Orchard, Dennis Ramsden, Ken Wynne, Tim Buckland and William Raymor.
1 March 1966   Frankie Howerd, Warren Mitchell, Beryl Reid, Arthur Mullard, Rita Webb, Valerie Bell, Felix Bowness, Henry Longhurst, Sheree Winton, James McManus, Emmett Hennessey and Keith Ashley.
8 March 1966   Frankie Howerd, John Le Mesurier, June Whitfield, Edwin Brown, Sheree Winton and Peggy Ann Clifford.
15 March 1966   Frankie Howerd, Nora Nicholson, Garry Marsh, Coral Atkins, Evelyn Lund, Harry Brunsing, Eddie Malin, Anita Moore, Ronald Alexander, George Myddleton and Peter Perry.
22 March 1966   Frankie Howerd, Peter Butterworth, Gretchen Franklin, Gerald Rowland, Alan Baulch, Bill Maxam, Marie Makino, George Hirste and Anthony Buckingham.
29 March 1966   Frankie Howerd, Hugh Paddick, Sheila Steafel, Arthur Mullard, Dennis Ramsden, Michael Robbins, Ian Trigger, Joan Ingram, Peter Diamond and Tim Buckland.

[Writers: Ray Galton and Alan Simpson]

The Canterville Ghost (US: ABC)

2 November 1966   Michael Redgrave (Sir Simon Canterville), Douglas Fairbanks Jr (Ambassador Otis), Peter Noone (David, Duke of Cheshire), Frankie Howerd, Natalie Schafer (Mrs Otis), David Charkham (Mark Otis), Mark Coleano (Matthew Otis) and Tippy Walker (Virginia Otis).

Frankie and Bruce's Christmas Show (ABC/ITV)

24 December 1966   Frankie Howerd, Bruce Forsyth, Cilla Black, Tommy Cooper, Tom Jones, The Kaye Sisters, Aleta Morrison and The Malcolm Goddard Dancers.

[Writers: Dick Hills and Sid Green]

Those Two Fellas (ATV/ITV)

5 May 1967   Dick Hills, Sid Green, Diane Rachelle and Frankie Howerd.

[Writers: Dick Hills and Sid Green]

Frankie and Bruce's Christmas Show (ABC/ITV)

23 December 1967   Frankie Howerd and Bruce Forsyth.

[Writers: Dick Hills and Sid Green]

Howerd's Hour (ABC/ITV)

12 May 1968   Frankie Howerd, Hattie Jacques and Patrick Wymark.

[Writer: Eric Sykes]

Frankie Howerd Meets the Bee Gees (Thames/ITV)

20 August 1968   Frankie Howerd, The Bee Gees, Arthur Mullard, Valentine Dyall and June Whitfield.

[Writers: Ray Galton and Alan Simpson]

The Frankie Howerd Show (Thames/ITV)

25 September 1968   Frankie Howerd, Diane Cilento, Cilla Black, Joe Brown, Bobby Moore, Lew Hoad, Ken Parry, Nosher Powell, Eric Delaney and The New Seekers.

[Writers: Dick Hills and Sid Green]

David Frost Presents . . . Frankie Howerd (Paradine/WNEW)

23 February 1969   David Frost, Frankie Howerd, Ronnie Corbett, Paul McCartney and Mary Hopkin.

Frankie Howerd at the Poco A Poco (Thames/ITV)

7 May 1969   Frankie Howerd and Patrick Wymark.

The Frankie Howerd Show (ATV/ITV)

9 August 1969   Frankie Howerd.
16 August 1969   Frankie Howerd.
23 August 1969   Frankie Howerd.
30 August 1969   Frankie Howerd.
6 September 1969   Frankie Howerd.
13 September 1969   Frankie Howerd.

[Writers: Dick Hills and Sid Green]

Up Pompeii *pilot episode* (BBC 1) *V*

17 September 1969   Frankie Howerd (Lurcio), Max Adrian (Ludicrus Sextus), Elizabeth Larner (Ammonia), John Junkin (Odius), Aubrey Woods (Captain Bilius), Kerry Gardner (Nausius), Julia Goodman (Cilla), Georgina Moon (Erotica), Ruth Harrison (Cassandra), Richard McNeff (Senator), Walter Horsbrugh (Plautus), Danny Daniels (Agrippa), Barbara Lindley, Valerie Stanton and Marie (Slavegirls).

[Writer: Talbot Rothwell]

Frost on Saturday (LWT/ITV)

22 November 1969   Dusty Springfield, Frankie Howerd, George Best, Barry Humphries and Manitas de Plata.

Carry On Christmas (Thames/ITV) *V*

24 December 1969   Sid James, Terry Scott, Charles Hawtrey, Hattie Jacques, Barbara Windsor, Bernard Bresslaw, Peter Butterworth and Frankie Howerd.

Up Pompeii! *Series one* (BBC 1) *V*

30 March 1970   Frankie Howerd (Lurcio), Max Adrian (Ludicrus Sextus), Kerry Gardner (Nausius), Elizabeth Larner (Ammonia), Jeanne Mockford (Senna), Leon Thau (Odius), Georgina Moon (Erotica), William Rushton (Plautus), Geoffrey Hughes (Pitius), Hugh Paddick (Priest), Penny Brahms (Tittia), Janet Mahoney (Virginia) and Trisha Noble (High Priestess of the Virgins), Sui Lin, Barbara Lindley, Anita Richardson, Joanna Ross, Valerie Stanton and Jeanette Wild.

6 April 1970   Frankie Howerd, Max Adrian (Ludicrus Sextus), Kerry Gardner (Nausius), Elizabeth Larner (Ammonia), Jeanne Mockford (Senna), Georgina Moon (Erotica), William Rushton (Plautus), Jeremy Young (Ponderus), Wendy Richard (Soppia), Robert Gillespie (Mucus), Nicholas Smith (Hidius), Michael Knowles (Caushus) and Colin Bean (Centurion).

13 April 1970   Frankie Howerd, Max Adrian (Ludicrus Sextus), Kerry Gardner (Nausius), Elizabeth Larner (Ammonia), Jeanne Mockford (Senna), William Rushton (Plautus), Derek Francis (Senator Lecherus), Norman Mitchell (Stovus Primus), Valerie Leon (Daili) and James Ottaway (Scrophulus).

20 April 1970   Frankie Howerd, Max Adrian (Ludicrus Sextus), Kerry Gardner (Nausius), Elizabeth Larner (Ammonia), Jeanne Mockford (Senna), Georgina Moon (Erotica), William Rushton (Plautus), Wallas Eaton (Sgt Jankus), Robin Hunter and Peter Needham (Britons), Fiona Kendall and Andi Ross (Camp Followers), and Stephen Churchett, David Hilton, Nigel Pegram, Michael Sharvell-Martin and Vic Taylor (Soldiers).

27 April 1970   Frankie Howerd, Max Adrian (Ludicrus Sextus), Kerry Gardner (Nausius), Elizabeth Larner (Ammonia), Jeanne Mockford (Senna), Georgina Moon (Erotica), William Rushton (Plautus), Olwen Griffiths (Hermione), Bill Maynard (Percentus), Audrey Nicholson (Hernia) and Douglas Ridley (Cuspidor).

4 May 1970   Frankie Howerd, Max Adrian (Ludicrus Sextus), Kerry Gardner (Nausius), Elizabeth Larner (Ammonia), Jeanne Mockford (Senna), William Rushton (Plautus), Shaun Curry (Spartacus), Wallas Eaton (Centurion Captain), Vic Taylor (Centurion Private), Larry Martyn (Gaoler) and Anita Richardson (Iris).

11 May 1970   Frankie Howerd, Max Adrian (Ludicrus Sextus), Kerry Gardner (Nausius), Elizabeth Larner (Ammonia), Jeanne Mockford (Senna), Georgina Moon (Erotica), William Rushton (Plautus), Lynda Baron (Ambrosia), David Kernan (Prodigius), John Ringham (Bumshus), Trisha Noble (Lusha), John Cater (Dr Castor Oilus), Mollie Sugden (Flavia), Queenie Watts (Lush's Maid) and Anita Richardson (Castor's Assistant).

[Writer: Talbot Rothwell]

List of Performances

Royal Television Gala Performance (BBC 1)

24 May 1970 Eric Morecambe, Ernie Wise, Frankie Howerd, Elizabeth Larner, Dave Allen, Dudley Moore, Cilla Black, Rod McKuen, Derek Fowlds, Vera Lynn and the cast of *Dad's Army*.

Up Pompeii! *Series two* (BBC 1) *V*

14 September 1970 Frankie Howerd (Lurcio), Wallas Eaton (Ludicrus Sextus), Kerry Gardner (Nausius), Elizabeth Larner (Ammonia), Georgina Moon (Erotica), Jeanne Mockford (Senna), Bunny May (Hermes), Pat Coombs (Tarta), William Corderoy (Gladiator) and Anita Richardson (Filfia).

21 September 1970 Frankie Howerd (Lurcio), Wallas Eaton (Ludicrus Sextus), Kerry Gardner (Nausius), Elizabeth Larner (Ammonia), Georgina Moon (Erotica), Jeanne Mockford (Senna), Kenneth J. Warren (Felonius), Grazina Frame (Letitia) and Penelope Charteris (Twiggia).

5 October 1970 Frankie Howerd (Lurcio), Wallas Eaton (Ludicrus Sextus), Kerry Gardner (Nausius), Elizabeth Larner (Ammonia), Jeanne Mockford (Senna), George Baker (James Bondus), Patricia Haines (Pussus Galoria) and Larry Martyn (Spurios).

12 October 1970 Frankie Howerd (Lurcio), Wallas Eaton (Ludicrus Sextus), Kerry Gardner (Nausius), Elizabeth Larner (Ammonia), Georgina Moon (Erotica), Jeanne Mockford (Senna), Alan Curtis (Captain Bumshus) and David Anderson (Lieutenant Preshus).

19 October 1970 Frankie Howerd (Lurcio), Wallas Eaton (Ludicrus Sextus), Kerry Gardner (Nausius), Elizabeth Larner (Ammonia), Georgina Moon (Erotica), Jeanne Mockford (Senna), Barbara Windsor (Nymphia), Michael Brennan (Ambi Dextrus) and Roy Stewart (Jeremy the Nubian).

26 October 1970 Frankie Howerd (Lurcio), Wallas Eaton (Ludicrus Sextus), Kerry Gardner (Nausius), Elizabeth Larner (Ammonia), Georgina Moon (Erotica), Jeanne Mockford (Senna), Bunny May (Hermes), Jean Kent (Aphrodite), Paul Whitsun-Jones (Nefarius) and Larry Martyn (Verminus).

[Writers: Talbot Rothwell and Sid Colin]

Cucumber Castle (BBC 2)

26 December 1970 Barry Gibb (Prince Frederick), Maurice Gibb (Prince Marmaduke), Eleanor Bron (Lady Marjorie Pee), Pat Coombs (Nurse Sarah), Julian Orchard (Julian the Lord Chamberlain), Frankie Howerd (The Dying King), Spike Milligan (The Court Jester), Vincent Price (Wicked Count Voxville), Lulu (Lulu the Cook), Peter Blyth (Narrator) and Blind Faith.

Frankie Howerd: The Laughing Stock of Television (Thames/ITV)

14 April 1971 Frankie Howerd, Hattie Jacques, Peter Copley, Patricia Hayes, Carmel McSharry, Arthur English, Michael Hawkins, George Tovey, John Bindon, George Roderick, Jenny Lee-Wright, Lesley Goldie and Richard McNeff.

[Writers: Marty Feldman and Barry Took, Ray Galton and Alan Simpson and Talbot Rothwell]

Parkinson (BBC 1)

28 November 1971 Frankie Howerd, Ralph Richardson and Marion Montgomery.

List of Performances

Frankie Howerd's Hour (Thames/ITV)

1 September 1971   Frankie Howerd.
29 September 1971   Frankie Howerd.

[Writers: Ray Galton and Alan Simpson]

Whoops Baghdad (BBC 1)

25 January 1973   Frankie Howerd (Ali Oopla), Derek Francis (Abu ben Ackers, the Wazir), Hilary Pritchard (Saccharine), Anna Brett (Boobiana), Larry Martyn (Derti Dhoti the Beggar), Norman Chappell (Imshi), Josephine Tewson (Fatima), Alan Curtis (Captain of the Guard), Valerie Stanton (Shanana) and Neville Simons (Ahmed).
1 February 1973   Frankie Howerd (Ali Oopla), Derek Francis (Wazir), Hilary Pritchard (Saccharine), Larry Martyn (Derti Dhoti), Bill Fraser (Wizard Prang), Alan Curtis (Fake Wizard), Ronnie Brody (Mustapha Shufti), Mark Nicholls (Short Guard), Lee Young (Tall Guard), Mahed Khairy (Belly Dancer) and Danny Gray (Juggler).
8 February 1973   Frankie Howerd (Ali Oopla), Derek Francis (Wazir), Hilary Pritchard (Saccharine), Anna Brett (Boobiana), Larry Martyn (Derti Dhoti), Lee Young (Genie), Gertan Klauber (Major Domo), Louis Mansi (Messenger), John Levene (Cassim), Jack Wright (Sultan) and Eric Kent (Wine Merchant).
15 February 1973   Frankie Howerd (Ali Oopla), Derek Francis (Wazir), Hilary Pritchard (Saccharine), Anna Brett (Boobiana), Norman Chappell (Imshi), Alan Curtis (Akbar the Vile), Janet Webb (Gigantima), Robert Bridges (Auctioneer), Jack Wright (Little Old Man), Douglas Emery (Beggar) and John A. Tinn (Chinaman).
22 February 1973   Frankie Howerd (Ali Oopla), Derek Francis (Wazir), Hilary Pritchard (Saccharine), Anna Brett (Boobiana), Larry Martyn (Derti Dhoti), Patrick Troughton (Tamberlane the Terrible), Alan Curtis (Avabanana), Robert Bridges (Chief Guard), Jane Murdoch (Tangerine), Jack Wright (Short Tribesman), John G. Hughman (Tall Tribesman) and Winifred Sabine (Crone).
1 March 1973   Frankie Howerd (Ali Oopla), Derek Francis (Wazir), Hilary Pritchard (Saccharine), Anna Brett (Boobiana), Larry Martyn (Derti Dhoti), Bill Fraser (Caliph), June Whitfield (Charisma), Alan Curtis (Captain of the Guard), Milton Reid (Sinbad), George Ballantine (Hairdresser) and Cherri Gilham (First Lady).

[Writers: Sid Colin with David McKellar and David Nobbs, Peter Vincent and Bob Hedley and Roy Tuvey and Maurice Sellar]

Frankie Howerd in Ulster (BBC 1)

14 March 1973   Frankie Howerd, June Whitfield, Wendy Richard, Allan Cuthbertson, Paul Haley, Elizabeth Larner, Andee Silver, The Tremeloes and Pan's People.

[Writers: Ray Galton and Alan Simpson, Johnny Speight, Chris Allen, Talbot Rothwell and Roy Tuvey and Maurice Sellar]

Russell Harty Plus (LWT/ITV)

17 March 1973   Frankie Howerd, Ruby Murray and Sheilah Graham.

An Evening With Francis Howerd (BBC 2)

30 April 1973   Frankie Howerd, June Whitfield, Norman Bird, Wolfe Morris, Pamela Cundell, Raymond Mason, Tricia Newby, Jacqueline Stanbury and Ken Alexis.
7 May 1973   Frankie Howerd, June Whitfield, Robert Keegan, Patricia Haines, Alan Curtis, Betty Duncan and Keith James.
14 May 1973   Frankie Howerd, June Whitfield, John Arnatt, Norman Bird, Alan Curtis, Allan Cuthbertson, Kerry Gardner, Keith James, Robert Lankesheer, Geoffrey Lumsden and Bernard Severn.

List of Performances

[Writers: Eric Merriman, Ray Galton and Alan Simpson, Peter Robinson, Chris Allen, David McKellar and David Nobbs, Tony Hare, Roy Tuvey and Maurice Sellar, Mike Craig, Lawrie Kinsley and Ron McDonnell and Dave Freeman]

Russell Harty Plus (LWT/ITV)

26 January 1974   Frankie Howerd, Cleo Laine and Johnny Dankworth.

Howerd's History of England (BBC 1)

30 April 1974   Frankie Howerd, Patrick Newell, Patrick Holt and John Cazabon.

[Writers: Barry Took and Michael Mills]

Francis Howerd in Concert (Yorkshire/ITV)

18 September 1974   Frankie Howerd, John Le Mesurier, Kenny Lynch and Julie Ege.

[Writers: Barry Cryer and Johnny Speight]

Further Up Pompeii! (BBC 1)

31 March 1975   Frankie Howerd (Lurcio), Mark Dignam (Ludicrus), Elizabeth Larner (Ammonia), Kerry Gardner (Nausius), John Cater (Pollux), Jeanne Mockford (Senna), Olwen Griffiths (Hernia), Jennifer Lonsdale (Erotica), Cyril Appleton (Claudius) and Lindsay Duncan (Scrubba).

[Writer: Talbot Rothwell]

Frankie and Bruce (Thames/ITV)

3 September 1975   Frankie Howerd, Bruce Forsyth, Marie Gordon Price, Jenny Lee-Wright, Isobel Hurll, Suzanne Danielle and Jim Clayton.

[Writers: Dick Hills and Sid Green and Barry Cryer]

Frankie Howerd's Tittertime (Thames/ITV)

1 October 1975   Frankie Howerd, Hughie Greene, Caterina Valente, The Anderson Sisters, Norman Chappell, Derek Seaton, Raymond Farrell, Michael Bangerter, Willi Bowman, Gideon Kolb, Peter Kodak and David Valentine.

[Writers: Ray Galton and Alan Simpson and Barry Cryer]

A Touch of the Casanovas (Thames/ITV)

31 December 1975   Frankie Howerd (Francesco), Stuart Damon (Casanova), Marguerite Hardiman (Isabella), Leon Greene (Captain of the Guard), John Cater (Bartoldi), Patsy Rowlands (Clemintina), Madeline Smith (Teresa), Roger Brierley (Count Pelligrini), Patricia Haines (Countess Pelligrini), Cyril Appleton (Count Malatesta) and Gregory Powell, Billy Horrigan and Terry Maidment (Doge's Guardsmen).

[Writers: Sid Colin and Hugh Stuckey]

This Is Your Life (Thames/ITV)

27 February 1976   Frankie Howerd, Eamonn Andrews and guests.

List of Performances

The Frankie Howerd Show [AKA: Oooh Canada!] (CBC, Canada)

26 February 1976   Frankie Howerd (Himself), Ruth Springford (Mrs Otterby the Landlady), Gary Files (Mrs Otterby's Son, Hardin I. Otterby), Jack Duffy (Wally Wheeler) and Peggy Mahon (Denise).
4 March 1976   Frankie Howerd (Himself), Ruth Springford (Mrs Otterby), Gary Files (Hardin I. Otterby), Jack Duffy (Wally Wheeler) and Peggy Mahon (Denise).
11 March 1976   Frankie Howerd (Himself), Ruth Springford (Mrs Otterby), Gary Files (Hardin I. Otterby), Jack Duffy (Wally Wheeler) and Peggy Mahon (Denise).
18 March 1976   Frankie Howerd (Himself), Ruth Springford (Mrs Otterby), Gary Files (Hardin I. Otterby), Jack Duffy (Wally Wheeler) and Peggy Mahon (Denise).
25 March 1976   Frankie Howerd (Himself), Ruth Springford (Mrs Otterby), Gary Files (Hardin I. Otterby), Jack Duffy (Wally Wheeler) and Peggy Mahon (Denise).
1 April 1976   Frankie Howerd (Himself), Ruth Springford (Mrs Otterby), Gary Files (Hardin I. Otterby), Jack Duffy (Wally Wheeler) and Peggy Mahon (Denise).
8 April 1976   Frankie Howerd (Himself), Ruth Springford (Mrs Otterby), Gary Files (Hardin I. Otterby), Jack Duffy (Wally Wheeler) and Peggy Mahon (Denise).
24 April 1976   Frankie Howerd (Himself), Ruth Springford (Mrs Otterby), Gary Files (Hardin I. Otterby), Jack Duffy (Wally Wheeler) and Peggy Mahon (Denise).
1 May 1976   Frankie Howerd (Himself), Ruth Springford (Mrs Otterby), Gary Files (Hardin I. Otterby), Jack Duffy (Wally Wheeler) and Peggy Mahon (Denise).
8 May 1976   Frankie Howerd (Himself), Ruth Springford (Mrs Otterby), Gary Files (Hardin I. Otterby), Jack Duffy (Wally Wheeler) and Peggy Mahon (Denise).
15 May 1976   Frankie Howerd (Himself), Ruth Springford (Mrs Otterby), Gary Files (Hardin I. Otterby), Jack Duffy (Wally Wheeler) and Peggy Mahon (Denise).
22 May 1976   Frankie Howerd (Himself), Ruth Springford (Mrs Otterby), Gary Files (Hardin I. Otterby), Jack Duffy (Wally Wheeler) and Peggy Mahon (Denise).
29 May 1976   Frankie Howerd (Himself), Ruth Springford (Mrs Otterby), Gary Files (Hardin I. Otterby), Jack Duffy (Wally Wheeler) and Peggy Mahon (Denise).
5 June 1976   Frankie Howerd (Himself), Ruth Springford (Mrs Otterby), Gary Files (Hardin I. Otterby), Jack Duffy (Wally Wheeler) and Peggy Mahon (Denise).

[Writers: Bill Lynn, Jerry O'Flanagan and Ken Finkleman]

Up the Convicts (Seven Network, Australia)

June 1976   Frankie Howerd (Jeremiah Shirk), Lee Young, Frank Thring, Carol Raye (Lady Fitzgibbon), Wallas Eaton, Crystal Redenko, Anne-Louise Lambert and Jacki Weaver.
June 1976   Frankie Howerd (Jeremiah Shirk), Lee Young, Frank Thring, Carol Raye (Lady Fitzgibbon), Wallas Eaton, Crystal Redenko, Anne-Louise Lambert and Jacki Weaver.
July 1976   Frankie Howerd (Jeremiah Shirk), Lee Young, Frank Thring, Carol Raye (Lady Fitzgibbon), Wallas Eaton, Crystal Redenko, Anne-Louise Lambert and Jacki Weaver.
July 1976   Frankie Howerd (Jeremiah Shirk), Lee Young, Frank Thring, Carol Raye (Lady Fitzgibbon), Wallas Eaton, Crystal Redenko, Anne-Louise Lambert and Jacki Weaver.

[Writers: Hugh Stuckey and Peter Robinson]

The Howerd Confessions (Thames/ITV)

2 September 1976   Frankie Howerd, Joan Sims, Charles Morgan, Ken Kitson, Virginia Balfour and Elspeth MacNaughton.
9 September 1976   Frankie Howerd, Caroline Munro, Alex Scott, Hans Meyer and Cyril Appleton.
16 September 1976   Frankie Howerd, Joan Sims, Madeline Smith, Nicholas McArdle, Tommy Godfrey, George Moon, Dorothy Frere, Jack Le White and Beverley Kay Jennings.
23 September 1976   Frankie Howerd, Joan Sims, John Junkin, Ruth Kettlewell, Ronnie Brody, Isabella Rye, Roland MacLeod and Kate Brown.
30 September 1976   Frankie Howerd, Alfie Bass, Linda Thorson, Alan Curtis and Bunny Reid.

7 October 1976   Frankie Howerd, Margaret Courtenay, Geoffrey Chater, April Olrich, Roger Brierley, Sarah Douglas, Mireille Allonville and Margaret Dalton.

[Writers: Dick Hills, Hugh Stuckey, Peter Robinson and Dave Freeman]

Good Afternoon (Thames/ITV)

7 October 1976   Mavis Nicholson and Frankie Howerd.

Russell Harty (LWT/ITV)

8 October 1976   Frankie Howerd and Leslie Caron.

Russell Harty (LWT/ITV)

14 April 1979   Frankie Howerd and Charlton Heston.

Just So Stories (Thames/ITV)

3 April 1979   Frankie Howerd (narrator)
10 April 1979   Frankie Howerd (narrator)
17 April 1979   Frankie Howerd (narrator)
24 April 1979   Frankie Howerd (narrator)
1 May 1979   Frankie Howerd (narrator)
8 May 1979   Frankie Howerd (narrator)

The Plank (Thames/ITV) *V*

17 December 1979   Eric Sykes (Larger Workman), Arthur Lowe (Plank Man), Lionel Blair (Smart Gent), Henry Cooper (Beer Drinker), Harry H. Corbett (Amorous Truck Driver), Bernard Cribbins (Door Painter), Robert Dorning, Diana Dors (Woman with Rose), Charlie Drake (Man with Cake), Jimmy Edwards (Policeman), Liza Goddard (Crossing Lady), Deryck Guyler (Milkman), Charles Hawtrey (Co-Driver), Frankie Howerd (Photographer), James Hunt, Wilfrid Hyde-White (Pedestrian), Joanna Lumley (Hitchhiker), Kenny Lynch (Dustman), Brian Murphy (Truck Driver), Kate O'Mara, Ann Sidney (Photographer's Model), Reg Varney (Window Cleaner), Frank Windsor (Car Driver) and Carroll Baker.

[Writer: Eric Sykes]

After Noon Plus (Thames/ITV)

29 March 1980   Mavis Nicholson, Trevor Hyett, Kenny Everett and Frankie Howerd.

Frankie Howerd Reveals All (Yorkshire/ITV)

10 October 1980   Frankie Howerd, Sheila Steafel, Henry McGee, Kenneth Connor and Brian Osborne.

[Writers: John Bartlett and Mike Goddard, with Laurie Rowley]

Parkinson (BBC 1)

3 December 1980   Frankie Howerd, Bryan Forbes and Trevor Nunn.

Frankie Howerd Strikes Again (Yorkshire/ITV)

1 September 1981   Frankie Howerd, Henry McGee, Linda Cunningham, Neil Innes, Norman Chappell, Claire Davenport and Sweet Substitute.
8 September 1981   Frankie Howerd, Henry McGee, Linda Cunningham, Neil Innes, David

Brierley, Rag Terrett, Jacqui Ross, Anneka Rice (billed as Annie Rice) and Muriel Rogers.

15 September 1981   Frankie Howerd, Henry McGee, Linda Cunningham, Neil Innes, Ronnie Brody, Lesley E. Bennet, Wendy King, Colin Meredith, Bartlett Mullins and Carl Gresham.

22 September 1981   Frankie Howerd, Henry McGee and Neil Innes.

29 September 1981   Frankie Howerd, Henry McGee, Linda Cunningham, Neil Innes and Jeanne Mockford.

6 October 1981   Frankie Howerd, Henry McGee, Linda Cunningham, Neil Innes, Ronnie Brody and Bartlett Mullins.

[Writers: John Bartlett with Mike Goddard, Barry Cryer and Spike Mullins]

Does The Team Think? (Thames/ITV)

12 January 1982   Tim Brooke-Taylor, Jimmy Edwards, Beryl Reid, William Rushton and Frankie Howerd.

19 January 1982   Tim Brooke-Taylor, Jimmy Edwards, Beryl Reid, William Rushton and Frankie Howerd.

26 January 1982   Tim Brooke-Taylor, Jimmy Edwards, Beryl Reid, William Rushton and Frankie Howerd.

2 February 1982   Tim Brooke-Taylor, Jimmy Edwards, Beryl Reid, William Rushton and Frankie Howerd.

9 February 1982   Tim Brooke-Taylor, Jimmy Edwards, Beryl Reid, William Rushton and Frankie Howerd.

16 February 1982   Tim Brooke-Taylor, Jimmy Edwards, Beryl Reid, William Rushton and Frankie Howerd.

23 February 1982   Tim Brooke-Taylor, Jimmy Edwards, Beryl Reid, William Rushton and Frankie Howerd.

2 March 1982   Tim Brooke-Taylor, Jimmy Edwards, Beryl Reid, William Rushton and Frankie Howerd.

16 March 1982   Tim Brooke-Taylor, Jimmy Edwards, Beryl Reid, William Rushton and Frankie Howerd.

Then Churchill Said To Me (BBC 2) *V*

1982★   Frankie Howerd (Private Potts/General Fearless Freddy Hollocks), Nicholas Courtney (Colonel Robin Witherton), Joanna Dunham (Petty Officer Joan Bottomley), Michael Attwell (Pte Norman Pain), Shaun Curry (Sgt. Major McRuckus), James Chase (Batman MacKensey), Linda Cunningham (Sally Perks) and Peggy Ann Clifford (Tea Lady).

[★Transmission postponed, reportedly because of the outbreak of the Falklands/Malvinas conflict: first broadcast on UK Gold, 1 March 1993; first broadcast on BBC 2, 8 April 2000.]

1982★   Frankie Howerd (Private Potts/General Fearless Freddy Hollocks), Nicholas Courtney (Colonel Robin Witherton), Joanna Dunham (Petty Officer Joan Bottomley), Michael Attwell (Pte Norman Pain), Shaun Curry (Sgt. Major McRuckus), James Chase (Batman MacKensey), Linda Cunningham (Sally Perks) and Peggy Ann Clifford (Tea Lady).

[★Transmission postponed: first broadcast on UK Gold, 8 March 1993; on BBC 2, 15 April 2000.]

1982★   Frankie Howerd (Private Potts/General Fearless Freddy Hollocks), Nicholas Courtney (Colonel Robin Witherton), Joanna Dunham (Petty Officer Joan Bottomley), Michael Attwell (Pte Norman Pain), Shaun Curry (Sgt. Major McRuckus), James Chase (Batman MacKensey), Linda Cunningham (Sally Perks) and Peggy Ann Clifford (Tea Lady).

[★Transmission postponed: first broadcast on UK Gold, 15 March 1993; on BBC 2, 22 April 2000.]

1982★   Frankie Howerd (Private Potts/General Fearless Freddy Hollocks), Nicholas Courtney (Colonel Robin Witherton), Joanna Dunham (Petty Officer Joan Bottomley), Michael Attwell (Pte Norman Pain), Shaun Curry (Sgt. Major McRuckus), James Chase (Batman MacKensey), Linda Cunningham (Sally Perks) and Peggy Ann Clifford (Tea Lady).

[★Transmission postponed: first broadcast on UK Gold, 22 March 1993; on BBC 2, 2 September 2000.]

1982★   Frankie Howerd (Private Potts/General Fearless Freddy Hollocks), Nicholas Courtney (Colonel Robin Witherton), Joanna Dunham (Petty Officer Joan Bottomley), Michael Attwell (Pte Norman Pain), Shaun Curry (Sgt. Major McRuckus), James Chase (Batman MacKensey), Linda Cunningham (Sally Perks) and Peggy Ann Clifford (Tea Lady).

[★Transmission postponed: first broadcast on UK Gold, 29 March 1993; on BBC 2, 10 September 2000.]

1982★   Frankie Howerd (Private Potts/General Fearless Freddy Hollocks), Nicholas Courtney (Colonel Robin Witherton), Joanna Dunham (Petty Officer Joan Bottomley), Michael Attwell (Pte Norman Pain), Shaun Curry (Sgt. Major McRuckus), James Chase (Batman MacKensey), Linda Cunningham (Sally Perks) and Peggy Ann Clifford (Tea Lady).

[★Transmission postponed: first broadcast on UK Gold, 5 April 1993; on BBC 2, 10 September 2000.]

[Writers: Maurice Sellar and Lou Jones]

HMS Pinafore (BBC 1) *V*

30 August 1983   Frankie Howerd (Sir Joseph Porter, KCB), Peter Marshall (Captain Corcoran), Della Jones (Mrs Cripps), Meryl Drower (Josephine Corcoran), Michael Bulman (Ralph Rackstraw), Alan Watt (Dick Deadeye), Gordon Sandison (Bill Bobstay) and Anne Mason (Cousin Hebe).

All the World's a Stage (BBC 2)

29 January 1984   Ronald Harwood, Tom Courtenay, Paul Rogers, John Gielgud, Eli Wallach, Colleen Dewhurst, Frankie Howerd, Peter Brook, Michael Frayn and Michael Billington.

12 February 1984   Ronald Harwood, Frankie Howerd, Peter Jones, Peter Woodthorpe, Ian Saynor, Peter Gale and the Greek Art Theatre.

Trial By Jury (BBC 1) *V*

3 June 1984   Frankie Howerd (The Learned Judge), Kate Flowers (Angelina), Ryland Davies (Edwin), Anne Dawson (Miss Anne Other), Tom McDonnell (Counsel for the Plaintiff), Roger Bryson (The Usher), Brian Donlan (Foreman of the Jury), Beryl Kaye (Skivvy), Eleanor McCready (Angelina's Mama) and Elise McDougall (1st Bridesmaid).

Wogan (BBC 1)

8 May 1985   Frankie Howerd.

The Gong Show (Channel 4)

9 December 1985   Barbara Windsor, Barry Cryer, Mike Newman and Frankie Howerd.

Wogan (BBC 1)

31 March 1986   Frankie Howerd.

Superfrank! (HTV/Channel 4)

12 January 1987   Frankie Howerd.

[Writers: Vince Powell, Miles Tredinnick and Andrew Nickolds]

Aspel & Co (LWT/ITV)

14 February 1987   Frankie Howerd, Lulu and Nigel Havers.

Wogan (BBC 1)

6 March 1987   Frankie Howerd.

Wogan (BBC 1)

1 July 1988   Frankie Howerd.

All Change (Yorkshire/ITV)

15 November 1989   Frankie Howerd (Uncle Bob), Roger Milner (Henry Herewith), Maggie Steed (Fabia London), William McGillivray (Julian London), Lisa Butler (Polly London), Donna Durkin (Vicky Oldfield), Robert Ellis (Nathan Oldfield), Andrew Normington (Hornbeam), Pam Ferris (Maggie Oldfield), Tony Haygarth (Brian Oldfield), David Quilter (Charles London).
22 November 1989   Frankie Howerd (Uncle Bob), Roger Milner (Henry Herewith), Maggie Steed (Fabia London), William McGillivray (Julian London), Lisa Butler (Polly London), Donna Durkin (Vicky Oldfield), Robert Ellis (Nathan Oldfield), Andrew Normington (Hornbeam), Pam Ferris (Maggie Oldfield), Tony Haygarth (Brian Oldfield), David Quilter (Charles London).
29 November 1989   Frankie Howerd (Uncle Bob), Roger Milner (Henry Herewith), Maggie Steed (Fabia London), William McGillivray (Julian London), Lisa Butler (Polly London), Donna Durkin (Vicky Oldfield), Robert Ellis (Nathan Oldfield), Andrew Normington (Hornbeam), Pam Ferris (Maggie Oldfield), Tony Haygarth (Brian Oldfield), David Quilter (Charles London).
8 December 1989   Frankie Howerd (Uncle Bob), Roger Milner (Henry Herewith), Maggie Steed (Fabia London), William McGillivray (Julian London), Lisa Butler (Polly London), Donna Durkin (Vicky Oldfield), Robert Ellis (Nathan Oldfield), Andrew Normington (Hornbeam), Pam Ferris (Maggie Oldfield), Tony Haygarth (Brian Oldfield), David Quilter (Charles London).
13 December 1989   Frankie Howerd (Uncle Bob), Roger Milner (Henry Herewith), Maggie Steed (Fabia London), William McGillivray (Julian London), Lisa Butler (Polly London), Donna Durkin (Vicky Oldfield), Robert Ellis (Nathan Oldfield), Andrew Normington (Hornbeam), Pam Ferris (Maggie Oldfield), Tony Haygarth (Brian Oldfield), David Quilter (Charles London).
20 December 1989   Frankie Howerd (Uncle Bob), Roger Milner (Henry Herewith), Maggie Steed (Fabia London), William McGillivray (Julian London), Lisa Butler (Polly London), Donna Durkin (Vicky Oldfield), Robert Ellis (Nathan Oldfield), Andrew Normington (Hornbeam), Pam Ferris (Maggie Oldfield), Tony Haygarth (Brian Oldfield), David Quilter (Charles London).

Wogan (BBC 1)

28 March 1990   Frankie Howerd.

List of Performances

Frankie Howerd On Campus (LWT/ITV) *V*

24 November 1990   Frankie Howerd.

[Writers: Barry Cryer, Dennis Berson, Steve Knight, Spike Mullins, Mike Whitehill, Peter Vincent and Galton and Simpson]

Aspel & Co (LWT/ITV)

2 February 1991   Frankie Howerd, Richard Attenborough and Natasha Richardson.

All Change *series two* (Yorkshire/ITV)

5 February 1991   Frankie Howerd (Uncle Bob), Roger Milner (Henry Herewith), Maggie Steed (Fabia London), William McGillivray (Julian London), Lisa Butler (Polly London), Donna Durkin (Vicky Oldfield), Robert Ellis (Nathan Oldfield), Andrew Normington (Hornbeam), Pam Ferris (Maggie Oldfield), Bobby Knutt (Brian Oldfield), Peggy Mount (Aunt Fanny), David Quilter (Charles London), Paul Barber (Driver).
12 February 1991   Frankie Howerd (Uncle Bob), Roger Milner (Henry Herewith), Maggie Steed (Fabia London), William McGillivray (Julian London), Lisa Butler (Polly London), Donna Durkin (Vicky Oldfield), Robert Ellis (Nathan Oldfield), Andrew Normington (Hornbeam), Pam Ferris (Maggie Oldfield), Bobby Knutt (Brian Oldfield), Peggy Mount (Aunt Fanny), David Quilter (Charles London), Paul Barber (Driver).
19 February 1991   Frankie Howerd (Uncle Bob), Roger Milner (Henry Herewith), Maggie Steed (Fabia London), William McGillivray (Julian London), Lisa Butler (Polly London), Donna Durkin (Vicky Oldfield), Robert Ellis (Nathan Oldfield), Andrew Normington (Hornbeam), Pam Ferris (Maggie Oldfield), Bobby Knutt (Brian Oldfield), Peggy Mount (Aunt Fanny), David Quilter (Charles London), Paul Barber (Driver).
26 February 1991   Frankie Howerd (Uncle Bob), Roger Milner (Henry Herewith), Maggie Steed (Fabia London), William McGillivray (Julian London), Lisa Butler (Polly London), Donna Durkin (Vicky Oldfield), Robert Ellis (Nathan Oldfield), Andrew Normington (Hornbeam), Pam Ferris (Maggie Oldfield), Bobby Knutt (Brian Oldfield), Peggy Mount (Aunt Fanny), David Quilter (Charles London), Paul Barber (Driver).
5 March 1991   Frankie Howerd (Uncle Bob), Roger Milner (Henry Herewith), Maggie Steed (Fabia London), William McGillivray (Julian London), Lisa Butler (Polly London), Donna Durkin (Vicky Oldfield), Robert Ellis (Nathan Oldfield), Andrew Normington (Hornbeam), Pam Ferris (Maggie Oldfield), Bobby Knutt (Brian Oldfield), Peggy Mount (Aunt Fanny), David Quilter (Charles London), Paul Barber (Driver).
12 March 1991   Frankie Howerd (Uncle Bob), Roger Milner (Henry Herewith), Maggie Steed (Fabia London), William McGillivray (Julian London), Lisa Butler (Polly London), Donna Durkin (Vicky Oldfield), Andrew Normington (Hornbeam), Robert Ellis (Nathan Oldfield), Pam Ferris (Maggie Oldfield), Bobby Knutt (Brian Oldfield), Peggy Mount (Aunt Fanny), David Quilter (Charles London), Paul Barber (Driver).

Tonight with Jonathan Ross (Channel 4)

29 March 1991   Frankie Howerd.

Des O'Connor Tonight (Thames/ITV)

23 October 1991   Frankie Howerd, Kiri Te Kanawa, Carl Davis and Paul Young.

Further Up Pompeii (LWT/ITV) *V*

14 December 1991   Frankie Howerd (Lurcio), Joanna Dickens (Colossa), Elizabeth Anson (Petunia), John Bardon (Villainus Brutus), Russell Gold (Noxius), Peter Geeves (Ambiguous), Roy Evans (Typhus), Tim Killick (Gluteus Maximus), Gary Rice (Umbilicus) and Barry James (Claudius).

[Writers: Paul Minett and Brian Leveson]

Frankie's On . . . (Central/ITV) *V*

21 June 1992   Frankie Howerd.

[Recorded on board the *Ark Royal*, Gibraltar]
28 June 1992   Frankie Howerd.

[Recorded at Cotgrave Colliery, Nottinghamshire]
5 July 1992   Frankie Howerd.

[Recorded at the Fire Service College, Moreton-in-Marsh, Gloucestershire]
12 July 1992   Frankie Howerd.

[Recorded at the Queen's Medical Centre, Nottingham]

[Writers: Mark Bussell, Paul Minett and Brian Leveson, with Ian Davidson, Steve Knight, Mike Whitehill, Dennis Berson, Marc Blake and Hugh Stuckey]

Documentaries

Arena: Oooh Er, Missus! The Frankie Howerd Story or Please Yourselves (BBC 1)

1 June 1990

Heroes of Comedy – Frankie Howerd (Channel 4)

1 January 1995

Legends – Frankie Howerd (Carlton/ITV)

9 August 2000

The Unforgettable – Frankie Howerd (Chrysalis/ITV)

18 December 2000

Reputations: Frankie Howerd (BBC 2)

15 June 2002

Sex, Secrets and Frankie Howerd (ITN – Visual Voodoo/Channel 4)

24 April 2004

List of Performances

MOVIES

The Runaway Bus Eros/Conquest-Guest 1954

Director Val Guest
Screenplay Val Guest
Cinematography Stanley Pavey
Editor Douglas Myers

Cast Frankie Howerd .... Percy Lamb
Margaret Rutherford .... Cynthia Beeston
Petula Clark .... Stewardess 'Nikki' Nicholls
Terence Alexander .... Pilot Peter Jones
Toke Townley .... Henry Waterman
George Coulouris .... Ernest Schroeder
Belinda Lee .... Janie Grey
John Horsley .... Inspector Henley
Reginald Beckwith .... Telephone man
Michael Gwynn .... Transport Dispatcher
Stringer Davis .... Transport officer
Sam Kydd .... Chief of Security
Richard Beynon .... Transport officer
Anthony Oliver .... Uniformed Senior Airport Official
Alastair Hunter .... Detective Spencer
Cyril Conway .... One of the Crooks
Arthur Lovegrove .... One of the Crooks
Marianne Stone .... Uniformed Airport Hostess
Lisa Gastoni .... Airline Clerk
Frank Phillips .... BBC Newscaster
James Brown .... (uncredited)
Ted Chapman .... (uncredited)
Lionel Murton .... One of the American Travellers (uncredited)
Jimmy (Lee) Young .... (uncredited)
Running time 78 minutes *V* (PAL/NTSC)

An Alligator Named Daisy Rank 1955

Director J. Lee Thompson
Screenplay Jack Davies
Cinematography Reginald H. Wyer
Editor John D. Guthridge

Cast Donald Sinden .... Peter Weston
Jeannie Carson .... Moira O'Shannon
James Robertson Justice .... Sir James Colebrook
Diana Dors .... Vanessa Colebrook
Roland Culver .... Colonel Weston
Stanley Holloway .... The General
Avice Landone .... Mrs Weston
Richard Wattis .... Hoskins
Stephen Boyd .... Albert O'Shannon
Ernest Thesiger .... Notcher
Henry Kendall .... Valet
Michael Shepley .... The Judge
Wilfrid Lawson .... Irishman
Charles Victor .... Sergeant

313

George Moon .... Al
Margaret Rutherford .... Prudence Croquet
Patrick Cargill .... Steward (uncredited)
Cyril Chamberlain .... Party Guest (uncredited)
Jimmy Edwards .... Alligator Owner (uncredited)
Gilbert Harding .... Unwilling Guest (uncredited)
Joan Hickson .... Piano Customer (uncredited)
Frankie Howerd .... M.C. at Alligator Rally (uncredited)
Nicholas Parsons .... News Interviewer (uncredited)
Una Pearl .... Bit Part (uncredited)
Tony Selby .... Boy With Stick (uncredited)
Ronnie Stevens .... Singer (uncredited)
George Woodbridge .... PC Jorkins (uncredited)
Joan Young .... Competitor 9 (uncredited)
Running time 85 minutes *V* (PAL)

The Ladykillers Ealing 1955

Director Alexander Mackendrick
Screenplay William Rose
Cinematography Otto Heller
Editor Jack Harris

Cast Alec Guinness .... Professor Marcus
Cecil Parker .... Claude (a.k.a. 'Major Courtney')
Herbert Lom .... Louis (a.k.a. 'Mr Harvey')
Peter Sellers .... Harry (a.k.a. 'Mr Robinson')
Danny Green .... One-Round (a.k.a. 'Mr Lawson')
Jack Warner .... The Superintendent
Katie Johnson .... Mrs Wilberforce
Philip Stainton .... Sergeant MacDonald
Frankie Howerd .... The Barrow Boy
Madge Brindley .... Bit Part (uncredited)
Hélène Burls .... Hypatia (uncredited)
Kenneth Connor .... Cab Driver (uncredited)
Michael Corcoran .... Bit Part (uncredited)
Harold Goodwin .... Parcels Clerk (uncredited)
Fred Griffiths .... Junk Man (uncredited)
Lucy Griffiths .... Bit Part (uncredited)
Phoebe Hodgson .... Guest (uncredited)
Stratford Johns .... Security Guard (uncredited)
Evelyn Kerry .... Bit Part (uncredited)
Sam Kydd .... Bit Part (uncredited)
Edie Martin .... Lettice (uncredited)
Jack Melford .... Detective (uncredited)
Robert Moore .... Bit Part (uncredited)
Arthur Mullard .... Bit Part (uncredited)
Ewan Roberts .... Constable (uncredited)
George Roderick .... Bit Part (uncredited)
John Rudling .... Bit Part (uncredited)
Leonard Sharp .... Pavement Artist (uncredited)
Peter Williams .... Detective at Parcels Office (uncredited)
Neil Wilson .... Bit Part (uncredited)
Running time 97 minutes *V, DVD* (PAL/DVD)

Jumping For Joy Rank 1955

Director John Paddy Carstairs
Screenplay Henry Blyth and Jack Davies
Cinematography Jack E. Cox
Editor John D. Guthridge

Cast Frankie Howerd .... Willie Joy
Stanley Holloway .... Captain Jack Montague
A.E. Matthews .... Lord Reginald Cranfield
Tony Wright .... Vincent
Alfie Bass .... Blagg
Joan Hickson .... Lady Emily Cranfield
Lionel Jeffries .... Bert Benton
Susan Beaumont .... Susan Storer
Terence Longdon .... John Wyndham
Colin Gordon .... Max, 1st Commentator
Richard Wattis .... Carruthers
Danny Green .... Plug Ugly
Barbara Archer .... Marlene
William Kendall .... Blenkinsop
Ewen Solon .... Haines
Reginald Beckwith .... Smithers
Ian Wilson .... Man in Phone Box During Fight
Gerald Campion .... Man with Ice Cream (uncredited)
Man Mountain Dean .... (uncredited)
Bill Fraser .... Drunk in Pool Hall (uncredited)
Tom Gill .... Barry, 2nd Commentator (uncredited)
David Hannaford .... (uncredited)
Charles Hawtrey .... Punter at Bar (uncredited)
Jack Lambert .... (uncredited)
Arthur Mullard .... Bruiser (uncredited)
Michael Ward .... Tailor (uncredited)
John Warren .... Race Announcer (uncredited)
Running time 91 minutes *V* (PAL)

A Touch of the Sun Eros 1956

Director Gordon Parry
Screenplay Alfred Shaughnessy
Cinematography Arthur Grant
Editor Charles Haas

Cast Frankie Howerd .... William Darling
Ruby Murray .... Ruby
Dennis Price .... Hatchard
Dorothy Bromiley .... Rose
Katherine Kath .... Lucienne
Gordon Harker .... Sid
Reginald Beckwith .... Hardcastle
Pierre Dudan .... Louis
Colin Gordon .... Cecil Flick
Richard Wattis .... Purchase
Alfie Bass .... May
Naomi Chance .... Mrs Lovejoy
Miriam Karlin .... American Tourist
Esma Cannon .... Theatregoer

315

Ann George	Chalet Maid
Jed Brownd	(uncredited)
Willoughby Goddard	(uncredited)
Lucy Griffith	(uncredited)
George Margo	(uncredited)
Edna Morris	(uncredited)
Aïché Nana	(uncredited)
Evelyn Roberts	(uncredited)
Marianne Stone	(uncredited)
Brian Summers	(uncredited)
John Vere	(uncredited)
Ian Whittaker	(uncredited)
Lee Young	(uncredited)

Running time 91 minutes *V* (PAL)

Further Up the Creek Byron/Hammer 1958

Director Val Guest
Screenplay Val Guest
      Len Heath
      John Warren
Cinematography Len Harris
Editor Bill Lenny

Cast	
Ballard Berkeley	Whacker Payne
Victor Brooks	Policeman
Esma Cannon	Maudie
Jan Conrad	Signalman
Max Day	Kentoni Brother
Basil Dignam	Flagship Commander
Shirley Eaton	Jane
Joe Gibbons	Taxi Driver
Tom Gill	Philippe
Michael Goodliffe	Lt. Commander
George Herbert	Algeroccan Officer
Thora Hird	Mrs Galloway
Patrick Holt	First Lieutenant
Frankie Howerd	Bos'n
Walter Hudd	British Consul
Lionel Jeffries	Steady Barker
Sam Kydd	Bates
Jack Le White	Kentoni Brother
Desmond Llewelyn	Chief Yeoman
Charles Lloyd Pack	El Diabolo
David Lodge	Scouse
Cavan Malone	Signalman
Wolfe Morris	Algeroccan Major
Lionel Murton	Perkins
Larry Noble	Postman
Eric Pohlmann	President
Michael Ripper	Ticket Collector
John Singer	Dispatch Rider
John Stuart	Admiral
David Tomlinson	Lt. Fairweather
John Warren	Cooky
Ian Whittaker	Lofty
Katherine Byrne	2nd Model (uncredited)

Amy Dalby .... Edie (uncredited)
Judith Furse .... Chief Wren (uncredited)
Mary Wilson .... 1st Model (uncredited)
Running time 91 minutes *DVD* (PAL)

Watch It, Sailor! Hammer 1961

Director Wolf Rilla
Screenplay Falkland L. Cary
       Philip King
Cinematography Arthur Grant
Editor Alfred Cox
    James Needs

Cast Dennis Price .... Lt. Cmdr Hardcastle
Liz Fraser .... Daphne
Irene Handl .... Edie Hornett
Vera Day .... Shirley Hornett
Graham Stark .... Carnoustie Bligh
John Meillon .... Albert Tufnell
Marjorie Rhodes .... Emma Hornett
Cyril Smith .... Henry Hornett
Frankie Howerd .... Church Organist (guest appearance)
Bobby Howes .... Drunk (guest appearance)
Brian Reece .... Solicitor (guest appearance)
Renee Houston .... Mrs Mottram (guest appearance)
Arthur Howard .... Vicar (guest appearance)
Miriam Karlin .... Mrs Lack
Running time 81 minutes

The Fast Lady Independent Artists 1962

Director Ken Annakin
Screenplay Jack Davies
       Henry Blyth
Cinematography Reg Wyler
Editor Ralph Sheldon

Cast James Robertson Justice .... Charles Chingford
Leslie Phillips .... Freddie Fox
Stanley Baxter .... Murdoch Troon
Kathleen Harrison .... Mrs Staggers
Julie Christie .... Claire Chingford
Eric Barker .... Wentworth
Oliver Johnston .... Bulmer
Allan Cuthbertson .... Bodley
Esma Cannon .... Lady on Zebra Crossing
Dick Emery .... Shingler
Deryck Guyler .... Dr Blake
Victor Brooks .... Policeman
Terence Alexander .... Policeman on Motorcycle
Danny Green .... Bandit
Michael Balfour .... Bandit
Eddie Leslie .... Bandit
Clive Dunn .... Old Gentleman in Burning House
Campbell Singer .... Kingscombe
Trevor Reid .... Examiner

Fred Emney .... 1st Golfer
Frankie Howerd .... Road Workman in Hole
Monsewer Eddie Gray .... Himself
Raymond Baxter .... Himself
Graham Hill .... Himself
John Bolster .... Himself
John Surtees .... Himself
Bill Fraser .... 3rd Golfer
Irene Barrie .... (uncredited)
Ann Beach .... (uncredited)
Anne Blake .... (uncredited)
Gerald Campion .... Actor in Scottish TV Show
John Dunbar .... (uncredited)
Heidi Erich .... (uncredited)
Harold Goodwin .... (uncredited)
Mark Heath .... (uncredited)
Martin Miller .... Man with Microscope
Anna Ostling-Thomas .... (uncredited)
May Ling Rahman .... Maya
Terence Scully .... (uncredited)
Marianne Stone .... (uncredited)
Toke Townley .... Angry Motorist
Bernard Cribbins .... Man on Stretcher (uncredited)
Running time 95 minutes *V, DVD* (PAL)

The Cool Mikado Gilbert & Sullivan Operas/United Artists 1963

Director Michael Winner
Screenplay Michael Winner
(based on an adaptation by Maurice Browning of the W.S. Gilbert and Arthur Sullivan opera, with additional material by Lew Schwartz and Philip and Robert White)
Cinematography Martin Curtis
           Dennis Ayling
Editor Frank Gilpin

Cast Frankie Howerd .... Ko-Ko Flintridge
       Stubby Kaye .... Judge Herbert Mikado/Charlie Hotfleisch
       Mike Winters .... Mike
       Bernie Winters .... Bernie
       Tommy Cooper .... Pooh-Bah, Private Detective
       Dennis Price .... Ronald Fortescue
       Jacqueline Jones .... Katie Shaw
       Kevin Scott .... Hank Mikado
       Jill Mai Meredith .... Yum-Yum
       Lionel Blair .... Nanki
       Pete Murray .... Man in Boudoir
       Tsai Chin .... Pitti-Sing
       Glen Mason .... Harry
       Al Mulder .... (uncredited)
       Dermot Walsh .... Elmer
       Carole Shelley .... Mrs Smith
       C. Denier Warren .... (uncredited)
       Murray Kash .... (uncredited)
       Yvonne Shima .... Peep-Bo
       Kenji Takaki .... Ho Ho
       Frank Olegarn .... (uncredited)
       The John Barry Seven .... (uncredited)

318

Ed Bishop .... Man (uncredited)
Burt Kwouk .... Man on Aeroplane (uncredited)
Marianne Stone .... Espresso Waitress (uncredited)
Michael Winner .... Himself (uncredited)
Running time 81 minutes *V* (PAL)

The Mouse on the Moon United Artists 1963

Director Richard Lester
Screenplay Michael Pertwee
(based on the novel by Leonard Wibberley)
Cinematography Wilkie Cooper
Editor Bill Lenny

Cast Margaret Rutherford .... Grand Duchess Gloriana
Ron Moody .... Prime Minister Mountjoy
Bernard Cribbins .... Vincent Mountjoy
David Kossoff .... Professor Kokintz
Terry-Thomas .... Spender (as Terry Thomas)
June Ritchie .... Cynthia
John Le Mesurier .... British Delegate
John Phillips .... American Delegate
Eric Barker .... MI5 Man
Roddy McMillan .... Benter
Tom Aldredge .... Wendover
Michael Trubshawe .... British Aide
Peter Sallis .... Russian Delegate
Clive Dunn .... Bandleader
Hugh Lloyd .... Plumber
Gerald Anderson .... Member of Whitehall Conference
Robin Bailey .... Member of Whitehall Conference
Jan Conrad .... Russian Aide
Archie Duncan .... American General
Graham Stark .... Standard Bearer
Mario Fabrizi .... Valet
John Bluthal .... Von Noldol
Guy Deghy .... Russian Scientist
Richard Marner .... Russian General
Allan Cuthbertson .... Member of Whitehall Conference
Gordon Phillott .... Civil Sergeant
John Wood .... Countryman
George Chisholm .... Wine Waiter
Rosemary Scott .... Launching Lady
Vincent Ball .... Pilot
Frank Duncan .... News Announcer
Ed Bishop .... American Astronaut
Bill Edwards .... American Astronaut
Laurence Herder .... Russian Astronaut
Harvey Hall .... Russian Astronaut
Frankie Howerd .... Himself
Beverly Bennett .... (uncredited)
Michael Caspi .... (uncredited)
Paul Cole .... (uncredited)
Larry Cross .... (uncredited)
Stringer Davis .... 1st Councillor (uncredited)
Lucy Griffiths .... Lady-in-Waiting (uncredited)
Sandra Hampton .... April (uncredited)

Robert Haynes .... (uncredited)
Murray Kash .... (uncredited)
Bruce Lacey .... Bandleader (uncredited)
Frank Lieberman .... American Civilian (uncredited)
Coral Morphew .... Peasant Girl (uncredited)
Carolyn Pertwee .... June (uncredited)
Stuart Saunders .... Sergeant (uncredited)
Kevin Scott .... American Journalist (uncredited)
Running time 82 minutes *V, DVD* (PAL/NTSC)

The Great St Trinian's Train Robbery Braywild 1966

Director Frank Launder
        Sidney Gilliat
Screenplay Frank Launder
        Ivor Herbert
(inspired by the drawings of Ronald Searle)
Cinematography Kenneth Hodges
Editor Geoffrey Foot

Cast Frankie Howerd .... Alphonse of Monte Carlo/Alfred Askett
        Dora Bryan .... Amber Spottiswood
        George Cole .... Flash Harry
        Reg Varney .... Gilbert
        Raymond Huntley .... Sir Horace, the Minister
        Richard Wattis .... Bassett
        Portland Mason .... Georgina
        Terry Scott .... Policeman
        Eric Barker .... Culpepper Brown
        Godfrey Winn .... Truelove
        Colin Gordon .... Noakes
        Desmond Walter-Ellis .... Leonard Edwards
        Arthur Mullard .... Big Jim
        Norman Mitchell .... William (Willy the Jelly-Man)
        Cyril Chamberlain .... Maxie
        Larry Martyn .... Chips
        Leon Thau .... Pakistani Porter
        Maureen Crombie .... Marcia Askett
        Barbara Couper .... Mabel Radnage
        Elspeth Duxbury .... Veronica Bledlow
        Carole Ann Ford .... Albertine
        Margaret Nolan .... Susie Naphill
        Maggie McGrath .... Magda O'Riley
        Jean St Clair .... Drunken Dolly
        Lisa Lee .... Miss Brenner
        Peter Gilmore .... Butters
        Michael Ripper .... The Liftman
        George Benson .... Gore-Blackwood
        Meredith Edwards .... Chairman
        Jeremy Clyde .... Monty
        Aubrey Morris .... Hutch
        William Kendall .... Mr Parker
        Edwina Coven .... Dr Judd
        Philip Buchel .... Tango Dancer
        Betty Buchel .... Tango Dancer
        Stratford Johns .... The Voice
        Ingrid Brett .... Schoolgirl (uncredited)

Sally-Jane Spencer .... Schoolgirl (uncredited)
Running time 93 minutes *V, DVD* (PAL/NTSC)

Carry On Doctor Rank 1967

Director Gerald Thomas
Screenplay Talbot Rothwell
Cinematography Alan Hume
Editor Alfred Roome

Cast Frankie Howerd .... Francis Bigger
Kenneth Williams .... Dr Kenneth Tinkle
Sid James .... Charlie Roper
Charles Hawtrey .... Mr Barron
Jim Dale .... Dr James Kilmore
Hattie Jacques .... Matron
Peter Butterworth .... Mr Smith
Bernard Bresslaw .... Ken Biddle
Barbara Windsor .... Nurse Sandra May
Joan Sims .... Chloe Gibson
Anita Harris .... Nurse Clarke
June Jago .... Sister Hoggett
Derek Francis .... Sir Edmund Burke
Dandy Nichols .... Mrs Roper
Peter Jones .... Chaplain
Deryck Guyler .... Hardcastle
Gwendolyn Watts .... Mrs Barron
Dilys Laye .... Mavis Winkle
Peter Gilmore .... Henry
Harry Locke .... Sam
Marianne Stone .... Mum
Jean St Clair .... Mrs Smith
Valerie Van Ost .... Nurse Parkin
Julian Orchard .... Fred
Brian Wilde .... Man from Cox & Carter
Lucy Griffiths .... Patient
Gertan Klauber .... Wash Orderly
Julian Holloway .... Simmons
Jenny White .... Nurse in Bath
Helen Ford .... Nurse
Gordon Rollings .... Night Porter
Patrick Allen .... Narrator
Bart Allison .... Grandad
Simon Cain .... Tea Orderly
Pat Coombs .... Anxious Patient
Alexandra Dane .... Female Instructor
Stephen Garlick .... Boy
Cheryl Molineaux .... Women's Ward Nurse
Jane Murdoch .... Nurse
Running time 94 minutes *V, DVD* (PAL/NTSC)

Carry On Up the Jungle Rank 1969

Director Gerald Thomas
Screenplay Talbot Rothwell
Cinematography Ernest Steward
Editor Alfred Roome

Cast Frankie Howerd .... Professor Inigo Tinkle
    Sid James .... Bill Boosey
    Charles Hawtrey .... King Tonka/Walter Bagley
    Joan Sims .... Lady Evelyn Bagley
    Kenneth Connor .... Claude Chumley
    Bernard Bresslaw .... Upsidasi
    Terry Scott .... Cecil the Jungle Boy
    Jacki Piper .... June
    Valerie Leon .... Leda
    Reuben Martin .... Gorilla
    Edwina Carroll .... Nerda
    Danny Daniels .... Nosha Chief
    Yemi Ajibadi .... Witch Doctor
    Valerie Moore .... Lubi Lieutenant
    Cathi March .... Lubi Lieutenant
    Nina Baden-Semper .... Girl Nosha
    Heather Emmanuel .... Pregnant Lubi
    Willie Jonah .... Nosha
    Chris Konyils .... Nosha
    Verna Lucille MacKenzie .... Gong Lubi
    Roy Stewart .... Nosha
    Lincoln Webb .... Nosha With Girl
    Ashley Alexander .... Nosha (uncredited)
Running time 89 minutes *V, DVD* (PAL/NTSC)

Up Pompeii Associated London Films 1970

Director Bob Kellett
Screenplay Sid Colin
(based on an idea by Talbot Rothwell)
Cinematography Ian Wilson
Editor Al Gell

Cast Frankie Howerd .... Lurcio
    Patrick Cargill .... Nero
    Michael Hordern .... Ludicrus Sextus
    Barbara Murray .... Ammonia
    Lance Percival .... Bilius
    Bill Fraser .... Prosperus Maximus
    Adrienne Posta .... Scrubba
    Julie Ege .... Voluptua
    Bernard Bresslaw .... Gorgo
    Royce Mills .... Nausius
    Madeline Smith .... Erotica
    Rita Webb .... Cassandra
    Ian Trigger .... Odius
    Aubrey Woods .... Villanus
    Hugh Paddick .... Priest
    Laraine Humphrys .... Flavia
    Roy Hudd .... M.C.
    George Woodbridge .... Fat Bather
    Derek Griffiths .... Steam Slave
    Veronica Clifford .... Boobia
    Barrie Gosney .... Major Domo
    Gaye Brown .... Biggia
    Kenneth Cranham .... First Christian
    Andy Forray .... Second Christian

Russell Hunter .... Jailer
Irlin Hall .... Plumpa
Lally Bowers .... Procuria
Ken Wynne .... Vinus
Mischa De La Motte .... Satyr
Kenny Rodway .... Rempus
Robert Tayman .... Noxius
Billy Walker .... Prodigius
Nicola Austin .... Naked Woman (uncredited)
Peter Dean .... Orgy Attendee (uncredited)
Sally Douglas .... Titta (uncredited)
Carol Hawkins .... Nero's Girl (uncredited)
David Prowse .... Man (uncredited)
Corinne Skinner-Carter .... Belly Dancer (uncredited)
Patsy Snell .... Rent-a-Girl (uncredited)
Valerie Stanton .... Virginia (uncredited)
Sammie Winmill .... Orgy Girl (uncredited)
Running time 90 minutes *V, DVD* (PAL/NTSC)

Up the Chastity Belt Associated London Films 1971

Director Bob Kellett
Screenplay Sid Colin
        Ray Galton
        Alan Simpson
Cinematography Ian Wilson
Editor Al Gell

Cast Frankie Howerd .... Lurkalot/Richard the Lionheart
Graham Crowden .... Sir Coward de Custard
David Kernan .... Troubador
Bill Fraser .... Sir Braggart de Bombast
Roy Hudd .... Nick the Pick
Hugh Paddick .... Robin Hood
Anna Quayle .... Lady Ashfodel
Eartha Kitt .... Scheherazade
Royce Mills .... Knotweed
Anne Aston .... Lobelia
Billy Walker .... Chopper
Lance Percival .... Reporter
Godfrey Winn .... Archbishop of all England
Nora Swinburne .... Mistress of the Bed Chamber/Lady-in-Waiting
Lally Bowers .... The Voice
David Battley .... Yokel
Derek Griffiths .... Saladin
Judy Huxtable .... Gretel
Iain Cuthbertson .... Teutonic Knight
Rita Webb .... Maid Marian
Aubrey Woods .... Vegetable Stall Owner
Long John Baldry .... Little John
Sam Kydd .... Locksmith
Alan Rebbeck .... Friar Tuck
Ian Trigger .... Lucky Charm Seller
Fred Emney .... Mortimer
Dave King .... Landlord
Serretta Wilson .... Serving Wench
Fred Griffiths .... Father at Burning

Winnie Holman	Mother at Burning
Martin Woodhams	Child
John Barrett	Peasant
Nicholas Bennett	Peasant
Barrie Gosney	Meat Stall Holder
Norman Beaton	Blacksmith
Jonathan Elsom	Horseman
Robert Tayman	Horseman
Mischa De La Motte	Major Domo
Toby Lenon	Squill
Bernard Sharpe	Will Scarlett
Christopher Sandford	Mutch
Alec Pleon	Man in Stocks
Peter Straker	Arab
David Prowse	Sir Grumbel de Grunt
Christopher Timothy	Vendor
Frank Thornton	Master of Ceremonies
John Gorman	Ist Man-at-Arms
Don Hawkins	2nd Man-at-Arms
Veronica Clifford	Winifred the Pooh
Johnny Vyvyan	Chestnut Man
Ian White	Lieutenant
Ken Wynne	First Man
Jimmy Gardner	Little Man
Nora Wipp	Belly Dancer
Niko Laski	Belly Dancer
Sammie Winmill	Waitress
Parnell McGarry	Battle-axe Wife
Jonathan Dennis	Young Man
Patricia Quinn	Wife

Running time 99 minutes *V, DVD* (PAL/NTSC)

Up the Front Associated London Films 1972

Director Bob Kellett
Screenplay Sid Colin
          Eddie Braben
(additional material by Roy Tuvey and Maurice Sellar, and Peter Vincent and Bob Hedley)
Cinematography Tony Spratling
Editor Al Gell

Cast Frankie Howerd	Lurk
Bill Fraser	Groping
William Mervyn	Lord Twithampton
Linda Gray	Lady Twithampton
Jonathan Cecil	Nigel Phipps-Fortescue
Madeline Smith	Fanny
Nicholas Bennett	Mallett
Mike Grady	Newsboy
Dora Bryan	Cora Crumpington
Stanley Holloway	Vincento
Veronica Clifford	Velma
Peter Greenwell	Leader of the Orchestra
Barrie Gosney	Stage Manager
Bob Hoskins	Recruiting Sergeant
Lance Percival	Von Gutz
Peter Bull	Kobler

Vernon Dobtcheff .... Muller
Ingo Mogendorf .... Capt. Hamburger
Gertan Klauber .... Donner
Stanley Lebor .... Blitzen
Percy Herbert .... Cpl. Lovechild
David Battley .... Midgeley the Cook
Andy Bradford .... Despatch Rider
Alan Rebbeck .... Winking Soldier
Hermione Baddeley .... Monique
Bozena .... Frou Frou
Ian Talbot .... Monique's Soldier
Parnell McGarry .... Fat Nurse
Leena Skoog .... Nurse
Toni Palmer .... 1st Buttercup Girl
Delia Sainsbury .... Can Can Dancer
Michael Brennan .... MP
Harvey Hall .... MP
Zsa Zsa Gabor .... Mata Hari
Patricia Quinn .... Magda, Mata Hari's Maid
Robert Coote .... Gen. Burke
Kenneth Fortescue .... Gen. Burke's ADC
Mischa De La Motte .... Diplomat
Madhav Sharma .... Indian Officer
Robert Gillespie .... French Officer
Derek Griffiths .... El Puncturo
Lesley Anderson .... Can Can Dancer
Judy Gridley .... Can Can Dancer
Maggie Vincent .... Can Can Dancer
Wendy Lukins .... Can Can Dancer
Nicola Rowley .... French Girl
Philip Miller .... Waiter
Sidney Kean .... Singing Soldier
Liz Gold .... Mademoiselle from Armentières (uncredited)
Andrew McCullough .... Soldier (uncredited)
Running time 89 minutes *V*, *DVD* (PAL)

The House in Nightmare Park Associated London Scripts/Extonation 1973

Director Peter Sykes
Screenplay Clive Exton
        Terry Nation
Cinematography Ian Wilson
Editor Bill Blunden

Cast Frankie Howerd .... Foster Twelvetrees
Ray Milland .... Stewart Henderson
Hugh Burden .... Reggie Henderson
Kenneth Griffith .... Ernest Henderson
John Bennett .... Patel
Rosalie Crutchley .... Jessica Henderson
Ruth Dunning .... Agnes Henderson
Elizabeth MacLennan .... Verity Henderson
Aimée Delamain .... Mother
Peter Munt .... Cabbie
Running time 100 minutes *V* (PAL/NTSC)

Sgt Pepper's Lonely Hearts Club Band RSO/Geria 1977

Director Michael Schultz
Screenplay Henry Edwards
Cinematography Owen Roizman
Editor Christopher Holmes

Cast Peter Frampton .... Billy Shears
Barry Gibb .... Mark Henderson
Robin Gibb .... Dave Henderson
Maurice Gibb .... Bob Henderson
Frankie Howerd .... Mr Mustard
Paul Nicholas .... Dougie Shears
Donald Pleasence .... B.D. Hoffler
Sandy Farina .... Strawberry Fields
Dianne Steinberg .... Lucy
Steve Martin .... Dr Maxwell Edison
Tom Hamilton .... Future Villain Band (FVB): Bass
Joey Kramer .... (FVB): Drums
Earth, Wind and Fire .... Themselves
Joe Perry .... (FVB): Lead Guitar
Steven Tyler .... (FVB): Lead Vocals
Alice Cooper .... Marvin Sunk (the 'Sun King')
Brad Whitford .... (FVB): Rhythm Guitar
Philip Bailey .... Earth, Wind & Fire
Billy Preston .... Sergeant Pepper
Debra Anderson .... The Diamonds (as Stargard)
Rochelle Runnells .... The Diamonds (as Stargard)
Janice Williams .... The Diamonds (as Stargard)
George Burns .... Mr Kite
Carel Struycken .... The Brute
Patti Jerome .... Saralinda Shears
Max Showalter .... Ernest Shears
John Wheeler .... Mr Fields
Jay W. MacIntosh .... Mrs Fields
Eleanor Zee .... Mrs Henderson
Scott Manners .... Young Sergeant Pepper
Stanley Coles .... Young Lonely Hearts Club Band
Stanley Sheldon .... Young Lonely Hearts Club Band
Bob Mayo .... Young Lonely Hearts Club Band
Woody Chambliss .... Old Sergeant Pepper
Hank Worden .... Old Lonely Hearts Club Band
Morgan Farley .... Old Lonely Hearts Club Band
Delos V. Smith Jr .... Old Lonely Hearts Club Band
Patrick Cranshaw .... Western Union Manager
Terri Lynn Wood .... Bonnie
Tracy Justrich .... Tippy
Anna Rodzianko .... The Computerettes/Dancer
Rosa Aragon .... The Computerettes/Dancer
Peter Allen .... Our Guests at Heartland
Keith Allison .... Our Guests at Heartland
George Benson .... Our Guests at Heartland
Keith Carradine .... Our Guests at Heartland
Carol Channing .... Our Guests at Heartland
Jim Dandy .... Our Guests at Heartland
Sarah Dash .... Our Guests at Heartland
Rick Derringer .... Our Guests at Heartland

Barbara Dickson .... Our Guests at Heartland
Donovan .... Our Guests at Heartland
Randy Edelman .... Our Guests at Heartland
Yvonne Elliman .... Our Guests at Heartland
José Feliciano .... Our Guests at Heartland
Leif Garrett .... Our Guests at Heartland
Geraldine Granger .... Our Guests at Heartland
Adrian Gurvitz .... Our Guests at Heartland
Billy Harper .... Our Guests at Heartland
Eddie Harris .... Our Guests at Heartland
Michael Derosier .... Our Guests at Heartland (as Heart)
Steve Fossen .... Our Guests at Heartland (as Heart)
Roger Fisher .... Our Guests at Heartland (as Heart)
Howard Leese .... Our Guests at Heartland (as Heart)
Ann Wilson .... Our Guests at Heartland (as Heart)
Nancy Wilson .... Our Guests at Heartland (as Heart)
Nona Hendryx .... Our Guests at Heartland
Barry Humphries ... Our Guests at Heartland (Dame Edna Everage)
Etta James .... Our Guests at Heartland
Dr John .... Our Guests at Heartland
Bruce Johnston .... Our Guests at Heartland
Joe Lala .... Our Guests at Heartland
D.C. LaRue .... Our Guests at Heartland
Jo Leb .... Our Guests at Heartland
Marcella Detroit .... Our Guests at Heartland (as Marcy Levy)
Mark Lindsay .... Our Guests at Heartland
Nils Lofgren .... Our Guests at Heartland
Jackie Lomax .... Our Guests at Heartland
John Mayall .... Our Guests at Heartland
Curtis Mayfield .... Our Guests at Heartland
'Cousin Brucie' Morrow .... Our Guests at Heartland (as
                                            Cousin Bruce Morrow)
Peter Noone .... Our Guests at Heartland
Alan O'Day .... Our Guests at Heartland
Lee Oskar .... Our Guests at Heartland
Andy Paley .... Our Guests at Heartland (as The Paley Brothers)
Robert Palmer .... Our Guests at Heartland
Wilson Pickett .... Our Guests at Heartland
Anita Pointer .... Our Guests at Heartland
Bonnie Raitt .... Our Guests at Heartland
Helen Reddy .... Our Guests at Heartland
Minnie Riperton .... Our Guests at Heartland
Chita Rivera .... Our Guests at Heartland
Johnny Rivers .... Our Guests at Heartland
Monti Rock III .... Our Guests at Heartland
Danielle Rowe .... Our Guests at Heartland
Sha-Na-Na .... Our Guests at Heartland
Del Shannon .... Our Guests at Heartland
Joe Simon .... Our Guests at Heartland
Jim Seals .... Our Guests at Heartland
Dash Crofts .... Our Guests at Heartland
Connie Stevens .... Our Guests at Heartland
John Stewart .... Our Guests at Heartland
Tina Turner .... Our Guests at Heartland
Frankie Valli .... Our Guests at Heartland
Gwen Verdon .... Our Guests at Heartland
Diane Vincent .... Our Guests at Heartland

Grover Washington Jr .... Our Guests at Heartland
Hank Williams Jr .... Our Guests at Heartland
Johnny Winter .... Our Guests at Heartland
Wolfman Jack .... Our Guests at Heartland
Bobby Womack .... Our Guests at Heartland
Alan White .... Our Guests at Heartland
Lenny White .... Our Guests at Heartland
Gary Wright .... Our Guests at Heartland
Barbi Alison .... Dancer
Helena Andreyko .... Dancer
Jennifer Buchanan .... Dancer
Leonard Connor .... Dancer
Sheryl Cooper .... Dancer
Carol Culver .... Dancer
Dennis Daniels .... Dancer
Tom Demenkoff .... Dancer
Cindy DeVore .... Dancer
Lionel Douglas .... Dancer
Larry Dusich .... Dancer
Deborah Fishman .... Dancer
John Robert Garrett .... Dancer
Ken Grant .... Dancer
Sandra Gray .... Dancer
Mary Ann Hay .... Dancer
Mimi Lieber .... Dancer
Ben Lokey .... Dancer
Kim Miyori .... Dancer
Sean Moran .... Dancer
JoAnn O'Rourke .... Dancer
Melinda Phelps .... Dancer
Kathy Pickle .... Dancer
Greg Rosatti .... Dancer
Andy Roth .... Dancer
Lou Spadaccini .... Dancer
Dennis Stewart .... Dancer
Judy Susman .... Dancer
Andy Tennant .... Dancer
Lulu Washington .... Dancer
Richard Weisman .... Dancer
Antoinette Yuskis .... Dancer
Jonathan Paley .... Our Guests at Heartland
Carolyn Stellar .... Our Guests at Heartland (uncredited)
Al Stewart .... Our Guests at Heartland (uncredited)
Running time 113 minutes *V, DVD* (PAL/NTSC)

RECORDINGS

Singles
'Three Little Fishes'/'I'm Nobody's Baby' (Harmony 78 rpm, A 1001), 1950
'English as She is Spoken'/'I'm The Man Who's Deputising For The Bull' (Philips 78 rpm, PB 214), 1950
'All's Going Well'/'Nymphs And Shepherds' (both with Margaret Rutherford) (Philips 78 rpm PB 214), 1954
'It's All Right With Me'/'Song And Dance Man' (Columbia 45 rpm, DB 4230), 1958
'Abracadabra'/'(Don't Let The) Kiddy Geddin' (Decca 45 rpm, 45F 10420),
'The Last Word On The Election' (2 parts) (Decca 45 rpm, F 12028), 1964

'Up Pompeii'/'Salute' (Columbia 45 rpm DB 8757), 1971
'Up Je T'Aime'/'All Through The Night' (both with June Whitfield) (Pye 45 rpm 7N 45061), 1971
'Three Little Fishes'/'Primeval Scream' (FISHEE, FISH E 1), 1989
'Oh No Missus'/'Oh No Missus (Halifax Mix)' (Fly 12 Flea 6), 1991

Albums
Frankie Howerd At The Establishment (Decca LK 4556), 1963
A Funny Thing Happened On The Way To The Forum (HMV CLP 1685/CSD 1518), 1963/1998
Frankie Howerd Tells The Story Of Peter And The Wolf (Polydor Carnival 2928 201), 1971
Please Yourselves (BBC REH 230), 1976
The Frankie Howerd Show (BBC double-cassette ZBBC 1398/BBC GOLD re-issue ZBBC 0563389648) 1992/1996
The Frankie Howerd Show 2 (BBC double-cassette ZBBC 1730), 1995
Frankie's On . . . (Laughing Stock double-cassette LAFFC 1897774753), 1996
The Frankie Howerd Song and Dance Collection (QED 282, MCPS), 1998
Get Your Titters Out (Hallmark CD 703272), 2002

Videos
Frankie Howerd At His Tittermost! (Sunset + Vine, SV 2008), 1991
Frankie Howerd On Campus (Video Collection, VC 6145), 1991
Titter Ye Not! (Sunset + Vine, SV 086 042 3), 1992
Comedy Greats:Frankie Howerd (BBC Worldwide, BBCV 6935), 2000
Masters of Comedy – Frankie Howerd (Granada Cinema Club, GV0346), 2002

DVDs
Comedy Greats: Frankie Howerd (Region 2: BBC Worldwide, B0001MIQ8A), 2004

Notes

Opening epigraph: Frankie Howerd, quoted by Terry Coleman, 'Frankie Howerd: Delusion, Love, and Work', *Movers & Shakers: Conversations With Uncommon Men* (London: André Deutsch, 1987), p.210.

THE PROLOGUE

1.   As it is not always possible, nor practical, to provide the original, definitive source for every reference to a comic line, joke or story once uttered by Frankie Howerd, I will try to supply the most readily available recorded version.

2.   See, for example, the range contained in G.J. Mellor's brief but informative *They Made Us Laugh* (Littleborough: George Kelsell, 1982).

3.   Most of these posthumous 'tributes' tended to betray both a short memory (with little or nothing on his achievements in radio) and an insensitive, immature and, in some cases, distinctly homophobic attitude.

4.   Frankie Howerd, quoted by David Nathan, *The Laughtermakers* (London: Peter Owen, 1971), p.192.

ACT I: FRANCIS

Chapter 1

1.   Whenever biographical details were requested, the birth date was always given as '6 March 1922'. In Howerd's autobiography, however, the evasion takes the novel form of a vague reference to having been born 'after the war'. See Frankie Howerd, *On The Way I Lost It* (London: W.H. Allen, 1976), p. 11.

2.   *Ibid.*

3.   During the course of a typically peripatetic military career, Frankie Howerd's paternal grandfather, Francis Alfred Percival Howard (originally from Taunton in Somerset), had lived for a period at Sandhurst in Army-owned accommodation alongside his wife, Ada (who hailed from Plumstead in Kent), and their three children, Francis, Sarah and Charles. The family was in residence there at the time of the 1891 English Census.

4.   Howerd would later claim (in *On The Way I Lost It*, pp.11–12) that the tumble left him with 'a permanent dread of heights'.

5.   Howerd, *ibid.*, pp.14 and 16.

6.   Howerd attended the school (named after the hero of Khartoum) from 1923 to 1928.

7.   Howerd, *op. cit.*, p.14.

8.   *Ibid.*

9.   The bitter irony for Edith was that the HQ of the Educational Corps was based, in those days, a short walk away at Eltham Palace.

10.   In an article in the British Music Hall's journal, *The Call Boy* (Winter 2004, vol. 40, no. 4, p.1), the actor Jonathan Cecil (who worked with Howerd in 1972) recalled being told by him of his father's 'sadistic' treatment. Howerd also confided to several close friends that his father had physically abused him in a sexual way, and one of them (whose identity is known to me) allowed the show-business writer William Hall to quote her – anonymously – on the subject in his book, *Titter Ye Not! The Life of Frankie Howerd* (London: Grafton, 1992, p.126). According to another source (who for professional reasons must remain nameless), he also repeated this claim in much greater detail during the course of his sessions with at least one of his psychoanalysts.

11.   My interviewees – all of whom were friends of Howerd – asked to remain nameless. Certain potentially relevant police and psychiatric records are not yet available.

12.   Howerd, *op. cit.*, p.14.

13.   *Ibid.*, pp.12–13 and 19–20. According to the informal checklist provided by the NSPCC, some of the signs to look for are: a fear of, and/or reluctance to be with, certain adult members of the family; the appearance of being depressed and/or withdrawn; and a tendency to be unusually clingy.

14.   Howerd was always vague and inconsistent when it came to dating the arrival of his speech impediment. In his autobiography (p.17), he implies that it was already in evidence during his 'pre-teen years', but he also told some interviewers that it developed at a slightly later date.

15.   Howerd, *op. cit.*, p.13.

16.   According to William Hall (in *Titter Ye Not!*, p.16), the condition had been 'brought on . . . by the dreaded gas swirling around the trenches of Passchendaele'. If true, this would have made the 30-year-old Frank Snr one of the unluckiest soldiers of the Great War, as he happened to be in an office on the outskirts of York at the time of that terrible battle in Flanders. In reality, his active combat career had ceased long before the introduction of chlorine gas as a weapon of war in 1915.

17.   *TV Times*, 11 September 1969, p.7.

18.   Howerd, *op. cit.*, p.14.

19.   *Ibid.*

20.   *Ibid.*, p.79.

21.   See Bert A. French's pamphlet, *Boyhood Memories of Eltham, 1928–1933* (London: Clare Corner Publications, 1995), pp.23–5. The church would subsequently be entirely rebuilt.

22.   *Ibid.*, p.17.

23.   *Ibid.*

24.   *Ibid.*

25.   *Ibid.*

26.   The name change took place in time for the academic year of 1934–35.

27.   Howerd, *op. cit.*, p.18.

28.   *Ibid.*

29.   *Ibid.*

30.   *Ibid.*, p.19.

31.   *Ibid.*, p.15.

32.   See Bert A. French, *op. cit.*, p.36.

33.   Jack Payne (Frankie Howerd's future manager – see Chapter 4) became the first leader of the BBC Dance Orchestra in 1928, and stayed in that position until 1932, when Henry

Hall succeeded him; *Radio Radiance* was first broadcast by the BBC in 1925 and went on to run for over a year; *Music Hall* began its exceptionally long run on BBC radio in 1930; *Myrtle and Bertie*, a domestic proto-sitcom starring Claude Hulbert and his real-life wife Enid Trevor, aired on Radio Luxembourg from 9 June to 22 December 1935.

34. See Howerd, *op. cit.*, p.16.

35. *Ibid.*, p.19.

36. *Ibid.*

37. *Ibid.*, p.30.

38. *Ibid.*, p.20. The play (itself based on Hay's 1913 novel, *Happy-Go-Lucky*) had recently (1931) inspired a movie version starring, rather ironically, Sydney Howard.

39. Val Gielgud directed Reith, among others, in a 1928 BBC Amateur Dramatic Society production at the Rudolf Steiner Hall.

40. Howerd, *op. cit.*, p.20.

41. *Ibid.*

42. *Ibid.*

43. *Ibid.*

44. *Ibid.*

45. *Ibid.*

46. *Ibid.*, p.21.

Chapter 2

1. Howerd, *op. cit.*, p.22.

2. According to the memory (recorded on the Shooters Hill page of the Friends Reunited website) of one who had been present, Frank Howard 'stole the show'.

3. Howerd, *op. cit.*, p.22.

4. *Ibid.*

5. *Ibid.*, p.23.

6. Sidney (or rather 'Sydney' as his name was registered officially) Howard began his long GPO career (initially as a clerk, later as a telephone engineer) in 1935.

7. Betty Howard started work in 1936 as an office junior.

8. Howerd, *op. cit.*, p.23.

9. Quoted by Hall from an undisclosed source, *op. cit.*, p.24.

10. Howerd, *op. cit.*, p.23.

11. *Ibid.*, p.24.

12. *Ibid.*, p.25.

13. *Ibid.*, p.24.

14. *Ibid.*, p.25.

15. *Ibid.*

16. *Ibid.*

17. *Ibid.*, p.26.

18. *Ibid.*

19. Quoted by Hall from an undisclosed source, *op. cit.*, p.27.

20. Howerd, *op. cit.*, p.30.

21. Quoted by Hall from an undisclosed source, *op. cit.*, p.27.

22. Howerd, *op. cit.*, p.26.

23. Frank Howard's name is listed under the 1935 school magazine's farewell *Valete*.

24. Philip Kane, who attended Shooters Hill during the early 1930s.

25. Howerd, *op. cit.*, p.27.

26. *Ibid.*, pp.27–8.

27. *Ibid.*, p.28.

28. *Ibid.*, p.29.

29. *Ibid.*

30. *Ibid.*

31. *Ibid.*, p.32.

32. Jimmy James (whose real name was James Casey) was born in Stockton-on-Tees in 1892. Usually dressed in a black top hat and tails, he was known both for his solo drunk act and his sketches with his two stooges, 'Hutton Conyers' and 'Bretton Woods'. He died in 1965. For a fine account of the nature of his appeal, see the essay in John Fisher's *Funny Way to be a Hero* (London: Frederick Muller, 1973), pp.185–95, and for samples of his sketches, see Mike Craig's *Look Back With Laughter*, vol. 1 (Manchester: Mike Craig Enterprises, 1996), pp.29–57. For his broader influence on other comedians, such as Eric Morecambe, see my *Morecambe & Wise* (London: Fourth Estate, 1999), pp.17–18; and for his influence on Frankie Howerd, see Chapter 6 of this book.

33. Howerd, *op. cit.*, p.31.

34. Howerd, *Radio Times*, June 1955.

Chapter 3

1. See Howerd, *op. cit.*, p.33. His suggested date is accepted without elaboration by Mick Middles – *Frankie Howerd: The Illustrated Biography* (London: Headline, 2000), p.21; Robert Ross – *The Complete Frankie Howerd* (London: Reynolds & Hearn, 2001), p.18; and Barry Took – *Star Turns: The Life and Times of Benny Hill & Frankie Howerd* (London: Weidenfeld & Nicolson, 1992), p.22. William Hall – in his *Titter Ye Not!* (*op. cit.*, p.33) – also appears to accept this date, although he does go on to acknowledge that it remains unclear 'why the War Office waited until February 1940' to enlist the 22-year-old.

2. The Military Training Act of 27 April 1939 – one strand of the Government's response to Hitler's threat of imminent German aggression in Europe – obliged all fit and able British men between the ages of 20 and 21 to commence six months' military training. With Britain's subsequent declaration of war against Germany, The National Service (Armed Forces) Act made all fit and able men between the ages of 18 and 41 liable immediately for conscription. Registration began on 21 October 1939 for those aged 20 to 23. Frank Howard, on this date, was aged 22 years and seven months.

3. Howerd never explained the delay in the arrival of his call-up papers, but such a gap between registration and enlistment was not particularly uncommon during this period.

4. ENSA had been formed in September 1939 with the intention of providing organised forms of entertainment, at home and abroad, for military personnel, factory workers and other groups of people engaged in the war effort. Based in London at the Theatre Royal, Drury Lane.

5. Howerd, *op. cit.*, p.32.

6. *Ibid.*, p.35.

7. Former Private Peter Enright, quoted by William Hall, *op. cit.*, p.33.

8. Howerd, *op. cit.*, p.34.

9. *Ibid.*, p.35.

10. *Ibid.*

11. *Ibid.*, p.37.

12. The joke would be repeated, with minor variations, throughout Howerd's professional career. For a recorded version, see the 'On Board' *Ark Royal* segment of *Frankie's On!* (video, Central Television, 1992; cassette, Laughing Stock, 1994). The novelty song 'Three Little Fishes' was recorded several times, each version slightly different, by Howerd; the first time as a 78 single (Harmony A1001, 1950), the final time as one of the tracks on his CD album, *Get Your Titters Out* (Hallmark 703272, 2002).

13. Howerd, *op. cit.*, p.39.

14. *Ibid.*, p.40.

15. Howerd, interviewed by the BBC during preparation for Helen Gallacher's *Arena* documentary, *Oooh Er, Missus! The Frankie Howerd Story or Please Yourselves* (first broadcast on BBC 1, 1 June 1990), unreleased and uncut recording.

16. Max Miller performed numerous variations on this joke during his career. For one version, see Eric Midwinter, *Make 'Em Laugh* (London: George Allen & Unwin, 1979), p.104.

17. Howerd explains the basic technique in the 1990 *Arena* tapes, *op. cit.*

18. Howerd, *op. cit.*, pp.41–2.

19. *Ibid.*, p.42.

20. *Ibid.*, p.44.

21. *Ibid.*

22. *Ibid.*

23. *Ibid.*

24. *Ibid.*, p.47.

25. See, for example, Susan Sontag's classic essay, 'Notes on "Camp"' (1964), reproduced in *A Susan Sontag Reader* (Harmondsworth: Penguin, 1982), pp.105–19.

26. See Nathan, *The Laughtermakers*, *op. cit.*, p.192; Midwinter, *Make 'Em Laugh*, *op. cit.*, pp.71–102; and Robb Wilton, *Robb Wilton's War* (Pavilion Records: PAST CD 7854, 2001).

27. Norman Evans, excerpted from his 'Over the Garden Wall' sketch. A version was included in the movie *Over the Garden Wall* (Mancunian Films, 1950).

28. See Mike Craig's informative chapter on Evans in *Look Back With Laughter*, *op. cit.*, vol. 2, pp.125–149.

29. Howerd, quoted by Nathan, *op. cit.*, p.192.

30. Howerd, *op. cit.*, p.50.

31. The Co-Odments was a concert party that toured the Southend area putting on shows for the troops in church halls, anti-aircraft sites and sometimes outside in parks or fields.

32. Howerd, *op. cit.*, p.43.

33. I have withheld the man's name out of respect for the wishes of his surviving family. The 'sissified' description was confirmed to me by two of Howerd's Army contemporaries, both of whom wished to remain anonymous.

34. Dudley Cave, quoted by Harry Cohen, 9 May 1996: *Hansard*, part 31, col. 497 (reported originally in *The Guardian*, 8 May 1996).

35. Interviewed by assistant producer Ines Cavill and producer-director David F. Turnbull for their BBC 2 *Reputations* documentary on Frankie Howerd, first broadcast on 15 June 2002.

36. *Ibid.*

37. Howerd, *op. cit.*, p.49.

38. *Ibid.*

39. There are many recorded versions of this routine. See, for example, *Superfrank!* (first broadcast on Channel 4, 12 January 1987).

40.   The list included Vera Roper, Lena Crisp, Blanche Moore and Sunny Rogers. Blanche Moore was probably the first regular, but, as she was married with a family in Southend-on-Sea, touring on a regular basis proved impractical, and so Vera Roper came to feature increasingly often in the routine, and Sunny Rogers was the most familiar stooge of the final thirty years.

41.   Howerd, *op. cit.*, p.52.

42.   *Stars in Battledress* (SIB) was instigated by Lieutenant-Colonel Basil Brown early in 1942. Unlike the civilian company ENSA, SIB was considered a more 'organic' form of military entertainment – by servicemen for servicemen – as well as more integral – it had access to areas prohibited to civilian performers. Among the many future stars who took part at some stage were Terry-Thomas, Benny Hill, Reg Varney, Charlie Chester, Harry Secombe and Spike Milligan. See John Graven Hughes' *The Greasepaint War*, (London: New English Library, 1976), and Bill Pertwee's entertaining anecdotal history, *Stars in Battledress* (London: Hodder & Stoughton, 1992).

43.   Howerd, *op. cit.*, p.52.

44.   *Ibid.*, p.53.

45.   *Ibid.*

46.   *Ibid.*

47.   *Ibid.*, p.54.

48.   *Ibid.*, p.55.

49.   *Ibid.*

50.   *Ibid.*, p.56.

51.   *Ibid.*, p.57.

52.   *Ibid.*, p.58.

53.   See Richard Stone, *You Should Have Been In Last Night* (Sussex: The Book Guild, 2000).

54.   See Ian Carmichael interview at the NFT, 8 December 2002: *http://www.bfi.org.uk/showing/nft/interviews/carmichael/*

55.   'A-Tisket, A-Tasket' (1938), written by Ella Fitzgerald and Van Alexander.

56.   Ian Carmichael, quoted in Bill Pertwee's *Stars in Battledress*, *op. cit.*, p.153.

57.   Ian Carmichael, interviewed by Clyde Jeavons at the National Film Theatre, London, 8 December 2002.

58.   Richard Stone, quoted by Pertwee, *op. cit.*, p.153.

59.   Benny Hill, quoted by his brother Leonard Hill, *Saucy Boy: The Life Story of Benny Hill* (London: Grafton, 1992), p.181.

60.   Howerd, quoted by Hill, *op. cit.*, p.181.

61.   Stone, *op. cit.*, p.52.

62.   Howerd, quoted by Took, *op. cit.*, p.24.

63.   Howerd, *op. cit.*, p.58.

ACT II: FRANKIE

Chapter 4

1.   Dale's many tales of his wartime achievements were not always taken as truths by his friends, let alone his enemies. Barry Took (who for a time was a client of Dale) said of him in *Star Turns* (*op. cit.*, p.34): 'He might have been a hero. On the other hand he may never have seen action. Nobody knew.' I can, however, confirm here that Dale (a pilot officer – number 169884 – in the Royal Air Force Volunteer Reserve, 158 Squadron) most definitely

did receive the DFC on 23 May 1944 for displaying 'a high degree of skill and resolution'. The award was recorded in the Third Supplement to *The London Gazette* of 19 May 1944, p.2348, published on 23 May 1944.

2. Alan Simpson, interview with the author, 15 March 2004.

3. See Freddie Hancock and David Nathan, *Hancock* (London: BBC, 1996), pp.67–8.

4. Bill Lyon-Shaw, speaking in the BBC 2 *Reputations* documentary on Frankie Howerd, *op. cit.*

5. Howerd, *op. cit.*, p.59.

6. *Ibid.*, p.61.

7. *Ibid.*

8. *Ibid.*

9. *Ibid.*

10. *Ibid.*, pp. 61–2. (Howard's and Dale's final exchange recounted by Barry Took, interview with the author, 17 May 2000.)

11. Bill Lyon-Shaw, interview with the author, 29 January 2004.

12. Howerd, *op. cit.*, p.62.

13. *Ibid.*, p.63.

14. *Ibid.*

15. *Ibid.*

16. *Ibid.*

17. *Ibid.*

18. *Ibid.*, pp.63–4 (italics are mine).

19. *Ibid.*, p.64.

20. Kenneth Tynan, 'Sid Field' (1950), reproduced in his *Profiles* (London: Nick Hern Books, 1989), p.12.

21. Howerd, *op. cit.*, p.67.

22. *Ibid.*, p.68.

23. *Ibid.*, pp.67–8.

24. *Ibid.*, p.65.

25. *Ibid.*

26. Lupino Lane, *How to Become a Comedian* (London: Frederick Muller, 1945), p.8.

27. Howerd, *op. cit.*, p.69.

28. *Ibid.*

29. Lyon-Shaw, interview with the author, 29 January 2004.

30. Max Bygraves, *Stars in My Eyes* (London: Robson, 2003), p.74.

31. Howerd, *op. cit.*, p.67.

32. *Ibid.*

33. Bygraves, *op. cit.*, p.35.

34. Nosmo King (1886–1949) – real name Vernon Watson – was a former bank clerk from Liverpool who had graduated from appearing in blackface to performing more conventional comedy monologues. His bill matter, bizarrely, was: 'Iceland's Antidote for the Deep Depression'.

35. Bygraves, *op. cit.*, p.179.

36. Bygraves told William Hall (*Titter Ye Not!*, *op. cit.*, p.51) that Howerd fell 'head over heels in love with Pam'. The date of this interview was not given, but it must have taken place prior to Howerd's death. Bygraves has not repeated his remarks about the relationship

since this time, nor has he spoken publicly about Howerd's homosexuality. The only mention that Denton received in Howerd's autobiography (*op. cit.*, p.66) referred to her merely as 'a girl contortionist . . . who finally got unknotted and left show-business'.

37.   Lyon-Shaw, interview with the author, 29 January 2004.

38.   *Ibid.*

39.   Bygraves, *op. cit.*, p.36.

40.   Recalled by Barry Took, interview with the author, 17 May 2000.

41.   Quoted by Hall, *op. cit.*, p.52.

42.   *Ibid.*, p.53.

43.   Howerd, *op. cit.*, p.69.

44.   *Ibid.*, p.71.

45.   BBC Written Archives Centre (WAC): Frankie Howerd: Artist's File 1 – 1947–52: Joy Russell-Smith, audition card for Frankie Howerd (no date).

46.   BBC WAC: Frankie Howerd: Artist's File 1 – 1947–52: Letter from Joy Russell-Smith to Frankie Howerd, c/o Scruffy Dale, 23 October 1946, ref. 03/V/JRS.

47.   See Howerd, *op. cit.*, p.71. Russell-Smith had previously written to Howerd on 30 October 1946, informing him that he had gained the requisite number of marks and passed the second and final audition: 'It now remains to be seen whether you can be used in broadcasts, when our [other] producers have heard the recording made of your act' (BBC WAC: Frankie Howerd File, 1946–52). The telegram (a copy of which no longer appears to exist) followed several days later.

Chapter 5

1.   Anon, 'Both Sides of the Microphone', *Radio Times*, 29 November 1946, p.9.

2.   See Howerd, *op. cit.*, p.71.

3.   The transcript of this routine is included in John Watt's collection *Radio Variety* (London: J.M. Dent, 1939), pp.19–23. Former schoolteacher Stainless Stephen (1892–1971) – whose real name was Arthur Clifford Baines – became a stand-up comic in the mid-1920s. An assured performer of what he liked to call 'audible punctuation', he broadcast occasionally on BBC radio during the late 1920s and early 1930s. See Gale Pedrick, 'Laughter in the Air', *BBC Year Book 1948* (London: BBC, 1948), p.54.

4.   Spike Milligan, quoted by David Bradbury and Joe McGrath, *Now That's Funny!* (London: Methuen, 1998), p.15.

5.   *Ibid.*

6.   Lyon-Shaw, interview with the author, 29 January 2004.

7.   Jack Benny's radio show ran from 1932–1955, Fred Allen's from 1932–1949. Their mock feud was sparked in 1936 when Fred Allen ad-libbed a sarcastic remark about Benny during one of his own shows; the following week, Benny's writers handed him a suitable comical response. The sequence developed from there, and was featured not only in each comedian's radio show but also in two fairly successful movies: *Love Thy Neighbor* (1940) and *It's in the Bag* (1945). Recorded examples of many of the shows and sketches are still freely available (in both CD and MP3 formats) from specialist 'old-time radio' retailers.

8.   Howerd, *op. cit.*, p.71.

9.   Sources: BBC WAC: Daily Listening Barometers between January and March 1947, and Gale Pedrick, *Radio Times*, 28 October 1949, p.6.

10.   Howerd, interviewed in 1990 by John Morrish; reproduced in Robert Ross, *The Complete Frankie Howerd*, *op. cit.*, p.26.

11.   Howerd, interviewed by David Nathan, *The Laughtermakers*, *op. cit.*, p.194.

12.   Howerd, *op. cit.*, p.77.

13. See Howerd, *ibid.*, p.73.

14. *Ibid.*

Chapter 6

1. Howerd, *op. cit.*, p.73.

2. *Ibid.*, p.74.

3. *Ibid.*

4. Howerd, interviewed by Jack de Manio, 12 October 1976 (BBC Sound Archive ref. LP37336).

5. *ITMA* (itself an abbreviation of the original title, *It's That Man Again*) ran on the BBC's various radio networks for twelve series, from 1939 to 1949. It was written by Ted Kavanagh, and starred Tommy Handley, with support from, among others, Jack Train, Dorothy Summers, Clarence Wright, Horace Percival and Deryck Guyler. At its peak, it was listened to by an audience of twenty million in Britain and thirty million worldwide.

6. The formal title of the 'private and confidential' internal guide – an informal version of which had already been brought to the attention of programme-makers – was *BBC Variety Programmes Policy Guide For Writers & Producers* (London: BBC, 1948). It was nicknamed 'The Green Book' simply because of the colour of its cloth.

7. *Ibid.*, p.4.

8. *Ibid.*, p.5.

9. *Ibid.*, p.13. The decision to ban impersonations of Churchill (and certain other elder statesmen) came from the upper echelons of the BBC. As for Lynn and Fields, the decision was forced upon the BBC by either the performers themselves or their management.

10. Howerd, *op. cit.*, p.76.

11. Gale Pedrick, 'Laughter in the Air', *op. cit.*, p.56.

12. Eric Sykes, *Eric Sykes' Comedy Heroes* (London: Virgin, 2003), p.92.

13. Sykes, interview with the author, 19 February 2004.

14. Howerd, quoted by David Nathan, *The Laughtermakers*, *op. cit.*, p.194.

15. Sykes, interview with the author, 19 February 2004.

16. Sykes, *Variety Bandbox*, circa 1948, reproduced here by kind permission of Eric Sykes.

17. Howerd, *op. cit.*, p.69.

18. Sykes, *Variety Bandbox*, 16 October 1949; included on the LP *50 Years of Radio Comedy* (BBC, REC 138M).

19. Sykes, interview with the author, 19 February 2004.

20. Sykes, *Variety Bandbox*, circa 1948. A recording of the routine was released subsequently as one side of the 78 rpm single, 'English As She Is Spoken'/'I'm The Man Who's Deputising For The Bull' (Columbia DB 2694), and an excerpt was included in the BBC Radio 2 documentary, *There'll Never Be Another*, first broadcast 1 August 2000.

21. See my *Morecambe & Wise*, *op. cit.*, pp.141–2 and Chapter XIV *passim*.

22. *Variety Bandbox*, first broadcast 19 February 1950; excerpt broadcast again in an edition of the BBC Radio 4 documentary series, *Radio Roots*, on 10 October 2000.

23. Source: BBC WAC: Daily Viewing Barometers for Sundays during 1948 (e.g. 5 December 1948).

24. Source: Post Office/National Television Licence Records Office.

25. BBC WAC: Frankie Howerd: Artist's File 1 – 1947–52: memo from Michael Standing, July 1949.

26. Eric Sykes, interview with the author, 19 February 2004. (See Howerd, *op. cit.*, p.82.)

27. Sykes, speaking on the BBC Radio 2 documentary, *There'll Never Be Another*, *op. cit.*

28. *Ibid.*

29. BBC WAC: Frankie Howerd: Artist's File 1 – 1947–52. (£66 in 1949 was equivalent to about £1,300 in 2004.)

30. See Howerd, *op. cit.*, p.77.

31. *Ibid.*, p.79.

32. *Ibid.*, p.77.

33. *Ibid.*, pp.77–8.

34. *Ibid.*, p.77.

35. *Ibid.*, pp. 86–7. (The 'half-Scottish' claim was actually an exaggeration: although the maternal side of Howerd's family has often been described as Scottish, only his grandfather, David Morrison, came from that country; Howerd's grandmother, Edith Morrison, hailed from Framlingham in Suffolk, and his mother came from York.)

36. *Ibid.*

37. *Ibid.*

38. Eric Sykes, interview with the author, 19 February 2004.

39. There is no formal, but plenty of anecdotal, evidence for this. See, for example, Howerd's autobiography, *op. cit.*, pp. 86–8 and 95.

40. BBC WAC: Frankie Howerd: Artist's File 1 – 1947–52: memo from Joy Russell-Smith to Pat Newman (then Variety Booking Manager), 25 May 1948.

41. Lyon-Shaw, interview with the author, 29 January 2004.

42. BBC WAC: Frankie Howerd File (1946–52): in a memo from Con Mahoney to Michael Standing, dated 29 December 1948, the prospect of Howerd refusing to sign another three-month extension to his contract was discussed as a serious possibility.

43. BBC WAC: Frankie Howerd: Artist's File 1 – 1947–52: The arrangement was explained in a memo (dated 28 February 1949) sent by the Head of Variety, Michael Standing, to his colleagues in Manchester. Warning them not to attempt to use Howerd on radio during his summer season in Blackpool, Standing explained: 'We have deliberately taken this artist out of "Bandbox" where he has made a spectacular success in order to give him a rest from radio and we wish to have him back in the same context in the autumn, I hope, refreshed.'

44. Howerd, interviewed by Gale Pedrick, *Radio Times*, 28 October 1949, p.6.

45. The Bishop of London, 27 January 1949, memorial service for Tommy Handley: quotation taken from cuttings contained in the section of the Mass-Observation Archive on 'Radio Listening 1939–49', Box TC 74/4/D: 'The death of Tommy Handley' (University of Sussex Library).

46. Sykes, speaking on the BBC Radio documentary, *Howerd's Way*, BBC Radio 2, first broadcast 1992.

47. Howerd, *op. cit.*, p.86.

INTERMISSION: THE YEARS OF DARKNESS

Chapter 7

1. BBC WAC: Frankie Howerd: Artist's File 1 – 1947–52.

2. Howerd, *op. cit.*, pp.90–1.

3. *Ibid.*, p.93.

4. *Ibid.*, p.94.

5. *Ibid.*, p.95.

6.   *Ibid.*, p.94.

7.   *Ibid.*, p.96.

8.   BBC WAC: Frankie Howerd: Artist's File 1 – 1947–52.

9.   *Ibid.*: letter from Michael Standing to Frankie Howerd, 3 August 1950.

10.   *Ibid.*: letter from Frankie Howerd to Michael Standing, 13 August 1950.

11.   Howerd's final broadcast on *Variety Bandbox* as resident comic had been on 2 April 1950 (the remainder of that year was devoted to stage commitments). He would, however, return to the show on several more occasions as a special guest, and also starred in the very last edition of the programme on 28 September 1952.

12.   BBC WAC: Frankie Howerd: Artist's File 1 – 1947–52: Handwritten note (undated) by Tom Ronald appended to a memo sent to him by Con Mahoney, the BBC's assistant to the Head of Variety, on 12 January 1951.

13.   Howerd, *ibid.*, p.96.

14.   The award was given by the *Daily Mail.*

15.   Eric Sykes, interview with the author, 19 February 2004.

16.   *Ibid.*

17.   Peter Brough would go on to say of Sykes: 'I'm not exaggerating when I declare that the timely arrival on the scene of Eric Sykes was to prove the key to the entire situation. Without him there might have never been an *Educating Archie* series at all' (quoted by Andy Foster and Steve Furst, *Radio Comedy 1938–1968* [London: Virgin, 1996], p.129).

18.   Howerd, *op. cit.*, p.97.

19.   Lyon-Shaw, interview with the author, 29 January 2004.

20.   Howerd recalled (*op. cit.*, p.99) that his television debut had been the 'next memorable date' in his career. He must, however, have misremembered, because his concert parties were broadcast by BBC radio (23 April–11 June 1952) *after* his television series was broadcast by BBC TV (12 January–8 March 1952). Howerd's error has since been accepted as fact by his biographers – see, for example, Ross (*op. cit.*, p.159) and Middles (*op. cit.*, pp.45 and 137) – as well as innumerable websites.

21.   The original post-war aim had been for television signals to reach 80 per cent of the country by 1954 (see Sir Noel Ashbridge, 'Television Comes to the Centre of England', *Radio Times*, 9 December 1949, pp.5–6).

22.   Quoted by Peter Black, *The Biggest Aspidistra in the World* (London: BBC, 1972), p.166.

23.   *Hi There!* was Hill's debut starring vehicle; it was a one-off show broadcast on 20 August 1951.

24.   *Vic's Grill* was a *Duffy's Tavern*-style sitcom, starring the comedian Vic Wise and Norman Wisdom, with support from Beryl Reid and Ernest Maxin, which ran (during Lyon-Shaw's spell as producer-director) from 18 April–27 June 1951.

25.   Wisdom had previously appeared in two Variety shows that were broadcast under the banner of *Wit and Wisdom* (18 October 1948 and 30 August 1950) and a sitcom pilot called *Cuckoo College* (13 May 1949).

26.   Lyon-Shaw, interview with the author, 29 January 2004.

27.   No form of recording of the show exists (to the best of my knowledge), and so I have relied on reports and cuttings in the BBC Written Archives Centre, along with conversations with Bill Lyon-Shaw, for my account of the show's reception.

28.   Peter Black, *op. cit.*, p.163.

29.   Tom Sloan made the remark about McGivern during a BBC lunchtime lecture delivered on 11 December 1969, and published subsequently in pamphlet form as *Television Light Entertainment* (London: BBC, 1969).

30.   BBC WAC: Frankie Howerd: TV File 1 – 1947–62: memo from Cecil McGivern to Ronald Waldman, 10 March 1952.

31.   Howerd, *op. cit.*, p.99.

32.   The transmission sequence, via the BBC Light Programme, was as follows: 23 April, Nicosia (venue unspecified); 30 April, The Canal Zone (venue unspecified); 7 May, The Canal Zone (New Garden Cinema); 14 May, Fayid (RAF station); 21 May, Benghazi (The Berka Theatre); 28 May, Tripoli (The Miramare Theatre); 4 June, Malta (The Australia Hall); and 11 June, Malta (Manoel Island).

33.   Howerd, *op. cit.*, p.98.

34.   *Ibid.*, p.102.

35.   Gale Pedrick, *Radio Times*, 28 October 1949, p.6.

36.   Kenneth Tynan, reproduced in *Persona Grata* (London: Wingate, 1953), p.59.

37.   *Television's Christmas Party* ran on BBC TV from 1951 to 1954. As many as 150 performers would be featured in a single show. *Christmas Night with the Stars* ran on BBC 1 from 1958 to 1972 (followed by an insufferably smug, and shamelessly ersatz, 'revival' on BBC 2 in 1994).

38.   Gale Pedrick, 'The Toughest Job', *Radio Times*, 4 December 1953, p.5.

39.   Arthur Askey appeared in three series of *Before Your Very Eyes* (1952–55); Terry-Thomas starred in five very successful, technically audacious and critically-admired series of *How Do You View?* (1949–52); and Norman Wisdom was being groomed for a series of his own via such one-off specials as *The Norman Wisdom Show* (27 February 1952) and *Norman Wisdom* (27 July 1952).

40.   BBC WAC: Morecambe and Wise: TV Artists' File 1 – 1948–61: memo from Holland Bennett to Ronald Waldman, 15 December 1953. Howerd was actually listed as sixth on Bennett's list, but this was misleading. The 'official' highest-paid act on television in 1953 was Jimmy Jewel and Ben Warriss, a very successful and well-established northern comedy double-act, who earned £210 per show – but this was shared between them; the second highest-paid was Terry-Thomas on £147; third was Arthur Askey on £131 (Jimmy James also received this sum, but it included payment of his two stooges); joint-fourth were Eric Barker and Donald Peers on £89 each; and Howerd came next with 80 guineas (£84).

41.   Ronald Waldman, *ibid.*

42.   BBC WAC: Frankie Howerd: TV File 1 – 1947–62: Ronald Waldman, letter to Frankie Howerd, 29 December 1952.

43.   *Daily Telegraph*, 17 March 1953, p.8.

44.   In 1957, Beyfus represented the left-wing Labour politicians Aneurin Bevan, Richard Crossman and Morgan Phillips in their libel case against *The Spectator* magazine, which had suggested that the trio had been drunk throughout much of a meeting of international socialists in Venice. In spite of the fact that at least one of the plaintiffs appeared worse for wear in court, and all three had reputations as enthusiastic drinkers, Beyfus won each of them £2,500. Two years later, Beyfus was engaged by the flamboyant pianist Liberace after the *Daily Mirror* columnist William Connor (writing under the by-line of 'Cassandra') had described him as, among many other things, 'the summit of sex – the pinnacle of masculine, feminine, and neuter,' who came across as a 'deadly, winking, sniggering, chromium-plated, scent-impregnated, luminous, quivering, giggling, fruit-flavoured, mincing, ice-covered heap of mother love'. Liberace (a closet homosexual) had thought this rather harsh, and so Beyfus contrived to send him 'laughing all the way to the bank' by winning him £8,000 in damages.

45.   Howerd, *op. cit.*, p.104.

46.   All of the quotations and claims have been taken from daily newspaper reports from the High Court. (See, for example, *The Times*, 17–21 March 1953.)

47.   *Daily Telegraph*, 17 March 1953, p.8.

48.   *Ibid.*

49.   See Iain Adamson, *The Old Fox: A Life of Gilbert Beyfus QC* (London: Frederick Muller, 1963).

50. Howerd, *op. cit.*, p.104.
51. See *The Daily Telegraph*, 17 March 1953, p.8.
52. See *The Times*, 21 March 1953, p.9.
53. *Ibid.*
54. Howerd, *op. cit.*, p.105.
55. £5,216 in 1953 was equivalent in value to about £86,600 in 2004.
56. See the reports in both *The Times* (p.9) and *The Daily Telegraph* (p.7), 21 March 1953.
57. Howerd, *op. cit.*, p.105.
58. *Daily Telegraph*, 21 March 1935, p.7.
59. Howerd, *op. cit.*, p.104.
60. Reported in *The Times*, 16 October 1953, p.13.
61. Howerd, *op. cit.*, p.105.
62. *Ibid.*
63. *Ibid.*

Chapter 8

1. See Freddie Hancock & David Nathan, *Hancock op. cit.* pp.67–8.
2. BBC WAC: Frankie Howerd: TV Artist's File 1 – 1947–62: letter sent by Stanley Dale/ Frankie Howerd Scripts Ltd, 29 August 1955, to a number of people within the BBC Light Entertainment Department.
3. Bill Lyon-Shaw, interview with the author, 29 January 2004.
4. Jim Dale, quoted by Barry Took, *Star Turns*, *op. cit.*, pp.34–5.
5. Recalled by Barry Took, interview with the author, 17 May 2000. (Howerd would eventually offload the books on to Took in lieu of 'payment' for some scripts.)
6. Eric Sykes, *Eric Sykes' Comedy Heroes*, *op. cit.*, p.96.
7. Quoted by William Hall, *op. cit.*, p.109.
8. Howerd, quoted by Cilla Black, *What's It All About?* (London: Ebury Press, 2003), p.312.
9. Howerd, quoted by Terry Coleman, *op. cit.*, p.210.
10. Quoted by William Hall, *op. cit.*, p.122.
11. *Ibid.*, p.123.
12. Howerd, quoted by Hall, *op. cit.*, p.147.
13. Bill Lyon-Shaw, interview with the author, 29 January 2004.
14. Howerd, *op. cit.*, p.144.
15. *Happy-Go-Lucky* starred Derek Roy and featured contributions from Bill Kerr, Peter Butterworth, Graham Stark and Tony Hancock. It ran for fourteen weeks, from 2 August to 10 December 1951, on the BBC Light Programme. After Roy Speer, a fine producer, suffered his collapse, Dennis Main Wilson took over for the final two shows.
16. Eric Sykes told me that he mentioned their names (interview with the author, 19 February 2004). Ray Galton and Alan Simpson themselves, however, while not certain of the identities involved, told me that they suspected that Dennis Main Wilson was the most plausible candidate (conversation with the author, 5 April 2004). No correspondence that has been preserved in the relevant files in the BBC Written Archives Centre clarifies the matter.
17. Eric Sykes, interview with the author, 19 February 2004.
18. *Ibid.*

19.   According to Beryl Vertue, the first secretary at ALS, the original name was 'Associated British Scripts', but when the local council ruled that the company was too small to call itself 'British', the founding directors settled for the slightly more parochial-sounding 'Associated London Scripts' instead. Alan Simpson claimed that the 'Associated' part of the name was chosen in order to ensure that the company could be found at the front of the telephone directory. See the two-part documentary *Associated London Scripts*, BBC Radio 4, 14–21 January 2003.

20.   Alan Simpson, interview with the author, 15 March 2004.

21.   See Norma Farnes, *Spike: An Intimate Memoir* (London: Fourth Estate, 2003), p.54.

22.   Eric Sykes, interview with the author, 19 February 2004.

23.   Alan Simpson, interview with the author, 15 March 2004.

24.   Ray Galton, interview with the author, 15 March 2004.

25.   Alan Simpson, interview with the author, 15 March 2004.

26.   Eric Sykes, interview with the author, 19 February 2004.

27.   Quoted by Howerd, *op. cit.*, p.113.

28.   Alan Simpson, speaking in the first part of the two-part documentary, *Associated London Scripts*, BBC Radio 4, 14 January 2003.

29.   The two shows did well: according to the BBC's daily viewing barometer, the first edition attracted approximately 19 per cent of the total population of the UK (in other words, about 9,680,500 viewers – which was the biggest audience of the day); it received a Reaction Index of 78 per cent. The second edition fared similarly well. (Source: BBC WAC: Audience Research Report, 11 June 1955 [VR/55/287, 27 June 1955].)

30.   Johnny Speight, *It Stands To Reason* (London: M. & J. Hobbs, 1973), p.225.

31.   Speight, speaking in the documentary *Howerd's Way*, *op. cit.*

32.   Speight, in a script for *The Frankie Howerd Show*, series three, BBC Light Programme, 2 October 1955–22 January 1956.

33.   Brad Ashton, interview with the author, 14 November 2000. (The scripts to which Ashton referred were part of the series, written by Peter Bishop and Charles Hart, called *Frankie Howerd!*, broadcast by the BBC Light Programme between 24 July–28 August 1966.)

34.   *Ibid.*

35.   Ray Galton, interview with the author, 15 March 2004.

36.   Johnny Speight, speaking in *Howerd's Way*, *op. cit.*

37.   See Chapter 12 for a detailed account of Howerd's movie career.

38.   Howerd, *op. cit.*, p.120.

39.   Quoted by Leonard Miall, *Inside The BBC* (London: Weidenfeld & Nicolson, 1994), p.114.

40.   See Wallace Reyburn, *Gilbert Harding: A Candid Portrayal* (London: Angus & Robertson, 1978), *passim*.

41.   Harding featured in an edition of *Variety Bandbox* broadcast in 1949 (date unknown), as well as in an edition of *The Frankie Howerd Show* that was broadcast on the BBC Light Programme on 27 November 1955.

42.   Howerd, *op. cit.*, p.90.

43.   Quoted by Reyburn, *op. cit.*, p.102.

44.   Howerd, *op. cit.*, p.90.

45.   *Ibid.*, p.113.

46.   *Ibid.*

47.   *Ibid.*, p.114. Guy Burgess and Donald Maclean were British diplomats who disappeared in 1951 and then resurfaced in Moscow in 1956; their old colleague and informant, Kim

Philby, joined them in the same year. George Blake was a British espionage agent who was sentenced in 1961 to forty-two years in prison for treason – the longest term ever imposed under English law during peacetime; five-and-a-half years later, he escaped from Wormwood Scrubs, and resurfaced in Moscow twelve months after that. Bruno Pontecorvo was a British-based nuclear physicist who defected to the USSR in the summer of 1950 – an act of betrayal that was regarded in Britain at the time as an important episode in the Cold War. Klaus Fuchs was a distinguished scientist, attached to the Harwell Atomic Research facility, who was charged, in February 1950, of having given atom bomb secrets to the Soviets (he was found guilty, served fourteen years, and then settled in East Germany).

48.   *Ibid.*, p.117.

Chapter 9

1.   Howerd, quoted by David Nathan, *The Laughtermakers, op. cit.*, p.195.

2.   Barry Cryer, speaking in the BBC Radio 2 documentary *Howerd's Way, op. cit.*

3.   The phrase was coined in 1950 by a critic from the *Daily Mail* (see John Fisher, *Funny Way to be a Hero, op. cit.*, p.236).

4.   Howerd, speaking on 'A Funny Thing Happened', *Kaleidoscope*, BBC Radio 4, first broadcast on 4 May 1987 (BBC Sound Archive reference TO83406).

5.   Eric Sykes, interview with the author, 19 February 2004.

6.   *The Observer*, quoted by Howerd, *op. cit.*, p.121.

7.   Howerd, *ibid.*, p.125.

8.   *Ibid.*

9.   *Ibid.*, p.127.

10.   *Ibid.*

11.   Guinness (who had first played the role on stage in the summer of 1956) went on to reprise it in the movie version, also called *Hotel Paradiso* (1966), with Gina Lollobrigida as the love object next door.

12.   Howerd, *op. cit.*, p.127.

13.   *Ibid.*

14.   Kingsley Amis, *Memoirs* (London: Hutchinson, 1991), p.180.

15.   William Shakespeare, *Hamlet*, Act III, scene ii.

16.   Howerd, *op. cit.*, p.133.

17.   Judi Dench, quoted by Ross, *op. cit.*, p.37.

18.   Peter Roberts, *Plays and Players*, February 1958, p.15. (See also Howerd, *op. cit.*, p.133; and Ross, *op. cit.*, p.37.)

19.   Howerd, quoted by Hall (no primary source given), *op. cit.*, p.145.

20.   Howerd, interviewed by Gale Pedrick, *Radio Times*, 28 March 1958, p.4.

21.   Roy Walker, *The Listener*, 10 April 1958, p.633.

22.   Independent Television (ITV) began broadcasting in the London area only at 7.15 p.m. on 22 September 1955. Subsequent regions came within reach of the transmitters one by one, but it would not be until 1962 that the commercial network was completed with the addition of the North and West Wales areas. The original franchise set-up, in sequence, was as follows: Associated-Rediffusion (weekdays, London, 1955); Associated Television/ATV (weekends, London, 1955; weekdays, Midlands, 1956); Associated British Corporation/ABC (weekends, Midlands and Northern England, 1956); Granada (weekdays, North of England, 1956); Scottish TV (Central Scotland, 1957); TWW (Wales and West England, 1958); Southern TV (South and South-East England, 1958); Tyne Tees (North-East England, 1959); Anglia (East of England, 1959); Ulster TV (Northern Ireland, 1959); Westward (South-West England, 1961); Border TV (Anglo-Scottish border and the Isle of Man, 1961); Grampian

(North of Scotland, 1961); Channel TV (Channel Islands, 1962); and WWN (North and West Wales, 1962).

23. Howerd, *op. cit.*, p.133.

24. *Ibid.*, pp.133–4.

25. *Ibid.*, p.135.

26. *Ibid.*

27. See Griff Rhys Jones, speaking in the documentary *Legends – Frankie Howerd* (Carlton/ITV), first broadcast on 9 August 2000.

28. Ray Galton, interview with the author, 15 March 2004.

29. Howerd, *op. cit.*, p.136.

30. *Ibid.*, p.138.

31. *Ibid.*, p. 136.

32. *Daily Telegraph*, 23 October 1958, p.11; Caryl Brahms, *Plays and Players*, December 1958, p.11.

33. Howerd, *op. cit.*, p.141.

34. *Ibid.*

35. *Ibid.*

36. BBC WAC: Frankie Howerd: TV File 1 – 1947–62: memo from Kenneth Adam to Eric Maschwitz, 10 November 1958.

37. Howerd, *op. cit.*, p.142.

38. *Ibid.*, p.143.

39. *Ibid.*

40. *Ibid.*

41. BBC WAC: Frankie Howerd: TV File 1 – 1947–62: letter from Eric Maschwitz to Stanley Dale, dated 3 February 1959.

42. Eric Sykes, interview with the author, 19 February 2004.

43. Interview with the author, 15 March 2004.

44. Carlisle's previous production credits included *The Jimmy Wheeler Show* (1956), which featured Jimmy Wheeler and Thora Hird, and *Scott Free* (1957), a sitcom that starred Terry Scott and Norman Vaughan.

45. Howerd, interviewed by Rowan Ayers, *Radio Times*, 24 April 1959, p.11.

46. Brad Ashton, interview with the author, 14 November 2000.

47. Howerd, *op. cit.*, p.150.

48. *Ibid.*, p.151.

49. *Ibid.*, p.150.

50. *Ibid.*, p.158.

51. *Ibid.*, p.160.

52. Memo from John Simmonds to the BBC's Assistant Head of Variety, 19 April 1957; quoted by Barry Took, *Star Turns*, *op. cit.*, p.62.

53. Eric Sykes, interview with the author, 19 February 2004.

54. Barry Took, interview with the author, 17 May 2000, and *Star Turns*, *op. cit.*, p.97.

55. Brad Ashton, interview with the author, 14 November 2000.

56. George Martin, *All You Need Is Ears* (New York: St Martin's Press, 1994), p.100.

57. Eric Sykes, interview with the author, 19 February 2004.

58. Howerd, quoted by Hall, *op. cit.*, p.104.

59. Howerd, *op. cit.*, p.173.
60. Howerd, quoted by Terry Coleman, *op. cit.*, p.209.

ACT III: THE COMEBACK

Chapter 10

1. Bruce Forsyth, quoted by Ross, *op. cit.*, p.42 (no primary source acknowledged).
2. Kenneth Bailey, *Sunday People*, 25 April 1954, p.8. See Chapter VI of my book *Morecambe & Wise*, *op.cit.*, for a detailed account of the show, which was called *Running Wild*.
3. Ernie Wise, interviewed by William Hall, *op. cit.*, p.112.
4. Howerd, speaking on the unedited *Arena* documentary, *op. cit.*
5. Howerd, *op. cit.*, p.169.
6. *Ibid.*, p.174.
7. *Ibid.*, p.169.
8. Bill Cotton, interview with the author, 6 June 2000.
9. The respective reigns of Maschwitz and Sloan are often confused in histories of this period. Officially, Maschwitz was Head of Light Entertainment from 1958 to 1963; Sloan was Head from 1963 until his untimely death in 1970. In 1961, however, Sloan became the *de facto* Head while Maschwitz took on the additional role of consultant to the Director of Television (he left the Corporation in 1963, having tired of its internal politics, to join Associated-Rediffusion as producer of special projects).
10. Recalled by Barry Took, interview with the author, 17 May 2000.
11. Bill Cotton, interview with the author, 6 June 2000.
12. Ray Galton, interview with the author, 15 March 2004.
13. Howerd, interviewed by Malcolm Winton, 'The art of being perfectly Frankie', *Radio Times*, 26 March 1970, p.10.
14. Howerd, *op. cit.*, p.177.
15. *Ibid.*
16. Peter Cook, speaking in *Howerd's Way*, *op. cit.*
17. Howerd, *op. cit.*, p. 178.
18. Beryl Vertue, speaking in the BBC 2 *Reputations* documentary, *op. cit.*
19. Beryl Vertue, speaking in *There'll Never Be Another*, *op. cit.*
20. Howerd, *op. cit.*, p.180.
21. *Ibid.*
22. *Ibid.*, pp.180–2.
23. *Ibid.*, p.182.
24. *Ibid.*, p.183.
25. Beryl Vertue, speaking in the BBC 2 documentary *Reputations*, *op. cit.*
26. Howerd, quoted by Nathan, *op. cit.*, p.196.
27. Howerd, *op. cit.*, pp.170–1.
28. *Ibid.*, p.171.
29. Doris Collins, quoted by Hall (no primary source acknowledged), *op. cit.*, p.174.
30. My source, who treated Howerd for a period, asked to remain anonymous.
31. Alan Simpson, interview with the author, 15 March 2004.
32. Sigmund Freud, *Outline of Psycho-Analysis* (New York: W.W. Norton & Co., 1989), pp.30–1.

33. See Chapter XI of my book, *Cary Grant: A Class Apart* (London: Fourth Estate, 1996).

34. See Stanislav Grof, *LSD Psychotherapy* (California: Hunter House, 1980); H.A. Sandison *et al.*, 'The Therapeutic Value of Lysergic Acid Diethylamide in Mental Illness', *Journal of Mental Science*, 100: 491–507; Michael Hollingshead, *The Man Who Turned On the World* (London: Blond and Briggs, 1973); and Jay Stevens, *Storming Heaven* (London: Flamingo, 1993).

35. Thomas M. Ling and John Buckman, *Lysergic Acid & Ritalin in the Treatment of Neurosis* (London: Lambarde Press, 1963), p.17.

36. *Ibid.*, p.22.

37. *Ibid.*, p.24.

38. *Ibid.*, p.21.

39. My sources for these details only agreed to provide them on condition that their identities would not be revealed, but I can confirm that all of them either knew Howerd extremely well during this period or were associated in some way or other with the specific sessions that he underwent.

40. Howerd, *op. cit.*, p.186.

41. See the chapters on Bruce in Steve Allen's *Funny People* (New York: Stein and Day, 1981) and Kenneth Tynan, *Profiles* (London: Nick Hern Books, 1989). Bruce died, as a result of drugs, in 1966.

42. Eric Sykes, interview with the author, 19 February 2004.

43. Alan Simpson, interview with the author, 15 March 2004.

44. See *Howerd's Way*, *op. cit.*

45. Transcribed from the recording *Frankie Howerd At The Establishment* (Decca 4556, 1963).

46. Howerd, *op. cit.*, p.188.

47. J.W.M. Thompson, *London Evening Standard*, 7 September 1962, p.4.

48. See Nicholas Luard, in Lin Cook, ed., *Something Like Fire: Peter Cook Remembered* (London: Methuen, 1996), pp.43–4.

49. Kenneth Williams, in Russell Davies, ed., *The Kenneth Williams Diaries* (London: Harper-Collins, 1993), p.198.

50. Transcribed from *Frankie Howerd At The Establishment*.

51. Howerd, interviewed by Nathan, *The Laughtermakers*, *op. cit.*, p.198.

52. Howerd, *op. cit.*, p.184.

53. *Ibid.*, p.189.

54. Transcribed from a tape of *That Was The Week That Was*, broadcast on BBC TV on 6 April 1963.

55. James Casey, speaking in the documentary *There'll Never Be Another*, *op. cit.*

56. Ned Sherrin, speaking in the documentary *Howerd's Way*, *op. cit.*

Chapter 11

1. Alan Simpson, interview with the author, 15 March 2004.

2. Ray Galton, interview with the author, 15 March 2004.

3. Eric Sykes, interview with the author, 19 February 2004.

4. Howerd, *op. cit.*, p.190.

5. *Ibid.*, p.192.

6. Louis Calta, 'British Comedian Is Here to Study Mostel', *New York Times*, 11 May 1963, p.14.

7. *Ibid.*

8. Howerd, *op. cit.*, p.200.

9. *Ibid.*, p.202.

10. *Ibid.*, p.203.

11. Howerd, interviewed by Denise Richards, *London Evening Standard*, 4 October 1963, p.18.

12. Howerd, *op. cit.*, p.204.

13. *Ibid.*, p.205.

14. Milton Shulman, *London Evening Standard*, 4 October 1963, p.4.

15. Clive Barnes, *Plays and Players*, December 1963, p.36.

16. Howerd, interviewed by Denise Richards, *op. cit.*, p.18.

17. *Ibid.*

18. Transcribed from *A Last Word on the Election*, written by Galton and Simpson *et al.*, first broadcast on BBC 1 on 18 October 1964.

19. Frankie Howerd, *A Last Word on the Election* (Decca 12028, 1964).

20. BBC WAC: Audience Research Report on *The Frankie Howerd Show*, 11 December 1964 (VR/64/663, 4 January 1965).

21. The first edition of the first series, on 11 December 1964, was watched by an estimated 20.6 per cent of the then-total population of the UK (in other words, 11,196,100 – the biggest BBC audience of the night), and received a Reaction Index of 66 per cent. The final edition, on 15 January 1965, attracted 19.7 per cent of the total population (10,706,950), with an RI of 59. The first edition of the second series, on 22 February 1966, drew in 25.1 per cent of the total population (13,641,850), with an RI of 67; the final edition, shown on 29 March 1966, attracted 20 per cent of the population (10,870,000), with an RI of 65.

22. Ray Galton, interview with the author, 15 March 2004.

23. BBC WAC: Frankie Howerd: Artist's File III – 1963–67: Dr J. Sharp Grant sent the BBC a letter on 31 March 1964, together with a doctor's certificate, confirming that he had seen Howerd several times recently, and that 'there is no doubt that he is becoming increasingly tired mentally and physically'.

24. Howerd, *op. cit.*, p.220.

Chapter 12

1. An example from Benny's radio show: walking down the street with his colleague, the announcer Don Wilson, Benny encounters a teenager who asks for his autograph; as Benny obliges, the boy says, 'You know, Mr Benny, you're so great, why didn't you make any more movies?' Wilson starts to say, 'Oh, but he did, he made movies like *The Horn Blows –*' but Benny interrupts and hurries the boy away. When Wilson asks why he stopped him from putting the fan right, Benny replies: 'Just think, Don, isn't it wonderful – a whole new generation that doesn't know.' (See Milt Josefsberg, *The Jack Benny Show* [New York: Arlington House, 1977], pp.415–16.)

2. Frankie Howerd, interviewed by Tony Williams in 1978 (published in the US magazine *Psychotronic Video*, issue 34, March 2001, p.60).

3. Dialogue transcribed from the movie. Anyone interested in obtaining a copy of *The Runaway Bus* should be aware that most of the prints that have so far either been shown on television or transferred to video *omit* this improvised section. The phone box scene *is* included, however, in the 78-minute, NTSC, 'Video Images' version (number 219) released in 1998 by Video Yesterday (Box C, Sandy Hook, CT 06482, USA).

4. *Picturegoer*, 4 February 1954.

5. *Monthly Film Bulletin*, no. 242, vol. 21, March 1954, p.42.

6. Howerd, interviewed by Tony Williams, *op. cit.*, p.61.

7. *Ibid.*, p.60.

8. *Ibid.*

9. Howerd socialised with Lennon, McCartney, Harrison and Starr in 1963 at and after a concert given by their mutual friend, Alma Cogan, at the Talk of the Town in London, and met again on other occasions at Cogan's *soirées*. He was also visited in his dressing-room, during the same year, by Paul McCartney when he was performing in cabaret at a Manchester club called Mr Smith's. All four members of the band remained on good terms with him, and both Lennon and McCartney, in particular, continued to follow his career and express their support.

10. Howerd, *op. cit.*, p.211. It appears that no footage of this scene has been preserved. I have based my summary on the official 'novelisation' (written in tandem with the shooting of the movie) by Al Hine, called *The Beatles in HELP!* (New York: Dell Publishing Co., 1965), along with a set of surviving stills.

11. Howerd, *op. cit.*, p.215.

12. *Ibid.*, p.225.

13. Kenneth Williams, diary entry dated 10 August 1967, *The Kenneth Williams Diaries, op. cit.*, p.309. (Williams went on to record in his diary, five days later, the news that he had received a telegram from Peter Rogers 'saying Frankie Howerd out, and offering me the part!!' His response appears to have been to tell Rogers that such a switch was 'impossible', and he resigned himself to his original role.)

14. Howerd, *op. cit.*, p.252.

15. Howerd, letter to Peter Rogers, 21 November 1969, quoted by Ross, *op. cit.*, p.134.

16. Eric Sykes, interview with the author, 19 February 2004.

17. Ray Galton, interview with the author, 15 March 2004.

18. Hugh Leonard, *Plays and Players*, January 1967, pp.24–5. (Apart from being responsible for numerous plays, articles, books and essays, Hugh Leonard also wrote the BBC 1 sitcom *Me Mammy*, as a vehicle for Milo O'Shea – it ran for three series, from 1969 to 1971 – as well as the 1971 ITV Ronnie Barker showcase, *Six Dates With Barker.*)

19. Elizabeth Taylor, quoted by Howerd, *op. cit.*, p.230, and Hall, *op. cit.*, p.89.

20. Howerd, *op. cit.*, p.230.

ACT IV: THE CULT

Chapter 13

1. Michael Billington, in a review of the 1973 London Palladium production of *Jack and the Beanstalk,* reproduced in *One Night Stands* (London: Nick Hern Books, 1993), p.37.

2. Howerd, *op. cit.*, p.124.

3. *Ibid.*

4. *Ibid.*

5. *Ibid.*, p.140.

6. Howerd, speaking in the uncut version of the *Arena* documentary, *op. cit.*

7. See *The Times*, 24 February 1968, p.12.

8. See Norma Farnes, *Spike, op. cit.*, for a first-hand account of this period.

9. Beryl Vertue, both during and after the time of ALS, proved herself to be one of the most imaginative, innovative and audacious agents and producers in the history of British broadcasting: not only pioneering the now-common practice of selling formats to Europe and the US (including *Steptoe and Son* – which was remade by the Dutch as *Stiefbeen en*

Zoon, by the Swedish as *Albert och Herbert*, by the Portuguese as *Camilo y Filho* and the Americans as *Sanford and Son* – and *Till Death Us Do Part* – which was remade by the Dutch as *Tot de dood ons scheidt*, by the Germans as *Ein Herz und eine Seele* and the Americans as *All in the Family*) but also – as head, from 1992, of her own company, Hartswood – helping to devise and/or produce many popular shows for Britain.

10.   BBC WAC: Frankie Howerd: TV Artist's File – 1963–70: After the disappointment of failing to secure Howerd for a new internally-made BBC project, and also being outbid (it seems) for the Bee Gees special, Bill Cotton wrote to Beryl Vertue on 31 May 1968, saying 'how much I regret that we were unable to come to a deal with regard to the *Frankie Howerd Meets the Bee Gees* special', but he also reiterated his keenness to discuss doing another series or special with the comedian in the near future. Vertue wrote back on 4 June, saying that it would be difficult to make any firm plans during the next few months, as Howerd was about to set off to Broadway.

11.   Howerd, *op. cit.*, p.233.

12.   Ann Hamilton (who is married to Tony Clayton), interview with the author, 21 April 2004.

13.   Barbara Windsor, quoted by Hall, *op. cit.*, p.150 (no primary source acknowledged).

14.   Ann Hamilton, interview with the author, 21 April 2004.

15.   David Merrick, quoted by Ross, *op. cit.*, p.49 (no primary source acknowledged).

16.   Howerd, quoted by Ray Galton, interview with the author, 15 March 2004.

17.   Howerd, quoted by Louis Calta, *New York Times*, *op. cit.*

18.   See my book, *Morecambe & Wise*, *op. cit.*, pp.227–8.

19.   Alan Simpson, *In Conversation with . . .*, broadcast on BBC Radio 4, 29 March 2000. (*Kelly* opened on 6 February 1965 at the Broadhurst Theatre, and then closed at the end of the first performance.)

20.   Ray Galton, interview with the author, 15 March 2004.

21.   I am grateful to Annie Clayton (née Hamilton) for supplying me with these details.

22.   Ray Galton, interview with the author, 15 March 2004.

23.   Ann Hamilton, interview with the author, 21 April 2004.

24.   Kevin Kelly, *Boston Globe*, 17 September 1968; Samuel Hirsch, *Boston Herald Traveler*, 17 September 1968; Elliot Norton, *Boston Record American*, 17 September 1968. (My thanks to Annie and Tony Clayton for providing me with these cuttings.)

25.   Alan Simpson, interview with the author, 15 March 2004.

26.   Ray Galton, interview with the author, 15 March 2004.

27.   Richard L. Coe, *Washington Post*, 6 October 1968, p. K2.

28.   See, for example, Harry MacArthur's review in *The Evening Star* (Washington), 1 October 1968, p.A-16.

29.   The presence of the FBI caused particular problems for Ann Hamilton. 'I was the one whose character, at a certain stage in the play, fired a rifle out into the audience, and so on the nights when Lady Bird Johnson came there were five or six FBI special agents in the prop room inspecting the rifles and checking that they all had blanks. They insisted on being the ones who handed them to me, and on those two particular nights, not one of those guns fired. So I just said: "Bang!" What else could I have done? It was very embarrassing' (interview with the author, 21 April 2004).

30.   Alan Simpson, interview with the author, 15 March 2004.

31.   Ray Galton, interview with the author, 15 March 2004.

32.   Ann Hamilton, interview with the author, 21 April 2004.

33.   Howerd, *op. cit.*, pp.236–7.

34.   Ray Galton, interview with the author, 15 March 2004.

35. *Ibid.*

36. Clive Barnes, *New York Times*, 25 October 1968, p.37.

37. *Ibid.*

38. Ray Galton, interview with the author, 15 March 2004.

39. Alan Simpson, interview with the author, 15 March 2004.

40. *The Flip Side* opened at the Booth Theater, New York, on 11 October and closed on 12 October 1968.

41. Howerd, *op. cit.*, p.239.

42. Elizabeth, the Queen Mother, quoted by Hall, *op. cit.*, p.177 (no primary source acknowledged).

43. Michael Mills, quoted by Barry Took, interview with the author, 17 May 2000.

44. *Ibid.*

45. Howerd, *op. cit.*, p.253.

46. *Ibid.*, p.254.

47. Transcribed from a recording of the 1968 Royal Variety Show.

48. *Ibid.*, p.241.

49. Quoted by David Nathan, *The Laughtermakers*, *op. cit.*, p.199.

50. Transcribed, with one minor correction, from the pilot episode of *Up Pompeii*, written by Talbot Rothwell, first broadcast on BBC 1 on 17 September 1969. (Howerd actually misremembered his lines, missing out the reference to citizens and addressing the plebeians as 'noble' – but no one seemed to notice and the recording carried on.)

51. Nathan, *op. cit.*, p.202.

52. Michael Billington, quoted by Ross, *op. cit.*, p.34 (no primary source acknowledged).

53. BBC Daily Viewing Barometer, 17 September 1969.

54. Mary Whitehouse, *The Times*, 18 September 1969, p.3.

55. Nathan, *op. cit.*, p.201.

56. Quoted by Howerd, *op. cit.*, p.258.

57. BBC WAC: Audience Research Report on the pilot edition of *Up Pompeii!*, 17 September 1969 (VR/69/533, 13 November 1969).

58. Howerd, quoted by Malcolm Winton, *op. cit.*, p.10.

59. *Ibid.*

Chapter 14

1. Howerd, quoted by David Nathan, *op. cit.*, p.203.

2. See Hugh Leonard, *op. cit.*, p.25; Bernard Levin, quoted by Nathan, *op. cit.*, p.191; and Kenneth Tynan, 'Frankie Howerd', *op. cit.* (no page number).

3. Peter O'Toole, interviewed by Kenneth Tynan for *Playboy*, September 1965, p.96.

4. Terry Coleman, *op. cit.*, p.208.

5. Howerd, speaking in the uncut version of the *Arena* documentary, *op. cit.*

6. Howerd, *op. cit.*, p.264.

7. *Ibid.*, p.267.

8. *Ibid.*, pp.261–2.

9. Barry Took, *Star Turns*, *op. cit.*, p.66.

10. *Ibid.*

11. June Whitfield, *. . . and June Whitfield* (London: Corgi, 2001), p.220.

12. Barry Took, *op. cit.*, p.67.

13. Howerd, quoted by Hall, *op. cit.*, p.131 (no primary source acknowledged).

14. Ray Galton, interview with the author, 15 March 2004.

15. Shirley Abicair, interviewed by Ines Cavill for the BBC 2 *Reputations* documentary, *op. cit.*

16. Margaret Courtenay, quoted by Hall, *op. cit.*, p.93 (no primary source acknowledged).

17. Ray Milland, quoted by Howerd, *op. cit.*, p.273.

18. Among Sykes' recent credits were Hammer's *Demons of the Mind* (1972) and the sitcom spin-off *Steptoe and Son Ride Again* (1973).

19. See Howerd, *op. cit.*, pp.274–9; and his interview with Tony Williams, *op. cit.*, p.62.

20. Transcribed from the 1973 BBC 2 show, *An Evening With Francis Howerd*, an excerpt of which is included in the BBC Worldwide video and DVD *BBC Comedy Greats: Frankie Howerd*.

21. Eric Morecambe, see his joint autobiography with Ernie Wise, *Eric & Ernie* (London: W.H. Allen, 1973), p.159.

22. Michael Grade, speaking in the radio documentary *There'll Never Be Another*, *op. cit.*

23. Michael Billington, *op. cit.*, p.37.

24. The project was first discussed in 1970, but it was not until 1974 that a screenplay was completed. The cast, according to a variety of reports and rumours in the industry papers, was set to include James Mason, Mia Farrow, Topol, Frankie Howerd, Malcolm McDowell and Michael York, with Jack Cardiff signed up as cinematographer, Gerald Scarfe as designer and André Previn as composer of the score. Some of the backing, it seems, was due to be provided by Frixos Constantine & Costas Caryiannis, and shooting was due to start in Rhodes on 5 March 1975, but the project collapsed before then.

25. *Oooh, Canada*, as it was first called, featured Howerd as a British immigrant based in Toronto. Somewhat Hancock-like in tone, it was broadcast on CBC during 1976 from 26 February to 8 April, and then from 24 April to 5 June.

26. *Up the Convicts* featured Howerd as Jeremiah Stark, an ex-convict situated in Sydney Cove in the early 1800s. Planned originally by the Channel 7 Network as a six-episode series, it was broadcast eventually in four large chunks from 18 June to 19 July 1976.

27. Howerd, *op. cit.*, p.285.

28. *Ibid.*, p.286.

29. *Ibid.*

30. *Ibid.*

31. Frankie Howerd would leave an estate valued at more than £1m in his will (£1, 327,198 gross, £1,213, 141 net). The main beneficiaries were Dennis Heymer and Betty Howard (the will also said that Cilla Black and June Whitfield should each choose one of Howerd's possessions – valued at less than £1,000 – by which to remember him; Black chose a framed poster of *The House in Nightmare Park*, Whitfield selected a marquetry table). See *The Guardian*, 29 July 1992, p.3.

32. Howerd, *op. cit.*, p.287.

33. *Ibid.*, p.288.

34. On 27 July 1967, the Sexual Offences Act received Royal Assent (ending the total ban on sex between men which had existed since 1885). It did not, contrary to popular belief, legalise homosexuality as such, but it did exempt homosexual acts from criminal prosecution if they took place in private between two consenting males aged twenty-one or over.

35. Barry Took, who was Head of Light Entertainment at LWT at the time, recalled this incident in *Star Turns*, *op. cit.*, pp.36–7.

36. Bill Lyon-Shaw, interview with the author, 13 February 2004.

37.   See Wallace Reyburn, *Gilbert Harding, op. cit.*, pp.110–11.

38.   *The Times*, 22 October 1953, p.5.

39.   See *The Times*, 22 November 1962, p.5; 6 December, p.9; and 13 December, p.17.

40.   Howerd, recalled by a former friend and colleague who wished to remain anonymous.

41.   Fact-checking rarely seems to have figured very highly in the minds of those who have dedicated entire programmes to the repetition of these rumours. Howerd was indeed, at certain times in his adult life, unusually promiscuous in his sexual activity, but by no means all of the notorious stories deserve to be treated, *ab initio*, as indubitably real and true. In 1993, for example, Bob Monkhouse wrote of a harrowing-sounding encounter with Howerd during a summer season in Great Yarmouth in 1961. He claimed that Howerd lured him into his apartment on the pretext of needing advice about a plan to propose marriage to Joan Greenwood, and then attempted, unsuccessfully, to seduce him (Bob Monkhouse, *Crying With Laughter*, London: Arrow, 1994, pp.183–8). The problem with this story is that, though it may well have happened (and there is no evidence to suggest that Monkhouse, a kind and honourable man, wilfully invented the whole unhappy incident), the detailed reference to a supposed marriage proposal to Joan Greenwood makes no sense whatsoever – because she had already married André Morell the previous year. So this much-repeated story appears to have been at least partly embellished, imagined or misremembered.

42.   Tommy Cooper, quoted by Hall, *op. cit.*, pp.120–1 (no primary source acknowledged).

43.   Clive James, speaking in the ITV documentary *What a Performance!* (Carlton/Watchmaker) first broadcast on 12 May 1999. (Similarly, in his memoir *Adventures of a Suburban Boy* – London: Faber and Faber, 2003, pp.58–9 – the movie director John Boorman recalled following Howerd around the music-hall circuit as one of his most avid teenaged fans: 'We certainly had no idea Frankie Howerd was gay'.)

44.   Howerd, *op. cit.*, p.84.

45.   *Ibid.*, pp.83–4.

46.   *Ibid.*

47.   *Ibid.*, p.84.

48.   Victoria Glendinning refers to this exchange between Howerd and West in her biography of the novelist, *Rebecca West: A Life* (London: Weidenfeld & Nicolson, 1987), p.35.

Chapter 15

1.   Howerd, quoted by Barry Took, *Star Turns, op. cit.*, p.150.

2.   Howerd was the subject of the edition of *This Is Your Life* (whose code word had been 'FORUM') that was broadcast by ITV on 27 February 1976; he was awarded an OBE in the Queen's New Year's Honours List, and collected his medal on 2 March 1977 ('I never thought,' it was widely reported that he had said tearfully to the Queen Mother, 'I would be coming back for this honour.')

3.   Howerd, quoted by Hall, *op. cit.*, p.176 (no primary source acknowledged).

4.   Howerd, interviewed by Kenneth Passingham, 'The prologue of one Francis Howerd', *TV Times*, 25 September 1975, p.5.

5.   EOKA (the National Organisation of Cypriot Fighters) had started a guerrilla campaign against British colonial rule – aimed at self-determination and union with Greece – on 1 April 1955. The campaign, which lasted until 1959, caused the death of more Greek Cypriot civilians than it did British soldiers. Diplomatic efforts eventually effected a compromise, which saw the Greek-Cypriots abandon their demands for union with Greece and accept instead the establishment of Cyprus as an independent republic; Britain retained control of two Sovereign Base areas, at Akrotiri and Dhekelia.

6.   Derek Agutter, quoted by Hall, *op. cit.*, p.169 (no primary source acknowledged). General Sir Geoffrey Howlett made a similar point in a letter to *The Times* (23 April 1992, p.15) a

few days after Howerd's death: 'There was nowhere Frankie Howerd would not go: danger seemed irrelevant to him.'

7.   Howerd, *op. cit.*, p.283.

8.   Howerd, interviewed by Denise Richards, *London Evening Standard*, 4 October 1963, p.18.

9.   Jeanne Mockford, quoted by Hall, *op. cit.*, p.176 (no primary source acknowledged).

10.   Howerd, quoted by Griff Rhys Jones, 'Naughty but nice', *Radio Times*, 24–30 April 2004, p.26.

11.   Richard Willcox, quoted by Hall, *op. cit.*, p.156 (no primary source acknowledged).

12.   *Ibid*.

13.   An opinion expressed by Rory McGrath in the Channel 4 documentary *Sex, Secrets and Frankie Howerd*, first broadcast on 24 April 2004.

14.   According to June Whitfield (*op. cit.*, p.220), it was actually in Howerd's contract, during the last few years of his stage act, that 'he should be given a double brandy and soda with lots of ice' for the interval.

15.   Transcribed from certain editions of *The Frankie Howerd Variety Show*, broadcast on BBC Radio 2 from 10 October 1978 to 18 September 1979.

16.   Griff Rhys Jones, speaking in the Carlton/ITV 'Legends' documentary, 9 August 2000.

17.   Rhys Jones, 'Naughty but nice', *Radio Times*, 24–30 April 2004, p.25.

18.   Rhys Jones, speaking in the BBC 2 *Reputations* documentary, *op. cit.*

19.   Howerd chose the following for *Desert Island Discs* on 28 September 1959: 1. Parry, 'Jerusalem'; 2. Kalman, 'Love's Sweet Song' (from *The Gypsy Princess*); 3. 'Lilliburlero' (RAF Central Band); 4. O. Straus, 'Waltz Dream'; 5. 'My Very Good Friend the Milkman' (Fats Waller); 6. 'Torna a Surriento'(Beniamino Gigli); 7. 'Song and Dance Man' (Frankie Howerd); 8. 'Abide with Me' (Bach Choir). LUXURY: Photographs. BOOK: Leo Tolstoy, *War and Peace*. On 23 January 1982, he chose the following: 1. 'Knees Up, Mother Brown' (audience of the Metropolitan, Edgware Road, London); 2. Chopin, Nocturne in C minor (opus 48, no. 1); 3. Beethoven, Symphony No. 9 in D minor (opus 125); 4. 'Autumn Leaves' (sung by Nat 'King' Cole); 5. Puccini, 'Love and Music' (from *Tosca*); 6. Sondheim, 'Send in the Clowns' (from *A Little Night Music*); 7. J. Strauss, 'Brüderlein und Schwesterlein' (from *Die Fledermaus*); 8. Parry/Blake, 'Jerusalem'. LUXURY: A little cross given to him by his mother. BOOK: Charles Dickens, *David Copperfield*. Source: Roy Plomley, *Desert Island Lists* (London: Hutchinson, 1984).

20.   Set in the Second World War, *Then Churchill Said To Me* was recorded in the autumn of 1981 for transmission in the late winter/early spring of the following year. The BBC never gave a very clear formal explanation as to why the show was shelved, but the reason that was most widely reported concerned Britain's involvement in the conflict with Argentina over sovereignty of the Falkland Islands/Malvinas; as odd as it might initially sound, the BBC probably *was* fairly anxious to avoid the presence of any war-related themes in its entertainment shows during this time, because even such a silly show as this could potentially have caused offence had it coincided with news of the death of British soldiers. Anecdotal evidence suggested, however, that there was little faith in the series, considered purely in terms of its quality as a sitcom, within the Corporation – and when the series was finally screened (first on the cable/satellite station UK Gold in 1993, and then on BBC 2 in 2000) it was easy to see why.

21.   Kenneth Williams, diary entry for 10 January 1977, *op. cit.*, p.533.

22.   Quoted by Barry Cryer, *Pigs Can Fly* (London: Orion, 2003), p.49.

23.   Released by Automata in 1984 for use, initially, on 48k Sinclair Spectrum computers, the game (which won the CTA 'game of the year' award for 1985) was introduced by Jon Pertwee, who informed the player that, because of an 'accident' which saw a mouse leave an organic deposit within the machine just before it expired, a mutant creature is now growing within the confines of this complex mechanism; the task of the player, therefore,

is to guide the mutant through its 'weird' life by keeping its existence a secret from the all-seeing and all-knowing machine in which it now lives. Howerd contributed the voice of the 'Defect Police' – who had to be avoided at all costs – to this peculiar piece of sci-fi distraction (see the review in *Your Spectrum*, 10, December 1984).

24.   Quoted by Hall, *op. cit.*, p.124 (no primary source acknowledged).

25.   Barry Took, interview with the author, 17 May 2000.

26.   *The Times*, 14 November 1986.

27.   *Daily Mirror*, 20 April 1992, p.5.

28.   Helen Walters – a former colleague of Le Bars from RSO (and the wife of the distinguished broadcaster and radio producer John Walters) – conversation with the author, 14 June 2004.

29.   John McCready, conversation with the author, 11 February 2004.

30.   Howerd, *op. cit.*, p.256.

31.   Jack Rossiter, quoted by Hall, *op. cit.*, p. 172 (no primary source acknowledged).

32.   *Ibid.*, p.173 (no primary source acknowledged).

33.   Sid Vicious, quoted by Barry Took, interview with the author, 17 May 2000; see also Ross, *op. cit.*, p.81 (no primary source acknowledged).

34.   Eric Woolfson was a singer and writer with The Alan Parsons Project – a 'prog-rock' band known for its sequence of extremely grand, and arguably somewhat pompous, concept albums (on such topics as Edgar Alan Poe, the sci-fi of Isaac Asimov and the architecture of Gaudi) in the 1970s and 80s. *Freudiana* – which was intended originally to form part of the Parsons *oeuvre* – continued to be developed by Woolfson after he left the band for conceptual reasons. The studio album, featuring Howerd, Kiki Dee, Eric Stewart, Marti Webb, John Miles, Graham Dye, Chris Rainbow, The Flying Pickets and Woolfson himself, was released in 1990 by EMI (Parlophone Odeon CDP 79 5415 2), followed at the end of the year by a version for the stage (which premièred in December in Vienna).

35.   Howerd, speaking in the uncut version of the BBC *Arena* documentary, *op. cit.*

36.   *Ibid.*

37.   Transcribed from *Frankie Howerd On Campus* (Video Collection, VC 6145), 1991.

38.   Reported by Jonathan Sale (in his review of a performance at the Lyceum), 'Playing hoots and titters', *Sunday Times*, Arts (Section E), 8 April 1990, p.4.

39.   Howerd, quoted by Hall, *op. cit.*, p.174 (no primary source acknowledged).

40.   *Ibid.*

41.   Transcribed from the recording *Frankie Howerd On Campus*, first broadcast on ITV 24 November 1990, and released subsequently on video (Video Collection, VC 6145) in 1991.

42.   *Frankie Howerd At His Tittermost!* (Sunset + Vine, SV 2008), 1991.

43.   Barry Took, *Star Turns*, *op. cit.*, p.131.

44.   See Valerie Grove, 'Give the lad a joke, he'll cast the spell himself', *Sunday Times*, News Review (Section C), 8 April 1990, p.7.

45.   Max Bygraves, *Stars in My Eyes*, *op. cit.*, pp.36–7.

46.   *London Evening Standard*, 7 April 1992, p.3.

47.   Howerd, quoted by Hall, *op. cit.*, p.180 (no primary source acknowledged).

48.   *Daily Telegraph*, 9 July 1992, p.3.

49.   Marks, quoted by Hall, *op. cit.*, p.181 (no primary source acknowledged).

50.   *Daily Mirror*, 20 April 1992, p.1.

51.   Widely reported in the national papers, including *The Times*, 9 July 1992, p.3.

THE EPILOGUE

1. Howerd, *op. cit.*, p.288.

2. *Ibid.*

3. Ralph Waldo Emerson, 'Compensation', in *Essays and Poems* (London: J.M. Dent, 1995), p.59.

4. *Daily Mirror*, 20 April 1992, p.5, and *The Times*, 20 April 1992, p.14.

5. Eric Sykes, speaking in the radio documentary *Howerd's Way*, *op. cit.*

6. Johnny Speight, quoted by William Greaves, 'Titter ye not!' *Radio Times*, 26 May 1990, p. 8.

7. Barry Took, quoted by Hall, *op. cit.*, p.183 (no primary source acknowledged, but the comment was widely reported at the time).

8. Barry Cryer, speaking in the radio documentary *Howerd's Way*, *op. cit.*

9. Howerd, interviewed by Passingham, 'The prologue of one Francis Howerd', *op. cit.*, pp.2 and 4.

10. Alan Simpson, interview with the author, 15 March 2004.

11. Ray Galton, interview with the author, 15 March 2004.

12. Eric Sykes, interview with the author, 19 February 2004.

Bibliography

Frankie Howerd

Coleman, Terry, 'Frankie Howerd: Delusion, Love and Work', *Movers & Shakers: Conversations With Uncommon Men* (London: André Deutsch, 1987)

Fisher, John, 'And the Best of Luck!', *Funny Way to be a Hero* (London: Frederick Muller, 1973), pp.234–44

Hall, William, *Titter Ye Not! The Life of Frankie Howerd* (London: Grafton, 1992)

Hardy, Frances, 'Howerd's outrageous ways', *Daily Mail* (Weekend supplement), 8 June 2002, pp.17–18

Howerd, Frankie, *On The Way I Lost It* (London: W.H. Allen, 1976)

   Trumps! – and how to come up (London: J.M. Dent, 1982)

   Howerd's Howlers (London: Octopus, 1985)

Middles, Mick, *Frankie Howerd: The Illustrated Biography* (London: Headline, 2000)

Midwinter, Eric, 'Frankie Howerd: A Gossip for the Sixties', *Make 'Em Laugh* (London: George Allen & Unwin, 1979), pp.141–56

Nathan, David, 'Francis Howerd, Esquire', *The Laughtermakers* (London: Peter Owen, 1971), pp.190–203

Passingham, Kenneth, 'The prologue of one Francis Howerd', *TV Times*, 25 September 1975, pp.2–5

Pedrick, Gale, 'Frankie Howerd', *Radio Times*, 28 October 1949, p.6

Priestley, J.B., 'Frankie Howerd', *Particular Pleasures* (New York: Stein and Day, 1975), pp.174–5

Rhys Jones, Griff, 'Naughty but nice', *Radio Times*, 24–30 April 2004, pp.25–6

Ross, Maris, 'Top British Comedian to Try Luck Here', *Washington Post*, 6 August 1968, p.6

Ross, Robert, *The Complete Frankie Howerd* (London: Reynolds & Hearn, 2001)

Sykes, Eric, 'Frankie Howerd', *Eric Sykes' Comedy Heroes* (London: Virgin, 2003)

Took, Barry, *Star Turns: The Life and Times of Benny Hill & Frankie Howerd* (London: Weidenfeld & Nicolson, 1992)

Tynan, Kenneth, 'Frankie Howerd', *Persona Grata* (London: Wingate, 1953), p.59

Williams, Tony, 'Frankie Howerd', *Psychotronic*, pp.60–3

Winton, Malcolm, 'The art of being perfectly Frankie', *Radio Times*, 26 March 1970, p.10

General

Adamson, Iain, *The Old Fox: A Life of Gilbert Beyfus QC* (London: Frederick Muller, 1963)

Allen, Fred, *Treadmill to Oblivion* (Boston: Little, Brown, 1954)

Allen, Steve, *The Funny Men* (New York: Simon and Schuster, 1956)

Appleyard, Bryan, 'We pray you titter forever Frankie', *London Evening Standard*, 8 April 1992, pp.20–1

Askey, Arthur, *Before Your Very Eyes* (London: Woburn Press, 1975)

Beaton, Cecil and Kenneth Tynan, *Persona Grata* (London: Wingate, 1953)

Benny, Jack and Joan Benny, *Sunday Nights at Seven* (New York: Warner, 1990)

Billington, Michael, *One Night Stands* (London: Nick Hern Books, 1993)

Bibliography

Black, Cilla, *What's It All About?* (London: Ebury Press, 2003)

Black, Peter, *The Biggest Aspidistra in the World* (London: BBC, 1972)
  The Mirror in the Corner (London: Hutchinson, 1972)

Boorman, John, *Adventures of a Suburban Boy* (London: Faber and Faber, 2003)

Bradbury, David and Joe McGrath, *Now That's Funny!* (London: Methuen, 1998)

Brandreth, Gyles, *Brief Encounters* (London: Politico's, 2003)

Briggs, Asa, *The History of Broadcasting in the United Kingdom* (Oxford: Oxford University Press, 1961–1979):
  Vol.1: *The Birth of Broadcasting*, 1961
  Vol.2: *The Golden Age of Wireless*, 1965
  Vol.3: *The War of Words*, 1970
  Vol.4: *Sound and Vision*, 1979

Bygraves, Max, *Stars in My Eyes* (London: Robson, 2003)

Cardiff, David, 'Mass middlebrow laughter: The origins of BBC comedy', *Media, Culture & Society*, vol.10, no.1 (January 1988), pp.41–60

Cotton, Bill, *The BBC as an Entertainer* (London: BBC, 1977)
  Double Bill, (London: Fourth Estate, 2000)

Craig, Mike, *Look Back With Laughter*, vols 1 and 2 (Manchester: Mike Craig Enterprises, 1996)

Cryer, Barry, *Pigs Can Fly* (London: Orion, 2003)

Farnes, Norma, *Spike: An Intimate Memoir* (London: Fourth Estate, 2003)

Fisher, John, *Funny Way to be a Hero* (London: Frederick Muller, 1973)

Foster, Andy and Steve Furst, *Radio Comedy 1938–1968* (London: Virgin, 1996)

Frith, Simon, 'The pleasures of the hearth: the making of BBC light entertainment', in Tony Bennett *et al.* (eds), *Popular Culture and Social Relations* (Milton Keynes: Open University, 1983)

Gambaccini, Paul and Rod Taylor, *Television's Greatest Hits* (London: Network Books, 1993)

Glendinning, Victoria, *Rebecca West: A Life* (London: Weidenfeld & Nicolson, 1987)

Greene, Hugh Carleton, *The BBC as a Public Service* (London: BBC, 1960)

Grof, Stanislav, *LSD Psychotherapy* (California: Hunter House, 1980)

Hollingshead, Michael, *The Man Who Turned On the World* (London: Blond and Briggs, 1973)

Hudd, Roy, *Roy Hudd's Book of Music-Hall, Variety and Showbiz Anecdotes* (London: Virgin, 1994)

Hughes, John Graven, *The Greasepaint War* (London: New English Library, 1976)

James, Clive, *Clive James on Television* (London: Picador, 1991)

Jeffries, Stuart, *Mrs Slocombe's Pussy* (London: Flamingo, 2000)

Josefsberg, Milt, *The Jack Benny Show* (New York: Arlington House, 1977)

Keighron, Peter, 'Vertue rewarded', *Broadcast*, 23 April 2004, p.19

Lane, Lupino, *How to Become a Comedian* (London: Frederick Muller, 1945)

Lewisohn, Mark, *Radio Times Guide to TV Comedy* (London: BBC, 1998)

McCann, Graham, *Cary Grant: A Class Apart* (London: Fourth Estate, 1996)
  'Why the best sitcoms must be a class act', *London Evening Standard*, 21 May 1997, p.9
  'An offer we can refuse', *London Evening Standard*, 2 December 1998, p.8
  Morecambe & Wise (London: Fourth Estate, 1998)
  'Sit back and wait for the comedy', *Financial Times*, 24 November 1999, p.22
  'Don't bury your treasures', *Financial Times*, 28 June 2000, p.22
  Dad's Army: The Story of a Classic Television Show (London: Fourth Estate, 2001)
  'You never had it so good or so funny', *Financial Times*, 13 November 2002, p.17
  'How to define the indefinable', *Financial Times*, 20 March 2003, p.14
  'Bob Hope: The master of special delivery bows out', *Financial Times*, 29 July 2003, p.15
  'Steptoe and Son', *British Comedy Greats*, ed. Annabel Merullo and Neil Wenborn (London: Cassell Illustrated, 2003), pp.157–61
  'Johnny Speight', *Dictionary of National Biography* (Oxford: Oxford University Press, 2004)

McFarlane, Brian, *An Autobiography of British Cinema* (London: Methuen, 1997)

Mellor, G.J., *The Northern Music Hall* (Newcastle upon Tyne: Frank Graham, 1970)
  They Made Us Laugh (Littleborough: George Kelsell, 1982)

Bibliography

Miall, Leonard, *Inside The BBC* (London: Weidenfeld & Nicolson, 1994)

Midwinter, Eric, *Make 'Em Laugh* (London: George Allen & Unwin, 1979)

Monkhouse, Bob, *Crying With Laughter* (London: Arrow, 1994)

    Over The Limit (London: Century, 1998)

Morecambe, Eric and Ernie Wise, *Eric & Ernie* (London: W.H. Allen, 1973)

Muir, Frank, *Comedy in Television* (London: BBC, 1966)

Nathan, David, *The Laughtermakers* (London: Peter Owen, 1971)

Nobbs, David, *I Didn't Get Where I Am Today* (London: William Heinemann, 2003)

Pedrick, Gale, 'Laughter in the Air', *BBC Year Book 1948* (London: BBC, 1948), pp.53–6

Perret, Gene and Martha Bolton, *Talk About Hope* (Carmel, CA: Jester Press, 1998)

Pertwee, Bill, *Promenades and Pierrots* (Devon: Westbridge, 1979)

    A Funny Way to Make a Living! (London: Sunburst, 1996)

Plomley, Roy, *Desert Island Lists* (London: Hutchinson, 1984)

Priestley, J.B., *Particular Pleasures* (New York: Stein & Day, 1975)

Reyburn, Wallace, *Gilbert Harding: A Candid Portrayal* (Brighton: Angus & Robertson, 1978)

Richards, Jeffrey, *Visions of Yesteryear* (London: Routledge, 1973)

    Films and British National Identity (Manchester: Manchester University Press, 1997)

Rundall, Jeremy, 'They must be joking', *Plays and Players*, February 1967, pp.55–6

Sandison, H.A. *et al.*, 'The Therapeutic Value of Lysergic Acid Diethylamide in Mental Illness', *Journal of Mental Science*, 100: 491–507

Silvey, Roger, *Who's Listening? The Story of BBC Audience Research* (London: Allen & Unwin, 1974)

Sloan, Tom, *Television Light Entertainment* (London: BBC, 1969)

Sontag, Susan, 'Notes on "Camp"', (1964), *A Susan Sontag Reader* (Harmondsworth: Penguin, 1982)

Stevens, Jay, *Storming Heaven* (London: Flamingo, 1993)

Stone, Richard, *You Should Have Been In Last Night* (Sussex: The Book Guild, 2000)

Sykes, Eric, *Eric Sykes' Comedy Heroes* (London: Virgin, 2003)

Took, Barry, *Laughter in the Air* (London: Robson/BBC, 1976)

    'Whatever Happened to TV Comedy?' *The Listener*, 5 January 1984, pp.7–8, and 12 January 1984, pp.8–9

Tynan, Kenneth, *Profiles* (London: Nick Hern Books, 1989)

Watt, John (ed.), *Radio Variety* (London: J.M Dent, 1939)

Wheldon, Huw, *British Traditions in a World-Wide Medium* (London: BBC, 1973)

    The Achievement of Television (London: BBC, 1975)

    The British Experience in Television (London: BBC, 1976)

Whitfield, June, *. . . and June Whitfield* (London: Corgi, 2001)

Wilde, Larry, *The Great Comedians* (Secaucus, New Jersey: Citadel Press, 1973)

Williams, Kenneth, *The Kenneth Williams Diaries*, ed. Russell Davies (London: HarperCollins, 1993)

Wilmut, Roger, *Kindly Leave the Stage: The Story of Variety, 1918–60* (London: Methuen, 1985)

Windsor, Barbara, *All Of Me* (London: Headline, 2001)

Worthington, Kenneth, *Theatrical Agency On A Sensible Budget* (Sheffield: Harvester Press, 2002)

Wyndham Goldie, Grace, *Facing The Nation: Broadcasting and Politics 1936–1976* (London: Bodley Head, 1977)

Index

Index

Index